Scientific Method

'Barry Gower's book introduces students to the philosophy of science in a way I heartily applaud: scientific method, logic and probability are given centre-stage and are developed historically – through examination of the views of some of the greats: Galileo, Bacon, Newton, Bayes, Poincaré, . . ., and in close connection with developments in science itself. Theses and arguments are presented with great clarity and sound judgement.'

John Worral, LSE

The results, conclusions and claims of science are often taken to be reliable because they arise from the use of a distinctive method. Yet today, there is widespread scepticism as to whether we can validly talk of method in modern science. This outstanding new survey explains how this controversy has developed since the seventeenth century and explores its philosophical basis. *Scientific Method*

- introduces readers to controversies concerning method in the natural sciences
- provides an historical context to these issues
- shows that questions of method have played a vital role in the work of scientists
- challenges the current view that scientific method is a philosophical fiction.

Questions of scientific method are discussed through key figures such as Galileo, Bacon, Newton, Bayes, Darwin, Poincaré, Duhem, Popper and Carnap. The concluding chapter contains stimulating discussions of attacks on the idea of scientific method by key figures such as Kuhn, Lakatos, and Feyerabend.

Essential reading for students of history and the philosophy of science, *Scientific Method* will also appeal to anyone with an interest in what philosophers say about science.

Barry Gower teaches Philosophy of Science at Durham University.

Scientific Method

An historical and philosophical introduction

Barry Gower

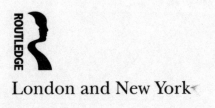

London and New York

First published 1997
by Routledge
11 New Fetter Lane, London EC4P 4EE

Simultaneously published in the USA and Canada
by Routledge
29 West 35th Street, New York, NY 10001

Typeset in Baskerville by
Ponting–Green Publishing Services, Chesham, Buckinghamshire

Printed and bound in Great Britain by
Clays Ltd, St Ives PLC

British Library Cataloguing in Publication Data
A catalogue record for this book is available from the
British Library. 10058520bo

Library of Congress Cataloguing in Publication Data
Gower, Barry.
    Scientific method: an historical and philosophical
introduction / Barry Gower.
        p.   cm.
    Includes bibliographical references and index.
    1. Science–Methodology.
    2. Science–Methodology–Philosophy.
    3. Science–Methodology–History.   I. Title.
Q175.G685   1996
502.8–dc20
96–7865
CIP

ISBN 0–415–12281–3 (hbk)
ISBN 0–415–12282–1 (pbk)

Contents

Preface

Those of my friends and colleagues who knew that I was writing a book about scientific method often expressed their surprise. Why, they said, should anyone wish to revive such a long-expired steed? People do not now believe in scientific method. Perhaps they should, for their dismissal is based more on specious rhetoric than on solid argument; but still, my friends told me, writers who would be read must address a real, rather than an ideal, world. My answer has been that the real world has a history, and to state the truth about it we must take account of that history. Scientific method – the logic of science – has occupied the attention of some of the greatest scientific and philosophical thinkers. If we dismiss what engaged their attention, then we had better be sure that we know why it engaged their attention. They were, no doubt, subject to prevailing cultural influences and attitudes of which they may have been unaware. But so are we, and if we can, with the help of history, exercise a degree of self-reflection, we may wish to circumscribe the influences which try to prevail over our thinking. Setting aside the radical scepticism of some philosophers, we can know something about the past, including something about how our predecessors have considered scientific method. But for our predecessors the future, including that future of theirs in which we live, is unknown. We should take advantage of that difference. We willingly assert that our predecessors would not have believed some of what their contemporaries urged them to believe about scientific method if they had known what we know about it; we should just as willingly assert that we would not believe some of what our contemporaries urge us to believe about scientific method if we knew what our predecessors had known about it.

Not unexpectedly, few friends have been persuaded. Many, though, have not only tolerated my persistence, but encouraged and helped me to promote my unfashionable view. This is my opportunity to thank them. But I must also record my intellectual debt to Bob MacGowan and Rom Harre who introduced me to the philosophy of science, and to David Knight with whom I have been teaching the history and philosophy of science for almost thirty years. For helpful comments and criticism of various chapters of this book I thank Vernon Armitage, Donald Gillies, Stathis Psillos, Geoffrey Scarre and Michael Sharratt. I have not always taken the advice they gave me, so, for that reason as well as others, the faults that remain are my faults. Thanks, too, to the Research Committee of Durham University and to my colleagues in the Philosophy Department for a period of leave in 1994 enabling me to begin work on the book. Chapters, or parts of chapters, have been read to audiences in Belfast, Dublin, London, Florence and Virginia, as well as in Durham, and I am grateful for the advice I have received on those occasions. For less direct but nevertheless invaluable help I thank Robin Hendry, Roger MacAdam, Holger Maehle, David Mossley, Kathleen Natrass and Wendy Short.

But the greatest encouragement has come from my students at Durham University, and therefore my most heartfelt thanks go to them. I have been very lucky in having the opportunity to introduce philosophy to students of the natural sciences. Their response, their questions, their suggestions and their critical judgement have been very much in my mind as I wrote. Such success as I have had in identifying, articulating and addressing the philosophical questions which are the subject of this book is due in large part to their aid.

In this book's concluding chapter I have adapted material which appeared in 'Method in methodology', *Methodology and Science* 18 (1985): 30–47, and in 'Chalmers on method', *British Journal for the Philosophy of Science* 39 (1988): 59–65. I am grateful to the editors of those journals for permission to recycle the required paragraphs.

Barry Gower
January 1996

1 Introduction

We have increasingly powerful reasons for acquiring some understanding of the natural sciences. Their influence on the technologies
that shape our lives has already been immense, and undoubtedly will
continue to grow. In peace and in war, in work and in leisure, in health
and in sickness, in each of the different stages of life, we cannot escape
that influence. This book is being written with the aid of an electronic
computer of a type which, as little as twenty years ago, was unavailable
and unimagined by most people. You could well be reading it in
circumstances equally unanticipated. On the surface at least, the most
prominent differences between our lives and those of earlier generations are differences which have come about as a result of discoveries,
investigations, explorations and inventions in the natural sciences. If
we compare our modes of transport or communication with those
available to previous generations, or compare our education with theirs,
we cannot help but be struck with the consequences, for good or for ill,
of scientific knowledge. On the credit side, that knowledge, but not that
knowledge alone, has resulted in such benefits as the elimination of
drudgery and repetitive work for some people, the eradication and
control of some life-threatening diseases, and increases in crop pro-
ductivity. For the sake of these and other benefits we have welcomed
science. But we also fear science because, on the debit side, scientific
knowledge, though not scientific knowledge alone, is responsible for
such harms as the damage suffered by our environment, and has led
to questionable experimental practices which need the control of
so-called 'ethics committees'. Without the scientist's knowledge of
theories, of laws, of techniques and, in general, of what is possible
and what is not, the circumstances in which we live our lives would
undoubtedly be different.

At a deeper level, too, we feel the effects of the growth of natural
science and its technological consequences. Many people feel uneasy
about, and some are alienated by, the impersonality of science, and
even more so by what they perceive as its inhumanity; the future
societies imagined by science-fiction writers tend to be uncomfortably

alien rather than reassuringly familiar. This sense of science being something apart from us becomes more apparent if we take a longer view and compare the role that the science of Shakespeare's England played in understanding the place and significance of people in the world with its present role. Four hundred years ago the natural sciences and the picture they presented were inconsequential. They engaged the attention of otherwise idle gentlemen of means and leisure, but there was no sense that they were initiating enquiries which could or would have significant practical effect on people's lives. Even Francis Bacon, who was more sensitive than most to the practical consequences of scientific knowledge, would be astonished today to find that Her Majesty's Government is spending ever larger sums of money on laboratories to create what he called 'experimental histories'. Until the beginning of the twentieth century, scientific knowledge was limited in its scope and therefore limited in its practical significance. Industrial-isation had affected some parts of western Europe, but it was the management of that process rather than the technology and science it used which raised moral and social issues. The discoveries of scientists were, it is true, interesting and sometimes entertaining, but for the most part neither they nor their effects presented a challenge which was more than intellectual. Now, though, at the end of that century, scientists know, or we think they know, so much about the natural world, including the species of animals we call human beings, that nothing important can be missing from the scientific picture of the world they present. The picture presented today by the scientific enterprise is so large and so comprehensive that we sometimes wonder whether there is room for anything else. Accordingly we raise questions about the role of creativity, sensitivity, feeling and reflection. We wonder, therefore, how and why the arts and music, literature, religion and philosophy can have a place in our lives. Sometimes these questions take a striking form in the work of artists, musicians, and writers themselves. The growth of science and technology makes many of us feel uneasy, not just because of its effect on the details of our lives but on account of its implications for the way we think about ourselves, our responsibilities and our place as individuals in an impersonal world where everything is weighed, counted, measured and, we think, under-stood. Our image of the scientist as philosopher, in some sense of that elastic term, is being replaced by the image of the scientist as account-ant. Both images have the capacity to disturb us.

The tension which underlies this uneasiness arises from the need we all feel to control and predict our environment. We want to improve the circumstances in which we live our lives; we want to secure our future. To achieve these ends we must understand our environment; we must be able to explain why our circumstances are as they are. The kind of explanation which has proved most helpful is that provided by science, particularly natural science. There is, then, a close connection between our desire to enhance and make secure the circumstances in which we live, and the quest for the knowledge which will enable us to explain our world scientifically. Yet we are social beings; we live with other people who form an essential part of our environment. In so far as we think of them as having an inner life which is as important to them as ours is to us, we do not seek to control and predict their behaviour. Often what we look for in others is autonomy rather than conformity, spontaneity rather than predictability. We wish to understand the people who share our environment, but a scientific explanation will, we feel, miss what is essential. No doubt much of what matters to us is illuminated by natural science. After all, natural science has been a subject of interest for many people for many hundreds of years. It is not an insignificant object of knowledge. But still there is much more which is not, and cannot be, illuminated in an appropriate way by natural science or by any other kind of science. The projects which have tried to enlighten us – religion, philosophy, art, music, literature – have engaged our attention for thousands of years. They contribute something other than knowledge which is nevertheless important to us. They have served needs which are not met by science, despite its pervasiveness and power.

We should not, though, think that science is some all-devouring monster growing by force of its own inner logic. We can control and shape the way in which scientific knowledge changes; we do so control and shape it, though we are seldom aware of what we are doing. We, or more usually politicians, bureaucrats, financiers and industrialists, influence the development of the natural sciences and thus that of the technologies with which they are coupled. There is, in short, influence the other way. To be sure, the personal circumstances of a scientist and the interests she or he is able to develop have an effect upon what the scientist achieves, but more importantly there are powerful social, economic and political circumstances which will shape that effect as well. If we know more about some aspects of our natural environment than we do about others, that is not so much because some things are easier to investigate than others, though that is no doubt true, but rather because some sorts of enquiries are deemed more important by those who pay for science.

What we know is, in this sense, influenced by and perhaps determined by socio-economic forces. There are a great number of things which could become the object of scientific knowledge; a proportion of them have become the object of scientific knowledge, and socio-economic considerations have affected the selection of that proportion. Scientific knowledge is, in this sense, 'socially contructed'. But what we know is what is true and, on the face of it, this is a matter of how the facts are, rather than of what social forces are operating. Scientific knowledge is, in this sense, not constructed, either socially or in any other way; what we or others might want to know or need to know in order to further a political agenda, or promote a social policy, or secure a financial advantage, is beside the point, for knowledge can only be of what is true. Similarly, when I buy a lottery ticket and choose a number, my choice is determined by many factors, some perhaps social, but the number chosen is not, or at least not for that reason, a social construct. What I choose, in the sense that it is my choice, is indeed 'constructed' by me rather than given to me. But what I choose, in the sense that it is a number, is given rather than 'constructed'.

There are, no doubt, complex issues about how in practice socio-economic forces work, and we need to assess them carefully. But we also need to exercise care in describing their effects. Our interest in these forces and our conviction that they play a crucial role can easily blind us to dimensions of the scientific enterprise that have been important in characterising it. Until relatively recently, social factors played a negligible role in that characterisation, and there is perhaps a temptation to suppose that, in order to give them proper prominence, we must urge the neglect of all other factors. We suppose, or argue, that natural science is entirely a creature of our own making and the responsibility for its effects on our lives and our thinking lies with the vested interests of multi-national corporations, neo-colonial powers and the so-called free market; science neither has, nor has need of, a 'logic'. We infer that the supposed intellectual content of natural science is spurious and is no more than a means of deceiving people into maintaining and enhancing the current role of science in a society which respects those intellectual values science is supposed to represent. But there is little merit in this supposition, or in what we infer from it. Science does sometimes succeed in stating the truth, or at least a good approximation to it, and that truth is independent of the wishes of anybody, however powerful. The facts that keep aircraft aloft are, fortunately for passengers, not socially determined but ascertained on the basis of evidence by logical reasoning. The truth that cigarette smoking increases susceptibility to lung cancer is, unfortunately for smokers, not socially determined but established on the basis of evidence by logical reasoning. We could, no doubt, use our reasoning powers to establish other conclusions about other matters, such as the prevalence of schizophrenia in Eskimos, or the facts about the forces driving weather systems in the North Atlantic. If we have not done so, then the responsibility may well lie with social, economic and political considerations. But even if the selection of a subject matter for scientific enquiry is determined by powers, sinister or benign, outside of science and its methods, the nature of the logical reasoning we use in that enquiry has a part to play in understanding science.

So, although the understanding of natural science that we need does depend upon the powerful political, economic and social forces which drive the activities producing it, we should not glibly set aside the methods enabling it to have a fact-stating capacity. In this respect, as in some others, the work of a scientist is analogous to that of a detective. A detective attempting to solve a crime is no doubt subject to many kinds of forces and influences, if only because he or she will be part of an organisation which acts upon, and reacts to, the society in which it exists. But when the detective successfully solves a crime, in the sense that he or she correctly identifies the person or persons responsible, an important part of the explanation for the success will be the extent to which the reasoning used to justify the identification is persuasive. If it were just a matter of identifying a person or persons then, no doubt, we could provide an adequate explanation for the choice made by reference to forces and influences of various kinds. However, correct identification would elude such an explanation. Similarly in the case of scientists. The sociologist or anthropologist can study the work of a scientist in the same kind of way that they study other human activity, such as playing football or participating in a religious ceremony. Some of that work will have a successful outcome in the sense that it will result in new knowledge; some will not. This difference will not matter to the sociologist or anthropologist. Their explanations will not discriminate between successful and unsuccessful science. If we wish to explain the success of the work of scientists we will have to refer to the methods they use; we will have to refer to the reasoning they use to justify their new knowledge.

So we need to know something about scientific method in order to understand the production of new knowledge. But it is also important when we turn to the distribution of that new knowledge. For it is a further important feature of the late twentieth century that an ever-increasing amount of information, including scientific information, is available to people. Information technology gives us access to much of what we might want to know and to even more of what we do not want to know. Even if we do not have a professional involvement with science we should, as responsible and effective citizens, have some knowledge of some science. But in order to transform scientific information into knowledge we have to understand and assess it, and this in turn requires a grasp of the kind of reasoning relevant in science. Often this knowledge is of practical value: knowledge of current research findings on causes of heart disease might have a practical effect on a person's diet and life style; knowledge of trials undertaken by a pharmaceutical company might have a practical effect on investment decisions; knowledge of successful biochemical techniques might affect a person's career development, etc. So understanding scientific reasoning – the methods of science – is not only an interesting and challenging task in itself; by undertaking it we will be better equipped to make the practical evaluative judgements that are required of us.

There is, then, a reason for paying some attention to scientific method. It is of course connected with the fact that many people have confidence in claims described as scientific. This is not to say that people think scientists are always right, even about scientific matters; they know perfectly well that scientists have made mistakes and that they will continue to make mistakes. Rather, it is to say that people think scientific claims are reliable. It is to say that, when faced with a choice between the predictions of an astrologer and an astronomer, many of us would place greater trust in the latter, even though we might think the former more interesting, more challenging, and indeed more relevant to our lives. It is to say that many of us find the geologist's account of the origin of the Earth more credible than the creationist's alternative account, even though we might recognise and respect the mythical, imaginative and emotional power of the latter. What, though, is the basis for this confidence? Setting aside the question whether we can justify confidence in scientific knowledge, we can take that confidence as a psychological fact and ask for its explanation. No doubt the authority of science is part of the answer: we trust scientific claims simply because they are scientific and therefore authoritative. But this is hardly helpful, for it simply invites a question about the basis of the supposed authority of science. A better answer to questions about the reliability of scientific claims, and hence their authority, directs our attention to the way in which they are established. Claims which count as scientific and therefore as reliable do so because they are established by means of a scientific method.

Associated with these ideas we sometimes find the view that the natural sciences are characterised not so much by their subject matter as by their methods. Thus we can, it is said, define physics as 'all that could be profitably studied by using a certain method'. This method of physics, we are told, was invented by Galileo and is experimental; an adequate understanding of physics depends on a grasp of this experimental Galilean method. That is why, in introducing novices to this science, and indeed to any science, it is thought important to refer to method. But there is a further implication that we should note. If scientists do need to know something about method in order to understand science, then it is also true that 'a scientific method cannot adequately be discussed if it is divided from the science to which it applies' (Toraldo di Francia 1981: 6–7).

So the study of scientific method should shed some light on the character customarily attributed, rightly or wrongly, to beliefs expressed in scientific statements. Individually considered, scientific beliefs are of course very various. Some are general in their scope, others are specific and particular; some are well established, others are more tentative; some are fundamental and central, others are less important. But despite these differences they have something in common which explains why we count them as scientific, namely the method by which they are established. The evidence which makes physicists believe Newton's law of gravity is quite different from the evidence which makes chemists believe that acids are electron acceptors, and yet in both cases the same kind of method is used to justify the beliefs on the basis of the relevant evidence. This means that, despite their difference, the beliefs share an important characteristic, and by describing them as scientific beliefs we show that we recognise that characteristic. To study this characteristic, and thereby to study what makes beliefs scientific, we have to turn our attention to the method used to justify them.

In the light of this background it is perhaps surprising that scientific method is currently neglected by philosophers of science. Many think the neglect justified. The interesting philosophical issues raised by examining scientific reasoning have been explored sufficiently thoroughly, and in any case a naturalistic approach to a subject which involves social co-operation rather than solitary ratiocination, calling on the insights of social scientists, is more appropriate. Part of the reason for resisting this facile response is that, until comparatively recently, scientific method occupied an important place in the study of both logic and the philosophy of science. For besides the connections often, and naturally, made between scientific method and science itself, there is a complex history which deserves our attention and interest. For a long time, analysing the logic of scientific reasoning has seemed important not only to those concerned with the scope of logic but also to those concerned with the scope of science. If we are to take seriously those who would have us believe that science has no logic, but is steered by rhetoric and ideology, we need to take this history into account. It is possible that all those analysing the logic of science were suffering from an illusion created by the psychological, social and ideological circumstances in which they found themselves. It is possible that there is no logic of science even though there is a long, sustained and coherent history of people who thought that there is such a logic. But possibilities are not always reasonable; we can and should ignore them unless they are shown to be reasonable. Moreover, there is a kind of arrogance involved in the claim that we are able, at last, to correct the mistake they made. Presumably we are as much influenced by our circumstances as they were by theirs; we are as liable as they to suffer from illusions. Of course, plausible tales can be told of the effects people's lives have on what they think. But this will not show that the possibilities envisaged are reasonable. For we can accept these tales without having to set aside other reasons why people think as they do, and some of them might be reasons of logic. To grasp the history of thinking about scientific method, and thereby illuminate current thinking, we cripple ourselves if we set aside the idea that the existence of real, objective, logical issues about the nature of scientific reasoning could have been an important reason why so much attention has been paid to scientific method.

Given its complexity, it is inevitable that the history traced in the chapters of this book is selective. My aim has not been comprehensiveness, even if that were possible. Rather, I have tried to tell a story which is coherent in the sense that certain ideas grew out of preceding suggestions and formed the basis for succeeding developments. Especial emphasis is placed on the role of ideas about probability in scientific method. One reason for this is that a great deal of interesting work has been done recently in recovering those ideas and relating them to the intellectual aspects of the historical contexts in which they emerged. A second reason is that current discussions of scientific method, even if they do not endorse the view that it is fundamentally probabilistic, cannot afford to ignore that view. This does, indeed, involve a certain distortion of history because, in describing and evaluating the contributions made by participants in that history, implicit use is made of information not available to them, namely, information about the fate of what they accomplished. Some distortion is, though, unavoidable if history is to connect with the present and help us understand it. One particular kind of distortion is readily apparent. It results from the omission of certain important thinkers and their ideas from this history. Thus, Aristotle's views about method are ignored, despite the influence that they exerted prior to the scientific revolution in the seventeenth century. In many respects we cannot properly appreciate the achievements of that century without information about those views, and about the very many ways in which they were received and modified. Nevertheless, the link with thinking about probability, which began to take shape in the seventeenth century, has meant that this history begins with Galileo and Bacon. There are other omissions. Descartes is a more important figure in the history of scientific method than is here acknowledged. In the nineteenth century there are several whose contributions are neglected, including Auguste Comte, Stanley Jevons, George Boole, John Dewey and Leslie Ellis. As for the twentieth century, the list of those neglected is embarrassingly long. To itemise it would be to invite further criticism and embarrassment. It does, though, include some important contributors that are unjustly ignored by others, such as W. E. Johnson.

In the past, both those we describe as philosophers and those we describe as scientists found it natural and important to reflect on the methods used in science. From the seventeenth century through to the nineteenth century, scientific beliefs were supplanting religious convictions, and it seemed important to clarify and explain the nature of the authority which enabled them to do that. Moreover, given that people were questioning, implicitly or explicitly, the authority of religious claims, it was entirely appropriate that they should question the authority of scientific claims. Galileo challenged the authority of the Church with respect to matters which, in his view, lay outside its scope. But he himself was attempting to draw conclusions about the real world, particularly about the structure of the celestial world, from evidence concerning the apparent world, the only world legitimately available to scientific investigation. Accordingly, he himself was challenged for laying claim to knowledge of matters outside the scope of his investigations. Similarly, Darwin challenged the power of the established English Church and claimed that with the aid of his theory of evolution, he could explain all those facts about the appearance, structure and behaviour of living creatures which had previously been thought to point to the existence of a designing creator. But critics of Darwin were quick to point out that if the only reason for believing the theory of evolution is its ability to account for such facts, then there can be no objection to other theories, including the theory postulating a designing creator, capable of accounting for the same facts. There is, as it were, more than one 'likely story' we can tell about the reason for the facts we observe; if Darwin's 'story' is to prevail over others, we need a good argument as to why it should.

Today, the motives for examining methods in science are different. We undertake such an examination, not because we seek to challenge the legitimacy of science, but because we wish to explain that legitimacy and, perhaps, to show that it is well grounded. For the most part, contemporary scientists do not find it either necessary or appropriate to turn to scientific method in defending the conclusions they state in their research reports. Reviewers and readers of such reports will take for granted what authors could have said about their method, and rightly so. There are, to be sure, occasions when these assumptions are mistaken, for scientists, like the rest of us, are sometimes economical with the truth. Reasons are found for setting aside data as 'untypical'. Sometimes the reasons are bad and, as a result, fraudulent claims are made. We may be led to believe that all relevant experimental evidence has been taken into account in reaching a certain conclusion whereas, in fact, evidence incompatible with the conclusion has been discarded for reasons which scientists may not have stated and may not be good. But those who deceive know that they are deceiving. They will know, that is, what conclusion they can legitimately draw, even if they fail to draw it.

In general, though, the point of paying attention to method is not to prevent or discourage fraud, or dishonesty, or carelessness. It is, rather, to enable us to see how the various sources of scientific knowledge contribute to the elaborate structures expressing that knowledge, and how we make judgements about the credibility of scientific conclusions. This appears to be the reason why scientists often find it appropriate to explain what they mean by scientific method in the textbooks they write for students. They will there emphasise, usually in an introductory chapter, the importance of observation, of data, and of evidence in general, in determining what conclusions scientists should reach. It is, they say, an essential characteristic of scientific conclusions that evidence should be relevant to their truth or falsity. Many make it clear that the most satisfactory form of evidence is experimental evidence, and that therefore scientific methods are essentially experimental. The evidence yielded by experiment is important both because scientists can reproduce it and because they can control it in such a way that it will yield answers to specific questions. Thus, the authors of a recent chemistry textbook write that, in the laboratory, 'nature is observed under controlled conditions so that the results of experiments are reproducible' (Brady, Humiston and Heikkinen 1982: 2). A similar view is expressed in a current physics textbook: 'In order to fulfil its objective, physics, as well as all natural sciences, both pure and applied, depends on ... experimentation [which] consists in the observation of a phenomenon under prearranged and carefully controlled conditions' (Alonso and Finn 1992: 4). In experiments, scientists interrogate rather than passively observe nature and are sometimes able to make their interrogations highly specific. Outside the laboratory they can do little more than observe and record the passing show of physical, chemical or biological phenomena, but inside the laboratory they can manipulate and control phenomena in order to answer the question: what would happen if ...? The analogies between scientific evidence and legal evidence, between the interrogation of nature in the laboratory and the interrogation of witnesses in courts of law, have not been lost on scientists. The writer of a biology textbook writes: 'As with legal evidence, scientific evidence can be strong and convincing, or merely suggestive, or poor' (Weisz 1961: 8). In the law, we seek to link conjectures about guilt or innocence with facts by interrogating witnesses and experts; in science, we seek to link our hypotheses and theories about nature with facts by interrogating nature in experiments.

Perhaps because it is expressed in such a general manner, the image of experiment which emerges from a reading of these accounts of how science is done is both misleadingly impoverished and disappointingly dull. The value and interest of a science depends, it would seem, entirely on its subject matter, on what is established rather than how it is established. And yet it takes little knowledge of a science or its history to realise that, often, experimentation is a source of evidence only because experimenters have exercised their manipulative skills, their imaginative powers and their patient persistence. Jakob Berzelius set new standards of experimental accuracy with his meticulous studies of the atomic weights of elements. Galileo, with an ingenious thought experiment, demonstrated brilliantly that objects falling freely from rest must travel the same distance in the same time. Michael Faraday established the identity of the different forms of electricity by means of a painstaking series of experimental investigations. But experimental know-how, ingenuity and determination are not inexhaustible, and consequently experiments are rarely decisive. Laboratory interrogations yield results which are often ambiguous and sometimes opaque. Part of the craft knowledge of a skilled experimentalist is to persuade us to adopt a particular interpretation of the evidence, to resolve the ambiguity in a particular way, to see despite the opacity. But when we come to form our own judgements about the conclusions that experiments are said to support, we try to resolve the uncertainties of the evidence before us and we are able to do so because, in part at least, we have balanced probabilities. The craft of the experimenter faces the critical judgement of those he or she wishes to persuade. Critical judgement will not always deliver the right answer but, by analysing the way it works, we will enrich our understanding of science as intellectually challenging.

So, although we construct and justify scientific knowledge on the basis of experimental evidence, the way that we do this is much more interesting, and much more problematic, than science textbooks suggest. The suggestion of these textbooks that to adopt a scientific method is to adopt a simple routine fails to do justice to the sophisticated skills which scientists use when they experiment and when they reason from evidence. Since the seventeenth century, philosophers have been trying to characterise the nature of these skills and, in the case of reasoning, they have made good progress. Less, though, has been achieved in understanding experimental skill. There are reasons – or excuses – for this. First, not all natural science lends itself to experiment. Astronomy throughout most of its history has been a conspicuous example, but in the earth sciences, too, fieldwork observation is sometimes more significant than laboratory experiment. Second, and more important, experimental expertise is closely tied to the subject matter of science. There are some general features which a good experiment in spectroscopy has in common with a good experiment in bacteriology, but the most interesting and the most important features are different. But third, the sheer variety of experiments defies any attempt to generalise. The language of experiment, or 'experimental discourse', is no longer confined to what we would ordinarily think of as science. We describe certain novels, plays, musical compositions and visual art as experiments; we refer to some political, social and economic programmes as experiments; and our everyday activities such as cooking or driving a car are sometimes described as experimental. What we mean when we use such descriptions is that what is described is in some sense out of the ordinary; it is unnatural. We know, or think we know, how a musical composition should sound, and when we hear music which fails to fit our expectations we describe it as experimental. We know, or think we know, what makes a political programme acceptable and practical, and when a programme is proposed which we think unacceptable or impractical we label it experimental. We know, or think we know, how to bake a cottage pie and we experiment when we depart, more or less radically, from the standard recipe. Such usages are not metaphorical; they signify, rather, that the scope of 'experimental discourse' is large. There is a complex network of similarities which bind these usages together, just as there is in usages of the term 'game'; but there is no single characteristic which they share and which could therefore serve as a definition of 'experiment'. It is not surprising, therefore, that the 'nature' of experimental investigation has proved elusive. Francis Bacon provided a sustained study of experiment in his *Novum Organum* but, until recently, very little had been added to it, perhaps because of the prevalent but unjust view that 'at least among philosophers of science Baconian method is now only taken seriously by the most provincial and illiterate' (Lakatos 1974: 259). Studies by historians and sociologists of science are now beginning to enrich our appreciation of the complexities and subtleties of 'experimental discourse'. Whether these studies will enable us to create an enlightening philosophy of experiment remains to be seen.

Textbook writers also give some attention to the way in which experimental evidence is used to justify conclusions about the scope of a novel technique, the worth of a tentative hypothesis, the reliability of a natural law, and the value of a scientific theory. We can find more sustained accounts of this reasoning in textbooks of logic, and in the work of philosophers of science who have offered analyses of the logical aspects of scientific methods. In the nineteenth century, certainly, studies of logic which aimed at comprehensiveness would have included as a matter of course some discussion of methods of scientific reasoning. And in the twentieth century a number of well known texts which are designed to introduce students to logic contain chapters on scientific method. A typical account tells us that, as a plausible basis of observations of some natural phenomena, scientists formulate a hypothesis. They will then use this hypothesis to predict what will happen in new, untried, circumstances. If possible these untried circumstances will be created in, and controlled by, an experiment. Prediction and experimental result can then be compared. If they agree then the hypothesis is confirmed, or substantiated; if they disagree the hypothesis must be modified or discarded. Continued confirmation of the hypothesis by experimental evidence will increase the scientists' confidence in its truth, and they may begin to think of it as a reliable law. This is no more than a roughly sketched outline of what is called 'the method of hypotheses' or 'the hypothetico-deductive method'; a detailed analysis is neither intended nor given. It is sufficient, nevertheless, to indicate where the crucial logical steps are taken.

Scientists, the textbooks say, have to derive testable predictions from their hypotheses. How, in practice, is this done? Lavoisier hypothesised that, when mercury is slowly burnt in a sample of air to form what we now call mercuric oxide, it appears to absorb part of that air. If he is right then, when we heat the mercuric oxide further so as to recover the mercury, we should find that the air released in the process is equal in quantity to the air absorbed. This prediction does follow from the hypothesis, but not from the hypothesis alone, for we need to make important if natural assumptions about what is happening in the experiment. As Lavoisier said, the slow burning of the mercury took place over a number of days and the reduction in the quantity of air remaining may have been due not to absorption of part of the air by the mercury but due to some overlooked fault in the experimental apparatus. In deriving the prediction to test, therefore, Lavoisier depended on the practical reliability of his equipment. The common and essential practice of testing and calibrating experimental equipment shows that scientists are fully aware of how important its reliability is in reaching secure conclusions.

Suppose, though, that an experimental test of the derived prediction is successful; the test and the prediction match. Lavoisier's evidence about the quantity of air released from heated mercuric oxide, for example, matched the prediction he derived from his oxygen hypothesis. In general, any coincidence between test result and prediction is not perfect, and it certainly was not perfect in this example. Tests are only more or less successful and we cannot define the borderline between a successful and an unsuccessful test, despite the weight we wish to place on the difference. Evidence from tests can be clear and decisive, leaving no doubt whether a prediction is true or false. But more usually it is difficult to obtain, ambiguous and indecisive. Often it has to stand alongside other evidence with which it may appear to conflict, and if we are unable to resolve the conflict our confidence in the evidence may be compromised. We cannot, therefore, assume that the scientist's judgement of a match between evidence and prediction is unproblematic; it will be made in the light of experience and will be fallible.

To these practical problems about the correct interpretation of experimental evidence we must add the logical difficulties we encounter when we try to draw a conclusion from a successful test of a hypothesis. The fact that we describe the test as successful suggests that our conclusion about the truth of the hypothesis should be positive. A successful test should increase our confidence in the truth of the hypothesis. But can it? Admittedly, this hypothesis enables us to derive a successful prediction, but there are other hypotheses which we could have used to derive the same successful prediction. Not all these hypotheses can be true, for there will be incompatibilities between them. Why, though, should we conclude that one rather than another is true, or that one rather than another is more likely to be true? If the only ground for concluding that a particular hypothesis is true is its ability to lead to one or more successful predictions, then the fact that there are other hypotheses which also lead to those same successful predictions seems to show that the conclusion is arbitrarily drawn. We might just as well have selected the hypothesis by lot, or randomly. Lavoisier's oxygen hypothesis did indeed lead to a successful prediction in the case of mercuric oxide, but we can make the contrary hypothesis that mercuric oxide absorbs a material substance – phlogiston – rather than releases oxygen, and it will lead us to the same successful prediction if we couple it with suitable other hypotheses. We have, so far, no reason for preferring either hypothesis over the other. In practice, of course, we normally have no difficulty in choosing one hypothesis rather than others as the one supported by the successful predictions to which they all lead. The difficulty arises when we try to explain the choice and to identify its rational basis.

Often, the reasoning which leads from a successful prediction to the conclusion that the hypothesis which generated it is likely to be true, or is more likely to be true than it was prior to the prediction, is described as 'inductive' reasoning. The 'method of hypotheses', that is to say, is an inductive method. If, by induction, we mean reasoning which leads from true premises to a more or less probable conclusion, or probable reasoning, then this description is correct. Such reasoning is not truth-preserving, for it does not guarantee a true conclusion when true premises are provided. But it is ampliative, for the conclusions it yields make claims which go beyond what is claimed in the premises. We are risking a false conclusion when we reason inductively, but if the conclusion is true then it can be of considerable value to us and we may think that the risk is worth taking. Much will depend upon our being able to claim that the premises of the inductive argument make the conclusion probably true to a high degree. But it is just this claim that is challenged. There are other conclusions which we can draw from the same premises; why should we think any one more probable than any other? The method of hypotheses allows us to 'justify' any number of distinct and incompatible hypotheses, in the sense that we can derive these hypotheses using this method. Nothing, so far, entitles us to favour one over any other. So inductive, or probable, reasoning seems impotent. If the conclusion yielded by an inductive argument with given true premises is probable, it is no more probable than any number of other conclusions that we can draw from those same premises, so we have no reason for accepting it in preference to any of those other conclusions.

One way of responding to this difficulty is to eschew the method of hypothesis altogether. It is unreliable and cannot legitimately justify the adoption of any scientific belief. Should we justify any belief by using this method, it will fail to count as scientific. This response is found in many philosophers and scientists since the seventeenth century. Galileo and Newton both recognised that the weakness of the method meant that no proposition defended by it could have a claim on our allegiance. If we consider hypotheses as propositions justified by this method then, according to Galileo and Newton, hypotheses have no proper place in science. Resistance to, or at least suspicion of, the method has persisted. In the twentieth century, we find philosophers of science such as Reichenbach and Popper developing accounts of scientific method which avoid dependence on the method of hypotheses. Scientists, too, have sometimes tended to doubt or ignore the supposed implications of a successful prediction for the truth of a hypothesis, though they have accepted the implications of an unsuccessful prediction for the falsity of a hypothesis. Thus, the physicist Richard Feynman said that, in science, we compute consequences of a proposed new law and compare the result with experiment 'to see if it works'. 'If,' he continued, 'it disagrees with experiment it is wrong. In that simple statement is the key to science' (Feynman 1965: 156). Significantly, he did not say what follows if computation and experiment agree.

A second way of responding has been to turn to ideas about probability. Henri Poincaré declared, of the mathematical calculus of probability, that without it 'science would be impossible' (Poincaré, 1952: 186). And Bertrand Russell was equally forthright: 'we cannot understand scientific method,' he said, 'without a previous investigation of the different kinds of probability' (Russell 1948: 354). The claim is that, prior to our having any information about the success or otherwise of a prediction implied by a hypothesis, we can make a judgement about how probable the hypothesis is. But we will make different judgements about different hypotheses, even though they are all capable of implying the prediction. The effect of this is that, after the prediction is known to be successful, we will be able to identify one hypothesis as the most probable. We will be able to assign a new probability to the hypothesis selected in the light of the successful prediction. Further successful predictions will further enhance this probability. There are, though, difficulties with this approach, for if these probabilities are going to justify our belief that a hypothesis is true we must show that they have a rational basis. We must show, that is, that our judgements of 'prior' probabilities are rational judgements. Philosophers and probabilists, such as Leibniz, the Bernoullis, Bayes and Laplace, suggested that our reason could provide a sufficient ground for the rationality of our judgements; that prior probabilities are a priori probabilities. But during the course of the nineteenth century their project began to founder as it became clear that reason does not always speak with a single consistent voice when consulted about probabilities. In the twentieth century, philosophers of science have sought to meet this challenge by developing a so-called subjective or personalist Bayesianism. This identifies constraints on prior probabilities which, though much weaker than those which had been proposed, are claimed sufficient to deliver rational judgements. But, despite the efforts that have been made over a long period of time to analyse probable reasoning, there are some who doubt that those efforts will help us to understand scientific method: 'probability', according to one influential contemporary philosopher of science, 'is a distinctly minor note in the history of scientific argument' (Glymour 1980: 66).

A third response is to urge that we recognise the role played by the historical and social context within which any scientist must work and make decisions. We cannot understand any important part of what a scientist does by appealing to logic or to scientific method. The weakness of the method of hypothesis simply shows that scientists can decide nothing of significance by reference to it. This is not to say that scientists are illogical or unmethodical; it is to say that logic and method are totally inadequate when what we seek is an understanding of the construction of scientific knowledge. We are persuaded to accept scientific claims in the same way that we are persuaded to accept non-scientific claims, namely by means of interests and rhetoric rather than reason or experiment. In science, as in politics, religion, philosophy, etc., our beliefs are consequences of complex historical, psychological and social processes and interactions. The power of these processes and interactions makes the attempt to identify a method for science misleading and unnecessary.

In the chapters which follow, these issues will recur in one form or another. The logical character of scientific method has tended to dominate the thinking of both scientists and philosophers, and the issues that have arisen are prominent in most chapters. Isaac Newton laid great stress on the need for rules of reasoning in science, and was very clear that some kinds of arguments used to justify conclusions are superior to others. His eighteenth-century successors turned to rapidly developing ideas about chance and probability in their exploration of the limits of legitimate reasoning. Nineteenth-century debates about scientific method grew out of this exploration and gave a sharper edge to the issues. Disagreements, with practical implications, emerged; the reasoning used to justify a theory was a legitimate target for those defending alternative theories. In the twentieth century, logical techniques have helped to illuminate and clarify some important questions, though they have also led to idealisations which sometimes seem to have only a remote connection with real scientific reasoning. Artificial, idealised languages may be conducive to clarity and precision, but arguments in science are expressed in natural languages which, though they may be supplemented with carefully defined scientific terminology, invariably contain obscurities and imprecisions. Many of the questions addressed by philosophers of science during the last fifty years have acquired a life of their own, in the sense that they have seemed worth solving irrespective of their relevance to real scientific enquiry. There is, that is to say, a philosopher's agenda which has to some extent developed independently of the practical questions which were its original basis.

The experimental character of scientific method has, until recently, received less attention. It has been enough to say that scientists simply assemble data relating to phenomena yielded by experiments, and then use those data to test theories and hypotheses. Thus Galileo used data from experiments with inclined planes to support his hypothesis that the speed reached by a falling object is proportional to the square of the time taken to fall from rest; Thomas Young, in his attempts to support a wave theory of light, used data derived from experiments in which an interference pattern was observed as a result of monochromatic light being passed through two narrow but close-together slits in a screen; Millikan used data from a series of experiments in order to show that each electron carries a discrete electrical charge. These examples, all from physics, are matched by similar examples from other natural sciences. In the eighteenth century, Stephen Hales devised experiments with results showing that the sap does not circulate in plants as blood does in animals but rather ebbs and flows in a regular daily manner; and towards the end of the nineteenth century, Louis Pasteur used data from his experiments on what we now call vaccines to test his ideas about how they work in protecting people from the effects of viruses (see Harré 1983: 52–8, 96–104).

Such cursory accounts are, however, insufficient, and we will have an opportunity to see why in the chapters about Galileo and Bacon. They knew well that experimental discourse has a grammar which requires a more sensitive appreciation of the skills and abilities which experimentalists bring to bear in their laboratories. Their contributions were, though, very different. Galileo is often hailed as the first experimental physicist, and there is much in his published and unpublished writings which justifies that description. It was his consummate ingenuity in calling on evidence from experiments, sometimes quite simple experiments, which impressed his friends and followers, and which irritated his foes. Bacon, by contrast, had little or no skill in devising and using apparatus and measuring devices; yet he thought harder than most about why experiments are important. In them, he showed, we can bring together the practical arts and the theoretical sciences, and thereby promote the 'advancement of learning'.

During the last few years there has been a revival of interest in the philosophy of experiment. As a result of this interest, philosophers of science have begun to pay more attention to the vocabulary of 'data', 'results', 'observations', 'phenomena', etc. that we use to speak about experiments, and to distinctions previously overlooked, such as that between data and phenomena. They also take more account of the practical difficulties in obtaining 'good' data from experiments, and of how experimenters deal with data they judge not to be 'good'. Experiments are not simple events with clear beginnings and ends; they are human interventions in a world of numerous conflicting influences and forces, and have their origins in earlier related investigations and their termination in later explorations. It is not surprising that the data produced in laboratories are sometimes unreliable, often contradictory, and always ambiguous. Experimental enquiries do have a life of their own, independent of any theories or hypotheses to which they may be relevant. We will consider the outcome of this recent revival in the final chapter.

What, though, of the project of elucidating the methods used by scientists when they justify, to themselves or to others, the claims they make about how our world works? Has it been a misguided failure? Is the search for a characteristic logic of science doomed to be fruitless and unnecessary? Some would claim that, whatever else may be true about science, and however limited our success may so far have been, there must be criteria which scientists can use in order to judge whether the conclusions they reach are likely to represent the facts correctly. Otherwise there would be no better reason to believe the conclusions of scientists than the conclusions of pseudo-scientists, quacks and confidence tricksters. To identify these criteria is to identify the methods and logic of science; it is not a trivial task even though it is a matter of making explicit what is taken for granted. We may still be debating important details about how the methods and logic of science work. We may even still be debating some issues of principle. But this does not in itself show that the project is misconceived; it may instead be a project where both principles and details are immensely difficult to make explicit. After all, for most of recorded history people have reasoned in ways that were always regarded as acceptable even though no-one knew how to make explicit the rules which made the reasoning acceptable.

Others, though, will say that a project intended to identify scientific methods would reveal the presuppositions or prejudices of scientists only at particular times and in particular places. To dignify these prejudices with labels like 'logic of science' and 'scientific method' is to attempt to give them political weight by investing them with a spurious authority and permanence (see Fuller 1987: 150). Science is a social activity, and the means by which it is pursued are a matter for negotiation between scientists, and between them and those other members of their society who have some control over what they do. Accordingly, the methods of science are grounded in the needs and interests of the particular and different societies within which scientists work; they are not, as the philosophers would have us believe, grounded in universal requirements of rationality. It is, in short, not universal reason but the conventions agreed in particular societies which determine the legitimacy of the reasoning used by scientists in that society.

This issue, too, is relatively recent, though there are intimations of it in Poincaré. In the final chapter I will mount a defence of the project intended to identify and elucidate a logic for natural science. Such a project, I claim, meets a need which has, at least, a psychological basis. As earlier chapters will show, scientific method has played an important part in both logic and in the philosophy of science. Of late it has been neglected. Many have thought that, if there is anything interesting to be said about it, let psychologists or sociologists say it, for they have the appropriate concepts and they will know how to collect and analyse the relevant evidence. There are, no doubt, psychological and sociological aspects of scientific method which lend themselves to such scrutiny. Certainly it has historical aspects which deserve the attention of historians. But I do not doubt either that there are questions about scientific method which are philosophical questions. Such reasons as have been given for dismissing those questions as inadmissible are less than compelling. The contribution philosophers can make to our understanding of the natural sciences is, perhaps, modest. It is, nevertheless, legitimate, both as a contribution to that task and as an application of our ability to reflect upon, to question and to evaluate a characteristically human enterprise.

FURTHER READING

Cohen, M. R. and Nagel, E. (1949) *An Introduction to Logic and Scientific Method*, Book 2, London: Routledge and Kegan Paul.

Black, M. (1952) *Critical Thinking: An Introduction to Logic and Scientific Method*, Part 3, Englewood Cliffs, NJ: Prentice-Hall.

Carnap, R. (1966) *An Introduction to the Philosophy of Science*, edited by Martin Gardner, New York: Basic Books.

Giere, R. (1984) *Understanding Scientific Reasoning*, second edition, New York: Holt, Rinehart and Winston.

Fisher, A. (1988) *The Logic of Real Arguments*, Cambridge: Cambridge University Press.

Klemke, E. D., Hollinger, R. and Kline, A. D. (eds) (1988) *Introductory Reading in the Philosophy of Science*, revised edition, Buffalo, NY: Prometheus Books.

Burbidge, J. (1990) *Within Reason: A Guide to Non-Deductive Reasoning*, Peterborough, Ontario: Broadview Press.

Copi, I. M. and Cohen, C. (1990) *Introduction to Logic*, Part 3, eighth edition, London: Collier Macmillan.

Losee, J. (1993) *A Historical Introduction to the Philosophy of Science*, third edition, Oxford: Oxford University Press.

Gustason, W. (1994) *Reasoning from Evidence: Inductive Logic*, New York: Macmillan College Publishing Company.

2 Galileo Galilei
New methods for a new science

Because Galileo thought the way some of his predecessors thought and also anticipated the thinking of some of his successors, his views are of special interest in understanding scientific method. He sought respectable authority for his way of establishing conclusions in the writings of ancient Greek philosophers and mathematicians, and there are, too, connections between his ideas and those of his more immediate predecessors and contemporaries in Italy. But he also helped to develop the role of experiment, particularly as a useful means for discovering and exploring new connections in nature, and partly because of this we detect in him ideas and methods which were further developed by his successors. There is no doubt that his claims about what is true and why it is true were particularly influential in the seventeenth century. His ideas played an important part in the early development of scientific method although, as we shall see, the differences between Galileo's views and those familiar to us are at least as significant as the similarities.

He was born in 1564, the year of Michelangelo's death and of Shakespeare's birth. After studying and teaching mathematics at the University of Pisa, he became, in 1592, a teacher of mathematics at the prestigious University of Padua in the Venetian Republic. There he remained until he was forty-six years of age, when he received an invitation from one of his former pupils, Cosimo II de' Medici, the Grand Duke of Tuscany, to continue his scientific work in Florence as Chief Mathematician and Philosopher. He acquired, that is, a patron, just as artists and writers of the period also did, and it was during this period of service to the Tuscan court that he accomplished much of the scientific work that we associate with his name. In 1616, Galileo was instructed on the authority of Pope Paul V to abandon a theory for which he had been arguing with increasing skill and ingenuity, namely Nicholas Copernicus's theory that it is the Earth, rather than the Sun, that moves. A panel of ecclesiastical authorities had examined this theory and had decided that, because the theory 'contradicted Holy Scripture' and thereby challenged the authority of the Church, it should not be held or defended. Galileo accepted the decision and knew that disobedience would result in arrest and punishment. But it was not until 1632, sixteen years after the warning, when Galileo was elderly and infirm, that he received a summons to appear before officers of the Inquisition in Rome to answer allegations that in his *Dialogue Concerning Two Chief World Systems, Ptolemaic and Copernican*, published that year, he had ignored the ruling. The famous trial of Galileo took place in 1633; its result was that he was sentenced to life imprisonment and was required to acknowledge publicly the false and heretical nature of Copernicanism. In the event, imprisonment amounted to house arrest and, although Galileo's freedom was severely restricted, he was able to work, to enjoy the company of visitors, and to take advantage of the comforts provided by powerful patrons. The dialogue known as *Two New Sciences*, which was the culmination of more than thirty years of work and thought, was published during this period. His reputation was firmly established throughout Europe; his discoveries and opinions, declared one of his visitors, Thomas Hobbes, 'opened to us the gate of natural philosophy universal' (Hobbes 1839: vol. 1, viii). He died, early in 1642, in his villa – 'The Jewel' – at Arcetri near Florence, and is buried in that city's beautiful Santa Croce.

Hobbes's view of Galileo as a pioneer was shared by his contemporaries and has since been widely endorsed. A Paduan colleague described him as 'the father of experiments and of all their exactness' (Drake 1978: 367), and the eighteenth-century French *philosophe* Condorcet declared that he 'founded the first school . . . where all methods other than experiment and calculation were rejected with philosophical severity' (Condorcet 1955: 115). In the nineteenth century the Austrian philosopher-physicist Ernst Mach attributed to Galileo the introduction of experimental methods in physics. 'Only when Galileo . . . investigated the motion of falling experimentally,' he said, 'could the laws of the uniformly accelerated motion of falling appear in a purely quantitative form' (Mach 1960: 167). And in our own century Mach's view remains prevalent: an introductory textbook of physics castigates the Ancient Greeks for their supposed reliance on 'reason and faith', and identifies Galileo as the first to recognise 'the importance of doing experiments as a way of testing hypotheses' (Krane 1983: 12).

Although some have questioned the role of experiments in Galileo's method, there is no dispute about the innovative character of his claims. In *Two New Sciences*, for instance, he requires readers to consider familiar phenomena in an unfamiliar way, and many of his conclusions remain strikingly disconcerting in that they contradict common sense and subvert received wisdom. We cannot fail to notice, too, the powerful rhetoric he uses to state his arguments and their conclusions. This book, his last major publication, expressed ideas about motion which had preoccupied him since his days as a teacher in Pisa, and its conclusions had been reached with difficulty. In a modified form, those conclusions have survived to the present day and are familiar to anyone who has studied elementary dynamics. But what matters for our purposes is the presentation and justification of those conclusions, rather than their scientific content. Galileo took great pains to ensure that his readers would be persuaded that his conclusions were correct. His methods for achieving this were not those we would use today, but they are recognisably scientific and they do shed interesting light on what was expected of science in the seventeenth century. We need, therefore, to examine these methods. We will see that the important, but very new, role played by experiment in Galileo's work is largely concealed by the way he presents his conclusions. To understand why this is so we will need to consider more generally Galileo's thinking about experimentation.

The question of how motion should be studied was answered by Galileo's contemporaries in a different way than it would be answered today. We think that the scientific study of motion is an experimental and mathematical undertaking. We think, that is, that our knowledge of the laws governing the behaviour of objects in motion must in some way be founded on our knowledge, gained by means of experiment, of moving objects, and that these laws should be expressed in the precise language of mathematics. For example, we observe and measure various characteristics of objects as they roll down inclined planes, and on that basis we develop general laws which will be expressed in a mathematical form. But in the sixteenth and seventeenth centuries a different way of thinking prevailed. The science of motion was then understood to be a study of the causes of motion, and to be, like any genuine science, a 'demonstrative' kind of enquiry. That is to say, experiential knowledge of the facts of motion was superseded by rational knowledge of the causes of those facts, this being accomplished by deductions from fundamental principles, or 'common notions', and definitions which were accepted as true. These facts of motion were understood as expressions of common experience rather than as generalisations based upon experiments. This was because the results of the experiments that could be performed were sufficiently uncertain and ambiguous to prevent reliable generalisation; discrepancies between conclusions derived from principles, and experimental results, could be tolerated. The appropriate model of a demonstrative science was Euclidean geometry, where the credibility of a theorem about, say, triangles depends not on how well it fits what we can measure but on its derivability from the basic axioms and definitions of the geometry. Just as the real triangles we can construct and measure do not exactly display the characteristics of the ideal triangles of geometry, so also the results of experiments concerning moving objects do not have to correspond exactly to the features of such objects described in a demonstrative science of motion. Since this science should be applicable to the real world, no doubt there must be some relationship between it and the motions we can observe and measure. But, although the nature of this relationship may be puzzling, it is no more so in this case than it is in the case of other demonstrative sciences such as geometry.

For Galileo and his contemporaries there was a good reason why demonstration, or proof from first principles, rather than experiment, was required to establish general truths about motion. Any science – *scientia* – must yield knowledge of what Aristotle had called 'reasoned facts', i.e. truths which are both universal and necessary, and such knowledge – philosophical knowledge – can only be arrived at by demonstration. To have knowledge of a reasoned fact, such as the fact that the interior angles of any triangle must add to two right angles, or the fact that the distance travelled by a falling object from rest must be proportional to the square of the time for which it has been falling, is to have understanding of that fact; it is, in other words, to be able to explain it. But this means being able to derive it from what is already known and understood, for we can explain why a fact holds by showing how it follows from accepted principles. So scientific knowledge must be demonstrative knowledge. Particular experiments cannot provide knowledge of a reasoned fact because they lack universality and therefore cannot provide understanding of the fact; rather, we must use whatever knowledge we have of reasoned facts about motion to explain experimental results.

But, even independently of Aristotelian doctrine, the ability of a method to yield certain knowledge was crucial, for investigations that we now call scientific were in Galileo's time counted as part of philosophy – natural philosophy – and the authority of philosophy depended upon its capacity to provide us with knowledge rather than mere opinion about nature. Anyone could acquire opinions, or beliefs, about how nature works simply by observing. Such opinions, however, would often be unreliable and sometimes self-contradictory. For certain knowledge we need to exercise our reason rather than our senses. But, although the aim of certainty was agreed, the means for achieving it were disputed. In particular, there was a long-standing disagreement about the role that mathematics could play in natural philosophy, even though mathematics was able to give certain knowledge. For some, a proper science should not only be able to produce derivations of 'reasoned facts' about, say, the motion of freely falling objects; it should also be able to adduce the cause of those facts, for it is only by so doing that a genuine explanation can be given. But derivations effected by the use of mathematical techniques will not necessarily succeed in identifying causes. For example, it follows mathematically from the claim that the velocity of a freely falling object is proportional to the time for which it has been falling, that the distance travelled is proportional to the square of the time taken; but such a derivation gives no information about what causes freely falling objects to behave in this way. But for many of Galileo's contemporaries a science of motion which failed to be concerned with causes would not be a proper science at all. We need, they thought, to know why objects fall as they do, not just how they fall as they do.

During the period when Galileo was teaching at Padua there was a vigorous debate about whether a mathematical science, providing quantified descriptions rather than causal explanations, could be a real science. Some took the view that mathematics treats only of abstract matters, whereas natural philosophy is concerned with real things and the causes of their behaviour and characteristics. They thought that causes could only be identified by using Aristotelian syllogistic reasoning. For example, a straightforward syllogism concludes that the planets, unlike the stars, shine with a steady light on the basis of premises which state that all heavenly bodies which are near the Earth shine with a steady light and that the planets are near the Earth. The information in these premises, if accepted, does indeed explain why the planets shine with a steady light, for it gives the proximity of a planet to the Earth as the cause of that effect. Such reasoning was widely taught and understood; it provided, so it was believed, the only means by which causal explanations of physical matters could be reliably investigated. Admittedly, it lent itself to qualitative rather than quantitative conclusions, but there was no reason to think that this represented a limitation so far as physical enquiries were concerned; indeed, mathematical precision should not be expected in a science of motion any more than in other parts of philosophy. As Aristotle had remarked, we should not expect more precision in the treatment of any subject than the nature of the subject permits. In some contexts, notably astronomy and geometry, the more elaborate and intellectually demanding methods of mathematics were often useful and appropriate, but in such contexts it seemed clear that those methods were applicable in so far as what was needed were re-descriptions which could help people formulate accurate predictions. 'Hypotheses' which successfully 'saved the phenomena', in the sense that they could be used as starting points for derivations of accurate predictions, could meet this need. Such hypotheses did not have to be true, since it is quite possible for true conclusions to follow correctly from false hypotheses. In astronomy, especially, a sharp division had emerged between mathematical astronomy and physical astronomy. In the former, mathematical methods were used to perfect the accuracy of predictions, and questions about the physical plausibility of the hypotheses used as a basis for the predictions were set aside. Predictive accuracy was an important practical consideration, for reliable calendars were needed for astrological and navigational purposes. But the status of mathematical astronomy as a demonstrative science was questionable simply because its use of mathematical techniques prevented it from revealing causes; its hypotheses could be no more than 'likely stories'. Copernicus's claim that the universe was heliocentric rather than geocentric, for example, was regarded by some as no more than a false hypothesis which happened to be remarkably useful for accurate prediction and calculation. Physical astronomy, on the other hand, tried to provide true causal explanations for celestial phenomena, but its limitations so far as accurate prediction is concerned deprived it of practical employment.

The situation was similar with regard to the science of motion. So long as it needed to produce causal explanations of motion, it was appropriate that the demonstrative methods used were syllogistic. But some, among them Galileo, sought – as a complement to a physical enquiry into the causes of motion – to develop a mathematical enquiry into the characteristics of motion. Doubts and confusions about how freely falling objects moved or about how to describe the path of a projectile could be resolved, they hoped, by treating the science of motion as a branch of mathematics and studying it by means of the methods which had been used with so much success in other branches. Geometry, in particular, had been an outstandingly successful, progressive and useful part of mathematics since the time of the ancient Greek mathematician Euclid; its basic 'axioms', or 'common notions', together with its definitions, were universally accepted as true, and mathematicians used them to explore the geometrical properties of space. Confidence in the truth of the axioms, and the security of the steps by means of which we are led from them to theorems, ensured that knowledge of the geometrical properties of space counted as real, necessary and certain knowledge. Above all, the systematic approach of Euclid in his *Elements* made it possible to derive a large number of important, useful and sometimes surprising geometrical theorems from a very small number of axioms. Indeed, this power of the axioms to act as a source for so many theorems was an additional important reason for accepting them as true.

But Euclid's *Elements* is a mathematical rather than a scientific work, and although his theorems can be used in a scientific investigation it is by no means obvious that Euclid's 'axiomatic' method has a useful application in science. Correct conclusions about motion may be mathematically derived from certain assumptions, but that does not establish the truth of the assumptions, for the same conclusions may also be derivable from other, perhaps incompatible, assumptions. In geometry we avoid the difficulty by declaring the basic premises – the axioms, common notions and definitions – to be 'self-evident', but premises suitable for a science of motion cannot be established so readily.

It is in connection with such problems that the Greek mathematician Archimedes is important. His work was in the tradition of Euclid, building upon the foundations provided in the *Elements* to establish, for example, truths about the surface area and volume of a sphere. But he also laid the foundation of that part of mechanics we now call statics, the science of bodies in equilibrium. His extensive writings only became widely available to scholars in the sixteenth century, several editions of them being published in Venice. For Galileo, who was familiar with some of Archimedes' treatises, it was especially important that he had shown that the axiomatic method need not be confined to geometry or arithmetic but could also be used to reach new conclusions in mechanics. For example, in his treatise 'On the Equilibrium of Planes or Centres of Gravity of Planes', Archimedes identified several postulates to be used in the derivation of propositions about levers and balances. For example, the first postulate envisaged a simple ideal beam balance and stated 'that equal weights at equal distances [from the fulcrum] are in equilibrium, and that equal weights at unequal distances are not in equilibrium, but incline towards the weight which is at the greater distance.' The justification for the adoption of such a postulate was not that it leads to correct conclusions but rather that it expressed, or idealised, common universal experience. This is not to say that it was a generalisation based upon experience, for that suggests – wrongly – that it is the conclusion of a derivation using, as premises, experiential claims that are even more basic and secure. It would be better to think of the postulate as providing a definitional link between the concepts of 'equal weights' and 'objects which balance each other'. Like Euclid's geometrical postulates, they were not justified on the basis of some further, more secure, statements; they were intended, rather, to be self-justifying in the sense that they do no more than make explicit what we intuitively know on the basis of familiar experience. Our experience of objects with weight is such that we would not count weights as equal unless, when at equal distances from a fulcrum, they balanced each other. Archimedes showed, in short, that experience as well as reason is capable of guaranteeing the foundations of a demonstrative science.

Galileo declared his science of motion was new just because it attempted to use these Archimedean methods. The conclusions of this new science must, as he said at the beginning of the *Two New Sciences*, be 'all geometrically demonstrated', for although some of these conclusions 'have been noted by others, and first of all by Aristotle, . . . they were not proved by necessary demonstrations from their primary and unquestionable foundations', and 'I want to prove these to you demonstratively and not just persuade you of them by probable arguments' (Galileo 1989: 15–16). This meant that he would have to identify and defend, as expressions or idealisations of common experience, principles which could be used as starting points for mathematical demonstrations.

There were, though, daunting differences between what had been accomplished by demonstrative methods in geometry and in statics, and what was hoped for in the case of motion. Not the least of these differences was the greater difficulty of knowing what the facts about motion were. For, although we can readily measure the real triangles and circles we draw, construct and find, we need instruments and apparatus to measure the velocities and accelerations which characterise moving objects. Galileo invented or developed some ingenious devices to meet this need, but nevertheless accurate ways of measuring small intervals of time were not available. But there were similarities, too, one of them being that, in the case of motion as well as geometry, discrepancies between what is implied by axioms and the results of measurement can be tolerated provided the axioms we use are sufficiently secure. For some, indeed, such discrepancies reinforced the point that there is little prospect of our being able to use our fallible senses to provide real knowledge.

In the case of the motion displayed by freely falling objects we need, Galileo said, 'to seek out and clarify the definition that best agrees with that which nature employs' (Galileo 1989: 153). This was indeed the crucial task and it had taxed the minds of all who wished to see progress being made in the study of motion. After repeated efforts and several false starts, Galileo had succeeded in formulating a definition of naturally accelerated motion which, he believed, does apply to falling objects. 'I say that motion is equably or uniformly accelerated which, abandoning rest, adds on to itself equal momenta of swiftness in equal times' (Galileo 1989: 154). In modern terminology, uniformly accelerated motion is motion where the velocity of a freely falling object is proportional to the time for which it has been falling. It was this definition that Galileo used as his starting point in his demonstrative science of motion.

Why, though, should this definition be accepted? Even if we agree that all freely falling bodies fall with the same accelerated motion, why suppose that this definition of accelerated motion is the appropriate one to use in calculating how, say, distance fallen depends upon time elapsed? Would it not be just as reasonable to define uniformly accelerated motion as motion where the velocity reached by a freely falling object is proportional to the distance through which it has fallen? Does it matter which definition is used? To see how Galileo answered these questions we must attend, not just to the kind of reasoning that he used, but also to the role of experience and experiment in his science of motion.

There are two questions about Galileo's definition of naturally accelerated motion, both of which raise the issue of how far experimentation played a role in his method. The first asks how Galileo was led to the definition he proposes; what reasons did he have which favoured his proposal? This is an historical question; an answer to it turns on the investigation of the clues he left in his papers concerning the processes which enabled him to generate his definition. We can draw no conclusion about whether he believed that the reasons he had were good reasons from such an investigation. The second question asks how Galileo justified his definition; what reasons did he give in his *Two New Sciences* for adopting his definition? This question is also an historical question, but an answer to it does provide information about what he and his contemporaries considered to be a good reason. An answer to this question will shed light on the methods considered proper for good science.

So far as the first of these questions is concerned, it does not seem possible that common observations of familiar events and circumstances could have led Galileo to adopt his definition. Common observations tell us that the Sun rises daily, that fire burns, that bread nourishes, that heavy unsupported objects fall, and that the speed of a falling object increases with both distance and with time. But there are no ordinary observations which lead inevitably to the view that the speed of a falling object is proportional to time taken. And yet, such a claim clearly has some relation to experience. So, if experience had a role in the discovery and formulation of the definition, the concept of experience would have to have application beyond generalised observations about how things usually occur. We take it for granted that the concept of experience does have application to the observed results of a scientific experiment, but for seventeenth-century scientists it was by no means evident that this was so.

Nevertheless, experiment – as distinct from common observation – was undoubtedly important to Galileo. Those who have studied his manuscripts are convinced that specially designed experiments played an indispensable role in leading him to his definition. These documents reveal, for example, that care and ingenuity were used in devising experiments showing how the distance travelled by a falling object depends upon the time taken. There were, to be sure, practical limits to what could be achieved by experiment. Distances could be measured consistently, though not with the precision which has since come to be expected; but in the absence of accurate clocks it was more difficult to measure and compare small intervals of time. For example, a manuscript dating from the time when Galileo was teaching at Padua records the results of an experiment which seems to have involved rolling a ball down an inclined plane and determining the distances through which the ball travels in small equal intervals of time. Though Galileo does not explain his working, his records can best be understood as measurements of the distance traversed by the ball from rest. The inclined plane used for the experiment was probably about two metres long and its angle of inclination would have needed to be quite shallow so that the ball would take several seconds to travel down it. It has been suggested that Galileo could have established the equality of the approximately half-second intervals he used by singing a tune and beating time to its regular musical rhythm (Drake 1975: 98–104; Drake 1990: ch. 1). However that may be, it is evident from the manuscript that Galileo was seeking a pattern in the way the distance figures increased. He tried and rejected a simple arithmetical pattern before noticing that each success-ive distance number is proportional to the square of the time taken. In this way, Galileo discovered the familiar rule often known as the 'times-squared' rule, namely that the total distances travelled by freely falling objects are proportional to the squares of the times taken. This rule can easily be derived from the definition of naturally accelerated motion that Galileo adopted in his *Two New Sciences*; it is proved as Theorem II, and is followed by an account of the inclined plane experiment, which illustrates the theorem.

But, although experiments such as the inclined plane do seem to have been important in leading Galileo to his conclusions, we should not suppose that he could make the move from experimental results to a general conclusion with ease. Incautious generalisation could easily result in mistakes, and even when it did not there remained the problem of how the certainty of the conclusion could be established, as it must be if the conclusion was to serve as the basis for a science. To address this problem we need to turn to the second of our questions: what reasons did Galileo give for adopting his axioms and definition?

We take it for granted that the right method to use in establishing a science of motion is, in part at least, experimental. So the reasons that Galileo gave for defining naturally accelerated motion in the way he did should have been experimental reasons. And it is true that some experiments, including the inclined plane experiment, are described in the *Two New Sciences*. But their role was a limited one. For, in the first place, Galileo was unable to produce direct experimental evidence favouring his definition of naturally accelerated motion. The best he could do was to claim that his definition led to consequences which did have experimental support. This, though, gives only a probable argu-ment for the definition, for alternative definitions could have those same consequences. Experiment, therefore, was insufficient to establish principles for a science of motion. In the second place, the concept of an experiment, involving apparatus and measurement, was neither familiar nor well understood in the early part of the seventeenth century. Experimental discourse lacked the authority it has since acquired, and was commonly regarded as of little relevance to a sound 'philosophical' method. In the view of many, the result of a contrived experiment would either endorse what was already known on the basis of common experience, in which case it was superfluous, or it would purport to reveal something hitherto unknown or unexpected, i.e. something either inaccessible or contrary to common experience, in which case its provenance would need to be considered with some care. Natural philosophy, and especially a science of natural motion, was understood to be concerned with universal truths concerning natural phenomena, and there was a danger that erroneous conclusions would be drawn if reliance was placed on a particular experiment concerning artificial phenomena, especially when – as was often the case – the result of such an experiment was ambiguous and the weight to be placed on the testimony of its witnesses was uncertain.

It was for these reasons, no doubt, that there is nothing resembling an experimental report in the whole of the *Two New Sciences*. Galileo did give a reasonably detailed description of the apparatus he used in his inclined plane experiment, but it is not accompanied by reports of specific results which could be compared with predictions derivable from his principles.

It is not surprising, therefore, that in justifying his new science of motion Galileo placed little weight on the results of real experiments. He fully appreciated that, to use the theological idiom appropriate to the time, God could produce the same effect in many different ways. And he understood that experiments which were difficult to perform successfully, or which gave ambiguous or inconsistent results, would not succeed in convincing his readers of the truth of his claims. This is why the experiments he described would hardly count as experiments in our modern sense. They do not, that is, involve the use of apparatus, arranged in a more or less elaborate manner so as to yield a result which may or may not have been anticipated. They require, rather, that we envisage some very simple and schematic arrangement of familiar objects in circumstances which leave no room for doubt about what will happen. For with these thought experiments, or experiments per- formed in the laboratory of the mind, he could avoid some of the disadvantages of real experiments. With them he could provide assur- ance that observation, albeit observation by the mind's eye, had some controlling influence in his study of motion, as indeed observation must have in any science. His task was to propose a definition of naturally accelerated motion which would be universally accepted and which would not lead to consequences at odds with observations, including those yielded by thought experiments. Clearly the best way to achieve this double objective was to use the evidence from thought experiments in arguing the case for the acceptance of his proposal. As we shall see, this is exactly what he did.

Perhaps the most important feature of thought experiments is that, because they depend upon reason and imagination rather than upon the skilful use of apparatus, they yield results which are available to all. To this extent they have a force comparable to that of common observations. By using them in an ingenious and convincing manner, Galileo was able to broaden the scope of the concept of experience without compromising its validity. They enabled everyone, using common experience and simple reasoning, to know facts about motion which had not previously been known. And these facts would be both necessary and universal. For example, we can know that, contrary to what was commonly believed, even the heaviest of objects must be travelling only very slowly when they begin falling, for common experience tells us that, when using such an object to drive a stake into the ground, very little will be achieved by dropping it on to the head of the stake from the height of an inch or so, and this must be because, despite its weight, it is travelling only slowly when it hits the stake. In the light of this thought experiment we can know, without needing to perform any real experiment, that all heavy objects must travel slowly when they begin falling. This knowledge would be as secure as any of the familiar truths based directly on common experience.

But thought experiments are experiments. Often they require us to imagine circumstances which, like those of real experiments, are to some degree contrived rather than natural. In a well known example, Galileo invites us to consider two objects, one heavy, one light, simultaneously dropped from the top of a tower, and asks us which will reach the ground first. Suppose, as many believed, that the heavier will reach the ground first because it travels faster. If we now imagine the two objects to have been tied together before being released then, assuming that they would have travelled at different speeds if falling separately, the heavier of the two will tend to pull the lighter more quickly and the lighter of the two will tend to slow down the fall of the heavier. So if the heavier one were to fall with a speed of eight units when released by itself, then we would expect it to fall with a speed of less than eight units when it is tied to a lighter object. But the two objects tied together – perhaps glued together – will make an object which is heavier than either, and so this new object should fall with a speed greater than that of either. It, including the heavier of the two objects, will therefore fall with a speed greater than eight units rather than with a speed less than eight units. We have, in this way, derived a contradiction from the supposition that the heavier a falling object is the sooner it reaches the ground.

In another well-known thought experiment we are asked to imagine what would happen if an object were dropped from the top of a ship's vertical mast, while the ship was sailing smoothly but swiftly. Would the object hit the ship's deck at the foot of the mast? We do not expect to observe the events we are asked to imagine in such an experiment, but nevertheless the events could be created and observed. Our imaginations are subject to the control and correction of the real world, so Galileo's thought experiments have a real aspect to them in the sense that they could be, and sometimes were, actually performed. The ship–mast experiment was, it seems, performed by the seventeenth-century

French natural philosopher Pierre Gassendi. Sometimes, indeed, it is hard to be sure whether an experiment Galileo described was actually performed or was imagined. The uncertainty may be intentional, for it may have been part of his purpose to suggest that our confidence in the conclusions reached by means of thought experiments could also be justified in conclusions drawn from real experiments.

For Galileo, then, thought experiments secured a link between the real experiments which had led him to his belief in the principles of a new science of motion, and the common experiences which he would need to appeal to in order to justify those principles to his readers. To fulfil his Archimedean aims he would need to use thought experiments to show that his definition of naturally accelerated motion is an accurate expression of common experience. The best way to see how he did this is to look at the way he presented his ideas.

The literary genre Galileo chose to convey his thinking in the *Two New Sciences*, as in the earlier *Dialogue Concerning Two Chief World Systems, Ptolemaic and Copernican*, has the form of a dramatic dialogue. It was, therefore, particularly well suited to the presentation of controversial topics and to the development of argumentative strategies intended to persuade or influence readers. What better way to settle controversial matters than to invite readers to eavesdrop on a lively conversation in which, although the sides to the controversy are fairly represented, a solution is found and agreed?

There are three participants in the dialogues: Salviati, who is Galileo's persona and spokesman; Sagredo, who speaks as an intelligent layman and expresses an ideal reader's reactions and conclusions; and Simplicio, who defends a version of traditional Aristotelian views on natural philosophy. All three are based on real people known to Galileo. The model for Salviati was Filippo Salviati, a wealthy young Florentine and one of a number of philosophers who associated themselves with Galileo when he returned to Florence as the Grand Duke's mathematician and philosopher. Sagredo was based on Giovanni Francesco Sagredo, a Venetian nobleman, who was one of Galileo's students at Padua and remained a close friend. There were several models for Simplicio, one of them being Cesare Cremonini, an Aristotelian philosopher and Paduan friend of Galileo, who acquired some notoriety as the man who refused to use the newly invented telescope.

The chapter of the *Two New Sciences* which is entitled 'Third Day', and which begins the development of Galileo's new science of motion, starts with what is supposed to be an extract from a mathematical treatise on motion. This treatise expounds the new science and, during the course of the 'day', it is discussed by Salviati, Sagredo and Simplicio. Evidently readers were to understand that Galileo himself was the author of the treatise, though naturally he is not referred to by name. The subject of the opening extract is uniform, or 'equable', motion, and it is expounded in an Archimedean manner with a definition and axioms, from which follow several theorems which state straightforward properties of uniform motion. The definition and axioms are evident in the same way that Euclidean and Archimedean axioms are evident; everyone would agree on their truth and would judge argument in support of them to be unnecessary. There is nothing controversial about this opening extract and Simplicio, Sagredo and Salviati are content to accept it as it stands.

The introduction to this chapter was evidently designed to encourage readers to have confidence in the 'Academician', or 'Author' of the treatise that Salviati has invited Sagredo and Simplicio to consider. What follows tests that confidence. It is a further extract from the treatise, concerning 'naturally accelerated motion', by which is meant the motion displayed by freely falling objects. Salviati introduces the topic by declaring that he and the 'Author' have at last settled upon a definition of such motion. It is a definition recommended, he says, by its simplicity and by the agreement of its consequences with experimental results. Nevertheless, Sagredo's response to the proposed definition is to ask why it should be accepted as correct. So the first matter which must be settled is the suitability of the definition proposed in the treatise. Salviati cannot claim that it is an obviously correct expression of common universal experience. Common experience does assure us that speed increases with both time and distance; the further an object has fallen and the greater the time for which it has been falling, the greater its speed must be. But common experience does not directly tell us how much further a falling object must fall, or for how much longer it must fall, if its speed is to, say, double. Debate, though, could help to illuminate and resolve the issues; it could provide the natural setting for Galileo to introduce the view, recommended on grounds of simplicity, that to double its speed a falling object must either travel twice as far, or it must travel for twice as long, perhaps both. The dialogue structure helped Galileo to persuade his readers to share this view, for he makes Sagredo and Simplicio oppose Salviati's definition by drawing attention to the apparent reasonableness of a definition which requires distance to double for double speed. This alternative definition was as well justified by common experience as Salviati's. Perhaps, indeed, it was more self-evident and was better justified. For suppose a stone, dropped from a height, has an effect – say, that of driving a stake into the ground by a certain amount. If we wished to double this effect so that the stake would be driven twice as far into the ground, then it would be natural to suggest that this could be achieved by dropping the stone from double the original height. This implies that the contribution to the effect made by the stone's speed would be doubled when the distance through which it is allowed to fall is doubled. It is true that the definition proposed in the treatise and endorsed by Salviati does conform to the results of experiments, but who is to say that Sagredo's and Simplicio's alternative and intuitively reasonable definition does not conform just as well?

By representing the issue as a choice between his definition and an apparently plausible alternative, Galileo's task was eased. He did not, because he could not, attempt to show that these alternative proposals are the only ones that might be considered. Instead, he proceeded to his next step which was to appeal to experience in the form of a thought experiment to show that the definition which makes speed proportional to distance fallen leads to a contradiction. Suppose, he said, that this is the correct definition. It would follow that if two objects were released from rest, one from twice the distance of the other above a given point, the first would have double the speed of the second as they passed the point. But since speed is nothing other than a measure of distance travelled in a given time and the distance travelled by the first object is twice the distance travelled by the second, it follows that the two objects must, if released simultaneously, reach the point at the same time. But this is absurd; the only way that two objects dropped from different heights can reach a given point at the same time is if the object dropped from the greater height is released earlier. So Sagredo's and Simplicio's definition cannot be correct. On the other hand, no absurdity is generated by the supposition that the speed of a falling object is proportional to the time for which it has been falling. So the definition used in the treatise must be the right one to use for naturally accelerated motion.

This thought experiment served a double purpose; it showed not only that there was a choice to be made between two different definitions of naturally accelerated motion but also how that choice should be made. From a mathematical point of view it was important to make the distinction, but this reasoning and the thought experiment it contained was an effective way of showing to those who doubted the relevance of mathematical thinking to physical inquiries that the difference mattered. It was because it helped to reveal hitherto inaccessible facts about motion that Galileo's thought experiment succeeded in convincing readers. No real experiment, involving unfamiliar apparatus and ambiguous results, could have succeeded so well.

Logically, though, the reasoning is less conclusive than Galileo took it to be. We are not forced to concede that speed must be proportional to time taken just because it cannot be proportional to distance travelled. Other possible definitions, such as that it is proportional to the square of the time taken, may yield consequences that are obviously mistaken or that conflict with the results of experiments, but Galileo made no attempt to show that this is so. He did not, that is, show that his definition was the only definition capable of leading to theorems which agreed with experimental results. No doubt he realised that any attempt to show this would be doomed to fail, for there are, in principle, an indefinite number of alternative definitions which would need to be considered and dismissed. No doubt, too, almost all these possible alternatives are wildly improbable, but Galileo had made it plain that probable arguments were not adequate to a genuine science of motion.

The presentation of the issue in the context of a dialogue clearly helped to counter the inconclusiveness of the reasoning. Knowledgeable but sceptical men – Sagredo and Simplicio – challenge, unsuccessfully, Salviati's definition, and they propose, again unsuccessfully, an alternative definition. That being so, we, as readers, can hardly help but conclude that any reasonable person will accept what Salviati proposes. The skilful reasoning Galileo employed was evidently intended to convince all but the most determined sceptic that the definition represents, as it should if it is to serve its purpose, an intuitively grounded insight into the nature of the motion displayed by freely falling objects. And it is in the context of this persuasive discourse that Galileo refers to experiments and common observations. For, should any doubts remain, they can be dispelled by using the definition to demonstrate conclusions which experience or experiment shows to be true. As Salviati put it: 'if it shall be found that the events that then shall have been demonstrated are verified in the motion of naturally falling and accelerated heavy objects, we may deem that the definition assumed includes that motion of heavy things, and that it is true that their acceleration goes on increasing as the time and the duration of motion increases' (Galileo 1989: 159). This way of supporting the definition is mentioned only in passing, and it appears to play only a minor part in Galileo's strategy. And so it should, for the conclusions demonstrated with the help of the definition, however well verified, could not play a legitimate part in demonstrating and thus establishing the definition. As we have seen, Galileo knew well that the mere fact that premisses lead to a true conclusion does not show that the premisses are true. Accordingly, the main thrust of his method for the study of motion reflected the past success of the deductive reasoning used by Euclid and Archimedes. Only by using such a method could real knowledge of motion be obtained. Observations which show that demonstrated conclusions are verified have a useful confirming role but, in themselves, can contribute little to our knowledge of motion. That is why Galileo thought of motion as a mathematical concept rather than a physical and experimental one, and of what we call mechanics as a demonstrative rather than an experimental science. The laws governing the motion of objects falling freely will be justified not on the basis of experiments with inclined planes but by derivation from 'true and indubitable' axioms or general principles of motion. For only in this way can we obtain the certain knowledge which is needed for philosophical understanding. What could be more reasonable, especially given that experiments agreed with what could be deduced on the proposed basis? In Galileo's hands the persuasive power of the dialogue's dramatic structure made it inevitable that the implicit question: 'What could be more reasonable?' was left hanging in the air, unexamined and unanswered, with the reader answering, implicitly, 'Nothing'.

We can see, then, that the literary form of the 'Third Day' in the *Two New Sciences* enabled Galileo to use two distinct styles of reasoning. On the one hand there was the demonstrative mathematical reasoning of the treatise being discussed by the participants in the dialogue. To mark the formality and the traditional authority of this reasoning, he used Latin as the language of this treatise. Its demonstrative discourse provided readers with a powerful analytical device enabling them to see what must be true of naturally accelerating objects once certain assumptions are made; it facilitated the discovery of new truths about accelerating objects. On the other hand there is the dialectic of the dialogue itself, and for this he used the down-to-earth, immediate language of vernacular Italian. Just as in the dialogue there is no mathematical reasoning, so in the treatise there is no experimental reasoning. It is only in the dialogue that we find Galileo exploring the concept of experiment and creating a role for it in scientific method. Yet the debate in the dialogue is about the treatise and so, despite the sharp stylistic difference between the dialogue and the treatise, Galileo was able to bring together mathematical and experimental reasoning; it was exactly this which was his chief contribution to the development of scientific method in the seventeenth century.

What conclusions can we draw about Galileo's methodology? First, it is clear that Galileo is committed to deductive reasoning. In this respect his views were continuous with those not only of his immediate predecessors but also of classical Greek thinkers such as Aristotle, Euclid and Archimedes. Like them he firmly believed that any science, because it was a type or kind of philosophy, should yield knowledge, and that the only way to achieve this was by employing deductive reasoning from indubitable premises. Second, the kind of deductive reasoning which Galileo thought most appropriate and useful in natural philosophy was that exemplified in Euclid's geometry and, more particularly, in Archimedes' statics. It was this conviction which underlay his famous remark that the book of nature is written in the language of mathematics. This view was increasingly shared by Galileo's contemporaries; he himself will have encountered it in the effects of the teaching of the Collegio Romano on the education of Jesuits. A notable feature of this teaching was the attempt to blend traditional Aristotelian natural philosophy with mathematical methods. But nevertheless there were many who continued to subscribe to the more traditional view that natural philosophy is essentially concerned with the investigation of causes and that mathematical reasoning, being abstract, is inappropriate to such an investigation. Third, because of the prominence given to mathematical methods, there is a natural tendency – which begins to be apparent in Galileo – towards a stress on quantitative mathematical discourse. The attempt to move natural philosophy in this direction was certainly contentious. Indeed, part of the complex set of reasons for Galileo's condemnation for his Copernicanism is to be found in the ways he had used and developed the new approach which this discourse signifies. Fourth, an examination of the part played by experience in the use of demonstrative methods by Galileo shows that it developed a dual role. On the one hand, there is the concept of universal generalised experience which is expressed and idealised in the principles of a demonstrative science of motion, rather in the same way that such experience is expressed and idealised in Archimedes' demonstrative science of statics. On the other hand, universal experience – and also particular experiments – can be used to show that the conclusions reached by a demonstrative science are applicable to the real world.

We can see, as Galileo could not, that this last conclusion, with its acknowledgement of a role for experiment, prefigured a key development in the understanding of scientific method in the seventeenth century. For, despite the powerful ties with his predecessors, and despite his inability to see where he was going, he succeeded in holding together a way of using reason in science with a reconstituted concept of experience. It would not be right to claim that he canvassed an experimental programme for natural philosophy, but his brilliant use of thought experiments showed that there were ways of broadening the scope of common observation and experience so as to strengthen the foundations of a demonstrative science.

FURTHER READING

Useful background material for this chapter can be found in:
Burtt, E. A. (1932) *The Metaphysical Foundations of Modern Physical Science: a Historical and Critical Essay*, second edition, London: Routledge and Kegan Paul; ch. 3.
Gillispie, C. C. (1960) *The Edge of Objectivity: an Essay in the History of Scientific Ideas*, Princeton, NJ: Princeton University Press; ch. 1.
Hall, A. R. (1983) *The Revolution in Science 1500–1750*, second edition, London: Longman; ch. 4.

For more detail concerning the context within which Galileo worked, see:
Schmitt, C. B. (1975) 'Science in the Italian Universities in the Sixteenth and Early Seventeenth Centuries', in M. P. Crosland (ed.), *The Emergence of Science in Western Europe*, London: Macmillan. Reprinted in Schmitt 1984.
Schmitt, C. B. (1984) *The Aristotelian Tradition and Renaissance Universities*, London: Variorum Reprints.

Wallace, W. A. (1984) *Galileo and his Sources: The Heritage of the Collegio Romano in Galileo's Science*, Princeton, NJ: Princeton University Press.
Westfall, R. S. (1988) 'Galileo and the Jesuits', in R. S. Woolhouse (ed.), *Metaphysics and Philosophy of Science in the Seventeenth and Eighteenth Centuries: Essays in Honour of Gerd Buchdahl*, Dordrecht/Boston/London: Kluwer.

For Galileo himself, the best modern translations are provided by Stillman Drake, including:
Galileo, G. (1989) *Two New Sciences: Including Centres of Gravity and Force of Percussion*, translated, with a new introduction and notes, by S. Drake, second edition, Toronto: Wall and Thompson.

Studies of Galileo's life and work are given in:
Drake, S. (1978) *Galileo at Work: His Scientific Biography*, Chicago, Ill.: University of Chicago Press.
Sharratt, M. (1994) *Galileo: Decisive Innovator*, Oxford: Blackwell.

Continuing research by Drake has resulted in:
Drake, S. (1990) *Galileo: Pioneer Scientist*, Toronto: Toronto University Press.

A briefer biography is:
Drake, S. (1967) 'Galileo: a biographical sketch', in E. McMullin (ed.), *Galileo: Man of Science*, New York: Basic Books.

There is an account of the development of Galileo's scientific ideas in:
McMullin, E. (1967) 'Introduction: Galileo, man of science', in E. McMullin (ed.), *Galileo: Man of Science*, New York: Basic Books.

Galileo's scientific method is studied in:
McMullin, E. (1978) 'The conception of science in Galileo's work', in R. E. Butts and J. C. Pitt (eds), *New Perspectives on Galileo*, Dordrecht: Reidel.
Wisan, W. L. (1978) 'Galileo's scientific method', in R. E. Butts and J. C. Pitt (eds), *New Perspectives on Galileo*, Dordrecht: Reidel.
Naylor, R. H. (1989) 'Galileo's experimental discourse', in D. Gooding, T. Pinch and S. Schaffer (eds), *The Uses of Experiment: Studies in the Natural Sciences*, Cambridge: Cambridge University Press.

3 Francis Bacon
Why experiments matter

When Francis Bacon was born in London in 1561, Elizabeth had been Queen of England for just three years. Among her closest advisers were Francis's father, Sir Nicholas Bacon, and his uncle, Sir William Cecil, later to become Lord Burghley. By the end of her reign in 1603, Francis had been called to the bar, had served as a Member of Parliament, had advised the Queen and her Privy Councillors on legal matters, and had acquired a reputation as a skilful lawyer, able administrator and determined inquisitor. Like others he faced religious divisions which threatened the stability of the Elizabethan state. On the one hand there were the Protestant crusaders, or Puritans as they came to be known, promoting the reforming ideals of Luther and Calvin; on the other there were counter-reformation Catholic missionaries seeking to restore papal authority in England. Bacon's mother, Lady Anne, was an eloquent supporter of the Puritans' cause; his Cambridge tutor, John Whitgift, who later became Archbishop of Canterbury, was a powerful opponent of their more zealous activists. Bacon himself began his political career as a supporter of the Puritans, but he soon distanced himself from the more radical of them, and came to accept Whitgift's view that extreme sectarianism, whether of Protestant or of Catholic variety, was damaging to the unity and security of the state. When Elizabeth was succeeded by James I, Bacon sought and secured high office in government, eventually becoming England's most senior legal officer, Lord Chancellor. It was during this period, when he was promoting legal reform, that Bacon published his ideas about how the study of natural philosophy could also be reformed. In 1621, when he was sixty years of age, he was successfully accused of accepting bribes, and stripped of public office. His last years were devoted to the development of his ambitious philosophical plans. He died in 1626 of bronchitis brought about, so the seventeenth-century biographer John Aubrey tells us, by a chill acquired in an attempt at an experiment involving stuffing a chicken with snow.

Though Galileo and Bacon were contemporaries, they worked in very different contexts. Galileo's Italy was dominated politically by ecclesiastical authority, and culturally by a long and vigorous tradition of intellectual enquiry, including what we now call 'scientific' enquiry. In Bacon's England, by contrast, political reformations in the first half of the sixteenth century had replaced the papal power of Rome with royal authority, and the Elizabethan culture with which he grew up was renowned for its drama, poetry and music, not for its philosophy or science. Galileo began his career as a mathematician and, as we have seen, an important part of his thinking about science was influenced by his understanding of mathematical methods. Bacon began his career as a lawyer, and the forensic methods he used played an important role in his efforts to found a new and better method of reasoning about natural phenomena. Both, though, shared a distaste for the academic philosophy taught in the universities, which contented itself with summaries of earlier writings. But their positive achievements were quite distinct. Galileo was, first and foremost, an innovative scientist, and only by implication a pioneer of scientific method. But Bacon's reputation rested on his thinking about scientific method, whereas his science reflected a tradition of natural magic, alchemy and practical medicine which was discarded by many of his successors.

Bacon's guiding idea was what he called a 'Great Instauration', the aim of which was nothing less than 'a total reconstruction of sciences, arts, and all human knowledge, raised upon the proper foundations' (Bacon 1985: 4; Great Instauration, Proem). He had explained the need for such an 'instauration' or restoration, in *The Advancement of Learning* of 1605 (Bacon 1915), as being the consequence of deficiencies in the learning then available. For, in Bacon's view, too much attention had been given to the way things were said, rather than to the way things are, and even when learning did concern facts rather than words, it often degenerated into academic trivialities or, even worse, perpetuated superstition and false belief. And yet, he was convinced, if only people would use the right methods, much could be achieved by a sustained attempt to improve our understanding of nature and our control of its processes.

The Great Instauration was conceived as a six-part enterprise. The first part was to be a survey of the whole of learning, the aim of which was to identify areas of enquiry where little or nothing had so far been achieved. Bacon emphasised those areas that we now call science, particularly theoretical science. The reason why so little progress had been made in science was, he thought, an inadequate method. So, in the second part of the project, he intended to put forward a new method which would help us find out about the natural world. This would supplant the traditional Aristotelian accounts of reasoning in science. In particular, more attention would be paid to evidence derived from experiments. The third part would consist of detailed reports of the natural and experimental phenomena, enabling the new method to be used. These reports, or 'histories', would require much time and labour, for, although reasonably reliable 'histories' of animals, plants, minerals and other naturally occurring phenomena were available, 'histories' of phenomena artificially induced by experiments were rarer and more unreliable. The fourth part would show, by a variety of examples, how we could draw conclusions from such histories. The method proposed in the second part would be applied so as to provide, not just illustrations of specific features of the method, but instead thorough examples of its use. The fifth part would be 'for temporary use only', in that it would collect provisional findings together as 'Anticipations of the New Philosophy'. Such findings, even though provisional, could well have practical significance, and we should not neglect the opportunity to make use of them. The sixth and final part of the Great Instauration would set out in a comprehensive manner the results of an exhaustive application of the recommended method. Its completion, Bacon acknowledged, was 'above my strength and beyond my hopes'. The best he could expect was that others would see fit to adopt his plan of action and that they would eventually complete his ambitious project. He thought, indeed, that once the laborious but routine natural histories called for in the third part were available, 'the investigation of nature and all the sciences will be the work of a few years' (Bacon 1985: 272).

Only the first two parts of this project achieved anything like their final form. To serve as the first part, Bacon wrote his *De dignitate et augmentis scientiarum* (*Of the Dignity and Advancement of Learning*) (1623), which was a revised and elaborated version of the survey he had previously published as the Second Book of *The Advancement of Learning*. For the second part, he wrote his *Novum Organum* (*New Instrument*) (1620) – a title which alludes to what is sometimes known as the *Organum* of Aristotle, a group of his influential writings about logic and method. Both were published towards the end of his life, the *Novum Organum* in an unfinished form. It is to this *Novum Organum* that we will turn for an account of Bacon's thinking about scientific method. But before we do so, we need to appreciate those features of its context which will help us understand that book correctly. In particular, we should consider the position and role of science in Bacon's system for the classification of learning.

This elaborate system is the most conspicuous feature of Bacon's *Advancement of Learning* and of its later, expanded, Latin version. The reason for this is that the Renaissance revival of learning brought with it an influential conception of logic which saw teaching as the main function of logic. That is to say, logic was concerned less with disputation and more with effective ways of conveying knowledge from teacher to learner; reasoning was seen less as a means of convincing or persuading and more as a means of elucidating and explaining. Logic had, in effect, a sorting or classificatory function, and the way the classification worked depended on how knowledge was thought to be structured. It was widely accepted that the ancient Greeks had discovered most of what there is to know, so the broad outlines of this structure could be discerned even if there were important details which needed adding. Reasoning, in the sense of proving or demonstrating, played only a minor role in the understanding of logic; what mattered more was finding the definitions and the divisions appropriate to the adopted classification scheme.

Bacon's classification scheme exemplified this new logic. But it also challenged some of its assumptions. In the first place, his scheme depended on a way of structuring knowledge which was opposed to tradition in the way it dealt with the distinction between theoretical and practical knowledge. Traditional classifications made this distinction fundamental, in the sense that it applied to all knowledge, whereas Bacon used it only with respect to a part of knowledge – natural philosophy. Second, Bacon's scheme emphasised the deficiencies of current knowledge, for, as a result of his way of thinking about practical knowledge, he thought there were important parts of the structure of learning where ignorance and superstition prevailed. And third, the new logic was only part, and not the crucial part, of what was needed for a new organon to replace Aristotle's. Logic should be concerned not just with the presentation and teaching of what was known but also with the ways in which deficiencies in what was known could be made good.

In Bacon's system, natural philosophy has two parts: a theoretical or 'speculative' part resulting from 'inquisition of causes'; and a practical or 'operative' part resulting from 'production of effects' (Bacon 1915: 90). Theoretical natural philosophy itself has two sub-divisions, called 'physics' and 'metaphysics', which correspond to and are connected with two sub-divisions of practical natural philosophy, called 'mechanics' and 'magic'. Thus, 'physics' tells us, for example, that the direct and immediate cause of the whiteness of snow or of agitated water is a 'subtle intermixture of air and water', and 'mechanics' tells us, with the help of experiments, what other effects this cause may produce. 'Metaphysics', the other part of theoretical natural philosophy, tells us about the nature of whiteness itself, wherever it might occur, and 'magic', a practical skill, will make use of this knowledge in manipulating natural phenomena so as to produce effects which could sometimes seem unusual and, indeed, magical. The association of science with magic may appear surprising, but it arises from Bacon's view that there was a legitimate tradition of natural magic, associated with the practical experimental arts of alchemy, which included elements of what we call chemistry, and of the newer iatrochemistry, the use of chemical, rather than herbal, remedies for medical ailments.

This tradition, though sometimes perverted by tricksters and char-latans, was concerned with experimental investigations of nature's marvels and mysteries, and was therefore a potentially valuable source of information about how phenomena could be produced.

Although Bacon was probably unaware of Galileo's success in using mathematics to create a new science of motion, we would nevertheless expect a role for mathematics in any proposed structure for knowledge. In *The Advancement of Learning* of 1605 he had supposed mathematics to be a branch of metaphysics, but in the *De augmentis* of 1623 his view was that mathematical investigations were of great importance in all parts of natural philosophy, and therefore should be treated as essential to them all. However, mathematics must, he thought, remain subordinate to natural philosophy, because descriptions of natural phenomena, however mathematically adequate, could not and should not take the place of philosophical explanations. In astronomy, for example, we need not just a hypothesis which provides us with a mathematically accurate way of constructing reliable calendars, but an account of the heavens which enables us to explain what we observe. Mathematics is no doubt essential to that explanation, but we should not suppose that mathematics is all that is required. Mathematics is servant or 'hand-maid' to the need for explanation provided by physics; it should not dominate physical enquiries. As he put it in *Novum Organum*: 'natural philosophy . . . is tainted and corrupted . . . by mathematics, which ought only to give definiteness to natural philosophy, not to generate or give it birth' (Bacon 1985: 93; Book 1, Aphorism XCVI).

Bacon was clearly raising questions about the effect that mathematical kinds of reasoning had been having in natural philosophy. He was not questioning the usefulness or correctness of mathematics itself; nor was he doubting the cogency of the deductive reasoning used in mathematics. His claim was, rather, that the use of mathematical techniques had tended to obscure the real and proper aim of natural philosophy, which was the investigation of causes or, as Bacon expressed it, the investigation of form natures. This is not to say that mathematics could play no role in such an investigation, for Bacon acknowledged that among these form natures we should include number and shape, the subject matter of arithmetic and geometry. Number and shape are no doubt the most abstract, and in that sense the most other-worldly, of form natures, but they are, nevertheless, essential to a philosophical understanding of the phenomenal natures of things.

We can see, then, why mathematics played no role in Bacon's thinking about method in science. It was not that he was ignorant of mathematics, or that he was blind to what had been achieved by such men as Copernicus and Kepler in their use of mathematical methods. In his view, its power and influence were already too much exaggerated. Its very abstractness had encouraged its development, for its practitioners were thus able to indulge their propensity to generalise without fear that nature would prove them mistaken. In his view, from a natural philosophy pursued in accordance with his new method, 'better things are to be expected' than could ever be achieved by a natural philosophy pursued in accordance with a mathematical method.

An important feature of Bacon's classification system was that, by insisting that science is practical as well as theoretical, Bacon broke with a traditional and influential way of classifying different kinds of knowledge. Since Aristotle's time, the fundamental distinction was between those kinds of knowledge which were theoretical, such as metaphysics, physics, mathematics and logic, and those kinds which were practical, such as ethics, politics, economics, navigation, agriculture and medicine. This type of classification made it difficult to associate theoretical enquiry with practical applications, in the way that is needed when testing scientific ideas using experiments. It also made it difficult to ensure that practical knowledge, like that gained from acquiring expertise with experimental apparatus, would be treated as equal in importance to theoretical knowledge. Bacon's classification puts the study of 'causes', a traditional concern of theoretical natural philosophy, in close proximity to the study of 'effects', a traditional concern of the practical experimental arts. He was, therefore, able to assign a central role in scientific method to practical experimental investigations. This was an important innovation because, until the seventeenth century, the practical skills necessary for successful experimental investigation, such as those of various kinds of artists and craftsmen, had no clear connection with the theoretical concerns of natural philosophers. As a result, theory was prevented from properly engaging with the facts, and practical skills yielded information which was fragmentary and unsystematic.

There is a connection between Bacon's experience as a lawyer and his belief that theoretical and practical science are relevant to each other. He knew that his expertise as a reformer of the law was dependent upon the skills he had acquired as a practical lawyer, and to that extent the theory and practice of law are also coupled together. Those who concern themselves with the nature of justice and its relation to legitimate authority in a state need to reflect on the ways in which justice is administered, determined and delivered. In a similar way, those who would concern themselves with nature must have, or be prepared to acquire, knowledge of the ways in which nature works. If, to have that knowledge, they need experiments to make the world reveal its secrets, then there is a continuing parallel with the law in that, at least from Bacon's point of view, lawyers need inquisitions and trials to make justice prevail. As Bacon put it when drawing King James's attention to the expenses incurred by experimenters: 'as secretaries and spials [spies] of princes and states bring in bills for intelligence, so you must allow the spials and intelligencers of nature to bring in their bills' (Bacon 1915: 65). The value of experiments which exhibit nature under investigation lies in their ability to reveal the truths nature would otherwise conceal, just as the value of espionage and inquisition lies in their ability to reveal the truths people would otherwise conceal.

Bacon's new way of doing science emphasised the role of experiments serving this purpose. More particularly, it promoted new experiments, for, although there were some experimental histories, they were neither comprehensive nor reliable. Too often, he thought, investigators ignored experiments as trifling curiosities or dismissed them as distracting irrelevancies. And even when this was not the case, they experimented in a haphazard manner and did not pursue enquiries suggested by the results they obtained. 'The manner of making experiments which men now use,' he said, 'is blind and stupid'. The thorough-going, patiently acquired histories that constitute the third part of the Great Instauration should report 'experiments of the mechanical arts', because 'the nature of things betrays itself more readily under the vexations of art than in its natural freedom' (Bacon 1985: 67, 25; Book 1, Aphorism LXX).

We can see something of the way Bacon intended that histories of natural and experimental phenomena should be constructed by examining some writings which were intended as contributions towards part three of the Great Instauration. Bacon made it clear that compilers of these histories should concern themselves with assembling a large and various collection of facts, paying no attention to whether those facts are, or are not, of interest or use. Proper subjects for natural and experimental histories are, for example, agriculture, cookery, chemistry, but also manufacturing industries, such as glass- and gunpowder-making, and practical arts such as weaving and carpentry. A catalogue of suitable histories lists some 130 subjects, and not surprisingly there are a number of items in this catalogue which seem odd, and even eccentric – 'History of Jugglers and Mountebanks' and 'History of Tickling and Feathers' (as well as a separate 'History of Manufactures of Feathers') for instance. It also reflects Bacon's priorities; honey and sugar have separate histories, but metals and minerals have to share a history. Meteorological histories are prominent; so are medicinal. A significant number indicate that, for Bacon, the workshops of craftsmen and tradesmen were the laboratories of the new science. Nevertheless, many of the items do concern topics which later generations would recognise as scientific. There is a 'History of the Motions (if any be) of the Globe of Earth and Sea', a 'History of Water', a 'History of the Magnet', a 'History Medicinal of Diseases', a 'History of Hearing and Sound' and a 'History of Salts'.

Bacon attached great importance to these histories. As he explained in a preface to one of the few that he was himself able to compile, his new method, or *Organum*, would be useless without the data provided by histories, though histories without a good method for dealing with them would still be of some use. Of the six histories that he planned to write on a monthly schedule as his contributions to the third part of the Great Instauration, three were completed, but there are only prefaces to the remaining three. Two of the completed histories begin with extensive lists of questions and topics for investigation. Then follow the histories proper, which collect together relevant common knowledge, reliable hearsay evidence and some experimental evidence.

But although these histories do constitute the starting point for scientific conclusions, they are by no means random, disorganised compilations of experimental results. Such compilations are, Bacon said, the work of 'empirics', who 'take for the material of philosophy . . . a very little out of many things'. These 'men of experiment' are like ants assembling what they need in a haphazard manner, in contrast to spiders who, like 'men of dogma' when they take 'for the material of philosophy . . . a great deal out of a few things', extract from themselves the cobwebs they need; and in contrast, too, to bees which, like good Baconian investigators, digest and transform the material they gather. The experiments of a craftsman can be fruitful in a practical sense, but nevertheless what is needed are 'light-giving' experiments intended to clarify or resolve some theoretical issue (Bacon 1985: 59, 93; Book 1, Aphorisms LXII and XCV). The organisation of an experimental history must, therefore, depend on the way it interacts with the conclusions it generates and establishes. We must envisage a two-way process in which we are provided with a ladder, to use Bacon's imagery, which will enable us to climb up from experimental histories to conclusions, and a ladder we can use to descend from conclusions to new experiments. Iterations of this process will result in the enhancement of the experimental histories, and in the modification and eventual perfection of the conclusions. There is, to be sure, a certain optimism in this image, for there is nothing yet to suggest that perfect, or certain, conclusions can be produced. But the image is not obviously absurd. If we want to reach conclusions about the nature of, say, whiteness, then we need to make use of experimental histories which contain relevant data. From these histories, if they are sufficiently comprehensive, we will be able with the help of Bacon's new scientific method to generate a preliminary conclusion. It is very likely that this preliminary conclusion will suggest some new experiments, the results of which might indicate a revised conclusion. Gradually, by following this process, we will be able to generate conclusions which, because they fit an ever-growing experimental history, will be increasingly reliable when put to practical use.

What, though, does Bacon understand by an 'experiment'? Certainly, he thought of the practices and techniques of craftsmen as experiments, though on the whole they will be 'experiments of fruit', undertaken for practical purposes, rather than 'experiments of light', undertaken for the sake of theoretical clarification. But he also means those procedures, whether tried or proposed, which involve measurement and the use of specially constructed apparatus. In the *Novum Organum*, as well as in the natural and experimental histories, he gives examples of these 'artificial' investigations. Some of his reports appear to be of investigations which he himself undertook. A good example is an experiment designed to find out how much a liquid expands when it changes to a gaseous form. Bacon said that he filled a small glass 'phial, capable of holding about an ounce' with 'spirit of wine', or alcohol, and that he 'noted exactly the weight' of this filled container. He then took a 'bladder, capable of holding about a quart' and, after excluding air from it, carefully attached its mouth to that of the alcohol container so that the join would be as airtight as possible. He then heated the alcohol, collecting the 'steam or breath' which was produced in the bladder. When the bladder appeared to be full, the heat was removed and the weight of the remaining alcohol determined. This enabled him, he said, to calculate 'how much had been converted into steam', and to compare 'the space which the body had occupied while it was spirit of wine in the phial, with the space which it afterwards occupied when it had become pneumatic in the bladder'. The experiment showed, he reported, that the alcohol 'had acquired by the change a degree of expansion a hundred times greater than it had before'.

It is easy to criticise Bacon's experiment from our present vantage point: the apparatus and the method used are clumsy; there is clearly confusion between the weight and the volume of the evaporated alcohol; the attempt to quantify the conclusion is of little value given the vagueness of certain parameters. Yet there are indications that Bacon saw the need for care: 'I inserted the mouth of the phial within the mouth of the bladder, and tied the latter tightly round the former with a thread, smeared with wax in order that it might stick more closely and tie more firmly' (Bacon 1985: 210–12; Book 2, Aphorism XL). And there is a recognition that such an experiment does make quantitative reasoning possible; knowledge of the exact volume of the phial and of the bladder would enable him to draw a more reliable conclusion. But perhaps the most important feature of the experiment is that, even though it was performed with ordinary materials in a way that calls upon the skills that a craftsman might be expected to have, it was intended to illuminate a theoretical issue, namely the 'nature' of 'the Expansion or Coition of Matter in bodies compared with one another'. We may be puzzled by a theoretical question such as this, and wonder what an experimental answer to it is supposed to signify, but it is nevertheless plain from this example that Bacon's experiments play an important role in forging that link between theory and practice which was so important for his methodology.

Bacon was not alone in his advocacy of experimentation; his fellow countryman William Gilbert had already done so in a practical manner by reporting many experiments concerned with magnetic and electrical phenomena in his famous *De Magnete*, first published in 1600. Indeed, we might well think that there was no need for Bacon to tell seventeenth-century scientists what to do, for they had Gilbert to copy. However, matters cannot be quite so straightforward, if only because Bacon was openly critical of Gilbert's work. For, while he applauded the care with which the experiments were performed, he complained that the base they provided was not of the kind he recommended for the establishment of satisfactory conclusions. We mistake the real significance of Bacon's scientific method by ignoring this complaint and attributing his criticism to a misjudgement of the worth of Gilbert's science. For, despite the scope and ingenuity of the experiments described in *De Magnete*, the second and crucially important part of Bacon's plan for his Great Instauration made it plain that any experimental history must be conceived on a broader scale than Gilbert envisaged. It needs, in the first instance at least, to be as comprehensive as possible in its scope. And it needs to be seen not as standing by itself and as leading to its own conclusions, but as contributing to the larger enterprise of constructing such histories for every kind of phenomena. Scientists who seek to generate conclusions on the sole basis of experimental histories they themselves have compiled are like builders constructing houses solely out of the limited number of bricks they have themselves made; the scientists' conclusions, like these builders' houses, must either be disappointingly modest but safe, or laudably ambitious but insecure. The conclusions Gilbert drew, such as that the Earth itself is a magnet, may perhaps turn out to be correct, but in Bacon's view they were nevertheless drawn too precipitately. Like the 'chemists [who] out of a few experiments . . . built up a fantastic philosophy', Gilbert 'employed himself most laboriously in the study and observation of the loadstone [and] proceeded at once to construct an entire system in accordance with his favourite subject' (Bacon 1985: 54; Book 1, Aphorism LIV). The difference between a Baconian and a Gilbertian experimental history is not simply a difference of degree; it is the difference between what is sufficient and what is insufficient for the conclusions drawn.

The ancient image of nature as a book that we learn how to read has often been popular. As we have seen, it was used by Galileo and coupled with the idea that the language in which the book is written is mathematical. In general, though, to read and understand the language in which this book is written we need a dictionary or index which will enable us to interpret it. We could construct such a dictionary by a trial-and-error procedure; we guess at what words mean, and sometimes we are lucky, for when we put our guesses together we succeed in making sense of some passage in the book. Eventually, some people, like Gilbert and Galileo, acquire skill in making correct guesses and become adept readers, perhaps because the parts of the book they are interested in are written using words they find relatively easy to understand. But we might, not unreasonably, fear that by relying on ingenuity, guess-work and luck we risk the possibility that only an incomplete dictionary will ever be available. So we might consider that a better approach would be one which is more methodical and painstaking and which depends upon the co-operation of many hands patiently building up a comprehensive dictionary. Such a dictionary would enable scientists eventually to read the book of nature and show us how to make use of the information it contains. This alternative approach was, in effect, the one advocated by Bacon when he urged that comprehensive natural and experimental histories be compiled. And in his criticism of Gilbert he expressed his conviction that it is only by means of these histories that scientists can construct a dictionary for the book of nature.

If nature is like a book, and histories are like parts of a dictionary enabling scientists to read the book, then the question arises about what kind of information we expect the book to contain. Bacon's answer was expressed in terms of what he called 'forms'. The form of something is a physical property, or a set of physical properties, which makes it what it is rather than something else. So, the form of a particular oak tree is the set of characteristics which makes that tree the tree it is rather than some other oak tree; the form of gold is the characteristic or set of characteristics that defines that kind of metal. An oak tree, and gold as well, has what we can call a phenomenal nature. There will be, that is, the nature of the oak tree as it appears to us when we look at it, and the nature of gold as it appears to us when we think about it. We might, though, wonder about the nature of the oak tree, or the nature of gold, as it really is – as it is independently of how it appears to anyone. In Bacon's terms we would be wondering about the form nature of the oak tree, and about the form nature of gold. We would be wondering about how that matter which constitutes the oak tree, or which constitutes gold, has been organised and characterised so as to give rise to the phenomenal natures familiar to us. In one sense we know why it is part of the phenomenal nature of the oak tree that it is, say, leafless; we are looking at it in wintertime. We know why it is part of phenomenal nature of gold to appear yellow; it reflects light of the appropriate wavelength. These, though, are superficial 'physical' answers, whereas our questions are 'metaphysical'. For theoretical natural philosophy, being leafless cannot be what is important about this oak tree because, at other times of the year, it does have leaves; being yellow cannot be what is important about gold because plenty of yellow things are not gold and not all gold is yellow. What is important is the knowledge of how the matter of the oak has been characterised so as to ensure it will appear leafless in wintertime, and of how the matter of gold has been characterised so as to ensure that gold appears, for the most part, to be yellow. Such knowledge is knowledge of form natures.

But to expect scientists to investigate the form natures of particular things, or kinds of things, is unrealistic; they are far too numerous. However, although the same phenomenal nature can be attributed to a potentially indefinite number of particular things or kinds of things, each particular thing, such as an oak, and each kind of thing, such as gold, has, Bacon claimed, only a definite number of phenomenal natures to characterise it. This suggests that, while the form natures of particular things and of kinds of particular things correspond to the words used in the book of nature, the form natures of phenomenal natures correspond to the letters which make words. There are, Bacon thought, only a limited and manageable number of these phenomenal natures, and so the investigation of them is a feasible undertaking. 'To enquire the Form of a lion, of an oak, of gold, nay of water, of air, is a vain pursuit,' he said in *The Advancement of Learning*, 'but to enquire the Forms of sense, of voluntary motion, of vegetation, of colours, of gravity and levity, of density, of tenuity, of heat, of cold, and of all other natures and qualities, which like the alphabet are not many, and of which the essences ... of all creatures do consist; to inquire ... the true forms of these is that part of Metaphysic which we now define of' (Bacon 1915: 95). Natural and experimental histories, used in accordance with Bacon's scientific method, will help us to discover the meanings of some of the words in the book of nature, i.e. to find out about the forms of some particulars and kinds of particulars. But, although there are an indefinite number of different words used in the book, each word requires only a selection from a relatively small number of letters for its expression, so the ultimate aim of scientists in using the histories is not so much the meanings of words as the meanings of their component letters, i.e. the form natures. If scientists achieve this aim they will be able to read the book of nature. Bacon tried to show how, by following his method, scientists could achieve this aim.

Bacon's recommendation, then, was to examine phenomenal natures with a view to discovering their forms. He gave some lists of these natures which help to indicate what he had in mind. Gold, for example, has the following phenomenal natures: 'it is yellow in colour, heavy up to a certain weight, malleable or ductile to a certain degree of extension; it is not volatile and loses none of its substance by the action of fire; it turns into a liquid with a certain degree of fluidity; it is separated and dissolved by particular means; and so on for the other natures which meet in gold' (Bacon 1985: 124; Book 2, Aphorism V). Phenomenal natures, he indicated, come in pairs. He prepared a detailed natural and experimental history for one of these pairs – dense and rare – though without drawing conclusions about their forms; he intended to compile one for another – heavy and light; and he made extensive use of part of a third – hot and cold – to illustrate his scientific method in *Novum Organum*.

The connection Bacon made between forms and laws of nature reveals again a parallel between his thinking about legal practice and his thinking about scientific practice. He shared with many of his contemporaries the belief that, just as a state lays down laws for its citizens to follow, so God has determined laws for nature to follow. If, therefore, we wish to have power over nature and control her activities, we must discover and use these laws, just as those who wish to have power over citizens must know and use the laws of a state. So, if we want to produce a phenomenal nature such as whiteness, or density, or heat, we must find the laws that ensure, whatever the circumstances, their production; we must find out how God produces them. But in doing this we will find, in effect, the form natures of whiteness, density, heat, etc. And conversely, by finding the form nature of, say, whiteness, we find the law ordained by God for its production. Knowledge of nature's forms is closely coupled with power over nature's effects, and we see again how Bacon sought to bring theoretical knowledge and practical power into close relation with each other.

How, though, can we achieve the aim of identifying the forms of phenomenal natures and thus of the laws governing their production? Bacon's answer was that, once we are supplied with natural and experimental histories, there is a method which will enable us to use them to achieve that aim. This method is explained and illustrated, though in an incomplete manner, in the second part of the Great Instauration – the *Novum Organum*. The key features of this method are that it is inductive, that it is experimental, and that it yields conclusions which are certain.

By 'induction' we are to understand a process which leads from particular facts to a general conclusion. The simplest kind of induction requires the particular facts to be positive instances of the general conclusion. For example, in his natural and experimental history of 'dense and rare', Bacon included the generalisation 'every tangible [i.e. solid or liquid] body with us has a pneumatic [i.e. gaseous] body of spirit united and inclosed within it', and we might try to establish the truth of this claim on the basis of positive instances of it. It may sometimes happen that we can examine all instances of a general claim, in which case we can conclude that the general claim is true once we have established that each instance is positive. But usually we can examine only some instances of the generalisation, and in simple 'induction by enumeration', as it is called, we conclude that the generalisation is true if and only if all the examined instances are positive. Bacon made it clear that he rejected this kind of induction:

'the induction which proceeds by simple enumeration is childish; its conclusions are precarious and exposed to peril from a contradictory instance; and it generally decides on too small a number of facts, and on those only which are at hand' (Bacon 1985: 98–9; Book 1, Aphorism CV). There was nothing new in this complaint; it had been clearly expressed by the ancient Greek sceptic Sextus Empiricus, when he said that those trying to establish generalisation by reviewing only some of its instances will conclude with an insecure generalisation, whereas those who try to do it by reviewing all its instances will establish nothing because they can never complete such a review. Galileo, too, was well aware of the same difficulty; for him, induction by enumeration cannot yield certainty and so is useless.

Bacon proposed, instead, that we reason from particular facts to general conclusions and to laws of nature by using those facts which enable us to exclude or eliminate alternative general conclusions. It relies, that is to say, on the idea that a single negative instance is sufficient to eliminate a generalisation. As we have seen, the generalisations which Bacon wished to establish were laws associated with form natures. In finding the form nature of a phenomenal nature we identify a law connecting the one with the other. For example, if the form nature of whiteness is or arises from a simple proportion in the sizes of the particles which make up a white object, such as the particles of air and water in agitated water, or the particles of air and glass in powdered glass, then there is a law to the effect that, whenever the particles of an object are in that simple proportion, the object will be white, and whenever an object is white its particles will be in that simple proportion. But to establish this general law it is necessary, according to Bacon's method, to eliminate alternative general laws stating that whiteness has some other form. On the face of it, this might seem a hopeless, because unending, task. There are just too many false laws – too many false possibilities about the form of a phenomenal nature – for us to find the true law by eliminating them.

Bacon's answer to this was to propose that we organise the facts assembled in the histories into tables. We construct, first, a table of 'Essence and Presence', which lists all those phenomena, natural and experimental, where the phenomenal nature under investigation is present in some degree or another. This table will show that there are characteristics – perhaps a large number of characteristics – which accompany the phenomenal nature. Second, we construct a table of 'Deviation, or of Absence in Proximity', which provides a matching list of all those natural and experimental circumstances where the phenomenal nature is absent, even though the circumstances are similar in other respects to those where it is present. This table will show that some of the characteristics accompanying the phenomenal nature in the first table are not always accompanied by it. By putting the two tables together we will be able to conclude that one or other of a smaller number of characteristics is the form of the phenomenal nature. A third table, of 'Degrees, or Comparison', extracts from natural and experimental histories instances in which the phenomenal nature in question is found in different degrees. The characteristic to be selected as its form will have to vary in its degrees accordingly, because no characteristic 'can be taken as the true form, unless it always decrease when the nature in question decreases, and in like manner always increase when the nature in question increases' (Bacon 1985: 142; Book 2, Aphorism XIII). This table will enable us to limit still further the possible candidates for the form of the phenomenal nature, and may well suggest that an 'axiom' or, as we would say, a hypothesis be put forward and tested as to the form of the phenomenal nature. This preliminary hypothesis Bacon refers to as the 'first vintage' concerning the form, implying by this term that further refinement is required. In particular, further experimental evidence should be sought so as to resolve uncertainties and ambiguities. These new experiments will result in the correction and improvement of the hypothesis, so that eventually there will be nothing tentative about it; it will be certain.

The certainty achievable by the use of this method is not just psychological; Bacon believed that it was logical. We can see why he thought this by considering the data provided by tables of presence and absence more closely. Suppose we wish to identify the form of a nature, w. The table of presence will be a list of instances in each of which w, together with other characteristics or natures, say a, b, c, d, e, . . ., are present. The table of absence will be a list of matching instances in each of which w is absent though other natures are present. The two tables might be presented thus:

Presence	Absence
$a\ b\ c\ d\ w$	$a\ c\ d\ f$
$a\ b\ d\ f\ w$	$a\ d\ f\ g$
$b\ g\ h\ w$	$d\ g\ h\ x$
etc.	etc.

There is just one letter, besides w, which occurs in each of the instances in the table of presence, and which does not occur in any of the instances in the table of absence, namely b. In so far as such limited information suggests anything, it suggests that b is the form of w. This will be the 'first vintage' and will need further examination, because its worth depends crucially on whether we think, as we probably do in this case, that there is another nature, say b', not so far mentioned or perhaps even noticed, which is always present with w and always absent with w. For, if there were such a nature, then further instances of presence and absence would need to be examined in order to decide whether b or b' is the form of w. New experiments, which Bacon calls 'prerogative instances', are needed to resolve the uncertainty. Is it possible, though, that there will always be some uncertainty, however many 'prerogative instances' we examine? Not if Bacon was right in believing that there is only a relatively small and manageable number of natures. For in that case we can decide, of each of that number of natures, whether it is present or absent in the experimental circumstances we have examined, and we must examine only as many circumstances as are needed to derive a secure conclusion about which nature is the form of the nature in question. That is to say, on the assumption that the form of w is one of a relatively small number of natures, a or b or c or . . . or x or y or z, we can draw the certain conclusion that it is, as in the above schematic example, b by using 'prerogative instances' to eliminate each of the other natures. The assumption is, perhaps, a generous one to grant, but, as we have seen, Bacon does offer a defence of it and it might well seem, from a practical point of view at least, to be reasonable.

Bacon's elaborate discussion of prerogative instances occupies the larger part of the second book of *Novum Organum*. It is, in effect, a detailed account of the different ways in which experiments give information. He was well aware that, although the construction of the tables is a relatively routine matter in that it requires only the reorganisation of information available in the natural and experimental histories, we must take great care over the selection of 'prerogative instances'. In many cases, new experiments provide these instances and are thereby able to transform the conjectures yielded by the use of the tables into secure and certain conclusions. The use of the term 'prerogative' reminds us that analogies between the experimental investigation of nature and the judicial investigation of people was never far from Bacon's thinking. Just as the most weighty judges have certain prerogative powers and rights, so the most significant experiments also have special prerogative powers and rights. For example, experiments which involve accurate measurement or which use instruments such as telescopes or microscopes provide prerogative instances. Also, experiments which create the nature whose form is sought can be especially informative, as when we experimentally create whiteness by pounding transparent glass into a powder or by agitating transparent water to produce a froth. But perhaps the most important kind of experiment is the one he called 'instance of the fingerpost', later called a 'crucial experiment'. The value of such an experiment lies in its ability to help us choose between two possibilities as to the form of a nature by showing that one is not after all a possible form because its absence is compatible with the nature's presence, or because its presence is compatible with the nature's absence. If, in the schematic example above, we were to suppose that only b *or* b' can be the form of w, an instance of the fingerpost will enable the investigator to choose between them.

In the *Novum Organum*, Bacon explored in some detail an example which explained how, in practice, his method would work. In the example, the aim is to find the form, or form nature, of heat – one of the phenomenal natures occurring on his lists. The first task was to construct a 'Table of Essence and Presence', listing instances in which heat of some kind is found. Bacon's table contained such items as the rays of the Sun, boiling liquids, friction, chemical reactions, and even the burning sensation produced by 'keen and intense cold'. Second, a 'Table of Deviation, or of Absence in Proximity' was constructed in which he tried to match the positive instances of the first table with negative instances. So, for example, the Moon's rays, unlike the Sun's, do not give heat; nor does a liquid 'in its natural state', though it does when it is boiling. In some cases there are no obvious negative instances to match positive instances, e.g. friction and some chemical reactions, and Bacon suggested certain new experiments in the expectation that they might provide such instances. Third, he gave a 'Table of Degrees or Comparison' which listed more than forty instances where heat is to be found in different degrees. The next step was to use these three tables, limited though they were in their scope and accuracy, to begin finding the form nature of heat. Any nature which does not appear in all the instances in which heat is present cannot be its form nature; any nature which does appear in any instance in which heat is absent cannot be its form nature; any nature which does not increase and decrease as heat increases and decreases cannot be its form nature. For example, because the Moon's rays do not produce heat, light is rejected as the form nature of heat. As a consequence of these exclusions, Bacon hoped, an affirmative though tentative conclusion might be drawn – a 'first vintage' concerning the form nature of heat. And the conclusion justified by his tables was, he claimed, that the form nature of heat is motion. A flame is always in motion; so are boiling and simmering liquids. The motion produced by bellows and blasts increases heat, whereas compression and restriction extinguish fire and heat, as when we extinguish a candle flame by pressing the wick between our fingers. But heat is not just any motion; it is a 'rapid', 'expansive' and 'upward' motion, not of the whole hot body but of its 'smaller parts'. This motion is what heat really is, independently of any effect it may have on people. By finding ways of inducing this form nature in any body we will, Bacon claimed, be able to generate heat in that body. Theoretical knowledge of the form of heat thus yields practical power enabling us to make heat. But before we can accept this tentative conclusion as theoretical knowledge we must undertake further work. To ensure the certainty of the conclusion we must examine new experiments, giving prerogative instances. Bacon himself did not carry through his example sufficiently far to make his claim about the form nature of heat more than a likely story, albeit one which bears more than a passing similarity to subsequent ideas about heat. For one thing, he gave no indication as to how experiments could show that it is the motion of the particles of matter which is the form nature of heat. The inference involved here cannot be from instances, positive or negative, to a general law; rather it is, at best, an inference from facts to a supposedly good way of explaining those facts. Bacon's instincts, we may think, were sound, even if the details of the method he proposed do not altogether legitimate them (Bacon 1985: 130–62; Book 2, Aphorisms XI–XX). Bacon was not alone in believing that he could infer 'insensible motions' from experimental evidence; Robert Hooke explicitly stated that he could experimentally prove the truth of his claims about a vibrating aether. In Hooke's case, too, the inference can hardly be described as inductive in Bacon's sense.

Both the theory of forms and an eliminative type of inductive reasoning are prominent in the *Novum Organum*. But Bacon's contemporaries would not have considered either as particularly novel. The theory of forms was a variation on philosophical ideas current at the time; it is associated with the Aristotelian view that genuine science must give real philosophical understanding through the identification of real natures or definitions, and cannot, therefore, have more than a limited concern with the immediate practical causes of natural phenomena. Despite his intention to reform science by bringing practice and theory closer together, Bacon never doubted the correctness of this view. The method of induction by elimination, though it was not expressed so clearly or so forcibly by others, was certainly widely practised. Galileo and his Italian colleagues used eliminative inductive thinking to decide between alternatives; so did Gilbert in reasoning about the nature of magnetic and electrical phenomena. It is, in any case, not a specifically scientific method of reasoning; as Bacon himself acknowledged, it was used to good effect by Plato to resolve philosophical issues in his dialogues. The importance of Bacon's contribution lies, rather, in the encouragement he gave to an experimental style in science. Real practical experiments were, in his view, indispensable to an understanding of natural processes. We need to find out what happens to the period of a pendulum when raised to the top of a church steeple or lowered to the base of a mine, what happens to a candle flame when it is surrounded by a larger flame, whether spirit of wine has the capacity to melt butter or wax, and so on. Such experiments are to be tried, not in a random or haphazard manner for the sake of idle curiosity or for practical benefit; they are to be tried, rather, when their results will give specific answers to formulated questions. The natural histories which provide the starting point for Bacon's method did, indeed, contain information derived from experiments, but, on the whole, these were experiments only in the sense that they involved processes which were, to some extent, artificial; they reported on discoveries made, by design or by chance, in the 'laboratories' of craftsmen. These experiments differed from the scientific experiments which produced Bacon's prerogative instances, in that the latter were designed for the specific purpose of providing what he called 'light' rather than 'fruit', i.e. were intended to illuminate theoretical questions rather than simply feed practical needs.

Once again the legal analogy is useful. Legal enquiries begin with the judge listening, largely passively, to what the witness has to say, just as scientific enquiries begin with the scientist observing, largely passively, what nature does. As a result, certain tentative conclusions begin to form in the mind of the judge, and in the mind of the scientist. The judge, and the scientist, will want to test the truth of their tentative conclusions, and in order to do so will take care to question the witness, or nature, in such a way that will resolve specific doubts suggested by the conclusions. Just as the witness might have to be put under pressure if he or she is to give answers, so nature might have to be treated in a special way, as in an experiment, if it is to give answers. And just as skilful inquisitors are needed to ensure that the witness's answers are correct and do not mislead the judge, so also skilful experimenters are needed to ensure that nature's answers are correct and do not mislead the scientist.

Bacon does not seem to have been a skilful experimentalist himself. Nevertheless, he cannot have been a mere onlooker, for he demonstrated an awareness both of what had been and of what might be achieved by experiment. He was, indeed, tolerably well informed about the science of his day. But it is to his successors that we turn in order to see the consequences of his view about the role of experimentation in science. Both Robert Boyle and Robert Hooke shared Bacon's conviction that a reformed study of nature should be an experimental study of nature. Genuine, secure knowledge of nature could, they believed, be founded on experiment, because experiment revealed facts about nature. There might be any number of opinions, some more probable than others, about events and processes normally concealed from an observer, but an experiment which enabled scientists to observe such an event or process would thereby enable them to substitute fact for opinion. Thus, in the science of pneumatics, both men co-operated in devoting considerable time, energy and resources to the construction of air-pumps – one of the very few reliable types of scientific apparatus available in the seventeenth century. As was the case with the newly invented telescope and microscope, scientists were able to use the air-pump to obtain experimental data about events and processes otherwise inaccessible. For example, the several phenomena of cohesion, whereby the surfaces of flat marble or glass discs could be made so smooth with polishing that they would cohere with each other, raised several questions. Various opinions were available as to the reason why a considerable force was needed to prise apart two cohering discs, and Boyle used his air-pump to test the suggestion that air pressure held the discs together. The contrast between Boyle's experiments and Galileo's is striking. We now know that many of the experiments described by Galileo he did indeed perform, even though his descriptions sometimes encourage doubts; but the details incorporated into Boyle's experimental narratives are such that no-one is left in any doubt that he performed them, or witnessed the performance of them.

Baconian strategies were also pursued in a more general way. The Royal Society began to take shape in 1660, receiving its charter in 1662, and Hooke's appointment in that year as its Curator of Experiments shows that from the first it was committed to an experimental programme. As the person responsible for designing and displaying experiments for the Fellows of the Society, he acquired considerable manipulative skill and ingenuity. This indeed was exactly what many of the founders of the Society, with backgrounds in various more or less informal clubs for Baconian experimenters, wanted. Together with Boyle, Hooke was among those who determined that an important task for the Society would be the promotion of Bacon's ambitious scheme for a reform of natural philosophy, and that it should use its wide and active membership to create new natural and experimental histories of mechanical arts and crafts. Several such histories were printed in the early issues of the *Philosophical Transactions* of the Society. Hooke's famous *Micrographia*, which told readers of remarkable biological phenomena revealed by the new microscope, was commissioned by the Society, and its preface promised 'a Natural and Artificial History' which would eventually be 'useful for the raising of Axioms and Theories'. When it was published in 1665 there was warm praise for its display of the advantages of Baconian 'Experimental and Mechanical knowledge'. It was Hooke, too, who tried in a 'philosophick Algebra' to develop Bacon's method further, so that it would more clearly yield the demonstrative conclusions needed in natural philosophy. Though the workings of this 'Algebra' were never clearly explained, it seems that they involved the identification and systematic testing of hypotheses or 'Axioms' of a certain type. This being so, it is not surprising that he emphasised experimental investigations rather than the routine collection of data, and thought that only superficial conclusions about causes could be reached on the basis of histories.

As for the Royal Society itself, its large active membership in the seventeenth century is testimony to the appeal of its Baconian programme for a 'new philosophy', especially in the early years when the enthusiasms of its founders were fresh. The Society's first Secretary, Henry Oldenberg, urged his foreign correspondents to assist in the labour needed by the Great Instauration. And Thomas Sprat, in his manifesto for the society, declared Bacon's arguments to be 'the best . . . that can be produc'd for the defence of Experimental Philosophy; and the best directions, that are needful to promote it'. The statutes of the society made it clear that one of the prime functions of its weekly meetings was to consider experiments. For some Fellows in these early years, such as the diarist Samuel Pepys, the chief reason for paying subscriptions was the pleasure to be derived from attending meetings when good experiments were displayed. There can, indeed, be little doubt that a Baconian emphasis on experimentation was given full expression in the rhetoric of the Royal Society in its early years, as well as in the particular scientific achievements of investigators such as Boyle and Hooke.

But we should not suppose that opposition to a Baconian experimental philosophy was entirely absent. Many ridiculed the experimenting activities of the first Fellows of the Royal Society. No-one with sense, they said, would devise elaborate experiments to prove what everyone knew to be the case, such as that air was necessary to life. Who, they asked when *Micrographia* was published, could possibly be interested in magnified images of such trivial things as fleas and strands of human hair? Certainly not anyone who claimed to be a gentleman. Satirists, especially, made fun of what was often seen as the foolish, trivial and useless activities of experimentalists. A different and more philosophically significant criticism was expressed by Benedictus de Spinoza, the Dutch philosopher, when he was sent Robert Boyle's description of some chemical experiments. He responded by firmly rejecting the method used: 'Since Mr Boyle does not put forward his proofs as mathematical, there will be no need to enquire whether they are altogether convincing' (quoted in Golinski 1990: 387). It was not that Spinoza thought observation and experiment irrelevant to science; his point was, rather, that science, as part of philosophy, required demonstrations, and no satisfactory demonstration of scientific principles had or could proceed from experimental evidence. In England, that view was shared and bluntly expressed by Thomas Hobbes, particularly in connection with Boyle's air-pump experiments. Such experiments, he claimed, had not, would not and could not establish the claims they were said to establish. Disputes about whether a vacuum is possible, which some thought to have been resolved by Boyle's experiments, remained unresolved; probable hypotheses intended to explain pneumatic phenomena remained just as probable. The only legitimate way to do natural philosophy was philosophically, not experimentally (see Shapin and Schaffer 1985: 129). The kind of knowledge capable of being produced by experimentalists such as Boyle, Hooke and the Royal Society virtuosos could not count as genuine philosophical knowledge. In the conclusions he drew from experiments with his air-pump, Boyle failed to address the sorts of questions about the nature of body, air, space and vacuum that Hobbes and others tried to address with the aid of theoretical principles, and in his chemical experiments he avoided creating a general theoretical framework in terms of which his results could be understood with the help of mathematical proofs. It is true that Boyle would have claimed the title 'philosopher' for himself, because he thought he had good experimental grounds for his mechanical or corpuscular philosophy, which promoted the idea that matter consists of microscopic particles that interact with each other in accordance with mechanical laws. But it was as an experimentalist that he resisted, in good Baconian fashion, the temptation to jump to conclusions, and for his caution he was accused of ignoring those issues which, according to some of his contemporaries such as Hobbes and Spinoza, have to be resolved if we are to have secure philosophical knowledge of nature.

Thomas Hobbes's friend William Harvey, the physiologist who established that the blood circulates around the body, is alleged to have said of Bacon that he wrote philosophy 'like a Lord Chancellor'. Though this was probably intended as an uncomplimentary jibe, it contains an important truth. As Lord Chancellor, Bacon had the responsibility for reforming the law so that just principles of 'Policy' could be established; in his philosophy he assumed responsibility for reforming scientific method so that true principles of 'Nature' could be established. Just as the judicial process, correctly administered, would increase the knowledge and the power of the King's ministers and thus the King himself, so Bacon's method, correctly administered, would also increase knowledge and power. It is no wonder, then, that Bacon should have found the vocabulary appropriate to his position as Lord Chancellor. The language of judicial enquiry proved to be particularly useful in urging the claims of experimentation as a way of disclosing nature's secret ways. But the legal idiom was of limited use in explaining how, from experimental results, legitimate philosophical conclusions could be reached. Neither Bacon nor any of his successors was able to show how claims about the real character of natural processes could be established with the certainty required for philosophical status. Both he and they had some good reasons for thinking that it could be done, but others had doubts which were also well founded. The questions about how scientific knowledge should be secured were becoming clearer, even if the answers remained as elusive as ever.

FURTHER READING

For Bacon's writings, use:

Spedding, J., Ellis, R. L. and Heath, D. D. (eds) (1857–74) *The Works of Francis Bacon*, 14 vols, London: Longman and Co. This edition contains English translations of all those works, such as the *Novum Organum*, which were originally published in Latin. Most of the translations of philosophical works are in Volume 4. It has remained the source for most subsequent editions of Bacon's works.

Robertson, J. M. (ed.) (1905) *The Philosophical Works of Francis Bacon . . .*, London: George Routledge and Sons. This one-volume collection brings together all the English translations of Bacon's philosophical works, as published in the Spedding, Ellis and Heath edition. It contains Ellis's helpful introduction and notes.

Bacon, F. (1915) *The Advancement of Learning*, edited with an introduction by G. W. Kitchin, London: Dent.

Bacon, F. (1985) *The New Organon and Related Writings*, edited with an introduction by F. H. Anderson, New York: Macmillan. This edition reprints the standard translation in the Spedding, Ellis and Heath edition. In addition to *Novum Organum* itself, it contains 'The Great Instauration' and 'Preparative Toward a Natural and Experimental History'.

Bacon's philosophy of science is explained and discussed in:

Hesse, M. (1964) 'Francis Bacon's philosophy of science', in D. J. O'Connor (ed.), *A Critical History of Western Philosophy*, New York: Free Press.

Horton, M. (1973) 'In defence of Francis Bacon: a criticism of the critics of the inductive method', *Studies in the History and Philosophy of Science* 4: 241–78.

Urbach, P. (1987) *Francis Bacon's Philosophy of Science: An Account and a Reappraisal*, La Salle, Ill.: Open Court.

Pérez-Ramos, A. (1988) *Francis Bacon's Idea of Science and the Maker's Knowledge Tradition*, Oxford: Oxford University Press.

Woolhouse, R. S. (1988) *The Empiricists*, A History of Western Philosophy 5, Oxford: Oxford University Press; ch. 2.

For more detail concerning questions addressed by Bacon, see:

Bentham, M. A. (1937) 'Some seventeenth-century views concerning the nature of heat and cold', *Annals of Science* 2: 431–50.

Rees, G. (1986) 'Mathematics and Francis Bacon's natural philosophy', *Revue Internationale de Philosophie* 40: 399–426.

For relevant background, see:

Shapin, S. and Schaffer, P. (1985) *Leviathan and the Air-Pump: Hobbes, Boyle, and the Experimental Life*, Princeton, NJ: Princeton University Press.

Lindberg, D. C. and Westman, R. S. (eds) (1990) *Reappraisals of the Scientific Revolution*, Cambridge: Cambridge University Press.

4   Isaac Newton
Rules for reasoning scientifically

William Harvey, Bacon's physician, wrote of his discovery of the circulation of the blood in his *De motu cordis* (On the motion of the heart), published in 1628. Not long afterwards, René Descartes read the book and in his own first publication – the *Discourse on the Method* of 1637 – gave prominence to Harvey's discovery. Though there were some who rejected Harvey's claim, including a number of anatomists, Descartes made it quite plain that his own anatomical work had led him to the conclusion that the blood does circulate around the body. Where the two men disagreed was about why the blood circulates. The debate has a factual scientific side but, as both Harvey and Descartes realised, it also raised questions about scientific method. These questions show that, although Harvey's emphasis upon the role of what he called 'ocular experiments', or anatomical dissections and vivisections, make him seem Baconian in his method, the same emphasis suggests a close connection with aspects of Galileo's ideas about method. And they show, too, that, although Descartes assigned a role to reason in science which made him seem Galilean in his method, his criticisms of Harvey echo some features of the Baconian method in experimental science.

Plainly the heart was centrally involved in the circulation of the blood around the body, but how? Harvey's view was that the heart is a muscle which contracts in a regular manner, making it act like a pump: blood coming from the body's veins via the liver enters the right side of the heart, from where it is forced by contractions through the lungs and back to the left side of the heart, which pumps it into the aorta and the arterial system so that eventually it finds it way via the capillaries into the veins again. Descartes's view was that the heart was able to circulate blood because it was able to heat and so expand the blood which entered it. According to him, when anatomists observed the heart contracting and relaxing, they were in fact observing an effect brought about by the expansion, or 'rarefaction', of the blood in the heart and its subsequent expulsion. Though largely ignored by Harvey, the conspicuous change in the colour of the blood is, Descartes thought, evidence of this 'rarefaction'. The blood's expansion was caused, he claimed, by heat produced within the heart. He knew from everyday experience that the expansion we observe in boiling and fermentation is the effect of heat; it was therefore reasonable to believe that the expansion of the blood within the heart is also the effect of heat. After all, one of the conspicuous differences between a living body with a beating heart and a corpse is that the former is warm and the latter cold.

Descartes's explanation is mistaken; the heart does not contain a heat source which might enable it to 'boil' or 'vaporise' the blood. But he did have an interesting and important reason for thinking that Harvey could not be right. Harvey, he said, had appealed to a property of the heart – its capacity for regular muscular contractions. But such a capacity is utterly mysterious, for muscles are used to exercise control over motion which, for human beings, is voluntary. How can something called a muscle contract in such a regular and involuntary manner? In the absence of an answer to this question, the 'contractile' property of the heart can no more explain why it is able to circulate blood than an appeal to the digestive properties of the stomach – its capacity for turning food into nutrients – can explain why it is able to digest food. When anatomists observe the contraction of the heart they thereby observe it circulating blood; they cannot be said to be observing anything distinguishable from the circulation, namely its cause. Pseudo-explanations of this type were relics of outdated ways of thinking which Galileo, Bacon and Descartes wished to replace; they provided merely verbal attempts to understand, camouflaging ignorance. We need to understand a cause, and not just be able to refer to it, if we wish to use it to explain an effect. So for Descartes, a genuine understanding of the action of the heart could come only from knowledge of the cause of that action. Though he did not use Baconian terminology, his view was that we need to find the form nature of the heart's phenomenal nature as revealed by anatomists. We need to find, that is, what it is about the nature of the heart which enables it to act in the way anatomists observe it to act. Only if our search is successful will we have a proper scientific, or 'philosophical', understanding of the circulation of the blood.

Descartes's criticism of Harvey is very similar in form to a criticism he expressed, at about the same time, of Galileo. The *Two New Sciences*, he complained, does not explain anything because it does not consider 'the first causes of nature' (quoted in Gaukroger 1989: 105). In other words, Galileo told us what happens when, say, a ball travels down an inclined plane, but he did not tell us why it happens; and the importance of this omission is that we cannot have a proper explanation of the facts about the ball's motion unless we have an explanation of why those facts are as they are. Similarly, Harvey provided for the first time an accurate description of how the blood moves in a body, but he did not provide an explanation for the facts that his anatomical investigation revealed. To understand these facts we must explain them, and, even though Descartes's explanation is faulty, there must nevertheless be some yet-to-be-discovered alternative account of the nature of the heart which will enable us to understand.

Although Galileo's scientific method was mathematical whereas Harvey's was experimental, it seems that their methods placed similar limits on what could be claimed: in neither case, so Descartes alleged, was their method sufficiently powerful to provide a philosophical explanation as opposed to a mathematical or experimental description. It may be, of course, that there is no method capable of justifying what Descartes would have understood by a philosophical explanation. On the other hand, perhaps the method of Bacon's *Novum Organum*, thoroughly applied to comprehensive experimental histories, or the method described in Descartes's *Discourse on the Method*, are capable of achieving this aim. But given the ambition of this aim, it would not be at all surprising if some of its features had to be sacrificed. Thus Bacon's method may be capable of yielding conclusions about form natures which could be used to provide philosophical explanations; but, as we have seen, given the theoretical, if not practical, insecurity of the inductive reasoning Bacon proposed, these conclusions will lack the complete certainty which a philosophically acceptable conclusion should, ideally, have.

Descartes's method is similarly ambitious, and the price to be paid for its ambition is, again, the uncertainty of its conclusions. It supposes that the form natures of all physical phenomena are mathematical, i.e. they are either geometrical or arithmetical. We identify 'principles or first causes' which specify these mathematical form natures, and we use them to deduce descriptions of the physical phenomena we want explained. But, as Descartes was well aware, there are too many ways of deducing such descriptions from 'first principles'. God could have chosen any from a number of different sets of first principles as the cause of the blood circulating in the body, or as the cause of the size, shape and elevation of a rainbow, or as the cause of light being 'refracted' or bent when it enters water or glass. Perhaps, indeed, there are possible worlds other than the actual world in which these same phenomena are to be found but in which the correct philosophical explanation of their occurrence is quite different from the correct philosophical explanation of their occurrence in this actual world. Descartes used the image of a clock to express this point. We see a clock telling us the time, but we know that there are different ways of constructing a clock so that it can do this; either a spring or a weight can drive its hands, for example. Similarly, we observe natural phenomena but we know that God 'could have produced all that we see in several different ways' (Descartes 1984–5: vol. 1, 289). To find the 'first principles' which give us a correct philosophical understanding of the phenomena to be explained, we must, Descartes said, use experiments, for they provide us with the means for discriminating between alternatives. In the case of the human body and its characteristics, Descartes acknowledged that explanations in terms of mathematical first principles were beyond his reach. It would be necessary, therefore, to postulate as causes of those characteristics mechanisms which we could eventually understand in terms of such principles. We can propose different and incompatible postulates, and it is the task of natural philosophers to devise experiments which will enable them to choose between alternatives. So experimental evidence concerning, for example, the change in the colour of the blood passing through the heart–lung system showed that Harvey's supposed explanation was inadequate and should be rejected in favour of Descartes's explanation. However, although experimentation enables us to test conclusions, it cannot justify them as infallible; the most we can expect is 'moral certainty', or certainty sufficient for ordinary practical purposes. Consequently, Descartes's method – like Bacon's – falls short of the absolute certainty expected in natural philosophy. Descartes's reasoning in his dispute with Harvey is not without force, but it led him to a mistaken conclusion. It is quite true that Harvey ignored and did not try to explain the change in the blood's colour; but although Descartes tried to incorporate an explanation of this into his account, his explanation was wrong. Only with Lavoisier's discovery, late in the eighteenth century, of the role of oxygen in respiration was it possible to supplement Harvey's account so that it could explain the colour change.

Both Bacon and Descartes accepted that their method did not yield absolute certainty. Nevertheless, they still thought that their conclusions counted as knowledge rather than as mere opinion. They believed that they had found ways of combining the resources of reason and of experience so as to justify conclusions entitling us to real knowledge, by which they meant knowledge of 'first causes' or 'simple natures'. There are, to be sure, important differences between the ways they found, with Bacon placing the greater weight on experience and emphasising the role of experimental histories in his method, whilst Descartes placed greater weight on reason and emphasised the role of mathematics in his method. But they both sought certainty, because they thought that, without it, their conclusions would lack philosophical worth.

Galileo and Harvey chose a different path. Absolute certainty was their priority and, to achieve it, they were prepared to adopt methods, albeit quite different ones, yielding conclusions which were criticised for their modesty. Bacon's critique of the role of mathematics in science, and Descartes's observation that to describe is not to explain, show that for some at least Galileo's conclusions about motion and Harvey's about the circulation of the blood failed to answer the questions that a natural philosophy should answer. They failed, that is, to supply the only sort of knowledge recognised in natural philosophy, namely knowledge of causes. Not that either man would have accepted such a criticism; for Galileo the 'book of nature' is written in the language of mathematics, and consequently a mathematical demonstration of the facts of motion from accepted principles does provide real knowledge of nature; and for Harvey direct 'ocular experiments' gave knowledge which was as good and sufficient as any that philosophers could provide. For both, knowledge of causes was not the only sort of knowledge worth having in natural philosophy.

It seems, then, that there were at least two dimensions to the debate about scientific method in the seventeenth century. One of these dimensions was concerned with the roles of mathematics and experiment. Galileo and Descartes recognised a role for both in their accounts of method, though they placed the greater weight on mathematics. Their view was shared by Hobbes in England. Bacon, too, recognised a role for both mathematics and experiment, but both he and Harvey placed the greater weight on experiment. Their view was shared by Boyle, Hooke and other founders of the Royal Society. A second dimension was determined by reactions to conflicting conceptions about the aim of scientific method. Some, like Bacon and Descartes, sought to preserve the traditional view that science is concerned above all with knowledge of causes, and that methods should be devised which will help us achieve this aim. Others, such as Galileo and Harvey, took the view, also sanctioned by tradition, that the absolute certainty of conclusions reached is crucial, and methods should secure that aim. The distinction represented on this second dimension is the more extreme. With regard to the first, many were willing to recognise that both mathematics and experiment have important parts to play in scientific reasoning, even though it was difficult to see how a coherent account of scientific method could do proper justice to both. But with regard to the second, neither party to the dispute saw any way of compromising or modifying their position; both believed that certain knowledge was attainable with the methods they proposed.

The unresolved tensions in this two-dimensional picture form an appropriate background for an examination of Newton's views about scientific method. The mathematical natural philosophy of the *Principia* (1687) and the experimental natural philosophy of the *Opticks* (1704) are, in many ways, the crowning achievements of the scientific revolution, and both of these books contain important statements about how science should be done. Though they were not uncontroversial, these statements acquired considerable authority in the early years of the eighteenth century. They have remained important, not just for their historical significance, but as an expression of a fruitful way of thinking about the aims and methods of science. Newton was, he said, able to see further than his predecessors because he stood on the shoulders of giants, and we should understand him to mean not only that he was able to discern more of the truth about the world, but also able to discern more about what are appropriate methods to use in obtaining that truth.

Isaac Newton was born on Christmas Day 1642 at Woolsthorpe, a Lincolnshire village. After Grantham Grammar School, he was sent to Trinity College, Cambridge, and, in 1669, became the University's Lucasian Professor of Mathematics. He was in his early and middle twenties when he formulated the main outlines of his mathematical and physical ideas, the years 1665–66 – when he had to return to Lincolnshire because of the plague then raging in urban centres – being particularly productive. He first attracted widespread attention for his work on light and colour, but at least as significant for those who had access and could follow them were his innovative but unpublished discoveries in mathematics, which were to play an important part in the early development of the calculus. His discoveries in optics, including a description of his famous prism experiment, which convinced him that white light is a mixture of different colours, began to be published in the *Philosophical Transactions* of the Royal Society in 1672. His mathematical ideas, though they played a part in his optical investigations, became prominent in his work in astronomy. The *Principia*, which set out his conclusions in dynamics and astronomy, was composed in the 1680s and first published in 1687. Thereafter his mathematical activity was more and more confined to the revision, publication and defence of his earlier work. Following the success of the *Principia*, Newton seems to have gradually lost interest in his professorship, and with his appointment as Warden of the Mint in 1696 he became a civil servant. Nevertheless, he continued to enjoy a reputation as England's foremost scientist. He became President of the Royal Society in 1703 and, two years later, was knighted by Queen Anne. His *Opticks*, in which he presents the results of thirty years of work on light and colour, was first published in 1704. An acrimonious priority dispute with Leibniz, which served as an occasion for disreputable deceit, arrogance and spite, marred his final years. He died in London in 1727 and is buried in Westminster Abbey.

Though Newton never wrote a sustained and detailed account of his scientific method, there are a number of places in his published and unpublished writings where we find explicit statements of how he thought science should be done. In the *Principia*, both the 'Rules of Reasoning in Philosophy' with which the final book, Book III, begins and the 'General Scholium' with which it concludes contain such statements; in the *Opticks* we find them in the last of the 'Queries' which appear at the end of the book. Given the way in which ideas about scientific method had developed in the Scientific Revolution, it is not surprising that these sources reveal tensions in his thinking. What is, perhaps, surprising is that they are not as pronounced as they might have been. At any rate, his Newtonian successors found it possible to promote both a mathematical and an experimental way of doing science, and possible to advocate methods which would yield conclusions appropriate in their security and their content to natural philosophy.

In Book III of the *Principia*, or to give the work its full English title, *Mathematical Principles of Natural Philosophy*, Newton undertook the task of showing that the 'mathematical principles' he had developed in the first two books are principles of natural philosophy: 'such, namely, as we may build our reasonings upon in philosophical inquiries' (Newton 1934: 397). In the first two books he had provided a 'science of motions resulting from any forces whatsoever, and of the forces required to produce any motions, accurately proposed and demonstrated', and he intended to show how this 'rational mechanics' could be used to provide philosophically adequate answers to questions about natural phenomena (Newton 1934: xvii). His strategy was to 'demonstrate the frame of the System of the World' by deducing, with the help of his mathematical principles, 'the motions of the planets, the comets, the moon, and the sea'. In this way, he would, he said, give an 'example' of their use. But the generality of his principles, together with his belief that 'the phenomena of Nature . . . depend upon certain forces by which the particles of bodies . . . are either mutually impelled towards one another . . . or are repelled and recede from one another', gave him hope that he would be able to do more. Later, he returned to this hope and developed some ideas which would, he thought, bring it within the scope of experimental natural philosophy (Newton 1934: xviii).

He foresaw he would meet with objections to his method for deriving conclusions in natural philosophy in this book, and at one point Edmund Halley had to persuade him to continue with his intention to include it despite misgivings about the disputes it might engender. His critics would complain, he thought, that he was offering as demonstrated truths about nature claims which were no more than implausible hypotheses; that his so-called mathematical principles were no more than an 'ingenious Romance'. It was for this reason, no doubt, that he began Book III by identifying certain 'Rules of Reasoning in Philosophy', i.e. rules which should govern the reasoning processes used to establish conclusions in natural philosophy. In their final versions, the rules are:

Rule I: 'We are to admit no more causes of natural things than such as are both true and sufficient to explain their appearances'.

Rule II: 'Therefore to the same natural effects we must, as far as possible, assign the same causes'.

Rule III: 'The qualities of bodies, which admit neither intensification nor remission of degrees, and which are found to belong to all bodies within the reach of our experiments, are to be esteemed the universal qualities of bodies whatsoever'.

Rule IV: 'In experimental philosophy we are to look upon propositions inferred by general induction from phenomena as accurately or very nearly true, notwithstanding any contrary hypotheses that may be imagined, till such time as other phenomena occur, by which they may either be made more accurate, or liable to exceptions' (Newton 1934: 398–400).

The first two of these rules are concerned with the kind of conclusion we should be looking for in natural philosophy. In them, Newton made it clear that, like Bacon and Descartes, he believed that conclusions had to provide information about causes. The third rule, new in the 1713 edition of the *Principia*, expressed Newton's endorsement of a certain kind of restricted inductive reasoning which entitles us to generalise some of our knowledge about things 'within the reach of experiments', so as to be able to make claims about things which, because they are too small or too remote, are outside the reach of experiments. Newton made it clear that we can only generalise from our experimental knowledge in those cases where the knowledge is of properties belonging to all objects. So, although we can claim, using this rule, that unobserved, and even unobservable, objects have 'extension, hardness, impenetrability, mobility, and inertia', we cannot claim that all or indeed any such objects have colour or taste or smell or a definite degree of heat, because not all objects we encounter in experiments have these characteristics. Clear glass and plain water, for example, have neither colour, nor taste, nor smell, and the same water can feel both cold (to a warm hand) and warm (to a cold hand) at the same time. In effect, Newton's third rule enabled natural philosophers to identify the limited number of form natures, as Bacon had called them, which were ultimately responsible for the multitude of phenomenal natures. And like Bacon, Newton considered his limited list of privileged qualities to characterise the nature of things in relation to the universe rather than in relation to human beings with certain contingent perceptual capacities.

The fourth rule, which was new to the third, 1726, edition of the *Principia*, refers to induction in the more general sense of reasoning, from 'phenomena' to 'general propositions', and comments on the confidence we can place in its conclusions. In the brief remark which Newton added to his statement of this rule – 'This rule we must follow, that the argument of induction may not be evaded by hypotheses' – he made it clear that there is an important difference between reasoning from the truth of consequences to the truth of the premisses from which they are drawn, or hypothetical reasoning, and reasoning from phenomena to generalisations of phenomena, or inductive reasoning. Rule IV licenses the latter, but not the former.

Perhaps because these rules seemed so reasonable, Newton provided little or no argument for them. In the case of the first, he simply drew attention to its consonance with the belief of philosophers that 'Nature does nothing in vain . . . and affects not the pomp of superfluous causes'. In support of the second he offered no more than the perfunctory 'Therefore' with which it begins, suggesting that in some unexplained way the first rule supports the second. There is a lengthy explanation attached to the third rule, but ultimately the appeal is to authority or general consensus – 'this is the foundation of all philosophy', by which he meant, of course, 'of all natural philosophy'. And in the case of the fourth rule, as we have seen, Newton simply assumed that his readers would never reject an inductive argument just because it was 'evaded by hypotheses'. But the absence of proper justifications for the rules is not so surprising, given that their function was not so much to defend as to explain what Newton did. He wanted, in particular, to assure critical readers that he understood as well as they did what was required in natural philosophy and what was needed to achieve it. It may be, of course, that Newton did not do what, according to these rules, he should have done, in which case their explanatory role is undermined. If, on the other hand, he can show that they had some significant part to play in the achievement of his scientific results, then he will, to that extent, have vindicated them.

But there are remarkably few references to these rules in the *Principia*. Newton used the first and second rules, usually together, to justify the claim that the 'same sort of cause', namely a gravitational force, must be responsible for the behaviour of heavy terrestrial objects, for the Moon's orbiting the Earth, for the planets' orbiting the Sun, and for the satellites of Saturn and Jupiter orbiting their planets. Roger Cotes, who wrote a preface to the second edition of the *Principia* with the express purpose of explaining the 'method of this philosophy', drew attention to the important role of the rules, particularly the second rule, in Newton's reasoning. The third rule is invoked just once in support of the claim that we should count gravity among the universal properties of bodies, i.e. that the inverse square law is a universal law. Cotes's preface emphasised this rule, too. Newton used the fourth rule also only once, in conjunction with the first two rules, to support the general proposition that whatever causes the Moon to retain its orbit will also affect all the planets (Newton 1934: 408–10, 413). But what is even more surprising is that none of these rules refers to the type of reasoning which is characteristic of Book III of the *Principia*. The

'Propositions' concerning planets and their satellites that Newton established are derived from astronomical 'Phenomena', but not in accordance with the inductive process mentioned in Rule IV. For the six 'Phenomena' listed immediately after the rules are already expressed in general terms, so presumably they have already been inferred by induction from specific observations. And in any case, the reasoning from 'Phenomena' to 'Propositions' is deductive rather than inductive. For example, 'Phenomenon IV' states a version of what is known as Kepler's third law of planetary motion, namely, '. . . the periodic times of the five planets [Mercury, Venus, Mars, Saturn, Jupiter], and . . . of the earth about the sun, are as the ³⁄₂th power of their mean distances from the sun'. And 'Proposition II' states that '. . . the forces by which the . . . planets are . . . retained in their proper orbits . . . are inversely as the square of the distances of the places of those planets from the sun's centre'. Using a mathematical theorem he had proved in Book I, Newton deduced this proposition, the famous inverse square law of gravitational attraction, from Kepler's law (Newton 1934: 402–4).

As explained in the 'General Scholium', added in the 1713 second edition to the end of the *Principia*, Newton's own view was that he had indeed used 'deduction from the phenomena' when he had derived his inverse square law. The mathematical principles he had stated at the beginning of Book I of the *Principia* were, therefore, entitled to be called principles of natural philosophy, because they had enabled him to deduce causes from effects. The effects in question were stated as 'Phenomena' – for example, Kepler's third law – and the cause of these 'Phenomena' was a force of gravity which his third rule of reasoning had enabled him to make universal. The operation of a force of gravity is not, then, a 'hypothesis' in the sense that it is one among many ways of explaining the phenomena. Newton's statement in the General Scholium was quite explicit in rejecting what we might call hypothetical reasoning in experimental natural philosophy: 'whatever is not deduced from the phenomena is to be called an hypothesis; and hypotheses, whether metaphysical or physical, whether of occult qualities or mechanical, have no place in experimental philosophy' (Newton 1934: 547). Just because we can use a hypothesis to explain phenomena is no good reason, Newton thought, for believing that hypothesis to be true. The only kinds of reasoning allowable in experimental philosophy were deductive reasoning, which might well depend on powerful mathematical results like those established in Books I and II of the *Principia*, and inductive reasoning of the types specified in Rules of Reasoning III and IV.

Newton was right to anticipate controversy. Critics did claim that he had failed to follow the scientific method he had specified, and that his inverse square law was, despite his disclaimers, no more than a 'hypothesis'. They claimed, too, that it was a highly implausible hypothesis in that it involved the idea that a gravitational force could be the cause of one object, say the Sun, affecting the motion of another object, say a planet, even though it had neither direct nor indirect contact with that other object; it involved, that is, the supposition of 'action at a distance'. They could not accept that Newton's method was both sufficiently austere to satisfy the demand that its conclusions be certain and also sufficiently strong to yield conclusions about real causes. Either 'deduction from the phenomena' licenses conclusions which are not derived from the phenomena but are, instead, hypotheses, or alternatively the conclusions it licenses are not conclusions about real causes.

The German philosopher Gottfried Wilhelm Leibniz was among Newton's sharpest critics in this respect. He objected that the conclusion that every body is attracted to every other body by a gravitational force was not 'deduced from the phenomena' as Newton had claimed. The same point was put to Newton by Roger Cotes when he was preparing his preface. In particular, the essential 'mutuality' of gravitational attraction, which requires that the Earth attract the Sun as well as the Sun attract the Earth, could not be deduced from the Kepler laws. Newton's answer to this objection invoked his third law of motion, which required equality of action and reaction, but it is not clear that this is applicable in a case of action at a distance and that the objection was satisfactorily answered. If, as Leibniz believed, universal gravity was not 'deduced from the phenomena', then it must be a hypothesis; it must, that is, be put forward as an explanatory cause of the observed phenomena. Leibniz did not share Newton's hostility to hypotheses in experimental philosophy, but he did object to the kind of cause that was being proposed. Consider, he said, a body which is subject to a law, perhaps Newton's inverse square law, according to which it circulated around a fixed point. To understand this behaviour we must either suppose that it is in the nature of the body concerned to circulate in this way rather than, say, to move in a straight line; or we suppose that there is an agency, natural or supernatural, which makes it circulate rather than behave in the way that its nature requires. But, in the case of gravitational phenomena, which specify just such behaviour, Newton had not claimed that the behaviour was natural to the gravitating bodies, for that would be to claim that gravity was 'essential' to bodies. Newton's view was, quite clearly, that the planets, for example, were made to circulate around the Sun rather than did so of their own accord. But his 'hypothesis' of universal gravitation provides, Leibniz claimed, no information about any natural agency which could make circulating bodies circulate. To say that a gravitational force makes them circulate does not identify a natural agency; it simply reports, in other words, what happens. So, Leibniz concluded, if Newton is not willing to make gravity an essential or 'scholastic occult' quality as well as a universal quality of bodies, he must suppose that gravitational phenomena are produced by a continual miracle and have therefore a supernatural cause (Alexander 1956: 184).

But Newton was adamant: a gravitational force is the cause of the motion of the planets and we can derive its nature, i.e. the inverse square law, from observed astronomical phenomena. There are, perhaps, some puzzling aspects of a gravitational force which enables objects to act where they are not, and it may be that only an enquiry into the cause of the gravitational force itself will enable us to solve those puzzles. 'I have not been able,' he said in the General Scholium, 'to discover the cause of those properties of gravity from phenomena'. But the fact that we have not yet discovered the cause of gravity should not prevent us from claiming that it is the natural agency which causes the observed motion of the planets, any more than Harvey's inability to specify a cause for the regular muscular contractions of the heart should have prevented him from claiming that those contractions are the natural agency which causes the circulation of the blood. 'We have', Newton said, 'explained the phenomena of the heavens and of our sea by the power of gravity', even if we 'have not yet assigned the cause of this power'. And so far as 'deduction from the phenomena' is concerned, provided we understand this phrase in terms of either strictly deductive methods, as used in the mathematics of Books I and II of the *Principia*, or inductive methods as specified in the Rules of Reasoning, then there should be no possibility of confusion with hypothetical reasoning (Newton 1934: 546–7).

In the Rules of Reasoning and in the General Scholium Newton was trying, with some success, to find a suitable way of reconciling the demand that his conclusions be certain with the demand that they concern real causes. So far as the demand for certainty was concerned, his strategy was to reject hypothetical reasoning and to insist upon a method which used only what he called 'deduction from the phenomena'. He recognised that such a method does not always yield absolute certainty, not so much because phenomena can be deceptive as because Newtonian deduction encompasses the inductive reasoning referred to in Rules III and IV, and arguing from observed phenomena to unobserved and to unobservable phenomena in the simple 'enumerative' manner Newton appears to have envisaged is, as Bacon had pointed out, notoriously fallible. Nevertheless, Newton thought that the kind of reasoning he advocated, even though it fell short of the demand for absolute certainty, was capable of producing 'the highest evidence that propositions can have in this [experimental] philosophy' (Thayer 1953: 6). It met, that is to say, the most stringent legitimate demand that could be made of 'deduction from the phenomena'. And, so far as the demand for real causes was concerned, Newton thought he could successfully and reasonably resist the criticism by denying that real causes had to be ultimate causes. In particular, the causal 'story' about gravitation may be a long one, and perhaps we know only a tiny fragment of its beginning, but that should not prevent us from telling the beginning of the story, or from believing it. We can understand gravity to be the cause of the motion of the planets, of our Moon, and of the sea, even if we do not know what it is about gravity that enables it to have these effects. It would, as Newton recognised, be easy to cut the story short by declaring gravity to be not only a universal quality of matter but an essential quality of matter, which would amount to the concession that matter could no more exist without gravitating than it could exist without size or shape. But to succumb to this temptation would be to fall into the trap of providing a merely verbal explanation: gravitational attraction explains gravitational phenomena but what we mean by gravitational attraction is exhausted by our accounts of that gravitational phenomena.

In the *Opticks* of 1704 we find this same view reiterated and re-inforced. Newton emphasised, in particular, his rejection of hypo-thetical reasoning in favour of a method which enables us to reason, deductively and inductively, from experimental evidence. As he said at the very beginning of the *Opticks*, 'My Design in this Book [i.e. the first of the three books which comprise the *Opticks*] is not to explain the Properties of Light by Hypotheses, but to propose and prove them by Reason and Experiments' (Newton 1979: 1). Throughout Book I the emphasis is upon experimental 'proofs' of 'Theorems' and experi-mental solutions to 'Problems', rather than upon mathematical demon-strations, but this does not mean that Newton's scientific method altered when he turned his attention to optical phenomena. For the method he had called 'deduction from the phenomena' in the *Principia* does not differ in essence from the method he called 'Proof by Experiments' in the *Opticks*. This is made clear in the last of the 'Queries' appended, in the 1706 Latin edition, to the third book. There he explained that 'in Natural Philosophy' we should undertake 'the Investigation of difficult Things by the Method of Analysis', which consists, he said, 'in making Experiments and Observations, and in drawing general Conclusions from them by Induction, and admitting of no Objections against the Conclusions, but such as are taken from Experiments, or other certain Truths'. To underline his conviction that only experimental objections could count, he went on to repeat his belief that 'Hypotheses are not to be regarded in experimental Philo-sophy' and that 'the arguing from Experiments and Observations by Induction . . . is the best way of arguing which the Nature of Things admits of' (Newton 1979: 404). These are the same views that he had conveyed in the Rules of Reasoning and the General Scholium of the *Principia*.

The emphasis on experimentation in the *Opticks* created fresh problems for Newton. In Book I, some thirty-five experiments are listed, including what is perhaps the most famous, namely his experiment showing that the colours produced by prisms are not caused by light being modified or weakened by the prisms (Newton 1979: 45f; cf. 73, 122). This experiment is what Bacon would have called an 'Experiment of the Fingerpost', producing a 'Prerogative Instance'. Newton himself regarded it as a 'crucial experiment', though he did not call it so in the *Opticks*. It is easy to describe in outline: Newton arranged for sunlight to pass through a triangular prism and for the familiar colour spectrum it produces to appear on an opaque board; he made a small hole in this board so that rays from a small part of the spectrum could pass through it and on to the side of a second prism; beyond this second prism he placed a second board to see whether the second prism modified or changed the light entering it; he found that it did not. The colours produced by the first prism 'could not be changed by Refraction', i.e. by viewing them through a second prism. But this is exactly what should happen if the 'modification' view about prisms were correct. Contrary to what this view anticipates, 'If any Part of the red Light was refracted, it remained totally of the same Colour as before', and 'No orange, no yellow, no green or blue, no other new Colour was produced by that Refraction' (Newton 1979: 122).

One question posed by this experiment is whether its role was purely negative, in that it showed the 'modification' theory to be wrong, or whether Newton was right in thinking that he could use this experiment to prove a positive conclusion, namely that sunlight is a mixture of rays of different refrangibility. Of course, if the 'modification' theory were the only alternative to Newton's view, then a positive conclusion could be drawn. But Newton does not seem to have wanted his argument to be eliminative in the way that Bacon had suggested. He believed that his conclusion was proved by experiment and that no questionable hypothesis claiming that it was the only alternative to the 'modification' theory was required. Much depends upon how we understand Newton's conclusion. The 'modification' theory was connected with what everyone regarded as hypotheses about the nature of light, in particular the hypothesis that light should be understood as a disturbance, or as a 'pulse', propagated in an aetherial medium in rather the way that a stone thrown into a pond creates a disturbance which is propagated in the form of ripples on its surface. Similarly, Newton's conclusion that sunlight is not pure and simple but a mixture of different coloured rays of light was associated with hypotheses, in particular the hypothesis that rays of light consist of light particles. This hypothesis is not proved by his experiments and he was careful not to claim that it was. But he thought that the truth of his conclusion was not dependent on the acceptability of any such hypothesis and that he could therefore claim that it was proved by experiment without the aid of any hypothesis.

Descriptions of Newton's 'crucial' experiment give the impression that it was a great deal easier and more straightforward to perform than was in fact the case. He had first described the experiment in 1672, and it is apparent from the criticisms expressed shortly afterwards that many investigators found his result very difficult to reproduce. Experimenters had to obtain good quality prisms and use careful experimental techniques. But there were no accepted standards for what could count as a 'good quality prism' or as 'careful experimental techniques'. Consequently, if experimenters failed to replicate his result, Newton could and did attribute their failure to inadequacies in the prisms or in the experimental techniques, just as readily as others attributed the failure to the non-existence of Newton's result. At a time when Newton's reputation had yet to be established, he could not assume that his explanation of failure would be accepted. He could, and did, produce more elaborate directions for performing the experiment, but not all were convinced. Evidence of the complaints Newton encountered is to be found in the very first 'Problem' he considers and solves in the *Opticks*, namely how 'To separate from one another the hetero-geneous Rays of compound Light' (Newton 1979: 64). For if the 'crucial experiment' is to show that homogeneous light, e.g. red light, is not 'modified' by the second prism, it is essential that there should be a means of obtaining such light. Part of the reason why experimenters had not been able to replicate his result was, Newton thought, that they had not taken sufficient care to ensure that a 'well parted ray' was delivered to the second prism. The experimental solution Newton proposed to his 'Problem' tried to overcome this problem. He added to it some advice about the quality of prisms needed for a successful experiment, saying they must 'be well wrought, being made of Glass free from Bubbles and Veins', and, after providing some suggestions about experimental techniques, said disarmingly: 'In trying these Things, so much diligence is not altogether necessary, but it will promote the Success of the Experiments, and by a very scrupulous Examiner of Things deserves to be apply'd'. Even so, when repetitions of this and other experiments were reported in the Royal Society's *Philosophical Transactions* for 1716, further details of apparatus and procedure were added (Newton 1979: 72; cf. Schaffer 1989: 67–104).

There were, then, some important questions about the capacity of 'Proofs by Experiment' to produce secure conclusions, and Newton's response to these questions was not always convincing. This is not to cast any doubt on his acumen and skill at devising appropriate ex-periments. It is, rather, to suggest that his 'philosophy' of experiment was in some respects naive. In particular, he assumed too easily that experimental evidence had the authority it needed to guarantee the conclusions drawn from it. When, as in the *Principia*, the emphasis was upon the application of mathematical results to experimental or observational evidence, there was less of a problem, because the evidence was seen as an extension of common experience. But in the *Opticks*, phenomena were subjected to a Baconian style 'inquisition' intended to uncover 'secrets', with the accompanying danger that, unless suitable precautions are taken, what the phenomena reveal will be misleading. Whereas Bacon had shown some sensitivity to the need for precaution and was eager to develop strategies which recognised it, Newton's attitude, like Galileo's before him, was to turn to rhetoric. The sheer ingenuity of the experiments Newton described in the *Opticks*, together with their appearance in a context which could not fail to remind readers of the successes of the *Principia*, made them seem so powerful that it would be superfluous to perform them for oneself. It was, in fact, more than forty years after some of the experiments were first described that accounts of them were given which would enable experimenters to replicate Newton's results reliably.

There is a further feature of the *Opticks* which seems remarkable in the light of Newton's very clear rejection of hypothetical reasoning. This is the fact that its third and final book concludes with a list of thirty-one 'Queries', in some of which hypotheses do seem to be proposed and defended. For example, 'Query 29' begins by asking, 'Are not the Rays of Light very small Bodies emitted from shining substances?' and continues with a substantial discussion of how a corpuscular theory of light might be able to explain various optical phenomena. It certainly seems as if Newton was here suggesting and examining a hypothesis, thereby violating the claim that he made only a few pages later that 'Hypotheses are not to be regarded in experimental Philosophy' (Newton 1979: 404). In other 'Queries', speculations about a space-pervading aether, and about the ultimate constituents of matter being 'solid, massy, hard, impenetrable, moveable Particles', are explored. But there would only be an inconsistency between his method and his practice if, in the 'Queries', he was doing experimental philosophy. It seems rather doubtful whether Newton would have thought so. In the first place, the 'Queries' are introduced with the remark that they are added 'in order to a farther search to be made by others'. They were intended, that is, not as contributions to experimental philosophy but as aids to anyone who might wish to resolve the issues they raise using the experimental method. Second, the preceding part of Book III consists entirely of 'Observations' concerning what we now call 'inter-ference' phenomena. It would appear that Newton was not satisfied with these 'Observations', for he intended, he said, 'to repeat most of them with more care and exactness, and to make some new ones for determining the manner how the Rays of Light are bent in their passage by Bodies, for making the Fringes of Colours with the dark lines between them' (Newton 1979: 338). There is, therefore, a question as to whether any part of Book III would have counted for him as experimental philosophy. And finally, it was only with respect to the first of the three books making up the *Opticks* that Newton explicitly declared that he was engaged in proving by means of 'Reason and Experiment', i.e. engaged in experimental philosophy. It is, moreover, noticeable that only in this book do we find 'Propositions' accompanied by experimental proofs. There are, then, doubts about whether experimental philosophy is to be found elsewhere than in Book I, and certainly doubts about whether what is written in the 'Queries' counts as experimental philosophy. Hypothetical reasoning may have no legitimate place in experimental philosophy, as Newton claimed in both the *Principia* and the *Opticks*, but that is not to say that the 'probable opinions' which he associated with such reasoning cannot be interesting, or suggestive, or in some other way helpful to anyone whose aim is the establishment of certain knowledge using the experimental method.

Newton's achievement so far as scientific method is concerned, then, was to identify and use a method which gave scope for emphasis upon the use of mathematical results, as in the *Principia*, and for emphasis upon experimental evidence, as in the *Opticks*. The method is called 'deduction from the phenomena' in the *Principia*, and 'experimental philosophy' in the *Opticks*, but its essential features are the same in both treatises. It uses nothing other than deductive reasoning from basic principles or from 'Phenomena', these principles and these 'Phenomena' being established by the two kinds of induction recognised in the third and fourth Rules of Reasoning. So far as the mathematical–experimental dimension is concerned, then, Newton's view is not radically different to that of his immediate predecessors and contemporaries, such as Galileo and Descartes, and Bacon and Harvey, though it is expressed more explicitly and worked out in more detail. They supposed that both mathematics and experiment have important roles in scientific method; Newton showed by precept and example how it was possible for them to have such roles.

The aims of Newton's method were to produce genuine philosophical knowledge by investigating the real causes of natural phenomena, and to do this by establishing conclusions with as much certainty as is appropriate in experimental philosophy. However, the ultimate cause of everything is God, and He has the power to bring about the same effects in any number of different ways unknowable to us; we must therefore be willing to accept intermediate causes such as gravitational forces without understanding how they are able to produce the effects we observe. As for certainty, Newton made it clear in his fourth rule of reasoning that additional evidence might show that a conclusion needed to be modified, and in the *Opticks* acknowledged that 'arguing . . . by Induction [is] no Demonstration of general Conclusions' (Newton 1979: 404). The conclusions of the method do not have, and do not need to have, absolute certainty; but they do have, or can be made to have, the practical or 'moral' certainty that they do need. If properly applied, Newton's method can establish conclusions beyond reasonable doubt. So far as this dimension is concerned, then, Newton's view is distinct from that of Galileo and Harvey, who were willing to sacrifice knowledge of causes in order to achieve certainty, and from that of Bacon and Descartes, who were willing to sacrifice certainty in order to achieve knowledge of causes. According to Newton, if they are correctly understood, knowledge of both causes and certainty is obtainable.

Newton's method was steadfastly opposed to hypothetical reasoning, or reasoning which supposes that some hypothesis is true just because if it were true it would explain phenomena. Such reasoning is capable of yielding only 'probable opinion', and is therefore worthless in natural philosophy, where the aim is certain knowledge. But few of Newton's contemporaries adopted such a dismissive attitude, and Newton himself seems to have used hypothetical reasoning, though not within experimental philosophy. Among those who took a favourable view of hypothetical reasoning was Christian Huygens, the Dutch natural philosopher. In the Preface to his *Treatise on Light* (1690; Huygens 1962) he recognised that the 'demonstrations' he had provided in the book 'do not produce as great a certitude as those of Geometry' and explained that this was because 'Geometers prove their Propositions by fixed and incontestable Principles', whereas the principles he proposed were to be 'verified by the conclusions drawn from them'. Nevertheless, Huygens claimed, these verifications had enabled him to 'attain thereby to a degree of probability which very often is scarcely less than complete proof'. In particular, where the conclusions drawn were in perfect agreement with a 'great number' of observations resulting from experiments, and, moreover, the conclusions drawn had been used to anticipate 'new phenomena' correctly, then there is 'strong confirmation' of the truth of the conclusions 'and it must be ill if the facts are not pretty much as I represent them' (Huygens 1962: vi–vii). By adopting such a method, Huygens hoped that he would be able to identify the cause of optical phenomena, such as the fact that light travels in straight lines and that rays of light are able to cross each other without hindrance, for which no one had yet given even a probable explanation. Unfortunately, the conclusions Huygens reached by means of his method were incompatible with the conclusions that Newton had reached using his method. To an extent, then, the controversy about the nature of light – whether it is corpuscular or a wave motion in an invisible aether – was connected with the controversy about scientific method – whether it allows only 'deduction from the phenomena' or also allows hypothetical reasoning. Newton was able to have the last word, for the time being at least, about the nature of light in his *Opticks*, for it was first published after Huygens's death, and, as we have seen, he took that opportunity to declare that his view about method should prevail.

The famous English philosopher John Locke, a contemporary admirer of Newton, was prepared to allow a place for hypothetical reasoning in natural philosophy, but he also thought natural philosophy, whether or not it used this method, incapable of providing genuine knowledge. The reason for this was that he adopted a strict definition of knowledge which made it impossible to count anything which was less than absolutely certain – and therefore any conclusion in natural philosophy – as knowledge. Where knowledge was impossible, 'judgement' had to suffice. Judgement, for Locke, always involved an element of 'presumption' or conjecture or hypothesis. Accordingly, the conclusions reached in natural philosophy, however carefully derived, would be judgements having one or another degree of probability. But hypothetical reasoning was capable of yielding probable judgements, and so it could count as a legitimate method of reasoning. Naturally, confidence in any conclusion reached with the aid of hypothetical reasoning must depend upon the care with which it is used. A case in point is Locke's qualified approval of the corpuscular hypothesis – the hypothesis favoured by Robert Boyle and others that matter consists of small invisible and indivisible particles whose size, shape and motion are causally responsible for the observed qualities of matter. In such speculations about what is unobservable we may use 'wary Reasoning from Analogy' (Locke 1975: 666) with what falls within the scope of our experience, in rather the way that Newton had proposed in his third rule of reasoning. But what really made this hypothesis worth examining, for Locke as well as others, was its potential for providing causal explanations. Scepticism about the truth of this or any other hypothesis was, nevertheless, always legitimate. For Locke could not see, any more than Newton could, how any of the methods available to a natural philosopher could produce conclusions immune to sceptical doubt. It may be, as Newton thought, that some methods are more reliable than others, but Locke was less interested than Newton in discriminating degrees of immunity to doubt. As a result, Locke's Newtonianism was a helpful counter, despite its pessimism about what natural philosophy could achieve, to the austerity of scientific method explained, defended and used in the *Principia* and the *Opticks*.

FURTHER READING

For background reading, use:

Burtt, E. A. (1932) *The Metaphysical Foundations of Modern Physical Science*, revised edition, London: Routledge and Kegan Paul; chs 4 and 7.

Mandelbaum, M. (1964) *Philosophy, Science, and Sense Perception: Historical and Critical Studies*, Baltimore, Md.: The Johns Hopkins University Press; ch. 2.

For Descartes, use:
Clarke, D. M. (1982) *Descartes' Philosophy of Science*, Pennsylvania: Pennsylvania State University Press.
Descartes, R. (1984–5) *The Philosophical Writings*, translated by J. Cottingham, R. Stoothoff and D. Murdoch, 2 vols, Cambridge: Cambridge University Press.

Newton's major scientific works are:
Newton, I. (1934) *Mathematical Principles of Natural Philosophy*, translated by A. Motte, revised by F. Cajori, Berkeley and Los Angeles, Calif.: University of California Press.
Newton, I. (1979) *Opticks, or A Treatise of the Reflections, Refractions, Inflections and Colours of Light*, based on the fourth edition, London, 1730; New York: Dover Publications.

Helpful guides are provided by:
Cohen, I. B. (1971) *Introduction to Newton's 'Principia'*, Cambridge: Cambridge University Press.
Shapiro, A. E. (1993) *Fits, Passions, and Paroxysms: Physics, Method, and Chemistry and Newton's Theories of Coloured Bodies and Fits of Easy Reflection*, Cambridge: Cambridge University Press.

Many of the crucial passages in the *Principia* and the *Opticks*, together with important and relevant letters, are reprinted in:
Thayer, H. S. (ed.) (1953) *Newton's Philosophy of Nature: Selections from his Writings*, New York: Macmillan.
Alexander, H. G. (ed.) (1956) *The Leibniz–Clarke Correspondence*, Manchester: Manchester University Press.

A useful collection of modern essays on general aspects of Newton's life and work is:
Fauvel, J., Flood, R., Shortland, M. and Wilson, R. (eds) (1988) *Let Newton Be!: A New Perspective on his Life and Works*, Oxford: Oxford University Press.

A more specialised collection, dealing with philosophical issues, is:
Bricker, P. and Hughes, R. I. G. (eds) (1990) *Philosophical Perspectives on Newtonian Science*, Cambridge, Mass.: MIT Press.

Two recent biographies of Newton are:
Westfall, R. (1980) *Never at Rest: A Biography of Isaac Newton*, Cambridge: Cambridge University Press.
Hall, A. R. (1992) *Isaac Newton: Adventurer in Thought*, Oxford: Blackwell.

5   The Bernoullis and Thomas Bayes

Probability and scientific method

John Locke's view that scientific knowledge is not attainable in natural philosophy was understood in a variety of ways. Locke himself imposed severe restrictions on what could count as scientific knowledge, but he allowed a generous variety of legitimate methods in natural philosophy. Newton, as we have seen, used a less restricted conception of scientific knowledge; it required 'moral' or practical certainty, rather than 'metaphysical' or absolute certainty. And he combined this with a conviction that natural philosophy can and should be reformed so that only methods capable of yielding scientific knowledge count as legitimate. Because they had different understandings of what kind of certainty is required in scientific knowledge, and of what kinds of methods are legitimate in natural philosophy, the views of Locke and Newton were not inconsistent, and nor were they meant to be. Nevertheless, there was a difference of emphasis. Locke's concept of scientific knowledge involved absolute certainty, and because absolute certainty cannot be a matter of degree he was able to preserve a sharp distinction between, on the one hand scientific knowledge, and on the other hand 'judgement', this being his term for what had been called 'probable opinion'. Newton, however, in common with most of his immediate predecessors and contemporaries, used a concept of scientific knowledge involving practical certainty. But practical certainty is a matter of degree, and to acknowledge degrees of certainty is to acknowledge degrees of probability. Consequently, for Newton and those who shared his understanding of certainty a sharp distinction between scientific knowledge and probable opinion could not be maintained. Newton himself tried to counter the effects of this by insisting on a distinction between established principles and imaginary hypotheses. He wanted, that is, to preserve the integrity of experimental natural philosophy as a provider of real knowledge, while at the same time conceding that this knowledge does not have absolute certainty. Given the way in which real knowledge was traditionally understood, his task would be seen by some as incoherent, and it is not surprising that he had to supplement logic with rhetoric in order to sustain his distinction.

Others in the seventeenth century, such as Christian Huygens, promoted the kind of reasoning Newton rejected, because they were willing to accept the consequence that he resisted. There is, they conceded, no sharp distinction between the knowledge of nature that we count as scientific and the judgements about nature that we count as being probable. Most reasoning recognised in scientific method, including the reasoning endorsed by Newton, is probable reasoning, in the sense that it generates conclusions which have one or another degree of certainty and therefore one or another degree of probability. And as the idea of using evidence, including experimental evidence, to argue for the truth, or at least the credibility, of conclusions gained ground in the seventeenth century, so the concept of probability became associated with the idea of something being credible or believable in the light of evidence. Investigators, whether they be of nature, of history, or of law, could set aside authority in favour of evidence, though evidence may still need the testimony of witnesses, with appropriate authority, in order to do its work of making conclusions believable.

Even so, not every conclusion yielded by probable reasoning is acceptable; only some have degrees of certainty or probability which are worth having. If, therefore, scientific method is to permit probable reasoning, we need some account of when and why such reasoning is acceptable. For this purpose we must find ways of measuring or 'weighing' degrees of probability which will show how a conclusion should be qualified. Huygens himself contributed to such an understanding when, in 1657, he published what is recognised as the first textbook treatment of quantitative probabilistic reasoning in games of chance. He was not attempting to quantify degrees of probability; indeed, words customarily used to signify the probability concept are absent from his tract. Nevertheless he, like us, made those connections between chance and probability that we find so natural.

Some important preliminary steps in understanding the qualitative aspects of probability were taken by Leibniz. Like others of his generation, he accepted that, if natural philosophy was to be promoted as Galileo and Bacon hoped, then investigators must recognise that absolute certainty is an ideal they can rarely achieve. But practical certainty, implying degrees of probability, is regularly achieved and is an appropriate aim for scientific method. We should, therefore, embrace rather than reject reasoning which gives probable conclusions. For Leibniz, probability is a relation between the evidence disclosed by investigators and the conclusions they draw. It would, therefore, make sense to think in terms of degrees of probability, because the link between evidence and conclusion can be more or less strong. This suggested to Leibniz that a jurisprudential model might be appropriate for a logic of probable reasoning. Indeed, there were many seventeenth-

and eighteenth-century writers who associated probabilistic reasoning in science with legal reasoning. Evidence was, after all, primarily a legal notion, and it could, as in scientific contexts, be more or less reliable. As Bacon had pointed out, there is an illuminating analogy between skilled attorneys examining and testing the testimony of witnesses, and skilled experimenters examining and testing the testimony of nature. In law, the aim of judicial enquiry was truth beyond reasonable doubt; in science, that same aim was also seen as appropriate. 'We need', Leibniz said, 'a new *logic* in order to know degrees of probability, since this is necessary in judging the proofs of matters of fact and of morals' (Leibniz 1969: 260). Such a logic could, he thought, be created by bringing together the ideas of jurists and the arithmetic of games of chance. The chances for and against a particular outcome in a game of chance could be calculated; why then should we not calculate the degrees of probability for and against a proposition in the light of evidence relevant to it, whether the proposition be about the guilt of a defendant or about the cause of a natural phenomenon? Certainly, the prospects for a clearer understanding of probabilistic reasoning in legal and scientific contexts would thereby be much enhanced, and some interesting and important steps towards an understanding of scientific method were taken by those eighteenth-century thinkers who explored this suggestion.

Although Leibniz never created a formal jurisprudential logic, he did study the subject of *jus conditionale*, where a legal right to, say, property is neither absolute nor void, but dependent on the satisfaction of conditions. If, for example, Titius has an absolute right to a property worth a certain sum, then a fair price to pay for this right is just that sum, and if this right is null and void then it is valueless. But if Titius has a conditional right to the property, then its fair price, or 'expected value' as Huygens had called it, is determined by the probability that the condition upon which the right depends will be satisfied. To compute this probability it would be necessary to divide the possible circumstances into those in which the condition for this right is satisfied and those in which it is not. Clearly, though, this will enable us to calculate a fair price only if the enumerated possibilities are equally easily realised, i.e. if all the circumstances resulting in the right being satisfied can occur just as easily as each other and as easily as each of the circumstances resulting in the right not being satisfied. Leibniz was well aware of this requirement and it was, no doubt, the practical difficulties involved in trying to meet it that prevented him from supplying realistic examples of his jurisprudential logic. However, in games of chance, the analogy of this requirement can often be readily satisfied; a die can be and usually is unbiased, and a shuffled pack of cards can, and usually does, produce a random order. That is to say, each of the sides of an unbiased die are 'realised' equally easily when

we roll the die; each of the cards in a randomly ordered pack is
'realised' equally easily when we select, say, the top card. To create a
mathematical 'doctrine' of legal probabilities analogous to the mathematical 'doctrine of chances' then being developed, it would be
necessary to find ways of using the idea of equally easily realised
outcomes, or equipossibility, in jurisprudence. There might, then, be
ways of adapting the result so as to throw some light on probable
reasoning in scientific contexts.

While Leibniz was exploring, for the first time, the philosophy of
probability, the Swiss mathematician Jakob Bernoulli was achieving
some success by pursuing this practical line of thought. In his post-
humously published *Ars conjectandi* (Art of Conjecture), he defined
probability as 'a degree of certainty . . . [which] differs from it as
a part from the whole' (Bernoulli 1975: 239), and when he came to
apply probability to matters of 'civil, moral and economic life', he used
legal examples to illustrate his thinking about degrees of certainty,
representing a probable argument in law as a set of equipossible 'cases'.
Suppose, for example, Titius inherits an estate only if the father of
his young wife Caja dies before she does. Evidently the two possibilities
of his father-in-law predeceasing Caja, and of Caja predeceasing the
father-in-law, are not equally easily 'realised in nature'. Perhaps,
though, we can assume that, for every two equally realised 'cases' which
result in the death of Caja's father, there is just one equally realised
'case' which results in her own death. If so, we can calculate the
probabilities and determine the value of Titius's expectation. There
are, as it were, three equally easily realised 'cases' of a probable
argument, two of which give the conclusion that Titius inherits the
estate. Titius's expectation is, therefore, worth two-thirds of the value
of the estate. Of course, it is unlikely that such a simple assumption
about the numbers of equally easily realised, or equipossible, 'cases' is
justified. But Bernoulli believed that a more realistic one can be
obtained with the aid of statistical investigations of human mortality,
which would reveal the ratio of the number of equipossible 'cases'
resulting in the father-in-law's death to the number of such 'cases'
resulting in Caja's death. If, for example, extensive statistical investigations were to reveal that the ratio of men of the father-in-law's age and
state of health who predecease their daughter when those daughters
are of Caja's age and state of health, to such fathers-in-law who do not
predecease such daughters, is 10 to 1, then, Bernoulli thought, it is ten
times more probable that the father-in-law will predecease Caja than
that he will not. There would, therefore, be eleven 'equipossible' cases,
in ten of which Titius inherits the estate, and his expectation is worth
ten-elevenths of the value of the estate. In fact, this reasoning involves
fallaciously inverting a theorem proved by Bernoulli, for, in arguing
from observed frequencies to the probabilities which cause those

frequencies, we need to use ideas developed later in the eighteenth century by Thomas Bayes (see Daston 1988: 232–3).

Some parts of Bernoulli's discussion make it clear that he was concerned with probabilistic reasoning from effects to causes, which is also the concern of hypothetical reasoning in science. Accordingly, he used as examples cases where different causes can produce the same effect, and the argument from effect to cause must therefore be probabilistic. Consider, for instance, Gracchus, who is suspected of perpetrating a crime. He turns pale when accused, and on the basis of this fact we construct an argument for his guilt. But it can only be a probable argument, because Gracchus's pallor may have a cause other than the presumed guilt. This probable argument, Bernoulli suggested, can be resolved into a number, n, of equipossible 'cases'. In one out of these n cases, Gracchus's pallor proves his guilt because in this case the guilt really is the cause of the pallor. In the remaining $n - 1$ other cases of the argument, his pallor does not prove his guilt, because then it has some other cause. There are, as it were, n cases; each is as probable as any other; $n - 1$ leave the matter of Gracchus's guilt or innocence undecided; just one case proves his guilt; none of the cases prove his innocence.

This idea can be extended to cover circumstances where more than one probable argument is available. For suppose Gracchus is one of m people who fit the description we have of the crime's perpetrator. This information gives us a second argument for Gracchus's guilt, but it is a probable argument because, although Gracchus fits the description we have of the criminal, so do $m - 1$ other people, and if any of them are guilty then Gracchus is innocent. There are, as it were, m cases in all; each is as probable as any other; $m - 1$ prove Gracchus's innocence; just one proves his guilt; none leave the matter undecided. We can now use this second probable argument to divide the $n - 1$ undecided cases of the first probable argument into those cases that prove Gracchus's guilt and those that prove his innocence. Clearly, a proportion $1/m$ of these $n - 1$ undecided cases will prove his guilt, and $(m - 1)/m$ of them will prove his innocence. So, taking both arguments together, we have $1 + (n - 1)/m$ out of a total of n cases which prove Gracchus's guilt. We can therefore represent the combined probability for Gracchus's guilt as $[1 + (n - 1)/m]/n$, or $(m + n - 1)/mn$. If, for example, there were just four suspects who satisfied the description, and we judged on the basis of experience that guilt can be correctly inferred from pallor one out of every ten times, then the combined arguments yield a probability of $13/40$ in favour of Gracchus's guilt (see Shafer 1978).

To see the relevance of Bernoulli's thinking to scientific method, consider a problem discussed by one of Jakob Bernoulli's nephews, Daniel Bernoulli. The inclinations of the planetary orbits to the ecliptic are all very small. There is a strong argument from the existence of this phenomenon to the existence of a cause which would explain this effect. It could be, as Descartes and his followers thought, that there is an aether which rotates around the Sun and changes the planes of planetary orbits so that they tend to coincide with its equatorial plane. Or it could be, as Newton and his followers thought, that this phenomenon can only be explained as an effect of divine choice and is therefore evidence of God's existence. But the argument for the conclusion that the phenomenon must have some such explanation is a probable argument because it could be that there is no single cause for the uniformity. If Newton's inverse square law is true, the orbital plane of any planet could have any orientation, and the fact that they all have a similar orientation could be simply a coincidence. To measure or estimate the degree of probability of the conclusion that the phenomenon has a single cause, we suppose, following Jakob's suggestion, that there are a definite number of equipossible 'cases', in some of which there is a single cause operating to produce this planetary phenomenon, and in others of which no such cause operates. In order to assess the probability of the argument for the conclusion that the planetary phenomenon does have a single cause, we need to find a way of calculating the ratio of the number of 'cases' of the first kind to the number of 'cases' of the second kind. How can this be done given that we have no way of even enumerating the alternatives, let alone of making those alternatives equally possible in the sense of equal ease of realisability in nature? In his winning contribution for a prize offered by the Paris Académie des Sciences in 1732, Daniel thought that this could be done by calculating how probable it is that the inclinations of the planetary orbits would be as small as they are if they were the result of coincidence. He supposed, that is, that if the phenomenon were coincidental then the orbit of any planet could have any orientation, and using this assumption together with the arithmetical 'doctrine of chances' he worked out what would be the probability that the inclinations of the planetary orbits would be as astronomers find them to be. In fact Daniel produced three calculations, the choice between them depending on which parameter was selected as the one whose values are equally realised in nature. Each of these calculations yielded a number which was so small that he was able to conclude that the effect in question should not be attributed to coincidence but to a real, if unknown, cause. In effect, he calculated the ratio required and used his calculation as a measure of the degree of certainty of this conclusion of his probable argument. In gambling terms, if someone had contracted to receive a certain sum of money in the event of there being a single cause for the small mutual inclinations of the planetary orbits, the value of that contract would be almost as much as the sum of money staked (see Gower 1987).

Daniel's technique was ingenious, and it resulted in one of the earliest attempts to produce a quantitative estimate of a degree of certainty for the conclusion of a probable argument. In a different context, a similar technique had been used earlier in the eighteenth century by John Arbuthnot, physician to Queen Anne and friend of fellow satirist Jonathan Swift. His topic was demographic rather than astronomical, and his calculations related to the recorded fact that, in London in each of the eighty-two years prior to 1711, more male than female children had been born. It could be that there was no single cause which explained this state of affairs and that it was no more than a coincidence; it could be, as Arbuthnot put it, that 'chance . . . governs' whether a birth be of a boy or of a girl. On the other hand it could be that there was some single cause, even if we are unable to say what it might be, that explains the state of affairs; it could be that 'art . . . governs' whether a boy or girl is born. If the record is not of a coincidence then we would expect the small preponderance of male births to appear in other populations at other places and other times. Both of the suggested conclusions were uncertain, and the question arose whether their degrees of uncertainty could be expressed in a quantitative form. Arbuthnot thought that they could. For he could easily calculate, on the assumption that there is no single reason why in any year more males than females should be born, and that the probability of either outcome was equal to the probability of the other, the probability that in each of the eighty-two years more males would be born than females. This probability is, of course, the same as the probability that a fair coin will show eighty-two heads when thrown eighty-two times. The calculation showed, in effect, that there were almost five hundred million billion equipossible 'cases', in only one of which was the observed state of affairs produced in the absence of a single cause. We can, therefore, assign a high degree of certainty to the conclusion that there must be some single cause for the facts recorded in London's bills of mortality (see Hacking 1975: ch. 18; cf. Shoesmith 1987).

Such techniques, though, could not be generalised to all probable reasoning. In most cases there is no reasonable and reliable way to determine the ratio of the number of equipossible 'cases' which favour the conclusion to the number of such 'cases' which do not favour it. There is therefore no way in which Jakob Bernoulli's ideas can be used to estimate the degree of certainty or probability appropriate to the conclusion. For consider simple enumerative induction, i.e. the reasoning by which we conclude that all A's are B's on the basis of the evidence that observed A's have, without exception, been B's. A straightforward example of such reasoning would be that in which we conclude, with Newton and his followers, that because experiments show that all observed bodies are subject to gravitational attraction, all bodies, whether or not they be the subject of experiment, and however small or however remote in space they might be, are subject to gravitational attraction by other bodies. Such reasoning is clearly probabilistic in the sense that, though we may be quite sure the conclusion is correct, our certainty is practical rather than absolute. This is shown by noticing that, unlike the conclusion, the evidence we have does not make it impossible for the next A we examine not to be a B. Bodies beyond the reach of our experiments because they are too small or too remote might not be gravitationally attracted to every other body. The conclusion we draw has, therefore, a more or less high degree of practical certainty, and since probabilities measure degrees of certainty, the reasoning for the conclusion is probable reasoning. We can express the same point by saying that there are a large number, indeed an indefinitely large number, of other conclusions which could be drawn from the same evidence. We could, for example, conclude that half of all A's are B's and suppose that, for some reason, only those A's which belong to the half that are B's have been observed. Or we could conclude that only a tiny minority of all the very many A's are B's, and for some reason the only A's we have observed are members of that tiny minority. Jakob Bernoulli was fully aware that, because the reasoning was probabilistic, these other conclusions could be drawn from the evidence provided. But he urged that they should be rejected in favour of the conclusion favoured by common sense. He shared the belief we all naturally have that the reasonable conclusion to draw is that all A's are B's rather than that half of them are, or that a small minority are. But he could not prove that this conclusion has a higher degree of certainty, or of probability, than those other conclusions. Moreover, for all that Jakob could show, the conclusion that all A's are B's could be the most reasonable one to draw and yet have such a low degree of certainty, or even such a low degree of probability, that no reasonable person who was aware of it would wish to place any confidence in it. There was no way for him to produce estimates of the degrees of probability involved, because there did not seem to be any way of using the idea of 'cases' equally realisable in nature, some favouring the conclusion drawn, others disfavouring it.

The inductive conclusion that all A's are B's is a suggestion about the underlying inaccessible cause of all observed A's being B's; all observed A's are B's because of the underlying fact that 100 per cent of A's are B's. Clearly, though, there could be other causes for the same observations. The underlying fact which causes all observed A's to be B's could be that some other percentage of A's are B's. It could be, for example, that only 10 per cent of A's are B's, and that for some reason the only A's that have been observed belong to that 10 per cent. If we think, as perhaps we should, that there are an indefinite number of these alternative underlying facts about percentages and that each of them should be treated as an equipossible 'case', then because only one of these 'cases' is favourable to the conclusion we have drawn, the degree of certainty of that conclusion is indefinitely small. But this seems unacceptable, or at least counterintuitive; the degree of certainty we would naturally attach to inductive conclusions is high rather than low. This shows that, in practice, we do not regard the indefinite number of 'cases' as equipossible; we do not think that they are equally realisable in nature. Like Jakob Bernoulli and many others we believe that 'nature follows the simplest paths' and that therefore some 'cases' or 'paths' are more easily realised than others. If this is right, it would explain why the degrees of certainty we attach to inductive conclusions, or at least to some of them, are high rather than low. But it would not explain how such degrees of certainty might be measured.

Perhaps, indeed, the very idea of measurable degrees of certainty is misguided, and the attempt to boost confidence in probable reasoning by developing a quantitative logic of reasoning is misconceived. For certainty is, in part, a psychological concept; people with different psychological characteristics may well attribute different degrees of certainty to the conclusion of a probable argument, and the same person may attribute different degrees of certainty to that conclusion at different times. Thus a person with a cautious psychological disposition is likely to attribute a lower degree of certainty to a conclusion than is a person with a more adventurous disposition. Qualitative judgements about a person's degree of certainty, as compared with that of another person, provide psychological information but they do not in themselves give any information about what degree of certainty would be reasonable. Quantitative judgements would be no better in this respect, and would tend to give a spurious air of precision to the psychological information. What is needed is the degree of certainty which a reasonable person would have in the conclusion of a probable argument. This, we might think, depends only on the logical relation between the evidence and the conclusion, and not at all upon the variable psychological characteristics of people. The quantitative arguments of Arbuthnot and of Daniel Bernoulli seem to be concerned with degrees of certainty in this normative sense, for they both suppose that a reasonable person is a person who, using only the evidence given, calculates the probability of the conclusion drawn. But, it might be argued, though reasonable people do calculate degrees of certainty in accordance with the mathematical 'doctrine of chances', not everyone who so calculates counts as being a reasonable person. There are, that is to say, considerations other than the logical relations between evidence and conclusions that have an effect upon the degree of certainty a reasonable person will have in the conclusion.

This general issue was debated in the 1760s by Daniel Bernoulli and Jean d'Alembert. The occasion for the debate was an essay by Bernoulli concerning the degree of certainty that a reasonable person should have in the efficacy of inoculation against smallpox. The risk posed by this disease in its 'natural' form is indicated by the fact that, during epidemics, about one in ten of the populations of London and Paris died from its effects; it disfigured many others. On the other hand, inoculation against the disease was by no means risk-free; those inoculated acquired a more or less mild, or 'artificial', form of the disease and there was a chance of, perhaps, one in 200 that they would die of its effects within a month or two, whereas anyone not inoculated stood a one in seven chance of dying from the disease at some time in their life. Bernoulli used probability calculations to set out the reasoning for and against inoculation. The statistical evidence available to him, though unsatisfactory and incomplete in several respects, enabled him to calculate that inoculation increased a person's life expectancy by about four years. The rational person would, Bernoulli implied, choose to be inoculated because, in the light of the evidence, the degree of certainty in evading smallpox was greater with inoculation than without it, and the probability calculations in terms of life expectancy were a measure of the difference in degree. This is like arguing that a rational person will choose to bet on getting seven when two dice are thrown rather than twelve because the degree of certainty that a seven will be thrown is greater than the degree of certainty that a twelve will be thrown, and the probability calculations giving the difference between the expectations of a seven and of a twelve are a measure of the difference in degree of certainty.

D'Alembert accepted that reasonable people should choose inoculation. But he disputed the cogency of Bernoulli's argument. Reasonable people are not just calculators; they have psychological dispositions which have a bearing on the conclusions they reach. It may not be possible to give a quantitative form to these dispositions but we cannot and should not ignore them. For example, a reasonable person exercising reasonable caution would not exchange the certain prospect of one pound for a one in ten thousand chance of ten thousand pounds, even though the expected values of these prospects are, according to Bernoulli's methods of calculation, identical. Even more strikingly, no reasonable person would willingly participate in a lottery knowing that half the ticket holders would be guaranteed a lifespan of double their average life expectancy while the other half were put to death immediately. Yet, again, Bernoulli's methods implied that the expected value of choosing to participate in such a lottery is the same as the expected value of refusing to participate. In the inoculation case, we know that the risk of smallpox resulting from inoculation is small, but nevertheless the expected value of inoculation to a person in the prime of his or her life might not be so great simply because the prospect of four further years at the end of a life could be seen as less advantageous than the prospect of an immediate future free from the risks of inoculation.

D'Alembert expressed the difficulty by insisting that, in comparing risks, we must compare like with like. An inoculated person runs the risk of dying from the inoculation, but that risk is of short duration – perhaps one month – and thereafter he or she runs no risk of contracting smallpox. A non-inoculated person runs a risk of dying from smallpox, but that risk is small if we consider it limited to one month rather than the remainder of the person's life; it is indeed smaller than the risk from inoculation. Consequently, 'during the whole course of one's life one will never reach a month in which inoculation is really less to be feared than natural smallpox'. D'Alembert recognised that this argument is specious but, he claimed, in order to make a proper comparison of the risks of 'natural' versus 'artificial' smallpox we would have to find a way of adding the small risk of dying from 'natural' smallpox during the next month to the risks for all subsequent months in a person's lifetime. There is no way, d'Alembert said, of calculating this total risk. Data from bills of mortality may enable us to estimate the risk of death from 'natural' smallpox for each separate month, but 'how would we estimate the total risk resulting from the sum of these separate risks, which become weaker as they become more distant, not only by the distance from which we see them, which . . . makes them uncertain and softens the view, but by the length of time which must precede them, during which we should enjoy the advantage of living' (Bradley 1971: 30, 58–9; cf. Emch-Deriaz 1982; Maehle 1995). In effect, d'Alembert was drawing attention to the psychological aspects of probabilistic reasoning, and arguing that, because the mathematical calculation proposed by Bernoulli did not represent our experience of these aspects, it was of little worth.

The attack on Bernoulli's justification of inoculation was part of an extensive campaign by d'Alembert against the way his contemporaries were using the mathematical 'doctrine of chances'. Earlier, he had criticised Bernoulli's calculations relating to the inclinations of the planetary orbits. It is true that, if the orientations of the planetary orbits are a matter of chance or coincidence, then the observed small inclinations are very improbable. But that does not entitle us to conclude that the planetary orientations are not a matter of chance or coincidence, because any particular arrangement of the inclinations – not just the observed inclinations – is equally improbable. D'Alembert's objection was, then, that if Bernoulli's mathematical reasoning is allowed, there will be no possible way in which the planetary orbits could be inclined to each other which would give a high degree of certainty to the conclusion that no single cause was operating and that the observed facts being as they were supposed to be was a coincidence. As in the case of inoculation, d'Alembert's objection was not to the conclusion drawn, but rather to the attempt to quantify the degree of certainty of the conclusion.

In questioning the role of mathematics in assessing probable reasoning, d'Alembert contributed a new element to thinking about scientific method. The Newtonian ideal of 'moral' certainty obtained by deduction from the phenomena remained attractive, but with the development of the mathematical 'doctrine of chances' investigators could, or so it seemed, evaluate the degrees of certainty attributable to conclusions of probable arguments, at least in some cases. It appeared, therefore, that, despite the misgivings of Newton and many others, probable arguments, including the much criticised hypothetical reasoning, could play a part in scientific method. But d'Alembert's doubts about the applicability of mathematical probability raised questions about the cogency of this development. In identifying modes of reasoning which are legitimate in science we are, in effect, identifying the modes of reasoning which a reasonable and rational investigator would use, and d'Alembert's view was that mathematical calculations do not always reflect the reasoning of such an investigator. It is of course true that investigators are not always reasonable and rational, but nevertheless their experience cannot be discounted and, in so far as mathematically derived assessments of degrees of certainty fail to conform to that experience, their worth must be doubted. As an important contributor to the development of rational mechanics in the eighteenth century, d'Alembert would have acknowledged Galileo's claim that the book of nature is written in the language of mathematics, but he would not have accepted that the criteria for a correct interpretation of that language are exclusively mathematical.

While d'Alembert debated with Daniel Bernoulli in rationalist France, the general issue about the role of probable reasoning in scientific method was being addressed in a rather different way in empiricist Britain. David Hume, by expressing scepticism about probable reasoning in a particularly trenchant form, had not only reaffirmed traditional views about the limited scope of real knowledge (see Milton 1987; Gower 1991), but had raised doubts about whether any degree of certainty could be attributed justifiably to the conclusion of any such reasoning. Suppose, for instance, that someone were to deny the conclusion of a probable argument. That person's denial, Hume pointed out, is not contradicted by any evidence currently available to him or her, and so any argument we might use to persuade such a person to withdraw their denial could not be deductive or 'demonstrative'; it must therefore be an inductive or probable argument. But if the reason for the denial in the first place was lack of confidence in probable arguments, we cannot succeed in our attempt at persuasion. We would be taking for granted what is at issue, namely the capacity of probable arguments to yield believable conclusions. Even Newtonian 'deduction from the phenomena' was susceptible to this scepticism, for it led to conclusions with, supposedly, 'moral' rather than

'metaphysical' certainty. Hume acknowledged that we are psychologically constrained to reason from available evidence to conclusions
such as that the Sun rises, that fire burns, that water drowns, etc.; so
indeed might any reasonable person be so constrained. Nevertheless,
we are not thereby shown to be rationally justified in reasoning from
that evidence to those conclusions. Perhaps, as Hume thought, we must
be content with a psychological explanation of our propensity to use
probable reasoning and forgo any rational justification of the practice.
That, though, would be a hard conclusion to accept for those who saw
such reasoning as important in scientific method. For the reform of
scientific method promoted by Galileo and Bacon in the seventeenth
century depended not on the naturalness, in psychological terms, of
probable reasoning, but upon its rationality. Experimental natural
philosophy depended upon experimental inductive methods, and if we
cannot defend these methods from scepticism then we put in question
the value and the legitimacy of that philosophy.

Hume was no expert in mathematical probability. He agreed with
Leibniz that, though 'systems of logic' are 'very copious' when they
explain demonstrative reasoning, they are 'too concise' when they
concern probable arguments (Hume 1955: 184). As we have seen, those
who had mathematical expertise assumed that probability measured the
degree of certainty that a reasonable person should have in a statement.
It seemed possible, therefore, that Hume's challenge might be met by
justifying this assumption. If it could be shown that the probability of
the conclusion of an experimental argument is indeed a measure of
the degree of certainty that a reasonable person should have in that
conclusion then it will be possible to show that anyone who accepts the
premisses of the argument but denies its conclusion is judging unreasonably, though not inconsistently. This seems to have been the
strategy of Richard Price, an acquaintance of Hume, in drawing
attention to the work of his friend and fellow Presbyterian clergyman,
Thomas Bayes.

Bayes, a mathematician and a Fellow of the Royal Society, had written
an essay on a problem which he expressed using the language of the
'doctrine of chances': '*Given* the number of times in which an unknown
event has happened and failed: *Required* the chance that the probability
of its happening in a single trial lies somewhere between any two
degrees of probability that can be named'. So expressed, the problem
might well seem to have little if anything to do with Hume's scepticism.
However, we can readily understand the 'given' in his problem as an
observed effect, and understand what he 'required' as the unobserved
or unobservable cause of this effect. Suppose, for example, that
unknown to an investigator, a coin is in fact double-headed. The
investigator can indirectly detect this property of the coin by using
evidence about how many times a head shows when the coin is thrown.

But the argument used to do this will be a probable argument from an observed effect to an unobserved cause. The degree of certainty of the conclusion drawn by the investigator is measured by the probability of the conclusion. And by probability, Bayes explained, he meant a measure of rational acceptance: 'The *probability of any event* is the ratio between the value at which an expectation depending on the happening of an event ought to be computed, and the value of the thing expected upon it's happening' (Bayes 1763: 376). If, for instance, I stand to win £30 if a six turns up on the single throw of an unbiased six-sided die, then as a rational person I should value my expectation at £5, that being the price at which I would be prepared to sell my opportunity. The ratio of £5 to £30, which is the 'value of the thing expected upon it's happening', is 1/6 and this, of course, is the probability that a six will turn up. So even though Bayes's terminology was mathematical rather than philosophical, and his models were games of chance rather than scientific inferences, he was, in Price's view at least, addressing Hume's philosophical doubts about the rationality of accepting the conclusions of probable arguments.

Bayes's essay dealing with this problem was not published during his lifetime. It was found by his friend Richard Price, who provided the essay with an introduction and an appendix when it was printed in the *Transactions* of the Royal Society in 1763. In his introduction, Price pointed out that the problem addressed by Bayes 'is by no means merely a curious speculation in the doctrine of chances, but necessary to be solved in order to be a sure foundation for all our reasonings concerning past facts, and what is likely to be hereafter'. So Price was certainly alert to the wider significance of Bayes's problem. 'We cannot', he added, 'determine, at least not to any nicety, in what degree repeated experiments confirm a conclusion, without the particular discussion of the beforementioned problem; which, therefore is necessary to be considered by any one who would give a clear account of *analogical* or *inductive reasoning*'. Though Price does not mention Hume by name, perhaps because mathematical readers of the *Transactions* were not likely to have been familiar with his views, these remarks indicate that Price discerned a close connection between Bayes's problem and Hume's inductive scepticism (Bayes 1763: 371–2; cf. Price 1764; cf. Gillies 1987).

Bayes treated his 'given' and his 'required' as two events, and he first established what would be needed in order to calculate the probability of the 'required' event when we know that the 'given' event has occurred. Such a calculation would involve 'inverse' inference if the 'given' is an effect, and the 'required' is its cause. Bayes showed that the probability of the supposed cause in the light of its supposed effect, which we can write as p(cause, effect), is equal to the ratio of the probability of the cause and its effect to the probability of the effect, i.e. p(cause & effect)/p(effect). There is nothing controversial about this claim; in modern versions of the probability calculus it would count as a definition of what we are to understand by the conditional probability p(cause, effect). Indeed, by combining this equality with its equally uncontroversial partner, namely p(effect, cause) = p(effect & cause)/p(cause), we easily obtain

$$p(\text{cause, effect}) = \frac{p(\text{cause}) \; p(\text{effect, cause})}{p(\text{effect})} \qquad (1)$$

which is a simple version of what is today called 'Bayes's theorem' applied to reasoning from effect to cause. If we suppose that one of n possible causes – say cause$_k$ – is responsible for the observed effect, then we can easily derive the following, using rules recognised by Bayes:

$$p(\text{cause}_k, \text{effect}) = \frac{p(\text{cause}_k) \; p(\text{effect, cause}_k)}{[p(\text{cause}_1) \; p(\text{effect, cause}_1)] + \ldots \atop + \; [p(\text{cause}_n) \; p(\text{effect, cause}_n)]} \qquad (2)$$

Neither of these equations, however, is to be found in Bayes's essay. At most we have statements which readily imply them.

Bayes then turned to consider an ingenious and interesting example where we have two events, one of which is the given effect and the other the required cause. We consider a square level table, ABCD, with sides of unit length, and we let AB be the x-axis (see Figure 1). Suppose that, as the first of the two events to be considered, a ball has been thrown on to this table and has come to rest at a certain point. Through that point an imaginary line, *fg*, is drawn parallel to AD. Later a second ball is thrown on to the table in a random manner a number, n, times. We are given that of these n throws, m result in the ball coming to rest between AD and the imaginary line, the remainder resulting in the ball coming to rest on the other side of the line. This is the second of the two events. We know, for example, that, out of ten throws, six have resulted in the ball coming to rest between the line and AD; we wish to know the position of the line. What we know is an effect; what we wish to know is its cause. The inference we make from effect to cause is a probable inference; our hypothesis as to the cause will be a probable hypothesis, and the degree of its probability is given by $p(h_f, e)$, where h_f is the hypothesised cause or the event consisting in the first ball coming to rest at a point on a line parallel to AD meeting AB at f, and e is the given effect, or the event consisting in the second ball coming to rest at a point between the line and AD in m out of n throws.

To calculate the inverse probability $p(h_f, e)$, Bayes needed to show how we could, at least in theory, evaluate $p(h_f \; \& \; e)$ and $p(e)$. He first proved that $p(e)$ is equivalent to the area between the curve A*i*B and the edge, AB, of the square table, the equation of the curve being $y = E \; x^m (1 - x)^{n-m}$, where E is a coefficient of the term in which occurs

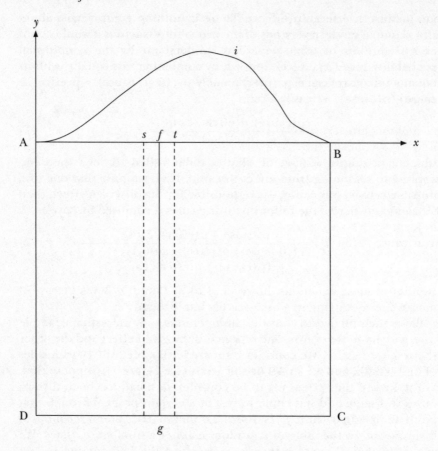

Figure 1 A simplified version of the diagram used by Bayes to explain his problem and its solution.

$a^m b^{n-m}$, when the formula $(a + b)^{m + (n - m)}$, i.e. $(a + b)^n$, is expanded. According to the binomial theorem

$$(a+b)^n = a^n + na^{n-1} b + [n(n-1)/2.1] \, a^{n-2}b^2 + [n(n-1)(n-2)/3.2.1] \, a^{n-3}b^3 + [n(n-1)(n-2)(n-3)/4.3.2.1] \, a^{n-4}b^4 + \ldots + b^n.$$

So, if the ball has been thrown on to the table ten times and it has come to rest between the line and AD six times, the equation of the curve is

$$[10.9.8.7/4.3.2.1] \, x^6(1 - x)^4, \text{ or } 210x^6(1 - x)^4.$$

To find $p(h_f \,\&\, e)$ Bayes showed that we must determine a part of the area under the curve, namely that part which corresponds to h_f. Of course, if h_f is precisely specified, then it will correspond to a line only and the area in question will be zero. But if we specify some limits within which h_f is to fall, then it will correspond to an area under the curve bounded by these limits. The inverse probability we seek will then have a finite non-zero value equal to the ratio of these two areas.

Suppose, then, that the second ball has come to rest between the line and AD m times in n throws; what is the probability, given this information, that a specific hypothesis about the position of the line is correct? Much will depend upon the values of m and n, which means that the shape of the curve $y = \mathrm{E}\, x^m(1 - x)^{n-m}$ is important. But, as we have noticed, the answer to the question is also dependent upon how precisely we specify the hypothesis. If we specify it absolutely precisely, then our hypothesis will almost certainly be false; its probability will be zero. So we need to consider a hypothesis which claims that the position of the line falls between an upper and a lower limit, say s and t on Fig. 1. Bayes then proved that the probability we seek is the ratio of the area under the curve AiB lying between $x = s$ and $x = t$ to the whole of the area under that curve. In modern mathematical treatments these two areas would be expressed as integrals and the probability we require would be represented by their ratio. So

$$
p(h_f, e) = \frac{\displaystyle\int_s^t \mathrm{E}\, x^m (1 - x)^{n-m}\, dx}{\displaystyle\int_0^1 \mathrm{E}\, x^m (1 - x)^{n-m}\, dx} \tag{3}
$$

This, too, is a formula frequently referred to as 'Bayes's theorem', though it, too, does not occur in Bayes's essay.

Version (3) of Bayes's theorem incorporates a concealed assumption which, because it was identified and justified by Bayes, explains why his name has been associated with it. To see what this assumption is, suppose that we consider only a limited number of hypotheses concerning the position of the line *fg*. We divide the unit line AB into k equal sections and claim that the position of the line *fg* corresponds to one of these sections. To a reasonable approximation, the probability $p(h_f, e)$ is the area of a rectangle of width $1/k$ and height determined either by the solution of the equation of the curve AiB given, or by knowledge of m, n and x. Let y_f denote the height of this rectangle in the case of the hypothesis h_f. Also, to a reasonable approximation, $p(e)$ corresponds to the sum of the areas of the k rectangles constructed on AB each of width $1/k$ and with varying heights depending on the calculated values for y. So

$$
p(e) = (y_1/k) + (y_2/k) + (y_3/k) + \ldots + (y_f/k) + \ldots + (y_k/k)
$$

Since $p(h_f, e) = p(h_f \& e)/p(e)$, we have

$$p(h_f, e) = \frac{y_f/k}{(y_1/k) + (y_2/k) + (y_3/k) + \ldots + (y_f/k) + \ldots + (y_k/k)} \quad (4)$$

As n increases, this approximates ever more closely to the ratio of integrals in (3). But we can also see that, if $p(h_f) = p(h_1) = p(h_2) = \ldots = p(h_n)$, and $(y_f k)$ etc. are taken as measures of the likelihoods of the observed effects, or evidence, given the proposed causes, or as in this case the proposed hypotheses, this equation is derivable from (2). The crucial step is, of course, the condition that each possible cause, or each possible hypothesis, is as probable as any other when it is considered 'prior' to the evidence *e*. There are circumstances in which this condition is satisfied, Bayes's table with balls being thrown 'at random' on to it being one of them. But in general we cannot assume that the prior probability of one cause of a given effect, or one hypothesis accounting for given data, is the same as the prior probability of any other. Nor did Bayes himself suppose that we could. The 'Scholium' which appears at the end of Proposition 9 explains that it is only in those cases where the unknown cause of a known effect is selected randomly that we can make use of an equation like (4). The 'experiment' involving throwing balls on to a table is one of those cases, since the cause of the observed effect is determined by the position where the first ball comes to rest when it is thrown, so that 'there shall be the same probability that it rests upon any one equal part of the plane as another' (Bayes 1763: 385). He knew, that is, that the position of the line *fg* was 'determined in such a manner as to give me no reason to think that, in a certain number of trials [with the second ball], it should rather happen [i.e. the second ball should fall between the line and AD] any one possible number of times than another' (Bayes 1763: 393). However, Bayes goes on to say at the end of the Scholium that he will 'take for granted' that a formula such as (4) 'is also . . . to be used in relation to any event concerning the probability of which nothing at all is known antecedently to any trials made or observed concerning it' (Bayes 1763: 393–4). But it is one thing to set these prior probabilities equal each to other when we know that there is no reason for assigning different probabilities; it is quite another to set prior probabilities equal to each other when there is no reason known to us for assigning different probabilities. Bayes's table is, we know, level, and the first ball is thrown, we also know, at random. So we know that there is no reason why it should come to rest at one point rather than another. In such circumstances it is legitimate for us to assign equal probabilities. But suppose we did not know that the table is level or that the ball is thrown at random, because we did not know anything about the relevant circumstances. Then, there is a question about whether we are entitled to assign equal probabilities to each of the possible positions where the ball could, so far as we know, come to rest. If the probabilities of outcomes are equal only when they are equally easily realised in nature, then it seems that we would not be entitled to assign equal probabilities on the basis of our ignorance. If, on the other hand, probabilities are equal when, perhaps because of ignorance, they are equally easily believed by us, then it seems that we would be entitled to assign equal probabilities.

It may be that Bayes decided not to publish his essay because he became uneasy about the legitimacy of what he was taking for granted. His friend Richard Price, however, seems to have had no misgivings about the scope of the Scholium, for he provided an appendix to the essay explaining in some detail how to apply Bayes's solution in a wide variety of contexts. Suppose, for example, that an experiment has been tried on a number of occasions and that the same particular result is obtained every time. From this information as our premiss we might conclude, by means of a probabilistic argument, that it is more likely than not that the same result will be obtained in the next trial of the experiment. What, though, is the degree of certainty, or degree of confidence, that we can place in this conclusion? How probable is it that we are right in our conclusion? There is a fixed, but unknown, probability that the same result will obtain. Perhaps there is a scientific law which will ensure that, when the experiment is tried again, the same result will happen; in which case the probability is maximal. All that we know, however, is that the experiment, with this result, has been tried on a number of occasions, and on that basis we have concluded that there is a more than 50:50 chance that a further experiment will produce the same result. How likely is it that we are right? The answer implied by Bayes's general solution is found by evaluating $A^{n+1} - B^{n+1}$, where A is the upper limit to the chance we have attributed to the occurrence of the result in the further experiment, B is its lower limit, and n is the number of trials of the experiment so far made. Bayes assumed a conventional probability scale according to which, in this example, $A = 1$ and $B = 1/2$, so if there have been ten trials the likelihood that we are right is $1 - 1/2^{11}$, which is approximately 0.9995. This figure measures the degree of certainty we are entitled to have in the conclusion we have drawn, namely that, after ten experiments have produced the same result, there is a greater than even chance that the next experiment will also produce that result. We could, of course, have drawn a more ambitious conclusion from the same evidence; for example, that there is a more than 0.9 chance that the next experiment will produce the result. In that case the likelihood we are right is $1 - 0.9^{11}$, or about 0.72. If, on the other hand, there was just one experimental result, and we drew the conclusion that there is a more than 0.5 chance that a second experiment will produce the same result, then the likelihood we would be right is $1 - 1/2^2$, which is 0.75, and this is the figure measuring the degree of certainty we should have in our conclusion.

Armed with such figures, Price said, 'we may determine what conclusion we ought to draw from a given number of experiments which are unopposed by contrary experiments' (Bayes 1763: 406). He gave some practical examples of probable reasoning in order to show that his calculations 'are all strictly applicable to the events and appearances of nature'. It is striking that his examples are very similar to those that Hume had used to illustrate his doubts about probable reasoning. Thus he asked us to imagine a person 'just brought forth into this world' who observes the Sun to rise and set and who, shortly afterwards, observes the return of the Sun. He, for the person referred to corresponds to the Adam whose deliberations Hume had considered (Hume 1955: 40–2), wonders whether the Sun, having returned once, will return a second time. If he concludes that the chance of its returning for that second time is greater than the chance of its not returning, then, according to Price's calculation, the degree of certainty that he is right is 0.75. This degree of certainty would decrease in a mathematically determined way if he concluded that the chance of its returning was two, three, four, etc. times the chance of its not returning. The degree of certainty in a further return would increase, again in a mathematically determined way, if he had observed not just one but several returns of the Sun. But no matter how many returns of the Sun had been observed, absolute certainty would never be achieved. For the formula $A^{n+1} - B^{n+1}$ measures the degree of certainty we should have in the conclusion of a probable argument, and this cannot ever equal one – which is required for the maximum degree of certainty – no matter how large n might be, provided only that B does not equal zero when A equals one. This proviso can safely be ignored because a probable argument which merely concluded that the unknown probability of an event occurring lay somewhere or other on the zero to one scale would be worthless.

Hume had claimed that 'all reasonings concerning matter of fact seem to be founded on the relation of *cause* and *effect*' (Hume 1955: 41), and the probable arguments with which Bayes and Price were concerned can indeed be understood as reasoning from effect to cause. Thus, the Sun having returned n times is an observed effect, and its cause is the unknown and unobserved chance of the Sun's returning. Some possible causes are more probable than others. If, for example, we were to propose that the cause is an unknown chance of less than 50:50, and we had observed ten returns of the Sun, the Bayes solution implies that the likelihood of our being right is $1/2^{11} - 0^{11}$, or approximately 0.0005. And since this likelihood, or probability, is intended as a measure of the degree of certainty that a reasonable person would have in the proposed conclusion, we can infer that this suggestion as to the possible cause should be rejected in favour of the alternative suggestion that the cause is an unknown chance of more than 50:50 that the Sun will return. In a similar way, we can compare the probability that the cause is an unknown chance lying between 0.5 and 0.75 with the probability it lies between 0.75 and one. Of course, if the unknown chance is one then it will be true that the Sun returns every day, and if the unknown chance is less than one it will be true that the Sun returns on less than every day, so attributing a degree of certainty to a conclusion about the unknown chance of the Sun returning is tantamount to attributing a degree of certainty to a generalisation, universal or statistical, about the Sun returning.

There were, though, certain assumptions adopted by Bayes and Price which were crucial to the success of their project. One of these, not explicitly noticed by either man, was that the unknown chance of an event occurring does not change over time or from place to place. They supposed, for example, that the chance of the Sun returning on any particular day, whatever it might be, is the same as its chance on any other day. In other words, they assumed that the events whose causes are to be established are subject to scientific laws, whether universal or statistical. There are, no doubt, good reasons for accepting this assumption, but we cannot be absolutely certain of its truth. And if the assumption is mistaken, then none of the calculations undertaken by Price has any force, and, indeed, no probable argument would generate any degree of certainty. Hume had, in effect, noticed the role of an assumption of this kind in any attempt to counter inductive scepticism when he pointed out that 'if there be any suspicion that the course of nature may change, and that the past may be no rule for the future, all experience becomes useless and can give rise to no inference or conclusion' (Hume 1955: 51). Any change that may take place in the 'course of nature' will result in a change in the chance that an event such as the Sun returning will occur. The defender of inductive scepticism, therefore, can claim that there are no considerations mentioned by Bayes or by Price which would prevent one from believing that, although the chance of the Sun returning on days prior to today has been greater than 50:50, the chance of the Sun returning is due to change today and tomorrow it will be less than 50:50. The Bayes–Price calculations would be impotent in the face of this claim, because they assume that the chance is stable from one time to another. Hume's concerns about probable reasoning, therefore, retain their force. Bayes and Price expressed in quantitative terms what degrees of certainty a reasonable investigator has in the conclusions he or she reaches. But they did not show that these are the degrees of certainty that a reasonable investigator must have.

As we have already noticed, a second assumption was explicitly recognised and defended with some care by Bayes himself. This is the assumption that the prior probabilities of the several possible causes of a given effect are equal. Bayes's ingenious but artificial example of throwing balls on to a table showed that there are clear cases when this assumption is justified; the table is perfectly flat and so the first ball could come to rest anywhere on it 'equally easily'. But when we wish to apply Bayes's solution to real practical situations, we certainly cannot take it for granted that the unknown probability we wish to determine can take any value 'equally easily'. Adam, equipped with reasoning powers but with no evidence, could not assume that just because of his ignorance the unknown probability of the Sun's returning could have any value 'equally easily'. For it may be that, unknown to Adam, there are physical circumstances which make it impossible for the unknown probability of the Sun's returning to take certain values. What Adam can do, though, is to compare the probability that the Sun will not return in the next n days with the probability that there will be one return of the Sun in the next n days with the probability that there will be two returns of the Sun, with the probability that there will be three returns, etc. Given that he knows nothing of what will happen on these n days, he will have to judge that each of the available possibilities can happen 'equally easily'. Thus, the probabilities of no return and of one return of the Sun, considering just the next day, are each 1/2; the probabilities of no return, of one return and of two returns of the Sun, considering two days, are each 1/3; the probabilities of no return, of one return, of two returns, and of three returns of the Sun, considering three days, are each 1/4, and so on. In general, for n days, the probability for any particular number of returns of the Sun will be $1/(n + 1)$. But in the case of Bayes's artificial application of his mathematical solution to a ball thrown on to a table, an exactly analogous idea also applies. For before we start trials with the second ball we can consider how many out of n trials will result in the ball coming to rest at a point nearer the left hand edge of the table than the unknown point reached by the first ball, and compare the probability that in none of the n trials will this happen with the probability that in one of the n trials this will happen, with the probability that in two of the n trials this will happen, etc. Given that the point reached by the first ball is completely unknown, we will have to judge that each of the available possibilities can happen 'equally easily' and that, therefore, each has the same probability, namely $1/(n + 1)$. And, Bayes claimed, since this feature of the artificial application carries over to real applications, like Adam's probable argument concerning the Sun's rising, we can infer that in real applications, as in the artificial one, the unknown probability can have, prior to any evidence which might help us to determine it, any one value just as easily as any other value. So, Adam's reasoning powers will be sufficient to inform him that, prior to any evidence being available to him, the unknown probability that the

Sun will return can have any one value just as easily as any other value. This, in Bayes's view, is a conclusion Adam can and should derive; it is not simply an assumption that Adam would have to make because, in his ignorance, he would have 'insufficient reason' for preferring one value to another.

Bayes had an argument, then, for his assumption that, prior to any relevant evidence being available, each of the hypotheses between which an investigator would have to choose has the same probability of being true. The argument is certainly secure in the case of the artificial example of throwing balls on to a table. It is rather less clear that the argument is sound in realistic cases of probable reasoning. One reason for this is that, in realistic cases of probable reasoning, the distinction between relevant and irrelevant evidence is not sharp, and consequently we are rarely if ever faced with determining probabilities prior to relevant evidence being available. The situation we have attributed to Adam is hardly a realistic one, and it cannot therefore be clear that his strategy in determining prior probabilities, even if justifiable in his case, is generally applicable. Real examples of probable arguments in science are far removed not only from Bayes's table, but also from the accounts given by Hume and Price of what reason would, or would not, be able to tell Adam about the return of the Sun. Subsequent developments in the eighteenth century ensured that the issues raised by this essential assumption would, sooner or later, be divisive for those who thought that the clarification of probable reasoning would contribute to our understanding of scientific method.

Bayes's solution to his problem was, and has remained, difficult to understand, and because of this Price's claim that it could be used to resolve the difficulties raised by Hume was ignored. It succeeded as a contribution to the mathematical 'doctrine of chances', which was perhaps all that Bayes intended, but it failed to illuminate obscure or controversial aspects of scientific method. Newtonian reservations about hypothetical reasoning, in which unobserved causes are assigned to observed effects, remained untouched. And as for Hume's radical scepticism, which encompassed the simple inductive arguments endorsed in Newton's rules of reasoning, the practical successes of Newtonian science in the eighteenth century were seen as sufficient answer, if indeed answer were needed to philosophical concerns which seemed increasingly distant from natural philosophy. Nevertheless, Bayes's pioneering ideas about probable arguments, which inferred causes from effects, or, as such arguments came to be called, inverse inferences, were revived later in the eighteenth century by a protégé of d'Alembert, Pierre Simon de Laplace.

According to Laplace, degrees of certainty could be quantified in a number of contexts where scientists used such probable arguments. An important example at the time was the determination of errors to which observations were subject. In trying to determine experimentally the value of a parameter, we have to reach a conclusion on the basis of observed values which will no doubt differ from each other. The observed values are the 'effects', the unknown real value being their 'cause'. Other examples discussed by Laplace include versions of Arbuthnot's argument about the cause of the observed ratio of male to female births, and of Daniel Bernoulli's argument about the cause of the observed inclinations of the planetary orbits. One general result, Laplace's rule of succession, is of particular interest. Like Bayes, he obtained a general formula for finding the probability that the unknown chance of an event happening in particular circumstances has a specified value, given that it has occurred in those circumstances a certain number of occasions and not occurred in those circumstances on other occasions. This formula can be applied to a case where we want to find the probability that a universal scientific law governing an event is true when we are given that the event has always happened in the relevant circumstances. We might, for instance, want to find the probability of the law that the Sun will always return, given that it has done so on every one of n occasions in the past. Laplace showed that his formula also enabled him to determine the probability that an event would happen in certain circumstances, given that it has happened in those circumstances on a certain number of occasions and not happened in those circumstances on other occasions. That being so, he was able to determine the probability that an event, such as the Sun returning tomorrow, will occur given that the Sun has returned on every one of n occasions in the past. The probability is, he claimed, $(n + 1)/(n + 2)$, so that if just one return of the Sun has been observed the probability that the Sun will return tomorrow is $2/3$, a fraction which will increase as the number of returns of the Sun increases, provided there are no occasions on which the Sun does not return. This result seems to offer the prospect of quantifying, at least in principle, the degree of certainty of simple inductions by enumeration; if we have observed n A's and all of them have been B's, then the probability that the next A will be a B is given by the rule of succession, $(n + 1)/(n + 2)$.

However, in deriving his general formula upon which this result depends, Laplace depended, as did Bayes, on the truth of certain assumptions. In particular, he needed to assume that, prior to any evidence being available, the unknown chance of an event could take any value and that no one value was any more likely to be true than any other. He needed, that is to say, the Leibniz–Jakob Bernoulli assumption that we could identify an appropriate number of 'cases' which could be equally easily 'realised' in nature. Leibniz had been unable to see how this assumption could be justified in practical scientific reasoning using probable argument. Bernoulli was only able to justify claims about the equal ease with which 'cases' could be realised on the basis of evidence. Perhaps, indeed, that is the only basis on which such claims can be justified, and it is misguided to suppose that they can be justified independently of evidence. Laplace, though, tried to bring some probable arguments in science within the scope of his mathematical formulae by suggesting that a principle of 'sufficient reason' entitles us to count all chances as equally probable when we judge them independently of any evidence, i.e. without any reason for preferring one chance to any other. We could judge Bernoulli's 'cases', that is to say, to be equally easily 'realised' in nature, because we have no reason for believing otherwise. The credibility and usefulness of this suggestion has subsequently been widely debated. Versions of it have been, and still are, defended and criticised. Laplace's confidence in the assumption was tempered, though, by his appreciation that with respect to 'the surest method which can guide us in the search for truth, [which] consists in rising by induction from phenomena to laws and from laws to forces ... it is almost always impossible to submit to calculus the probability of the results'. 'But', he added, 'the totality of the phenomena explained ... is sometimes such that without being able to appreciate the probability we cannot reasonably permit ourselves any doubt in regard to them' (Laplace 1951: 182–4; cf. Zabell 1989). This judicious caution, however, was not always in evidence among Laplace's followers.

FURTHER READING

There are excellent accounts of probable reasoning in the eighteenth century in:
Hacking, I. (1975) *The Emergence of Probability*, Cambridge: Cambridge University Press; chs 14–19.
Stigler, S. M. (1986) *The History of Statistics: The Measurement of Uncertainty before 1900*, Cambridge, Mass. and London: Harvard University Press; chs 2, 3.
Daston, L. (1988) *Classical Probability in the Enlightenment*, Princeton, NJ: Princeton University Press; ch. 5.

Unfortunately, Jakob Bernoulli's *Art of Conjecturing* has yet to be translated into English. The original Latin version has, however, recently been reprinted in:
Bernoulli, J. (1975) *Die Werke von Jakob Bernoulli*, vol. 3, Basel: Basel Naturforschende Gesellschaft.

Helpful translations of some passages, and a very useful guide, are provided in:
Shafer, G. (1978) 'Non-additive probabilities in the work of Bernoulli and Lambert', *Archive for the History of the Exact Sciences* 19: 309–70.

Much of Daniel Bernoulli's writings remain untranslated, but his ideas about probable reasoning are discussed in:
Bradley, L. (1971) *Smallpox Inoculation: An Eighteenth Century Mathematical Controversy*, Nottingham: Adult Education Department, University of Nottingham.

Sheynin, O. (1972) 'D. Bernoulli's work on probability', *Rete. Strukturgeschichte der Naturwissenschaften* 1: 273–99.

Gower, B. (1987) 'Planets and probability: Daniel Bernoulli on the inclinations of the planetary orbits', *Studies in the History and Philosophy of Science* 18: 441–54.

For d'Alembert, see:

Daston, L. (1979) 'D'Alembert's critique of probability theory', *Historia Mathematica* 6: 259–79.

Swijtink, Z. G. (1986) 'D'Alembert and the maturity of chances', *Studies in the History and Philosophy of Science* 17: 327–49.

For David Hume's famous argument about inductive or probable reasoning, see:

Hume, D. (1955) *An Inquiry Concerning Human Understandings*, edited with an introduction by C. W. Hendel, Indianapolis: Bobbs-Merrill.

Hacking, I. (1978) 'Hume's species of probability', *Philosophical Studies* 33: 21–37.

Milton, J. R. (1987) 'Induction before Hume', *British Journal for the Philosophy of Science* 38: 49–74.

Gower, B. (1991) 'Hume on probability', *British Journal for the Philosophy of Science* 42: 1–19.

For Bayes, see:

Bayes, T. (1763) 'An essay towards solving a problem in the doctrine of chances', *Philosophical Transactions of the Royal Society of London* 53: 370–418. Reprinted in *Biometrika* 45 (1958): 296–315, and in E. S. Pearson and M. G. Kendall (eds) (1970), *Studies in the History of Statistics and Probability*, London: Charles Griffin.

Analyses of Bayes's argument can be found in:

Stigler, S. M. (1982) 'Thomas Bayes's Bayesian inference', *Journal of the Royal Statistical Society* (A) 145: 250–8.

Gillies, D. (1987) 'Was Bayes a Bayesian', *Historia Mathematica* 14: 325–46.

Earman, J. (1992) *Bayes or Bust: A Critical Examination of Bayesian Confirmation Theory*, Cambridge, Mass.: MIT Press; ch. 1.

For Laplace, see:

Laplace, P. S. de (1951) *A Philosophical Essay on Probabilities*, translated by F. W. Truscott and F. L. Emory, New York: Dover.

Zabell, S. (1989) 'The rule of succession', *Erkenntnis* 31: 283–321.

6   John Herschel, John Stuart Mill and William Whewell

The uses of hypotheses

In 1767, just three years after the appearance of Thomas Bayes's solution of his problem in the 'doctrine of chances', the Royal Society published in its *Philosophical Transactions* an essay which attempted to apply that 'doctrine' to the question whether Newton's law of gravity extends to and governs the behaviour of the stars. Its author was John Michell, who has been described as the only natural philosopher of distinction working in Cambridge during the hundred years following Newton's death. His reasoning was that, if the stars were gravitationally attracted to one another, there would be more binary stars, and more clusters of stars, than would otherwise be the case. Of course, astronomers were aware that certain stars appeared close together, either as pairs or as clusters, but this in itself is of little significance because optically close stars can still be physically remote from each other. Observations of stars rotating about a fixed centre would suffice, but telescopes available at the time were insufficiently sensitive to enable astronomers to report such observations. So what Michell did was to construct a probable argument: 'The argument I intend to make use of', he said, 'is of that kind, which infers either design, or some general law, from a general analogy, and the greatness of the odds against things having been in the present situation, if it were not owing to some such cause'. He began his argument by calculating a numerical value for the probability that, if we were to scatter at random all the stars equal in brightness to the pair forming Beta-Capricorni, there would appear any two as close to each other as that pair. The small value of this probability, reinforced by other calculations relating to other pairs and clusters, led Michell to conclude that 'we may . . . with the highest probability conclude (the odds against the contrary opinion being many million millions to one) that the stars are really collected together in clusters in some places . . . to whatever cause this may be owing, whether to their mutual gravitation, or to some other law or appointment of the creator' (Michell 1767: 243, 249).

Michell's argument is not unlike others used in the eighteenth century to assign numerical values to the degrees of certainty of probable arguments. Like most of them, and like Bayes's theoretical essay on this topic, it seems to have attracted little attention, though this may be because it was accepted as a legitimate application of developing ideas about the mathematics of chance. In the nineteenth century, however, the argument became the focus of controversy. On the one hand there were those who understood it as an acceptable, if primitive, example of a form of reasoning in science – inverse probabilistic reasoning from effects to causes – which Laplace had quantitatively analysed and placed on a secure foundation. According to this view, the mathematical theory of probability provided a legitimate way of introducing a 'quantifying spirit' into evaluations of the strength of probable arguments. On the other hand there were those who, because they rejected quantitative analyses of inverse probabilistic reasoning from effects to causes, thought Michell's calculations worthless. In the view of critics, this exemplification of the 'quantifying spirit' gave a merely specious air of precision to judgements of the credibility of conclusions. The case against Michell's argument was put by James Forbes, Professor of Natural Philosophy at Edinburgh University and a well-respected geologist and physicist. 'I confess my inability', he said, 'to attach any idea to what would be the distribution of the stars or of anything else, if "fortuitously scattered", much more must I regard with doubt and hesitation any attempt to assign a numerical value to the antecedent probability of any given arrangement or grouping whatever' (Forbes 1849: 132). Forbes objected to Michell's implicit assumption that, to use Jakob Bernoulli's language, there is a definite and determinable number of equally easily realisable cases which can result from a scattering of stars called 'fortuitous'. We cannot possibly know that there is such a number or what it is, because we do not know what circumstances make a scattering 'fortuitous', and therefore cannot form a judgement about which 'cases', or resulting distributions, are equally easily realised by nature in those circumstances. Michell had assumed that, prior to any evidence being available, each specific distribution resulting from a 'fortuitous scattering' of the stars would have the same probability. He assumed, that is, that, prior to any observation of the stars, and given that they are randomly distributed, the probability of the observed distribution is the same as the probability of any other distribution. But though his numerical result depended on it, he offered no good grounds for the truth of this assumption, and in Forbes's view we should not, therefore, accept that result.

But whatever the merits of Michell's calculations, the conclusion he tried to establish – that there were physically double, or 'binary', stars – had been verified observationally by Sir William Herschel in 1796. His larger and more accurate telescopes enabled him to observe pairs of stars rotating around each other in accordance with Newton's law of gravitation. There was, therefore, no need to depend on Michell's curious, and perhaps questionable, probabilistic argument. True, William Herschel had referred, in approving terms, to this argument, but Forbes was in no doubt that it should have 'remained buried in the heavy quartos of the Philosophical Transactions' (Forbes 1850: 424). So it was ironic that the occasion for Forbes's critique was the publication in 1848 of a popular textbook of astronomy by John Herschel, William's son, which endorsed Michell's view that we can calculate the probability of two stars forming a binary pair if 'fortuitously scattered' (Herschel 1848: 564–9). As a consequence of Forbes's attack, John Herschel found himself obliged to defend the character, if not the details, of Michell's reasoning.

In part, the disagreement between the two men concerned the meaning of such terms as 'fortuitous scattering'. For Forbes, the use of words like 'fortuitous', 'accidental' and 'random' to describe a distribution precluded the possibility of assigning a numerical value to the antecedent probability of that distribution. For Herschel, on the other hand, we can 'assign a numerical value to the antecedent probability of any given arrangement or grouping of fortuitously scattered bodies', because in so doing 'we set out with a certain hypothesis as to the chances', namely that they are equal. Probability calculations concerned with 'one definite arrangement' are, he said, of 'no importance whatever'; the question is, rather, 'in the apparent proximity of the stars called "double", do we recognise the influence of any tendency to proximity, pointing to a cause exceptional to the abstract law of probability resulting from equality of chances as respects the area occupied by each star . . .?' (Herschel 1850: 36–7). But whereas for Michell the concept of equal chances would have been given a Bernoullian-style interpretation in terms of the equal ease with which 'cases' can occur in nature, Herschel's understanding of equal chances was in terms of what can occur equally easily so far as we know. The difficulty with Michell's interpretation was that, if 'fortuitous scattering' means that, in nature, a star could equally easily occupy one position as any other position, then any particular distribution, however striking, is as improbable as any other distribution, and therefore we can draw a conclusion against 'fortuitous scattering' on the basis of any distribution. On the other hand, Herschel's interpretation implies that by 'fortuitous scattering' we mean we know of no reason why a star occupies one position rather than any other. We can, he claimed, induce from the observed distribution of the stars that they have not been 'fortuitously scattered', but, as Forbes insisted, it is illusory to suppose that our ignorance can justify us in assigning a numerical value to the probability of that conclusion.

To some extent the Forbes/Michell controversy echoed the earlier debate between d'Alembert and Daniel Bernoulli. It was, though, made sharper by Laplace's promotion of a pronounced epistemological note to our understanding of probability. How can probable knowledge arise from ignorance? How can probability not measure the extent of our ignorance? Some sided with Forbes and argued that guesses about unobserved, or unobservable causes, and guesses about unverified, or unverifiable hypotheses, must remain guesses, for the assumptions we have to make in order to calculate probabilities are unjustifiable. Others sided with Herschel and claimed that guesses about causes and hypotheses are naturally recognised as being more or less good, and probabilities are ways of acknowledging degrees of that goodness. The disagreement persisted throughout the nineteenth century and is still discernible at the end of the twentieth.

At the time of his debate with Forbes about the possibility of in-verse probabilistic reasoning, John Herschel was at the height of his considerable powers. Like others of his contemporaries, he actively cultivated wide interests, in literature and in public policy for example, but his reputation rested chiefly on his accomplishments in chemistry, in optics, but above all in astronomy. He had, though, also acquired a responsibility as keeper of science's philosophical conscience, for earlier in his career he had contributed to Dionysius Lardner's *Cabinet Cyclopaedia*, a book on scientific method. The intended audience for this, as for other books comprising the *Cyclopaedia*, was the rapidly ex-panding number of people who wanted to share the knowledge which was producing power and wealth, as well as subservience and poverty, in Britain's expanding industrial centres. The title Herschel chose for his book – *Preliminary Discourse on the Study of Natural Philosophy* – indicated the role it was intended to play in Lardner's series, and it appropriately echoed the title d'Alembert chose for his introduction to the French *Encyclopédie* of 1751 – *Discours préliminaire de l'encyclopédie*.

Given Herschel's expertise and knowledge in physics and astronomy, we might expect that his account of 'the rules by which a systematic examination of nature should be conducted' (Herschel 1830: xxvi) would reflect an emphasis on mathematics rather than experiment. As a student at Cambridge he had been among those actively promoting the reform of mathematical notation in Britain and the use of analytical rather than geometrical methods in the calculus, so that the work of continental mathematicians and physicists such as the Bernoullis, Leonhard Euler, Joseph Louis Lagrange, Laplace and Carl Friedrich Gauss could become more accessible. We might expect, that is, an emphasis on the construction and elaboration of mathematical systems capable of representing, or idealising, the observed behaviour of planets and stars, the dynamics of gases and liquids and of objects moving in them, the interactions between rays of light, the transmission of sound and of heat, etc. Yet the *Discourse* presents a view of scientific method which is largely Baconian. Its title page portrays Francis Bacon, and it is quite clear that Herschel saw him as the guiding influence for scientific method as it was understood in Britain in the early nineteenth century. Yet he was aware of the tensions between the inductive experimental aspects of physical science and the increasingly successful use of deductive mathematical methods in theoretical physics. In chemistry, investigators could more easily repudiate theory, for experimentalists were responsible for much of the progress being made. But this was not the case in physics. The early decades of the nineteenth century witnessed the introduction of mathematical modes of thinking to topics which investigators had hitherto associated with experimental methods. Jean-Baptiste Fourier and Sadi Carnot initiated the use of mathematical ideas in the study of thermal phenomena; André Ampére and Siméon-Denis Poisson applied mathematics to electrical phenomena. There were exceptions such as Michael Faraday, but it seemed that more and more of what natural philosophers wished to read in the 'book of nature' was written in the language of mathematics, and that experimental expertise could not compensate for an inability to read that language.

Science begins, Herschel claimed, with the analysis of a composite observational or experimental phenomenon into its component phenomena. Such an analysis, like the analogous analysis of a chemist who wishes to distinguish the component ingredients of a chemical substance, is often provisional in the sense that it yields elements which resist, for the time being, further division. So we analyse a phenomenon, as a chemist analyses a substance, by extracting from its instances and examples those features present in them all. In the production of sound, for example, a preliminary analysis would reveal that there is always some sort of motion, detectable experimentally if not observationally, in the sounding body; always some medium capable of transmitting this motion to our ear; always some suitable mechanism for conveying the motion produced in the ear's membrane to the auditory nerves; and always a capacity for the result of this process to produce auditory sensations. Bacon, as we have seen, wrote of 'experimental histories' as providing the material for such analyses, and Herschel is equally clear that investigators need 'a sufficient quantity of well ascertained facts . . . affording us the means of examining the same subject in several points of view'. In Bacon's view, analyses would enable investigators to identify the 'form natures' of the 'phenomenal natures' explored in the experimental histories. Herschel's language was different: it was causes which he saw as the product of analyses. So, in the case of sound, the vibrating motion of a tuning fork is the cause of the sound it produces, and other kinds of motion of other sounding bodies are the causes of the sounds they produce. There are, of course, questions to ask about the cause of this cause, e.g. the cause of the vibrating motion. But this is just to say that there is an interconnected hierarchy of causes corresponding to increasingly elaborate analyses of phenomena. For just as we can ask, even if we cannot answer, questions about the causes of a cause, so we can also ask, though perhaps not answer, questions about the analysis of a component of a previous analysis. We can couple, therefore, the prospect of basic fundamental causes with the prospect of basic fundamental analytical elements; the task of discovering the basic fundamental causes of the phenomena of sound is the task of finding the basic fundamental analytical elements of those phenomena.

By 'induction' Herschel meant this process of analysis leading to the identification of causes. Like Bacon he understood it to be an iterative process enabling us to identify a hierarchy of causes. The analysis should proceed, he thought, by applying rules to assembled data, and the nine 'rules of philosophising' that he specified emphasise, in a good Baconian manner, the identification of a cause by the elimination of rivals. Several of the rules are used in an example which Herschel discussed in some detail, namely the experimental determination of the cause of dew and the construction of a theory to explain why dew forms. The theory had recently been developed by William Wells in *An Essay on Dew, and Several Appearances Connected With It* (1814). The right way to begin, Herschel said, is by assembling information about this phenomenon so that we will know of a variety of circumstances in which it occurs, and also of similar circumstances in which it does not occur. By judicious use of the rules we can manipulate this information so as to reveal the cause of dew, and 'we arrive at the general proximate cause of dew, in the cooling of the dewed surface by radiation faster than its heat can be restored to it, by communication with the ground, or by counter-radiation; so as to become colder than the air, and thereby to cause a condensation of its moisture'. Herschel evidently intended the example to exemplify a modernised form of Baconian reasoning; by applying rules to an 'experimental history' of dew, he was able to identify its 'form nature' (Herschel 1830: 152, 163).

Herschel's account of the causes of dew formation features prominently among the examples that John Stuart Mill used to illustrate the methods of experimental inquiry in his *System of Logic* (1843; Mill 1961). While still a young boy, Mill had been introduced to science and to ideas about reasoning in science by his father. He began working out his own ideas about logic when he was in his early twenties, but it was not until 1837, when he had studied Herschel's *Discourse* and also William Whewell's recently published *History of the Inductive Sciences*, that he was able to resolve the difficulties he had encountered in understanding induction. The chapter in *System of Logic* which explains the methods, or 'canons', of enquiry captures an important aspect of his resolution; it is, he declared in a letter to Herschel, 'the most important chapter of the book [and] is little more than an expansion & a more scientific statement of what you had previously stated in the more popular manner suited to the purpose of your "Introduction"' (Mill 1963: 583). For our purposes the important feature of the methods is their capacity to yield the certainty which was still as much a distinguishing mark of scientific knowledge as it had been in the seventeenth century.

Of the five methods explained by Mill, two – the methods of agreement and of difference – are fundamental. The reasoning they require is, in fact, deductive rather than inductive and there is therefore no question about the degree to which premisses make conclusions certain; in so far as we accept the premisses we must accept the conclusions. The form of the reasoning is what is sometimes called 'disjunctive syllogism', where one premiss claims that at least one of a number of statements is true, subsequent premisses claim that all except one are false, and the conclusion claims that the unfalsified statement must therefore be true. The initial disjunctive premiss is secured by implicit assumptions adopted when the methods are used, and the remaining premisses are established by observation or experiment. Consider, for example, an application of the method of agreement to find the cause of some phenomenon, say the formation of dew. We assume that the phenomenon does have a cause; we assume, in other words, that there is a true universal scientific law which links the phenomenon with its cause. We also assume that by a cause of the phenomenon we mean a necessary condition for its occurrence. That is to say, we assume that by the cause of the phenomenon we mean a condition which will always be present, or have been present, when the phenomenon is, and we rule out the possibility that the phenomenon could have different causes. And finally we assume that only one of a restricted and specified number of conditions is the true cause, so it can be identified by eliminating alternative conditions. The method of agreement claims that, if in two or more instances of the occurrence of the phenomenon we should find that only one of the specified conditions is also present, then that condition is necessary for, and thus the cause of, the occurrence of the phenomenon. Accordingly, experiments will be designed to vary circumstances in such a way as to show that, because each of the other conditions can be absent when the phenomenon is present, these alternatives are to be eliminated as real causes. The reasoning to the conclusion that identifies the cause is deductive because we cannot reject the conclusion without also rejecting one or other of the assumptions used by the method. For example, in the case of dew formation, an early stage in the investigation allows us to conclude, using agreement reasoning, that the relative coldness of a surface is its cause. The only way in which we could reject this conclusion is by rejecting at least one of the assumptions upon which it rests, which means rejecting either the assumption that there is a scientific law connecting this phenomenon with a cause, or the assumption that whatever is necessary for the occurrence of dew formation is its cause, or the assumption of a restricted number of possible causes for this effect. In many contexts, we can challenge one or other of these assumptions: relative coldness, though it always accompanies dew formation, may be its effect rather than its cause; the real cause might not be a single condition but, as Wells's theory showed, an assemblage of conditions; perhaps there are several different conditions each capable of causing the phenomenon; perhaps, finally, the real cause of the phenomenon is not included in the list of possible causes. But whatever the merits of such objections in specific contexts, we should notice that a successful challenge to an argument's assumptions, or premisses, is quite different from a successful challenge to its conclusiveness. Unless the premisses are acceptable, there may be no reason to believe the truth of the conclusion, despite the conclusiveness of the reasoning from premisses to conclusion, whereas even if an argument is inconclusive, its premisses, provided they are true, may still give some reason for believing its conclusion. So the certainty which Mill intended his methods to deliver was therefore bought at a price, that price being the vulnerability of the assumptions he needed.

Consider, second, the method of difference. We assume, again, that there is a scientific law connecting the phenomenon in question with its cause, which, for this method, is a condition both necessary and sufficient for the occurrence of the phenomenon. We also assume, as before, that one from a list of possible causes is the real cause. The observations we use in conjunction with these assumptions are of circumstances in which the phenomenon occurs and of circumstances in which it does not, the aim being to identify one of the possible causes as present when the phenomenon occurs and absent when it does not. To achieve this aim we have to vary the circumstances in which the phenomenon does and does not occur so that we can eliminate each of the possible causes other than the real one. For example, dew forms on polished glass but not on polished metals, though the conditions are the same. The cause of dew formation is among the many differences between glass and metal, and we draw up a list of possible causes with a view to collecting evidence which will enable us to eliminate all but one of the items on the list. Thus, transparency is a difference between glass and metals and might therefore appear on the list of possible causes; it is eliminated when we discover that dew forms on some polished opaque substances. The difference which survives elimination and is therefore identified as the condition necessary and sufficient for dew formation is the low thermal conductivity of polished glass as compared with polished metal. Once again, though, this conclusion is only as secure as the premisses, or assumptions, on which it is based. This method, like the method of agreement, has limitations, but they all derive from limits to the acceptability of its assumptions.

Mill's accounts of his methods of experimental enquiry are found in Book III of *System of Logic*, which bears the title 'Of Induction'. As we have seen, though, both agreement reasoning and difference reasoning have a deductive form. For Mill, then, inductive arguments were not always probable arguments in the sense that the truth of the premises made the conclusion probable to a greater or lesser extent. Developments in what Jakob Bernoulli had called 'the art of conjecture', at the hands of Bayes and Laplace, were therefore irrelevant to the internal cogency of Mill's methods. Hume's inductive scepticism had no more significance for these methods than it had for any other kind of deductive reasoning which used general empirical premises. As we have seen, Newton had insisted that reasoning in science – 'deduction from the phenomena' – could be both powerful and conclusive, and this insistence was an important part of his reason for resisting hypothetical reasoning, which, though powerful, was in his view too unreliable. Mill's view was similar; the reasoning employed in his experimental methods is powerful and conclusive, provided only that we accept the assumptions on which they depend. And, he too, was unimpressed by hypothetical reasoning or, as he called it, the Hypothetical Method. In this method, we assume or postulate a cause for the phenomenon under investigation; we then deduce a consequence which tells us what effect that cause will have in particular circumstances; finally we verify the truth of this consequence by observing that the facts correspond with this predicted effect. Our confidence in the postulate rests entirely on verifications of conclusions drawn from it; we do not attempt to prove that it is correct, perhaps because the nature of the postulate makes it impossible for us to have the experimental evidence which would provide a basis for a proof. For example, we could postulate that the cause of the elliptical orbits of the planets is a force operating on them which is directed towards the Sun. A consequence that we can deduce from this suggestion is that a planet operated on by such a force will describe equal areas in equal times as it moves in its elliptical orbit. This effect corresponds to one of Kepler's laws of planetary motion, and so we are able to verify a consequence of our postulate and thereby enhance our confidence that such a force really exists. Mill's view was that this mode of reasoning is unsatisfactory, for there will be other postulates we could have chosen with consequences we could have verified. We would do better, he thought, to adopt the 'Deductive Method', which makes the first step the 'direct induction' of a scientific law, rather than its postulation. By direct induction, Mill meant his methods of experimental enquiry. In his view we need to identify causes by these methods if verifications are to have significance. Thus, in his identification of a central force as the cause of the elliptical planetary orbits, Newton had not in fact used the questionable Hypothetical Method, but this Deductive Method. For he had shown not only that Kepler's area law was a consequence of the force being centrally directed, but also that a planet does not describe equal areas in equal times when the force is not centrally directed. In other words, when the central force is present, the area law holds, and when it is absent, the area law fails. In the light of this evidence we can use difference reasoning to draw the conclusion that a centrally directed force is the cause of the planets' motions (Mill 1961: 323–4; Book III, Chapter XIV, Section 4).

Herschel, though, seems to have had reservations about the role of rules in the discovery of causes. We should not be bound by the example of dew formation, where rules did lead to the identification of its cause. In our quest for 'ultimate facts', i.e. ultimate causes, we should not, he said 'be scrupulous as to how we reach to a knowledge of such general facts'. What really matters, it appears, is 'the verification of inductions'. Speculation about a cause is legitimate, provided only that we take steps to verify that it will 'perfectly account for every particular', so there is no reason why anyone should object to the postulation of a cause as the first step towards verification. The point was emphasised again when he turned his attention to what he called 'higher degrees of inductive generalisation', by which he meant theories built on general facts, or laws. In theorising, he said, we possess a 'liberty of speculation'; our reason is of more use to us than our experience because, in theorising about the hidden mechanisms of nature, our concern is with processes which are 'either too large or too small . . . to be immediately cognizable by our senses'. But our liberty and our reason are constrained; we must verify the reality of the agents we invoke in theories, and verify the laws which govern their behaviour by deducing from their existence and truth consequences which we can determine as correct. What matters 'is whether our theory truly represent all the facts, and include all the laws, to which observation and induction lead'. If a theory satisfies this condition, he claimed, 'it matters little how it has been originally framed'. The postulates of a theory do not have to be reached by applying rules, for so long as they 'lead us, by legitimate reasonings, to conclusions in exact accordance with numerous observations purposely made under a variety of circumstances as fairly to embrace the whole range of the phenomena which the theory is intended to account for, we cannot refuse to admit them' (Herschel 1830: 164, 190–1, 204, 208–9).

Herschel's view about this matter was not consistent. Elsewhere in the *Discourse* he referred to 'defects' of a method relying on verifications, as well as to 'defects' of induction, and made it clear that 'the inductive and deductive methods of enquiry . . . go hand in hand, the one verifying the conclusions deduced by the other' because 'the combination of experiment and theory, which may be thus brought to bear . . . forms an engine of discovery infinitely more powerful than either taken separately' (Herschel 1830: 181). The problem with relying exclusively on verification, he said, was that we may lack sufficiently sophisticated mathematics to enable us to apply a theory so as to be able to decide whether it is in accordance with the facts. For example, the intractability of the mathematical equations needed in hydrodynamics prevented investigators from determining whether the postulates used in this science are verified or not. Moreover, Herschel added, even if the technical mathematical difficulties could be overcome, lack of accurate empirical data would often inhibit the application of the mathematics. As for the 'defects' of induction, these derive, he said, from the need to rely on experimental measurements that cover only a limited range when investigating quantitative relations between physical variables, such as the volume and pressure of a gas, or the angles of incidence and refraction of a ray of light.

In one sense, Mill agreed with Herschel. In so far as scientific method is concerned with making discoveries, Mill accepted that it does not matter what sort of reasoning, if any, is used. Guesswork, invention, postulation, etc., are no worse than reasoning as methods of discovery. Hypotheses about causes which result from guesswork, invention and postulation are, he acknowledged, indispensable if we are to know what observations to make and what experiments to perform. But if our concern is not with methods of discovery but with methods we can use to establish or justify hypotheses as true, then Mill was quite clear that Herschel was wrong in supposing verifications are adequate. Sometimes hypotheses can be justified by deducing them from established principles, but failing that, they must be established by 'direct induction' using the methods of experimental enquiry. In terms of the contrast between experimental and mathematical approaches to scientific method, Mill sought to codify Bacon's unreflective experimentalism in so far as it related to methods for justifying scientific conclusions, and to acknowledge the achievements of mathematical methods in the physical sciences in so far as they related to methods for identifying those conclusions in the first place. For example, 'Mr Darwin's remarkable speculation on the *Origin of Species* is [an] unimpeachable example of a legitimate hypothesis'. But, Mill claimed, 'Mr Darwin has never pretended that his doctrine was proved'. The 'rules of Hypothesis', indeed, give us only an assumption, not a proof; for proof we must turn to the 'rules of Induction' (Mill 1961: 327–8; Book III, Chapter XIV, Section 5).

Herschel, being a defender of hypothetical reasoning as a way of justifying hypotheses, needed to distinguish between, on the one hand, convincing and effective examples of its use, and on the other hand, examples which display its fallaciousness. He was well aware that the verification of the consequences of a hypothesis by all known facts, though an important necessary condition for the truth of the hypothesis, was insufficient. Nevertheless, he believed that we would have good reasons for accepting the hypothesis as true if, in addition, it led to new and surprising facts which were subsequently verified. That is to say, hypothetical reasoning is convincing and effective if it incorporates verifications by new and unexpected facts. 'The surest and best characteristic of a well-founded and extensive induction', Herschel said, 'is when verifications of it spring up, as it were, spontaneously, into notice, from quarters where they might be least expected' (Herschel 1830: 170). One of Herschel's examples illustrates a way in which a verifying fact can be unexpected. The chemist Mitscherlich had proposed a law of isomorphism which claimed that the chemical compounds of elements belonging to the same isomorphic group crystallise in the same geometric form. The proposal met with difficulties in that the geometric forms of salt crystals of arsenate and phosphate of soda, which should have been identical, were not so. However, further and more careful investigation of apparent exceptions led to the discovery of new compounds of isomorphic elements which unexpectedly verified Mitscherlich's law. In this example, a prediction of a theory which we would not otherwise have anticipated, turned out to be true (Herschel 1830: 171).

But in another example Herschel gives, the verifying fact seems not so much unexpected as inexplicable in the absence of the verified hypothesis. Theoretical studies of the nature of sound and its propagation had made use of hypotheses which investigators could use to calculate the velocity of sound in air. However, there was a small but consistent difference between the calculated value for the velocity and its experimental determination. Laplace had explained this otherwise inexplicable discrepancy by elaborating the theory so as to take into account the thermal effects of the small but significant compressions and expansions of air which occur with the passage of sound waves. Because it is verified by facts inexplicable by (and inconsistent with) earlier versions of acoustic theory, we should accept the truth of Laplace's elaboration. Herschel's view, therefore, was that hypothetical reasoning is acceptable provided that it is verified by facts which are neither known nor expected, or by facts which, though known, are otherwise inexplicable (Herschel 1830: 171–2).

In the light of this we can see why Herschel wished to defend Michell's reasoning. The observed distribution of the stars, in particular the number of stars appearing in pairs or clusters, is surprising and hard to explain unless the hypothesis that stars are subject to gravitational forces is correct. There is, as it were, a discrepancy between the calculated consequences of the apparently sensible suggestion that stars are scattered randomly and what we observe to be the case when we examine their distribution carefully. We can remove the discrepancy by invoking the hypothesis that, though randomly scattered, the stars are subject to gravitational forces which result in the formation of binary pairs and physically related clusters. Without this hypothesis, we would not 'expect' the stars to be distributed as they are; with the hypothesis, we do. So, although the hypothesis is verified by facts which are known rather than new, we are nevertheless entitled to believe the hypothesis on the basis of that verification. Moreover, it would seem that we can quantify the degree to which a fact is expected. At one extreme we have maximum degree of expectedness belonging to facts deductively entailed by hypotheses; we expect that an effect must occur, or must have occurred, given the presence of its cause, provided that our hypothesis that the effect always happens in the presence of this cause is correct. At the other extreme we have minimum degree of expectedness belonging to facts inconsistent with a hypothesis; we expect that an effect must not occur, or must not have occurred, given the absence of its cause, provided that our hypothesis that the effect never happens in the absence of this cause is correct. Between these two extremes there are degrees of expectedness belonging to facts which are made probable by hypotheses, and if this probability is quantifiable, so is the degree of expectedness. If, therefore, the degree of expectedness of a fact given a hypothesis is low, we have a probable argument from that fact to the conclusion that the hypothesis is false, and our degree of confidence in that conclusion is correspondingly high. Michell's calculations were attempts to quantify the degrees of expectedness of observed facts concerning the closeness of star pairs and clusters, and because these degrees were so very small he was entitled to conclude, with a high degree of certainty, that the stars are not randomly distributed. But we should not confuse calculations of degrees of expectedness with calculations of degrees of certainty; just because the first is possible it does not follow that the second is. For it is only low degrees of expectedness which can have the kind of implication that Michell drew. It is only unexpected facts which have the power to verify hypotheses.

But Mill would have none of this reasoning. Investigators should not, he insisted, dispense with the first stage of his Deductive Method by inventing hypotheses subsequently used as the bases of predictions which, if fulfilled and especially if unexpectedly fulfilled, would verify them. In practice, we may find it necessary to begin by postulating a hypothesis, but we will have no secure argument for its truth until we find a way of using the methods of experimental enquiry so as to produce an induction of the hypothesis. A hypothesis can be consistent with all the known facts; perhaps it accounts for all the known facts and thus 'saves the phenomena'; perhaps it 'has led to the anticipation and prediction of [facts] which experience afterwards verified'. Even so, Mill claimed, we have no sufficient reason for believing the hypothesis true. 'Predictions and their fulfilment', especially if unexpected without the hypothesis, 'are, indeed, well calculated to impress the uninformed, whose faith in science rests solely on similar coincidences between its prophesies and what comes to pass'. But we should not mistake the psychological power of verified predictions for their logical power. The crucial issue is whether there is any significant difference between known and predicted facts, whether expected or unexpected, when we consider the strength of the reasoning from those facts to the truth of a hypothesis. And with regard to this issue, Mill's view is clear and unambiguous: whether the facts are known or predicted, expected or unexpected, the ability of a hypothesis to account for them does not by itself make the hypothesis believable, because there are many other, incompatible, hypotheses also able to account for them. What we need is a demonstration that consequences which we know are incorrect follow from the falsity of the favoured hypothesis. But this is just to say that the Hypothetical Method is inadequate, for by showing that the favoured hypothesis accounts for the facts whereas its competitors, because incompatible with it, are inconsistent with them, we are inducing its truth using agreement and difference reasoning, and so adopting Mill's Deductive Method. The Hypothetical Method, even though we enhance its psychological attractions by differentiating between verification by known and predicted facts, and by expected and unexpected facts, can only deliver 'probable conjectures'. The Deductive Method, however, can deliver 'proved truth' (Mill 1961: 331; Book III, Chapter XIV, Section 6).

The tradition of thinking about scientific method represented by John Herschel was liberal and accommodating. He had inherited from Bacon convictions about the central role in science of experimental evidence, particularly evidence having the power to promote theoretical progress by, for example, resolving theoretical disagreements. He had also adopted, with some refinement, Bacon's views about the kind of inductive reasoning capable of yielding scientific knowledge. But his Baconianism was tempered by his admiration for the post-Newtonian achievements of Continental scientists in astronomy and mechanics. In those contexts, deductive mathematical reasoning from first principles, even though it might yield conclusions which idealise experience, had successfully solved problems and enhanced understanding, and thereby provided verifications of those principles. Sometimes, then, we might be able to assemble evidence which will enable us to conform to Baconian strictures and induce theoretical conclusions. If we can, then in an ideal world we should. But sometimes it will be more expedient, and perhaps even necessary, to bypass those strictures and postulate a hypothesis, rather than derive an induction, which we can then accept or reject depending on whether observation and experiment verify its consequences. In the case of the mathematical sciences, where theoretical hypotheses can have only an indirect connection with observations, it may seem that this way of proceeding is the only way that is possible. Of course, verifications are inconclusive, so the reasoning from them to the truth of a postulate is probable reasoning. But nevertheless, investigations by probabilists of the 'art of conjecture' seemed to show that such reasoning could result in degrees of certainty sufficiently high to justify the acceptance of the conclusions drawn. Herschel wanted the conclusions reached by using scientific methods to count as scientific knowledge, and he believed that investigators could achieve this aim by verifications producing high degrees of certainty in conclusions, as well as by applying inductive rules to experimental data.

Mill's view was more rigorous. He modernised, without compromising, the ideals of Bacon, Newton and Locke. His methods of experimental enquiry were devised and formulated so that investigators could deduce conclusions from the phenomena in the way that Newton had intended. Of course, large assumptions had to be granted for the methods to work, but these assumptions often had a practical justification. In practice, investigators accepted without question that events always had causes and that they were linked with them by universal scientific laws; in practice, investigators were faced with a choice between different explanations of the facts. In theory, these justifications were questionable, but Mill was not concerned to defend scientific reasoning from radical scepticism like that expressed by Hume; in the face of philosophical doubts his account of such reasoning would fare no better than other accounts. But he was concerned to defend scientific reasoning against practical doubts, and to show that it did merit the confidence people placed in it. If only the necessary assumptions be granted, the methods of experimental enquiry will deliver conclusions of whose truth we can be confident because they are deduced from the experimental phenomena. Probable reasoning, on the other hand, is susceptible to practical doubts which cannot be countered by plausible assumptions. Verifications of a proposal about the cause of a phenomenon are a necessary condition of its truth, but they are not sufficient, and therefore, so long as the verified proposal remains a postulated hypothesis rather than an induction from the experimental facts, it will be subject to such doubts. Like Herschel, Mill wanted the conclusion reached by scientific method to count as scientific knowledge, but he believed that this would happen only if we insist that the conclusions are established on the basis of experimental data using agreement or difference reasoning in some suitable form. For him, therefore, it did matter how we reach claims about causes and their operation. The first step, in which we methodically seek to identify a cause, cannot be replaced by a conjecture, however expedient or enlightened. A conjectured cause may explain a phenomenon in the sense that it is verified by it, but for Mill as for Newton, scientific knowledge is of true causes and verifications are inadequate for this purpose.

It was not just Herschel's liberalism that Mill confronted with his austerity; vigorous and determined opposition was also provided by William Whewell. He, too, was a person of learning, energy and wide-ranging interests, writing on moral philosophy and on political economy as well as on science. His philosophy of science was informed by his expertise in astronomy, mechanics and mineralogy, together with a comprehensive knowledge of the historical development of these and other sciences. For the first time, Bacon's views about scientific method were set aside, for Whewell's key idea was that there can be no possibility of assembling facts concerned with things without using some theory resulting from thought. Scientific knowledge, he claimed, always requires the combination of elements which express a fundamental antithesis or opposition of facts and theories, things and thought, sensations and ideas, perceptions and conceptions, etc. A scientist's aim with respect to knowledge in, for example, optics will be to bring together the clearest and most coherent idea or conception of what light is with experimental data about light which in their accuracy and variety show that the idea is a perfect fit for the facts. Often, as in physical sciences like optics, the clarity and coherence of a theoretical idea will be assured by representing it as, or as part of, a deductive mathematical structure. For Whewell, then, mathematics is prominent in the physical sciences, not so much because the 'book of nature' happens to be written in the language of mathematics, but rather because the only way we can understand the book is by translating it into mathematical language. We become aware of the letters used to make the words written in the 'book of nature' just by looking around us, but we have to give these words meaning. The meaning of the text we try to read is that given to it by its author, the Creator, and is inaccessible to us. Therefore we have to give the text meaning, and sometimes it is appropriate and helpful to do this by using the resources of mathematics (Butts 1989: 48, 281). In general, the conceptual structures, whether mathematical or not, that we use to express theoretical ideas are contributed by us in order to understand nature rather than found by us as a result of investigating nature. But thought alone is not enough. Ideas, however clear and coherent, are useless unless we can show that they have application to natural phenomena. We must, then, find ways of comparing the theories we invent by thinking with the facts we discover about things. The quality of our theories will depend on the extent to which they agree with the facts they would explain. 'A Theory', Whewell declared, 'may be described as a Thought which is contemplated distinct from Things and seen to agree with them'. And, he continued, 'a Fact is a combination of our Thoughts with Things in so complete agreement that we do not regard them as separate' (Elkana 1984: 146). So, just as in scientific theories the form supplied by conceptual structures is a useless abstraction without the content supplied by experience, in scientific facts the content provided by the raw data of experience is never available to us without some form provided by our ideas or concepts. Thoughts are involved in things just as things are involved in thoughts.

One implication of this way of understanding scientific knowledge is that induction is seen as a process in which the mind provides a general idea or concept which enables us to interpret and explain the data of experience. That idea or concept is not in any way derivable from the data, and it is therefore useless to suppose, with Bacon, that we can start with data and somehow extract a general idea. For example, the general idea expressed in Newton's first law of motion that 'a body left to itself will move on with unaltered velocity' cannot be derived from experiential or experimental data, because no body has ever behaved in such a way. This idea provides us with a standard or an ideal 'created by us, not offered by nature', and with its aid 'we find that all actual cases are intelligible and explicable'. Even in a case where we might want to say that a general idea is derived from data, Whewell insisted that it is the generality of the idea which is its crucial feature, and this cannot be supplied by the data but only by the mind. For example, 'Kepler . . . in asserting that [Mars] moved in an ellipse . . . bound together particular observations of separate places of Mars by the . . . conception of an ellipse, which was supplied by his own mind'. 'To supply this conception', Whewell noted, 'required . . . a special activity in the mind of the discoverer'; it needed 'research, invention, resource' (Butts 1989: 47, 278).

If induction is interpretation and its results are 'inductive principles' expressing ideas supplied by the mind, then rules like those proposed by Mill are irrelevant for discovery. For, according to Whewell's 'antithetical' proposal, we can have facts about a phenomenon we wish to investigate only if we have already found a thought or conception which we can unite with perceptual experiences of things. We need conceptions before we can investigate; we should not expect them to emerge from investigations. But where do these ideas, these conceptions, these hypotheses, come from, if not from the facts themselves? To begin with, Whewell said, they are no more than 'happy guesses', and they come from the inventive resources of discoverers. 'Distinct and appropriate Conceptions', he said, are supplied by 'that peculiar Sagacity which belongs to the genius of a Discoverer'. And this sagacity 'cannot be limited by rules, or expressed in definitions' (Elkana 1984: 210). But there must be limits; of the conceptions or hypotheses we might use to 'bind together' the facts, at most one is true in the sense that it reflects the way reality is. And yet if all the information we have about reality, whether we describe that information as fact or as theory, incorporates elements contributed by us as well as elements contributed by reality, then any judgement we make about the truth of a hypothesis or conception will lack a proper basis. We can expect scientific method to deliver some of the truth about reality, in so far as it uses reasoning based upon facts which we can understand as representing reality. But if, as Whewell claimed, scientific knowledge, including knowledge of facts, has an antithetical structure, then we will have no grounds for thinking that reasoning from facts will deliver any of the truth about reality. Kepler's ellipse conception provides us with an effective way of interpreting and explaining data about planets, and we can use that way of interpreting the data to verify consequences of the ellipse conception. But it does not follow that the ellipse conception correctly represents reality, i.e. that the planets do really move in elliptical orbits. Other conceptions could supply equally effective ways of interpreting the same data which we could use to verify them. The problem would not be so pressing if we could understand data in their own terms, rather than in terms of a conception we supply, for in that case we might have good reasons for preferring one verified hypothesis to others. But Whewell's commitment to the antithetical character of science implies that we must either face and resolve the problem, or alternatively admit that scientific method does not provide us with a means of determining truth.

Whewell did not address the issue explicitly, but we can see his proposal that hypotheses should provide unexpected explanations and predictions as an implicit solution. A conception or a hypothesis must, he claimed, be true to reality when it enables us to predict consequences which are subsequently verified by observation and experiment, or when it enables us to explain things which it was not designed to explain. A favourite example was the recognition by astronomers that the conception of universal gravitation, originally introduced to interpret 'the Perturbations of the moon and the planets by the sun and by each other', could also be used to explain 'the fact, apparently altogether dissimilar and remote, of the Precession of the equinoxes'. Whewell's term for this unexpected support for a conception was 'consilience of inductions'. In general, verifications, though necessary for the acceptability of a conception or hypothesis, would not be sufficient; but some verifications, namely those producing 'consilience of inductions', were so striking as to be for practical purposes sufficient. If a conception enables us to produce satisfactory interpretations of data concerning two quite different kinds of phenomena, even though it was devised for the interpretation of only one, then we have consilience and a good reason for believing the conception true. It is possible that the conception is false and that the consilience is coincidental, but no reasonable person would believe that 'accident could give rise to such an extraordinary coincidence' and that a 'false supposition could, after being adjusted to one class of phenomena, exactly represent a different class, where the agreement was unforeseen and uncontemplated' (Butts 1989: 153).

We can, then, identify two issues at stake between Mill and Whewell. In the first place Mill asserted and Whewell denied that there are methods by means of which scientists can prove conclusively that a hypothesis is true on the basis of experimental evidence. Agreement reasoning and difference reasoning, Mill claimed, enable scientists to deduce conclusions from the phenomena. Such reasoning, Whewell retorted, makes essential use of large, questionable assumptions and it misrepresents real scientific reasoning by disregarding the antithetical character of facts and theories. In the second place Whewell asserted and Mill denied that verifications can be strong enough to ensure the truth of hypotheses. For Whewell, if a hypothesis successfully and unexpectedly explains what would otherwise be inexplicable and successfully and unexpectedly predicts what would otherwise not be predicted, then we have consilience of inductions and can be confident that the hypothesis is true. For Mill, although consilience of inductions has psychological power, it remains true that from a logical point of view other hypotheses could successfully and unexpectedly explain and predict, and until we have reason to eliminate them our preferred hypothesis will remain unjustified.

The two issues are connected: Mill and Whewell disagree about one because they disagree about the other. Neither man developed a position which did proper justice to the issues. Mill's commitment to his methods of experimental enquiry made it difficult for him to see that verifications have any logical power and thus difficult for him to explain why their psychological power can sometimes seem strong. Whewell's commitment to an antithetical account of scientific knowledge made it difficult for him to mount a satisfactory defence of his view that truth is attainable. Subsequent developments in the nineteenth century led to further divergence, with Mill's views about induction being incorporated into the developing genre of logic, and with Whewell's approach pointing towards ways of understanding reasoning in science which were responsive to real science.

FURTHER READING

For John Herschel's account of scientific method, see:

Herschel, J. F. W. (1830) *A Preliminary Discourse on the Study of Natural Philosophy*, London: Longmans, Rees, Orme, Brown, and Green. The 1987 reprint of this edition, published by the University of Chicago Press, contains a 'Foreword' by Arthur Fine which gives some details of Herschel's life and work.

For Mill's views, see:

Mill, J. S. (1961) *A System of Logic, Ratiocinative and Inductive: Being a Connected View of the Principles of Evidence and the Methods of Scientific Investigation*, London: Longmans, Green and Co. A critical edition with helpful notes can be found in J.S. Mill (1973–4) *Collected Works. Volumes VII–VIII A System of Logic*, J.M. Robson (ed.), Toronto: University of Toronto Press and Routledge and Kegan Paul. *A System of Logic* was first published in 1843.

There are many discussions and analyses of Mill's ideas about scientific method. Among the most recent is:

Skorupski, J. (1989) *John Stuart Mill*, London: Routledge; ch. 6.

The ideas of Mill and Herschel are compared in:

Strong, J. V. (1978) 'John Stuart Mill, John Herschel, and the "Probability of Causes"', in *PSA 1978* 1, East Lansing, Mich.: Philosophy of Science Association.

For Whewell's views, see:

Elkana, Y. (ed.) (1984) *William Whewell: Selected Writings on the History of Science*, Chicago: University of Chicago Press.

Butts, R. E. (ed.) (1989) *William Whewell: Theory of Scientific Method*, Indianapolis: Hackett.

His ideas have been examined in:

Laudan, L. (1971) 'William Whewell on the consilience of inductions', *Monist* 55: 368–91; reprinted in Laudan, L. (1981) *Science and Hypothesis*, Dordrecht: Reidel.

Fisch, M. (1991) *William Whewell: Philosopher of Science*, Oxford: Oxford University Press.

There is a discussion of the influence of Herschel's and Whewell's methodologies on Darwin's thinking in:

Ruse, M. (1975) 'Darwin's debt to philosophy: an examination of the influence of the philosophical ideas of John F. Herschel and William Whewell on the development of Charles Darwin's theory of evolution', *Studies in the History and Philosophy of Science* 6: 159–81.

The ideas of Herschel, Mill and Whewell are applied to controversies about the nature of light in:

Laudan, L. (1981) 'The medium and its message', in G. Cantor and M. Hodge (eds), *Conception of the Ether*, Cambridge: Cambridge University Press; reprinted as 'The epistemology of light: some methodological issues in the subtle fluids debate', in Laudan, L. (1981) *Science and Hypothesis*, Dordrecht: Reidel.

Worrall, J. (1989) 'Fresnel, Poisson and the white spot: the role of successful prediction in the acceptance of scientific theories', in D. Gooding, T. Pinch and S. Schaffer (eds), *The Uses of Experiment: Studies in the Natural Sciences*, Cambridge: Cambridge University Press.

Achinstein, P. (1990) 'Hypotheses, probability, and waves', *British Journal for the Philosophy of Science* 41: 73–102; reprinted in Achinstein, P. (1991) *Particles and Waves: Historical Essays in the Philosophy of Science*, Oxford: Oxford University Press.

Accounts of the nineteenth-century background to the work of Herschel, Mill and Whewell are given in:

Yeo, R. (1985) 'An idol of the marketplace: Baconianism in nineteenth-century Britain', *History of Science* 23: 251–98.
Yeo, R. (1986) 'Scientific method and the rhetoric of science in Britain, 1830–1917', in J. Schuster and R. Yeo (eds), *The Politics and Rhetoric of Scientific Method: Historical Studies*, Dordrecht: Reidel.

7 Henri Poincaré and Pierre Duhem
Conventions and scientific reasoning

By the middle of the nineteenth century the experimentalist approach to scientific method that we find in Bacon and Mill had begun to lose some of its power and influence. One reason for this was that the term 'science' had become more circumscribed and more specialised. It signified, primarily, physical science, and its previous associations with systematic, demonstrative knowledge in general were no longer as strong as they had been. 'Scientists' – a word coined by Whewell in 1834 – in this new sense are not really philosophers, or even natural philosophers. The poet, Samuel Coleridge, declared that he was 'half angry' with his friend Humphry Davy for 'prostituting the name of Philosopher ... to every Fellow who has made a lucky experiment' (quoted in Yeo 1991: 178). Experiment was indeed important, in varying degrees, to the physical sciences, but it was no longer a distinctive feature of them. Many other kinds of enquiry could boast of being experimental. What was distinctive of the physical sciences was their progressive character, and a proper understanding of scientific method should show how this had come about. Moreover, science in this new sense had become a profession. It was no longer the preserve of wealthy amateurs but of people who depended on its success for their livelihood. Scientists needed for practical purposes an understanding of scientific method; they needed, that is, guidance on how to pursue science successfully. New educational institutions were recognising and meeting the demand for trained scientists, and those responsible for their education saw it as one of their tasks to disseminate sound methodological principles. Not surprisingly, there was a feeling that the most reliable accounts of scientific method were those produced within the profession. Mill had indeed taken trouble to provide his readers with apt and scientific examples of his methods, as well as with a sophisticated analysis of the way they worked, but he was not a professional scientist; he was 'ignorant of science'. Because of this, his views, among scientists at least, counted for less than those of his adversary Whewell.

Another reason was the declining influence of Bacon. The Baconian spirit of cautious, sceptical empiricism remained prominent, but the specific recommendations of his methodology were seen by many as unworkable (see Ellis 1905; cf. Yeo 1985: 275). There could not be, as he had supposed, a set of mechanical rules that scientists should apply to experimental data so as to produce discoveries about causes and the laws of their operation. According to James Forbes, his attempts 'to systematise a positive method of discovery' were a failure; 'not only did he himself not succeed in any model-investigation, but the procedure he recommended was not followed by any natural philosopher' (Davie 1961: 184). Adequate data and sensible eliminative reasoning were no doubt as important in science as they were in other contexts, such as law, medicine, philology and even theology and metaphysics. But a theory about method in science must concern what is characteristic of science, and, except in its more general aspects, Bacon's theory was silent about the characteristics of successful physical science in the mid-nineteenth century. Though there was much in physical science that was practical, experimental and even popular, there was more that could only be grasped using techniques of mathematical analysis. Bacon's ideas about scientific method had not shown how these two aspects of scientific knowledge, the empirical and the a priori, could be brought together in a satisfactory manner.

A third reason was the ambiguous image of Newton. New ideas about light, contradicting some of his conclusions in the *Opticks*, tended to undermine the experimentalism of its methodology, whereas the mathematical emphasis of the *Principia*'s methodology was constantly reinforced by successful applications of its ideas. Mathematical analysis became a more reliable guide than experiment to what was beyond the reach of our senses. 'Models' of material atoms, of fluids, of ethers and of waves were used as sources of mathematically expressed hypotheses which could be put together to create theories capable of accounting for chemical, electrical, magnetic, optical, etc. phenomena. Admittedly, Newton did not himself use a 'model' in creating his theory of gravity; he claimed that he was able to deduce the theory from the phenomena. But nevertheless he created a mathematical theory which provided information, inaccessible to our senses, about the forces affecting the gravitational behaviour of terrestrial and astronomical objects. Progress had been made in the physical sciences by creating and verifying other mathematical theories which could similarly compensate for limitations in the ability of our senses to yield knowledge. Our understanding of scientific method, and indeed of Newton's accomplishment, should therefore acknowledge the increasingly important role played by hypotheses. Thus Whewell urged that we should see Newton's declared rejection of hypothetical reasoning as no more than an expression of a tendency 'prevalent in his time', and of his reaction to 'the rash and illicit general assumptions of Descartes'. In practice, Newton's suspicion of 'all elements of knowledge except observation ... was, however, in him so corrected and restrained by his own wonderful sagacity and mathematical habits, that it scarcely led to any opinion which we might not safely adopt' (Butts 1989: 323, 337). That is to say, a proper understanding of the widely misunderstood Rules of Reasoning, informed by familiarity with his practice, will show that Newton was not opposed to hypothetical reasoning and that his real views about scientific method were entirely in accord with those promoted by Whewell himself.

An experimentalist approach to scientific method is naturally associated with an empiricist view about scientific knowledge. It is associated, that is, with the philosophical idea that the propositions in which we express scientific knowledge represent the real world because the means by which we come to know and to justify these propositions is nothing other than direct experience of the real world. Our knowledge that there are binary stars, that oxygen is needed for combustion, that light is a transverse wave motion, that fossils record the presence of creatures now extinct, and so on, is empirical because it depends directly or indirectly only on sensory experience in some form or another. Often, as in these examples, scientists' claim to knowledge went beyond what is directly available in experience. This is because experience is always of particular things, events, processes, states of affairs, etc., whereas scientific knowledge is often expressed in general terms; experience is always of what can be observed, whereas scientific knowledge is sometimes of what cannot be observed. However, provided their experiential bases are adequate, we can justify these claims to knowledge, and in explaining the role of experiments methodologists are identifying criteria of adequacy for experiential bases. We may need reason, and perhaps mathematics, to justify the knowledge on the basis of experiment, but that simply means that the experimental evidence is processed or re-expressed, not that it is supplemented. Our experience is tied to particular places and times, and it is subject to constraints on our sensory capacities, but nevertheless experimental scientific method is capable of providing us with an account of reality which 'transcends' or goes beyond those limitations. It is capable, that is, of providing objective knowledge of reality – the knowledge that an omniscient God would have – and it does so because of the conviction that this objective knowledge is empirical knowledge.

In Britain, empiricist philosophies had, since the seventeenth century, implied such a view about scientific knowledge, and thereby sustained experimentalist accounts of scientific method. There are important differences between empiricists such as John Locke, David Hume and John Stuart Mill concerning the scope of empirical knowledge and about the nature of its justification, but they were agreed that scientific knowledge is empirical and that the contribution our minds make to our knowledge of reality does not add to the contribution made by reality itself, but simply enables us to organise it in ways that are effective for understanding, for prediction and for control of reality. We know that there are binary stars not because, or partly because, we are constrained to think in ways that lead us to this conclusion; we simply observe what is there to be observed and draw the conclusion which any being capable of thought would draw. How could scientific knowledge, since it is knowledge of the real world, be anything other than empirical knowledge based upon direct experience of the real world?

But empiricist theories of scientific knowledge were not uncontested. Experience, opponents claimed, is an entirely inappropriate basis for genuine knowledge, because genuine knowledge is stable and certain whereas experience is transitory and unreliable. Our senses often mislead us; to depend on the evidence they provide, however carefully that evidence is assembled and however extensive it is, is to forgo certainty and thus to forgo genuine knowledge. What we know must be true, but the conclusions attested by experience can be false; consequently conclusions attested by experience cannot count as knowledge. According to this view, versions of which were developed by Descartes and Leibniz, the source of genuine knowledge is not experience but reason. If, therefore, we can be said to have any knowledge of reality, it will be because the mind's reasoning powers can be the source of such knowledge. It may be that the knowledge reason provides is global and schematic, and that we need to use experience in order to determine how this knowledge applies to the local reality available to us in experience, but still the confidence we have in our knowledge of reality, whether global or local, will depend not on experience but on reason. How could real knowledge, including any scientific knowledge there might be, have anything other than reason as its basis?

According to many, including some empiricists, mathematics has provided the context for substantial, real, reason-based knowledge; mathematical knowledge is a priori and thus independent of experience. Since its beginnings in ancient Greece, it has proved remarkably useful to us in our practical, everyday dealings with the real world. It certainly appears to be applicable to reality even if it does not depend on our experience of reality. However, in so far as mathematical knowledge is knowledge of reality at all, it is concerned only with the most general and abstract features of it. We should not expect all, or even much, of what we count as scientific knowledge to be anything other than a priori mathematical knowledge. For experience will have an essential part to play in selecting those consequences of mathematical knowledge which have application to the experienced world. It is not at all surprising, therefore, that the theories in which we express our knowledge of reality are couched in mathematical terms. Reason alone justifies the most general and abstract principles of any topic about which we can have knowledge. These principles have consequences and, characteristically, they will be expressed in mathematical terms; we call the reason-based knowledge we have of these consequences 'mathematical knowledge'. By experiment and observation, we find that further consequences, also expressed in mathematical terms, are applicable to reality or to an idealised version of it; these further consequences are what scientists call hypotheses and, when we are able to verify that the specific predictions they entail are correct, then we can call the reason-based knowledge we have of these consequences 'scientific knowledge'. So far as reality itself is concerned, we can have no compelling grounds to suppose that it is mathematical or has a mathematical structure; rather, we are projecting a mathematical structure on reality, for that is the only way we can have of it what we are prepared to count as knowledge. Whatever may be the language in which the book of nature is written, we need the language of mathematics in order to understand it.

If the weakness of an empiricist theory of scientific knowledge arose from its failure to recognise and account for the part played by mathematics in the physical sciences, the corresponding weakness of this alternative theory was its failure to give due weight to the part played by experiment in the physical sciences, especially those which began as experimental or 'Baconian' sciences, such as chemistry, magnetism and electricity. Moreover, and despite strictures about the fallibility of sense experience, it is hard to resist the thought that perception, perhaps especially visual perception, does yield certainty – and thus knowledge – about what is perceived. Short of a thoroughgoing and corrosive scepticism, which might in any case affect what we claim to know on a priori as well as empirical grounds, many of the beliefs we acquire through sense experience have the practical certainty that is required for scientific knowledge. When we observe the patterns made by the stars, when we observe the interference fringes produced by passing monochromatic light through two adjacent slits, when we observe the fossil remains found in the Paris geological basin, we may be dreaming or hallucinating, but that possibility should not and does not deter us from claiming that, for all practical purposes, we are certain that stars, interference fringes and fossils exist and that they have at least some of the characteristics we attribute to them.

Henri Poincaré, the French mathematician, physicist and philosopher of science, expressed these contrasting views about scientific knowledge in terms of national character. The empirical, experimental approach he identified with the English; they, he said, 'wish to make the world out of what we see with the unaided eye'. The a priori, mathematical approach he identified with the French; they, he said, 'want to make it out of formulas'. 'Both', he added, 'would make the unknown out of the known, and their excuse is that there is no way of doing otherwise' (Poincaré 1946: 7).

Poincaré did not mention what could be described as the German contribution to this debate, namely Immanuel Kant's answer to the question about how it is possible for us to have a priori knowledge of matters of fact. On the face of it, this is impossible: if we know something a priori, or independently of experience, then that knowledge cannot be of what is synthetic, or factually true. David Hume had insisted that any true proposition is either a truth of reason, and knowable a priori, or a truth of fact, established by observation or experiment, and therefore knowable only empirically. If he is right, then the *apriorist* cannot correctly describe the scientist's task as one of identifying principles that are both factually true and demonstrable a priori, i.e. arrived at by mathematical reasoning but true of the world. In Kant's view, though, that description is correct even though the *apriorist* has failed to show how it could be; Hume was wrong to deny the existence of synthetic propositions known a priori. There are such propositions, and some of them are to be found in the physical sciences. There must be such propositions, Kant argued, because our experience of the world and the thoughts which we are able to express about it in physical science would not be possible without them. Geometrical and arithmetical truths, for example, make claims – no doubt general and abstract ones – about the world; they are, that is, synthetic. But they are not experimentally justified, and we would not, Kant thought, abandon them as false on the basis of evidence; they are, that is, a priori. Similarly, there are universal categories in terms of which we experience and think about reality. We have to experience and think of reality as causally determined, as consisting of substances, and as exemplifying what Kant called 'community'. These categories are realised in scientific principles of Newtonian science: causality is expressed in the law of inertia; substance is expressed in the law that matter is conserved; and community is expressed in the law that action and reaction are equal and opposite. These principles have factual content, but we do not depend on experience for our knowledge of their truth; rather, the possibility of experience presupposes their truth, and our knowledge of them is a priori. Kant's argument in support of these claims is complex and perhaps not altogether successful. That part of it which establishes that we impose a conceptual structure on our experience and our thought, so that they become experience and thought about an objective reality, is cogently and powerfully expressed. The propositions which express this conceptual structure would be synthetic truths which we know a priori. The less convincing part of the argument concerns the attempt to identify some key propositions in physical science – in Newton's mathematical physics in fact – as expressions of this conceptual structure (see Kant 1933: B169–B349; Kant 1953: 52–89).

Whatever we, with the benefit of hindsight, might think about the cogency of Kant's conclusions, he articulated with great insight the view of scientific knowledge and method which prevailed so successfully in continental Europe in the eighteenth century. The mathematical science of Newton's *Principia* yielded, he claimed, genuine knowledge of necessary truths about nature. This science was not simply a collection of 'empirical' laws. The inverse square law of gravitation, for example, is not a generalisation based upon observation or experiment; with the aid of principles which, though synthetic, are known a priori, we can – as Newton had claimed – deduce the law from phenomena. This law is, then, not a more or less probable conjecture or hypothesis which might be falsified or refuted by observation or experiment; we can be certain of its truth and we therefore count it as a scientific truth. By contrast, chemistry is not a 'proper natural science', but rather a 'systematic art or experimental doctrine'. This is because in chemistry 'the laws from which the given facts are explained ... are mere empirical laws [and] carry no consciousness of their necessity'. 'The principles of chemical phenomena', Kant declared, 'are incapable of the application of mathematics' (Kant 1970: 7–8).

Such a view, though not unreasonable if understood with reference to the eighteenth century, became increasingly implausible in the nineteenth century. In the first decade of the century John Dalton introduced the concept of atomic weight and began the mathematisation of chemistry. As a consequence, chemical laws began to seem as secure and as necessary as Newton's law of gravitation. It became apparent that the laws of chemical affinity, as well as laws of magnetic and electrostatic attraction, crystallisation, heat propagation, etc., could, like the law of gravitation, be formulated in mathematical terms. But Kant did not allow for the possibility that conclusions concerning knowledge and method in Newton's mathematical physics might need to apply also to knowledge and method in these new and rapidly developing sciences. With respect to nineteenth-century science the exclusivity of his conclusions made them seem less than convincing.

Despite its limitations, Kant's claim that real scientific knowledge contains a priori elements remained influential in the nineteenth century. A version of it was prominent in Whewell's idea that scientific knowledge requires that theories and facts, thought and things, are brought together. Experience provides the matter for our knowledge whereas conceptual structures provide the form; these structures consist of components supplied from our own resources, and our knowledge of their truth is a priori. He claimed that there were a certain limited number of 'Fundamental Ideas' which we use in creating conceptual structures and which made scientific knowledge possible.

For example, the Fundamental Idea of space makes geometrical knowledge possible; the Fundamental Idea of cause makes knowledge in the several mechanical sciences possible; the Fundamental Idea of likeness makes, he said, knowledge of systematic mineralogy possible. There are similarities with Kant's programme, but the differences are perhaps more conspicuous. Whewell's a priori 'ideas' were derived from the patterns he thought he could see in the history of science, whereas Kant's forms of intuition and categories have, he claimed, a basis in logic.

One effect of this move away from a traditional empiricist understanding of scientific knowledge, and from an experimentalist account of scientific method, was to direct attention to the nature of theory and hypothesis. It might still be possible to understand a true hypothesis as providing information about objective reality going beyond, or 'transcending', the information provided by observation or experiment. But it was difficult to see how hypotheses understood in this way could be justified as true. Hypothetical reasoning was, to be sure, a method of reasoning which purported to give investigators evidence-transcending information about reality, but from a logical point of view its cogency was questionable. Perhaps, though, we can have good reasons for accepting hypotheses if we understand them in a different way. If they express, not facts, but conditions for the possibility of experiencing and understanding objective facts, then we would expect to justify them by using deductive reasoning from first principles. Hypotheses, so-called, would not be 'evidence-transcending'; we would not, that is, suppose that by using our reasoning powers we could determine truths about objective reality inaccessible to perception. They would not be truths imposed upon us by reality but rather truths we impose upon reality. The empiricist ideal of scientific knowledge being knowledge of truths which straightforwardly represent reality, and of our having that knowledge on the basis of secure reasoning from experimental evidence, seemed unattainable. Its replacement was an ideal according to which scientific knowledge was knowledge of an objective reality by virtue of incorporating a priori elements. Different versions of this ideal identified different ways in which elements of our knowledge, including hypotheses, could be a priori. For Kant, hypotheses could be a priori because they stated conditions for the possibility of knowledge of an objective reality. In his view, for example, the hypothesis that the physical space in which we live has a Euclidean geometrical structure is true, not in the sense that it correctly records facts, including any evidence-transcending facts, about the geometrical structure of objective spatial reality, but rather in the sense that we could not have or understand our experience as experience of an objective geometrical reality unless it is true. For Whewell, hypotheses are a priori because all scientific knowledge is 'antithetical', involving thought as well as things, theories as well as facts, necessary truths as well as experiential truths, and hypotheses express the necessary truths deriving from the 'Fundamental Ideas' which we contribute to scientific knowledge.

Henri Poincaré proposed a modest version of this Kantian ideal. As a scientist he was aware of the power of experiment and of the impressive accomplishments of the experimental sciences in the nineteenth century. But he was also convinced that, as he put it, 'a reality completely independent of the mind which conceives it, sees or feels it, is an impossibility'. His suggestion was that, although some hypotheses are best understood as descriptions, true or false, of an objectively real world, other hypotheses are best understood as conventions. Some hypotheses are adopted, that is, not because we have derived them from experiment or because our cognitive powers are such that they cannot but be accepted, but rather because we have chosen to adopt them. Our choice of a convention 'is guided by experimental facts; but it remains free' (Poincaré 1952: 50). Principal among the hypotheses Poincaré counted as conventions were claims about the structure of physical space expressed in the axioms of Euclidean geometry. We choose to adopt these axioms because they implicitly define geometrical concepts in the most useful and convenient way. We could have chosen to adopt different, non-Euclidean, axioms such as those used by Lobatschewsky or by Riemann in the novel geometries they had developed earlier in the nineteenth century. Analogously, Poincaré claimed, we could have chosen to weigh things in kilogrammes rather than in pounds, ounces and other 'imperial' measures; we could have chosen to measure temperature in Celsius's units rather than in those of Fahrenheit. In geometry, as in these other cases, the choices we make are not arbitrary; they are influenced, but not determined, by experience, observation and experiment, for we may find the consequences of one choice easier, more convenient or simpler than the consequences of another. We do, to this extent, 'impose' a particular geometry on reality, rather than discover a geometry in reality.

Poincaré's conventionalism about geometry is closely associated with his 'relationist' view about space, which claimed that there is no such entity as space, over and above spatial relations of physical objects, which geometrical 'theories' – such as Euclid's – describe correctly or incorrectly. 'Space', he declared, 'is only a word that we have believed a thing' (Poincaré 1946: 5; cf. Stump 1989: 346). An important consequence of this is that the experience which guides the choice of a geometry is not direct experience of space itself, for there is no such thing, but rather experience of physical objects with geometrical shapes, and of rays of light which make straight lines. So, although the axioms and theorems of a geometry are conventions, they are not true by convention, because there is no such thing as space for them to be true of, even though the experience relevant to the conventions is experience of real things.

Poincaré's argument might seem of little relevance to science. Geometrical knowledge was usually considered immune to experimental or observational testing and not, therefore, a good example of scientific knowledge. To describe that knowledge as conventional, therefore, would not have important implications for scientific method. However, the creation of non-Euclidean geometries in the nineteenth century had shown that this way of thinking about geometry was unsatisfactory. It had shown that Kant was wrong in claiming that we have to experience and think about space in Euclidean terms; Euclidean geometry was, for the first time, recognised as a mathematical structure capable of functioning as a theory about physical space, and the theorems it contained might or might not be hypotheses correctly describing physical space. On the face of it, careful observation and experiment did seem to have a role to play in deciding whether this Euclidean geometry or one of its new competitors applied to real space. In good Baconian fashion, 'crucial' experiments were proposed to decide between Euclid and his competitors. Astronomical observations of the parallax of fixed stars, for example, might yield information which would oblige us to decide one way rather than another. Perhaps the correct geometry could be 'deduced from the phenomena'; perhaps investigators would need to employ hypothetical reasoning. But Poincaré was as sure that geometrical knowledge is not experimental as he was that it is not a priori. Kant was right in his conclusion that geometrical knowledge is independent of experience even if he was mistaken in his reasons for this conclusion. Geometrical knowledge is not knowledge at all; we no more know that the interior angles of a triangle sum to two right angles, and not to less than or more than two right angles, than we know that the temperature is 16 degrees Celsius, and not 61 degrees Fahrenheit. In the light of observation and experiment, investigators adopt the hypotheses of a geometry as conventions, but observation and experiment do not oblige investigators to accept these hypotheses as true or probably true descriptions of space. Prior to the discovery of non-Euclidean geometries, scientific method had only a minimal role in geometrical investigation. Poincaré's conventionalism showed that, despite that discovery, scientific method would still be of little help in geometrical investigations.

A second area in which conventions are prominent is classical mechanics. Here Poincaré's view was that, although Newton's three laws of motion have their origins in experiment, the role they play in mechanics is that of conventions. For example, the first law – the law of inertia – claims that objects not acted on by a force continue at rest or in uniform motion in a straight line. Inertial motion, that is to say, is uniform velocity. Newton certainly believed this law to have an experimental basis, and evidence relating to circumstances which approximate to those where the law applies does appear to support the law. But the law is used in mechanics in such a way that we would allow no experimental evidence to count against it; 'no one seriously thinks that the law . . . will ever be abandoned or amended' (Poincaré 1952: 95). In every case where a force seems to be acting on an object moving with uniform velocity we will claim that there is an equal and opposite force also acting; where an object is moving with non-uniform velocity we will take that fact as showing that a force is operating on the body, even if that force cannot be detected independently. But although the inertia law cannot be contradicted by experiment, it is not an a priori principle. It 'is not imposed upon us a priori' and there are other incompatible laws which are 'quite as compatible with . . . reason' (Poincaré 1952; 92).

In general, the laws of motion are 'truths founded on experiment and approximately verified'; but unlike other experimental laws they are 'regarded as rigorously true'. They 'possess a generality and a certainty which are lacking to the experimental verities whence they are drawn', because 'they reduce in the last analysis to a mere convention'. They are not, though, arbitrary in the sense that we could have adopted other conventions. They would only be arbitrary 'if we lost sight of the experiments which led the founders of the science [of mechanics] to adopt them, and which . . . were sufficient to justify their adoption' (Poincaré 1952: 110). We have adopted these conventions 'because certain experiments have shown us that it would be convenient'. Moreover, unlike geometrical conventions, we can describe the principles of mechanics as true. For the experimental basis on which we select conventions as convenient has to do with the properties and behaviour of solid objects. Indeed, 'our fundamental experiments are pre-eminently physiological experiments, which refer, not to the space which is the object that geometry must study, but to our body – that is to say, to the instrument which we use for that study'. Accordingly, 'the fundamental conventions of mechanics and the experiments which prove to us that they are convenient, certainly refer to the same objects or to analogous objects' (Poincaré 1952: 137). So, the three laws of motion, though conventions, are nevertheless true of the real world that we investigate before deciding to adopt them.

There is something puzzling in the idea that a principle or law correctly described as a convention can nevertheless have what appears to be a fact-stating role. Poincaré's geometrical conventionalism sits easily with, and to some extent is a consequence of, his view about space, namely that it is not something over and above the spatial relations between objects. But his mechanical conventionalism might seem to amount to little more than the claim that the Newtonian laws are particularly securely established. A convention is something we decide to adopt, and however firmly one insists that the decision to adopt a Newtonian law of motion is not arbitrary, it remains mysterious how something we decide to adopt can have a fact-stating function unless the decision to adopt it is based on its fulfilling that function. If we decide to adopt a Newtonian law because experiment shows that it fulfils a fact-stating function, then we should not describe it as a convention but as an experimental law; if, conversely, we describe it as a convention, then the decision to adopt it will be unconnected with experimental evidence about any fact-stating role it might have (see Sklar 1976: 119–46).

Perhaps this uncomfortable dilemma lay behind Poincaré's resistance to a thoroughgoing conventionalism. Not all hypotheses in science, and certainly not all scientific claims, are conventions; conventions are created by scientists, but facts including those stated in true scientific laws certainly are not. He identified Kepler's laws about the behaviour of planets, Newton's inverse square law, and the laws governing the relations between temperature, pressure and volume of gases as claims which are accepted on the basis of experiment and observation. These laws are hypothetical in that they provide information about circumstances which have not been, or cannot be, investigated. But our acceptance of them as stating the truth in those circumstances is a consequence not of a conventional decision but of probabilistic reasoning.

Poincaré could not, then, escape the question whether justification by probabilistic reasoning is satisfactory. His resource for answering this question was the 'calculus of probabilities', of which he was a prominent exponent. Thus, although we may find that all our observations are in accord with, say, Newton's gravitation law, it remains possible that this is a 'simple fact of chance' and that the law is in fact false. 'To this objection', he said, 'the only answer you can give is: It is very improbable'. Consequently, 'from this point of view all the sciences would only be unconscious applications of the calculus of probabilities' (Poincaré 1952: 186). When experiments reveal a uniformity, we reason probabilistically to the conclusion that the cause of this observed uniformity is a universal uniformity. And this reasoning, Poincaré claimed, is inverse probabilistic reasoning, or reasoning from the occurrence of an effect to the occurrence of its cause. A proposed cause has effects and successful detection of a sufficient number of them cannot, we think, be due to chance; so we conclude that this cause is responsible for those effects. Similarly, a proposed hypothesis has consequences and successful verification of a sufficient number of them enables us to 'declare that the hypothesis is confirmed, for so much success could not be due to chance'; we conclude, that is, that the truth of this hypothesis is the reason for the success of the verifications. It is because the probability of that success is so small given the falsity of the hypothesis, compared with its probability given the truth of the hypothesis, that we are entitled to accept the hypothesis. This sort of reasoning, he declared, must be legitimate, 'otherwise all science would be impossible' (Poincaré 1914: 89).

So Poincaré believed, as did Whewell, that surprising or unexpected phenomena provide powerful support for the hypotheses predicting them. If a hypothesis can explain existing data that would otherwise be inexplicable, or can successfully predict phenomena which would otherwise not be expected, then its probability is enhanced. We compare the probability of a phenomenon's occurrence given that a hypothesis is true with the probability of its occurrence given the hypothesis is false, and because the former is very much greater than the latter, we conclude that the probability of the hypothesis' truth given the phenomenon's occurrence is very much greater than the probability of its falsity given the same information. But the soundness of this inference depends crucially on it being the case that, before this information is considered, the hypothesis in question is just as likely to be false as it is likely to be true. It depends, that is, on the 'prior' probabilities being equal. Suppose, for example, that we have assembled experimental evidence concerning a new alloy, all of which is consistent with the hypothesis that there is a simple linear relationship between its temperature and its electrical resistance; if we double, or halve, the temperature, then electrical resistance will double or halve. It might well seem that because this evidence is improbable on the assumption that the hypothesis is false, but probable on the assumption that it is true, we should regard the evidence as supporting the truth of the hypothesis. We can, that is to say, reason from this evidence to the conclusion that a degree of certainty is attributable to the hypothesis. In effect, we are arguing from the evidence to a high probability for the proposed 'cause' of this evidence, namely the truth of the simple linear hypothesis. But this same evidence could have been the 'effect' of other 'causes' or hypotheses. If we are to calculate the probability of any cause, given certain of its supposed effects, we must determine 'in advance what is the *a priori* probability for the cause to come into play' (Poincaré 1952: 204). Certainly, any other available evidence should be taken into account in determining the required a priori, or prior, probability of the supposed cause or hypothesis. This other evidence may, after all, be incompatible with the existence of the cause or the truth of the hypothesis, in which case the prior probability of the cause's existence or the hypothesis' truth will be very small compared with the prior probability of non-existence or falsity. So, even though it is improbable that the cause is not responsible for the effect, or that the hypothesis is false, given the experimental evidence we have assembled, it could be even more improbable that the cause is responsible, or that the hypothesis is true, given all the relevant evidence.

Mill's objections apply to Poincaré just as much as they applied to Whewell. Even in the absence of other experimental evidence it is wrong to suppose that the prior probability of the truth of a hypothesis which explains evidence is equal or approximately equal to the prior probability of its falsity, even in the absence of other experimental evidence. For there will always be an indefinitely large number of hypotheses which fit the evidence just as well as the chosen hypothesis, but which must be false if it is true. There is, then, nothing at all to justify our selection of this hypothesis as the one whose prior probability exceeds the sum of the probabilities of all its competitors. Why indeed should its probability be any different from the probability of any of these competitors? If there is no good reason, and we recognise that the number of the competitors is very large, then the prior probability of the selected hypothesis will be, at best, very small. New evidence may augment this probability but we would still be a long way from achieving a respectable degree of certainty for the hypothesis.

Poincaré's response to these issues was to claim that judgements of prior probability are conventional judgements. We can only calculate the probability of a hypothesis given certain evidence if we have determined the probability of the hypothesis independently of that evidence. And this determination is a matter of adopting 'a convention more or less justified' (Poincaré 1952: 204). When we have no other relevant evidence and claim that the hypothesis is just as likely as not to be true, the justification for our claim is not our ignorance of reasons favouring or disfavouring its truth, but a conventional decision that the prior probabilities of truth and falsity are equal. But unlike the conventions of geometry and mechanics, this convention, as Poincaré acknowledged, is not 'guided' by what observation or experiment may indicate is convenient or simple. We may have recourse to the 'principle of sufficient reason' in choosing conventions about prior probabilities, but we need to appreciate that 'this principle is very vague and very elastic'. Consequently, any convention we choose in order to calculate a probability 'has always something arbitrary about it'. Nevertheless, in Poincaré's view this does not mean that the conclusions reached by probabilistic reasoning are useless and therefore unable to determine belief. For without these conventions, 'all science would be impossible' (Poincaré 1952: 210).

When, for example, we wish to determine a scientific law on the basis of experimental measurements, we reason from the measurements, as effects, to a law, as their cause. Different laws can give rise to the same measurements, just as different causes can give rise to the same effects. The problem we have to resolve is which of these different laws is the most probable. 'But', as Poincaré pointed out, 'the problem has no meaning if before the observations I had an *a priori* idea of the probability of this law or that' (Poincaré 1952: 205). This, though, does not seem to be a satisfactory way of defending the conventionality of judgements about prior probabilities. Perhaps we do need to use arbitrary conventions in order to reach conclusions, but that in itself will not make the conclusions acceptable. It may be, as Poincaré claimed, that some conventional decisions about prior probabilities, though arbitrary, have less influence on the conclusions reached than others, but again this will not make those conclusions which are more independent any more acceptable. How, we might ask, can a conclusion be independent of a convention if that conclusion could not be reached without the aid of the convention?

An appeal to the conventionality of prior probability judgements does not, then, seem to provide a convincing resolution of problems about applying inverse probabilistic reasoning to justify degrees of certainty for hypotheses. This is not surprising, given the long-standing debate about the use of probability in understanding and defending hypothetical reasoning in science. For Poincaré, the central issue was how far we can understand science as reporting on reality as we find it, and how far we can understand science as imposing conceptual structures on reality so that we can understand it. Theories of scientific method would have to reflect judgements on this issue, and any problems that might arise for such theories, though we would have to face and resolve them, would be of secondary concern. It is unsurprising, therefore, that Poincaré's theory of scientific method was not properly worked out and did not answer fundamental criticisms of hypothetical reasoning and the use of inverse probabilistic reasoning to justify it. His contemporary, Pierre Duhem, however, found an effective way of marginalising theories about scientific method and of evading any problems they engender. For he developed the idea of convention in science so that reasoning from experiment to the conclusion that a hypothesis is true assumed at best a minor role in his understanding of scientific method.

Though his interests and achievements lie in the history and philosophy of science, Duhem was educated and employed as a physicist. For most of his working life he was Professor of Physics at Bordeaux University. His work in hydrodynamics and in thermodynamics fell within the tradition promoted by French mathematical physicists such as Lagrange, Laplace and Fresnel in the early decades of the nineteenth century. It was uncompromising in its use of formal algebraic structures and in its resistance to mechanical hypotheses intended to exemplify these structures. Duhem wanted 'theory to be constructed with that logical rigour which the algebraists had taught us to admire'; but he also wanted to see theory as 'resting solidly on laws verified by experiment and completely exempt from those hypotheses about the structure of matter which Newton had condemned in his immortal General Scholium' (Duhem 1954: 276). For him, as for Poincaré, an abstract algebraic style was characteristic of Continental physics, whereas, despite Newton's strictures, British physicists such as James Clerk Maxwell and William Thompson (Lord Kelvin) favoured hypothetical models enabling one to interpret the mathematics. He realised, though, that the successes of British physics were encouraging some French and German scientists to abandon tradition, and wrote some of the more rhetorical passages of his *Aim and Structure of Physical Theory* in the hope that they would resist this trend. Partly because of his hostility to hypotheses and to mechanical models, he did not share the confidence of younger physicists such as Marie Curie and Jean Perrin in atomism. Consequently, he excluded himself from much that turned out to be at the forefront of physics in his lifetime. His hostile attitude to Einstein's momentous work on our concepts of space and time had similar consequences, though the reasons for it were different. Duhem seems to have set aside Einsteinian relativity because, in his view, it depended less on the discipline and understanding provided by an austere algebraic style than on the intuitive and imaginative appeal of a 'geometrical spirit'.

La théorie physique: son object et sa structure (The Aim and Structure of Physical Theory) first appeared as a sequence of connected essays in a philosophy journal, the *Revue de Philosophie*, for the years 1904 and 1905. It was published as a book in the following year. Duhem's view, though related to Poincaré's, was more radical in intention and was supported by quite different arguments. Reasoning in physical science, he claimed, was neither hypothetical, in the ordinary sense of that term, nor inductive. Hypotheses, as customarily understood, are claims about reality enabling us to understand the phenomena – or appearances – that we observe when we experiment. And if we allow that these hypotheses have a place in science, then we will suppose that scientific reasoning allows us to decide whether they are true, or probably true, accounts of that reality. To study hypothetical reasoning using ideas about how probabilities are measured or estimated is to study this kind of reasoning. But Duhem argued that physical theory does not and should not use hypotheses about reality. For the aim of physics is not to explain the appearances by making claims about an underlying and inaccessible reality, but simply to 'summarize and classify logically a group of experimental laws'. 'Our hypotheses', he declared, 'are not assumptions about the very nature of physical things'. Nothing is required of theories but that they provide for 'the economical condensation and classification of experimental laws' (Duhem 1954: 7, 219). Consequently, the choice of one hypothesis rather than another is not a matter of choosing between different descriptions of reality. Instead, it is a choice between more and less convenient ways of achieving the aim of the theory they contribute to. That is to say, the choice is a conventional choice. Scientific reasoning, in so far as it involves the choice of hypotheses, is not, therefore, probabilistic reasoning.

Duhem's argument against what he called 'the Newtonian method' provides further support for his claim about the conventionality of hypothesis choice. This method requires that any hypothesis 'be either a law drawn from observation by the sole use of . . . induction and generalization, or else a corollary mathematically deduced from such laws'. It corresponds to what Newton called 'deduction from the phenomena'. In the case of gravity, Kepler's three laws of planetary motion express the 'phenomena' and 'yield all the characteristics present in the action exerted by the sun on the planets'. In other words, deduction from these phenomena shows that each planet is attracted to the Sun by a force which is proportional to the product of the mass of the Sun and the mass of the planet, and inversely proportional to the square of the distance between the Sun and the planet. Finally, by legitimate generalisation of this conclusion, we arrive at the Newtonian law of gravitation, which states that every object – not just planets – is attracted to every other object – not just the Sun – by a force which is proportional to the product of their masses and inversely proportional to the square of the distance between them. But, Duhem declared, a closer and more careful examination of this reasoning shows that it is faulty. We cannot derive the principle of universal gravity from the Kepler laws, because that principle 'formally contradicts these laws'. 'If Newton's theory is correct', he said, 'Kepler's laws are necessarily false' (Duhem 1954: 190–3). The discrepancy arises because Newton's principle claims universal mutual attraction, so that the Sun is affected by a force exerted by a planet, however small, as well as each planet being affected by a force exerted by the Sun. If we could assume that the mass of the Sun is infinite compared with the mass of a planet, then there would be no discrepancy. But although this assumption is a reasonable approximation given the relative masses of the Sun and the planets, Duhem's claim of strict logical incompatibility remains correct.

The general point that Duhem insisted on was that it is impossible to base a general principle securely on observation or experimental evidence in the way that Newton and others had supposed. For we must first represent our observations and experimental evidence in a 'symbolic' form. We must represent them, that is, in an observational or experimental law. But there are always different ways of doing this, and some of the ways are incompatible not only with each other but with any general principle which we say is based on the evidence. Often we are tempted to suppose that there is only one way to generalise the evidence and to reach a conclusion about, say, the causes of the effects represented in the evidence. The Kepler–Newton example shows clearly that this is not so; some ways of symbolically representing the evidence are compatible with Newton's gravitation principle, but some, including the representations provided in Kepler's laws, are not. In this example, as in others, a choice faces us about how to represent evidence, and the fact that we can and do make that choice in a way that formally contradicts general principles shows that it is not evidence which forces the choice. We are, as Poincaré said in his discussions of geometry and mechanics, free to choose.

But Duhem's positive view is distinguishable from Poincaré's. In the first place, the generality of Duhem's arguments and thus the scope of his conventionalism is greater than Poincaré's. But, second, there are significant differences between the conventionalisms they proposed. In Poincaré's case, his insistence on a distinction between the conventionality of definitions in, say, geometry and the experimental character of laws and hypotheses in physics led him to deny that experimental evidence could ever result in a definition being abandoned. 'Euclidean geometry', he said, 'has nothing to fear from fresh experiments', because it is characterised by definitions of geometrical concepts which we have adopted as conventions (Poincaré 1952: 73). Duhem's conventionalism was different: for him, experimental evidence was certainly relevant to the adequacy of a hypothesis in physics, even though it could never force its acceptance or rejection. We always have to choose, but our choice is subject to constraints determined by available evidence, and since these constraints will vary from one time to another, our choice of convention can also vary from one time to another. If we take any individual hypothesis, we can bring evidence to bear on it only by employing, usually unconsciously, some other assumption, or hypothesis. Thus, to take a simple example, an experimental test of the claim that metals expand when they are heated will have to make use of an essential assumption, for unless we can assume that the test material is a metal, the experimental evidence concerning what happens when it is heated is not relevant. In the event of negative evidence, we have to decide how we should use it. In the example, if we are not prepared to abandon the claim that metals expand when heated, then, given that the test material has failed to expand when heated, we must relinquish the assumption that the test material is a metal. If, on the other hand, we are quite certain that the test material is a metal, then in those same circumstances we must give up the claim that all metals expand when heated. The evidence is relevant, but we have to choose how to use it, and that choice is conventional in the sense that it is determined by considerations of convenience and simplicity. 'Good sense' was Duhem's expression for the means by which scientists make choices about the distribution of relevant evidence, and what makes sense 'good' is judicious weighing of the available evidence. 'It is not enough', he said, 'to be a good mathematician and skilful experimenter; one must also be an impartial and faithful judge' (Duhem 1954: 218).

Can we, though, accept good sense as a reliable guide to truth? For example, creationists appeal to Biblical authority, together with more or less plausible assumptions about how that authority should be interpreted, in accounting for geological and biological facts. But good sense, we might think, indicates that we should prefer the explanations of those facts given by Charles Lyell and Charles Darwin. Nevertheless, even if we are right in so thinking, can we not still maintain the truth of creationism by refusing to concede that the good sense of uniformitarianism and the theory of natural selection obliges us to regard them as true? Theories have virtues other than that of truth, and we may wish to commend theories on account of such virtues. For Duhem, indeed, only these virtues should concern us in reaching scientific conclusions. For him, in adopting a theory, we look not for truth, which is in any case inaccessible to us, but for systematising power, for convenience, for simplicity. We are, of course, tempted to take these characteristics as indicators of truth, but in Duhem's view we can and should resist the temptation, for to succumb would be to step outside science and into metaphysics. These characteristics are worth having in a scientific theory, whether or not they signify truth. To this extent, then, the choices determined by good sense are scientifically valuable.

But even though we cannot assume that good sense will guide us towards truth, in appealing to it we assume we are appealing to objective standards. With respect to a particular decision, there are, no doubt, degrees of impartiality and faithfulness in the judgements scientists make using their good sense, but if those judgements varied from place to place, from time to time, or from person to person, they would have little value. We need to have some confidence that the conventional choices made by one person on the basis of good sense will be the same as, or at least very similar to, the choices made by another person. It seems doubtful, though, whether we can satisfy this requirement so long as we lack criteria to tell us when one theory is simpler, or more convenient, or more comprehensive, than another. Certainly we can use good sense to justify our adoption of 'conventional' scientific theories, but this is insufficient for rationality so long as creationists, flat-Earthers and others with 'unconventional' views can enlist their good sense to justify their choices.

Scientists often face conflicts between theory and evidence, and the question of when it is reasonable to abandon accepted hypotheses and when it is reasonable to change assumptions, including assumptions about the reliability of the evidence, is known as the 'Duhem problem'. Logic does not force scientists to take one course of action rather than another when such conflicts arise. They may nevertheless decide well or badly, reasonably or unreasonably, depending on whether they use good sense or not and on what they judge to be good sense. 'Certain opinions', Duhem said, 'which do not fall under the hammer of contradiction are in any case perfectly unreasonable'. But this is of little practical value in guiding decisions, so long as the reasons constituting good sense are, as Pascal had said, 'reasons which reason does not know' (Duhem 1954: 217). In the absence of an analysis of what good sense is, we have merely acknowledged, but not answered, Duhem's problem by referring to it.

We can express Duhem's answer to his problem, and the difficulties it presents, in terms of probabilities. For if the prior probability of an accepted hypothesis is high compared with the prior probability of auxiliary assumptions, we can reasonably blame those assumptions for any apparent conflict between evidence and hypothesis. If, on the other hand, the prior probability of a hypothesis is low compared with that of auxiliary assumptions, then it will be reasonable to abandon the hypothesis. However, unless we can give prior probability judgements an objective basis, the difficulty with good sense as a suitable basis for decisions will reappear. But proving an objective basis for prior probabilities means recourse to an a priori principle such as Leibniz's principle of sufficient reason. The alternative is that defenders of eccentric science will use their subjective judgements of prior probabilities to justify their beliefs, just as defenders of conventional science use their judgements of prior probabilities to justify their beliefs.

For example, before Augustin Fresnel's creation of a satisfactory wave theory of light in the 1820s, evidence which appeared to conflict with Newton's corpuscular theory was used to modify auxiliary assumptions rather than to refute the theory, because the prior probability of Newton's theory was much higher than the prior probability of those assumptions. Thus, experimental evidence concerning the diffraction of light could be reconciled with the theory by modifying assumptions. One important reason for the high prior probability of Newton's theory was the lack of a satisfactory alternative. The good sense and prior probability judgements of most scientists implied that the decisions taken, though conventional in the sense that they were not forced by evidence, were rational. There was, though, nothing to prevent a dissenting scientist from taking a different view about the requirements of good sense and about prior probabilities. Such a scientist could have concluded that the rational choice was to abandon Newton's theory in the light of the conflicting evidence. We can, it seems, resolve such a disagreement about what is rational only by making prior probabilities objective. To do this, however, we must overcome stubborn obstacles.

For both Poincaré and Duhem, hypothetical reasoning was the key to scientific method. Poincaré took the view that the scope for hypothetical reasoning was rather less than was commonly supposed, because some crucial scientific principles in geometry and mechanics were secured as conventions we decide to adopt rather than as hypotheses which evidence enables us to accept. There are, nevertheless, important parts of science where we must use probabilistic arguments to establish that conjectured hypotheses give a correct account of reality. Duhem's attitude to hypothetical reasoning was coloured by his view about hypotheses. Hypotheses, he argued, are not to be understood as correct or incorrect accounts of reality but simply as means for systematising evidence symbolised in experimental laws. It would, therefore, be a misconception to search for a type of reasoning which will enable us to tell whether, and to what extent, a hypothesis is probably true. This, no doubt, is why there is no discussion of probable reasoning in Duhem's philosophy of science. Nevertheless, hypothetical reasoning, properly understood, is reasoning in accordance with 'good sense', and results in decisions about which hypotheses should be accepted and which rejected. Probable reasoning, therefore, is essential for Duhem. As we have seen, his appeal to good sense is readily understood as an appeal to probabilities. Duhem's conventionalist account of scientific method does indeed entail new ideas about both experimental and theoretical discourse, but it supplements rather than supplants analyses of probable reasoning. It served, indeed, to highlight some questions which those analyses must address and which exercised an important role in the development of ideas about scientific method in the twentieth century.

FURTHER READING

For a useful broad view of conventionalism, see:
Gillies, D. (1993) *Philosophy of Science in the Twentieth Century: Four Central Themes*, Oxford: Blackwell; chs 3, 4 and 5.

For Poincaré's writings on the philosophy of science, see:
Poincaré, H. (1914) *Science and Method*, translated by F. Maitland, London: Thomas Nelson.
Poincaré, H. (1952) *Science and Hypothesis*, translated by W. J. G., New York: Dover.
Poincaré, H. (1958) *The Value of Science*, translated by W. J. G., New York: Dover.

The following contains other translations of all three of the above:
Poincaré, H. (1946) *The Foundations of Science: Science and Hypothesis; The Value of Science; Science and Method*, translated by G. B. Halsted, Lancaster, Pa.: The Science Press.

Poincaré's philosophy is discussed in:
Sklar, L. (1976) *Space, Time, and Spacetime*, Berkeley: University of California Press; ch. 2.
Giedymin, J. (1982) *Science and Convention: Essays on Henri Poincaré's Philosophy of Science and the Conventionalist Tradition*, Oxford: Pergamon Press.
Stump, D. (1989) 'Henri Poincaré's philosophy of science', *Studies in the History and Philosophy of Science* 20: 335–63.
Giedymin, J. (1991) 'Geometrical and physical conventionalism of Henri Poincaré in Epistemological Formulation', *Studies in the History and Philosophy of Science* 22: 1–22.

Psillos, S. (1996) 'Poincaré's conception of mechanical explanation', in G. Heinzmann *et al.* (eds), *Proceedings of the Congrés International Henri Poincaré*, Berlin/Paris: Akademie Verlag and Éditions Blanchard.

For Duhem's philosophy of science, see:
Duhem, P. (1954) *The Aim and Structure of Physical Theory*, translated by P. P. Wiener, Princeton, NJ.: Princeton University Press.
Duhem, P. (1969) *To Save the Phenomena*, translated by S. L. Jaki, Chicago: University of Chicago Press.

A biography of Duhem is provided in:
Jaki, S. L. (1987) *Uneasy Genius: The Life and Work of Pierre Duhem*, Dordrecht: Nijhoff.

Duhem's philosophy, and its relation to the recent views of Quine, is discussed in:
Vuillemin, J. (1986) 'On Duhem's and Quine's theses', in L. E. Hahn and P. A. Schilpp (eds), *The Philosophy of W. V. Quine*, Library of Living Philosophers, La Salle, Ill.: Open Court.

8   John Venn and Charles Peirce

Probabilities as frequencies

Throughout the nineteenth century there were scientists and logicians who shared Laplace's view that we could, at least in principle, measure and compare degrees of certainty in scientific conclusions using the mathematics of probability. Thus, in the *Philosophical Magazine*, a distinguished journal for the mathematical sciences, we find a contributor declaring in 1851 that 'every definite state of belief concerning a proposed hypothesis, is in itself capable of being represented by a numerical expression, however difficult or impractical it may be to ascertain its actual value' (Donkin 1851: 354). Many placed much confidence in the capacity of inverse probabilistic reasoning to yield quantitative degrees of belief, and to reassure those who doubted the legitimacy of inductive and hypothetical reasoning. The economist and logician W. Stanley Jevons explained the fundamental idea clearly. Deduction, he said, allows us to reason from general scientific claims to particular conclusions which we can check experimentally, and we should understand induction as the inverse of deduction, for by means of it we reason from particular experimental data to general scientific conclusions. In deductive reasoning we sometimes use the mathematical theory of probability, and when we do so we are using it in a direct manner. For example, the degree of certainty that we have in a particular conclusion deduced from general scientific premises will depend, in ways determined by the theory of probability, upon the degrees of certainty we attach to those premises. Thus, Darwin's theory of evolution had deductive implications for what the fossil record would reveal, and confidence in that theory would have an effect upon confidence in what the fossil record would show. But, just as we need probability theory in assessing the credibility of conclusions of deductive arguments, so we need probability theory in assessing the credibility of conclusions of inductive arguments, only in this case we have to use it in an inverse manner. Using inverse probabilistic reasoning, we may argue 'from the known character of certain events . . . to the probability of a certain law or condition governing those events'. And, 'having satisfactorily accomplished this work, we may [using direct probabilistic reasoning] calculate forwards to the probable character of future events happening under the same conditions' (Peirce 1931–58: 1.276).

One significant advantage of employing inverse probabilistic reasoning is that, because all such reasoning is mathematical and deductive, scientific method becomes exempt from the traditional criticism that it is rationally indefensible. The inductive reasoning that we use in scientific method is, we may say, an inverse application of deductive reasoning. Given the close association between Laplace and inverse probabilistic reasoning, it is not surprising, therefore, that he is sometimes credited with a justification of induction. David Hume, who first drew attention to the importance and the difficulty of justifying induction, had supposed that, in order to make our confidence in inductive conclusions rational, we need to adopt a general principle about the future being 'like' the past, or about nature being 'uniform'. The inductive scepticism he expressed was the result of acknowledging that such principles could only be adopted as inductive conclusions themselves. His successors, such as Bayes, Price and Laplace, had used the idea that confidence in inductive conclusions is a matter of degree, and that the theory of probability contains resources for measuring the degrees of confidence we are entitled to have in those conclusions. Experimental evidence does not enable us to give a conclusive proof of a general scientific claim, but by using inverse probabilistic reasoning we can, given the relevant evidence, assign a probability to the claim. And this probability is a measure of the degree of certainty that the evidence entitles us to have in the truth of the claim. The reasoning leading to this degree of certainty is mathematical and deductive; we have, therefore, justified inductive reasoning by showing that it is really disguised deductive reasoning.

However, although deductive arguments may be immune to doubts about whether their conclusions are true given that their premises are true, they are certainly not immune to doubt about whether their conclusions are true. For the conclusion of a deductive argument is only as secure as the premises from which it is drawn. So, if by inductive scepticism we understand the view that we have no good reason for attributing any degree of certainty to the truth of a general scientific claim, then we can sustain that scepticism by alleging that there is a false premiss among those justifying the attribution of such degrees of certainty. This was indeed the view taken by critics of inverse probabilistic reasoning, and to appreciate its force we need to be clear about the strengths and the weaknesses of such reasoning.

In science, when we seek to justify the acceptance of a law, or a hypothesis or a theory, we reason from facts that we count as known to the probable truth of a reason for those facts. Such reasoning is by no means confined to science. Detectives trying to solve a crime use it; so do bridge players when they make judgements about what contracts are possible; so do traffic accident investigators; so do medical practitioners diagnosing illnesses from symptoms; so do teachers using tests to assess the abilities of students; and so do many others. And in as much as detectives, card players, accident investigators, medical practitioners, teachers and others reason in ways that follow a pattern sanctioned in science, we can say that they use the scientific method. In general, whatever the facts might be, we will be able to account for them in different and incompatible ways. Thus Darwin's theory of evolution provides reasons for the facts about speciation which Darwin found so striking; but other theories provide other reasons for those same facts. How, in such circumstances, can we claim that the facts in question make Darwin's theory probably true, or more probable than other theories? Consider a different but simpler case in which we confront an analogous question. We are informed that a coin has been tossed ten times and has shown heads each time. Among the possible causes for this effect we have to consider only two: either the coin is double-headed, or it is a conventional unbiased coin with a head and a tail. How can we claim, as we unhesitatingly do, that in the light of the information provided it is probably true that the coin is double-headed? To answer this question we appeal to what Jevons called the 'principle of the inverse method' (Jevons 1874: 279): if an effect can be produced by any one of a certain number of different causes, the probabilities of the existence of these causes as inferred from the effect are proportional to the probabilities of the effect as derived from these causes. In our coin example, it is clear that the probability of the effect observed is very much greater if we assume that it is caused by the double-headed coin than if we assume that it is caused by the unbiased coin; consequently, given the observed sequence, the probability that the coin is double-headed is very much greater than the probability that it is unbiased.

But the general principle licensing this simple example of inverse probabilistic reasoning depends crucially upon an unstated assumption, namely that the prior probabilities of the alternative causes or reasons are equal. So, in the example, we have to assume that, if we knew the coin selected was either double-headed or unbiased but knew nothing of what would happen when it is tossed, we would judge the coin just as likely double-headed as unbiased. Suppose, though, that we knew that the coin producing the observed sequence was selected at random from a collection of more than two coins, only one of which was double-headed. Then our confidence in the conclusion we drew about the reason for the observed sequence would be reduced; the assumption of equal prior probabilities would no longer hold. Indeed, if the collection of coins was very large we might have no confidence in the conclusion that the double-headed coin had been selected, or at least no more confidence in this conclusion than in its alternative. We can measure the probability that the coin is double-headed if we know how large the collection of coins is, for then we will be able to say how much smaller the prior probability of the coin being double-headed is than the prior probability of it being unbiased. But this is possible only because the example is such that we can identify cases of equal prior probability: in supposing that the selection of a coin from the collection was at random we are supposing, reasonably enough in practice, that it is just as likely we will select any one coin as any other.

And now the difficulty of applying the principle of the inverse method in a scientific context becomes plain. We may know of several different ways in which we can account for certain experimental or observed facts. We may think that some, perhaps most, are unlikely to be true. We may find, that is, that we can make comparative judgements about the prior probabilities of these different reasons for the facts. But unless we are able to make quantitative judgements and to claim that the prior probability of one reason is so many times greater than the prior probability of some other reason, we cannot make use of the principle. For example, we can account for the appearance of pairs and clusters of stars by supposing that the stars are distributed randomly, or by supposing that stars have a tendency to cluster together because of the operation of the law of gravity. We may calculate the probability that the stars would appear in pairs and clusters if they were randomly distributed, and the probability that they would so appear if they were subject to gravitational tendencies. But such calculations are of no use in reaching conclusions about the probabilities of the alternative suppositions unless we can make quantitative comparisons of the prior probabilities of the suppositions. It might be claimed that, prior to observation of the stars, we cannot have any reason for preferring either supposition to the other, and that therefore we should assign the same prior probability to each. Our ignorance, that is, entitles us to distribute our confidence in alternative beliefs equally. As the author of the *Philosophical Magazine* article put it: 'When several hypotheses are presented to our mind, which we believe to be mutually exclusive and exhaustive, but about which we know nothing further, we distribute our belief equally amongst them' (Donkin 1851: 354). Suspicions as to the soundness of this suggestion are aroused once we notice that, while we can reach conclusions about the probabilities of the suppositions with its aid, we deprive ourselves of them if we deny our ignorance.

In the eighteenth century, probabilists had used the idea of alternative events being equally easily produced. Jakob Bernoulli, for example, wrote of our need to identify possible outcomes or 'cases' as equally easily 'realised' if we are to apply the mathematics of chance beyond games and gambling. He and his contemporaries, however, were under no illusions as to the difficulty we face in showing that 'cases' are equally easily 'realised'. They did not suppose that ignorance was an adequate basis on which to base conclusions. Thomas Bayes, as we have seen, devised an ingenious arrangement of a level table on to which a ball is thrown at random, and it is his description of what is done and of what happens, rather than our ignorance, which assures us that each outcome can be produced equally easily, and that therefore each has the same probability. If we try to use ignorance as a basis for judgements of probability, we generate contradictions by characterising our ignorance in different ways. For example, the probability of a ball taken from a bag of coloured balls being red will be one-half, if we base our judgement on our ignorance as to whether the ball drawn is red or not; but it will be one-third if the basis of our judgement is ignorance as to whether the ball is red or blue or neither. We should base our probability judgements on empirical knowledge of proportions and frequencies, even if that means that they are fallible and subject to inductive scepticism. If we want to know the probability of a red ball being drawn from a bag of balls, we should observe what happens when balls are drawn from the bag and use the frequency with which red balls are drawn as our guide to the probability. However, analogous investigations are not always possible. The universe is presented to us only once, and we have to judge probabilities without the aid of empirically observed proportions and frequencies. We observe the way the universe is – the way the stars are distributed, the fact that the Sun rises and sets each day, etc. – and we realise that what we observe could have come about in a variety of ways. But we cannot take each of these possible causes and find out how frequently each one results in the observed universe, and thereby make judgements about the prior probabilities of each possible cause. Yet we need these prior probabilities if we are to reason from effects to causes, and if ignorance or indifference cannot provide evaluations of them, then the project of a scientific method as conceived by Price, Laplace and others in the eighteenth century would seem to fail.

A specific target for those nineteenth-century writers sceptical of inverse probabilistic reasoning was Laplace's 'rule of succession', which, as we have seen, declared that if an event has occurred n times and has never failed to occur then the probability that it will occur on a further occasion is $(n+1)/(n+2)$. For of the possible reasons for the observed fact that in given circumstances an event has occurred n times and never failed to occur, there are some which entitle us to predict that when those circumstances next occur the same event will recur, and Laplace had shown that the probability of one or other of these reasons being true is given by this rule of succession. So, for example, if we adopt the (then) conventional assumption that the Earth's history began five thousand years, or '1826213 days', ago 'and the sun having risen constantly in the interval at each revolution of twenty-four hours, it is a bet of 1826214 to one that it will rise again tomorrow' (Laplace 1951: 19). Later in the nineteenth century, Jevons endorsed the Laplacian view that, because 'events come out like balls from the vast ballot-box of nature', the rule of succession is essential if observation of those events is to 'enable us to form some notion . . . of the contents of that ballot-box'. So, for example, 'on the first occasion on which a person sees a shark, and notices that it is accompanied by a little pilot fish, the odds are 1 to 1, or the probability 1/2, that the next shark will be so accompanied' (Jevons 1874: 275, 299).

Jevons's example shows that, in the inverse reasoning used to derive the rule of succession, large assumptions about prior probabilities were made. For when the event whose occurrence is predicted has yet to occur for the first time, and therefore n is zero, the probability of its occurrence, according to the rule of succession, is 1/2. The Cambridge logician John Venn, who gave the rule the name by which it is known, referred specifically to Jevons's illustration when expressing his scepticism. The rule, he declared, is 'hard to take seriously', and it seems to have been the quantitative aspects of the rule which he was unable to accept. 'I cannot see', he said, 'how the Inductive problem can be even intelligibly stated, for quantitative purposes, on the first occurrence of any event' (Venn 1962: 197–8). Others shared his misgivings. The American logician Charles Saunders Peirce, after also noticing that, according to Laplace's rule, 'the probability of a totally unknown event is 1/2', said that it also implies that 'of all theories proposed for examination one half are true'. But this, he observed, is unacceptable, for 'we know that . . . nothing like one half turn out to be true' (Peirce 1931–58: 2.744). And in the twentieth century the economist and probability theorist John Maynard Keynes added a *reductio ad absurdum.* For, he pointed out, the rule of succession is a special case of a more general rule of inverse reasoning which states that if, in certain conditions, an event has happened n times and failed to happen m times, then the probability that it will happen when those conditions next recur is $(n+1)/(n+m+2)$. According to this more general rule, Keynes said, 'in the case where on the only occasion on which the conditions were observed, the event did not occur, the probability is 1/3'. But this consequence is absurd. No reasonable person would suppose that this fraction is a measure of the probability of an event, 'in favour of which no positive argument exists, the like of which has never been observed, and which has failed to occur on the one occasion on which the hypothetical conditions were fulfilled'. Indeed, if anyone were rash enough to accept this consequence, they would be 'involved in contradictions, – for it is easy to imagine more than three incompatible events which satisfy these conditions' (Keynes 1921: 377–8).

John Venn was born in 1834, and spent the greater part of his life as Fellow and, later, President of Gonville and Caius College in

Cambridge. He died in 1923. Each of his three books on logic – *Logic of Chance* (1866), *Symbolic Logic* (1881) and *Principles of Empirical Logic* (1889) – was widely used and valued in the late nineteenth century and early twentieth century. The second of them explains and develops the well known method of representing arguments, Venn diagrams. In the first he established himself as a founder, together with Augustus De Morgan and George Boole, of probability theory in the nineteenth century, though he differed from them in adopting an uncompromisingly empiricist interpretation of probability. Following the lead of Leslie Ellis he identified the probability of events with their statistical frequency of occurrence in the class of events to which they belong, rather than with the degree of belief we should have in their occurrence. For him, the statistical frequency, and therefore the probability of a certain type of event, could be high, without our believing to any high degree that an event of that type will occur.

Venn's opposition to inverse probabilistic reasoning arose as a result of his conviction that we should interpret probability judgements as, primarily, judgements about frequencies in series. He was among the first to promote this view. According to him we can indeed quantify the probability of a fifty-year-old person dying before their fifty-first birthday, or of the card we are about to deal being an ace, etc., because there are ratios which measure the frequency with which fifty-year-old people do die before their next birthday, namely the proportion, in a suitably large population, of those reaching a fiftieth birthday who will survive to their fifty-first, or the frequency with which a card we are about to deal is an ace, namely the proportion, in a suitably extensive experience, of cards which have turned out to be aces. A probability is, then, a 'statistical frequency of events'. If we use a numerical fraction to express the degree of certainty we have in the occurrence of an event in certain circumstances, then that fraction is a probability only if our experience shows that it represents the frequency with which events of this type occur in those circumstances (Venn 1962: 137, 165–6).

Venn proposed his frequentist way of understanding probability and its measurement in conscious opposition to the 'classical' view that probability has to do with degrees of belief in, among other things, the truth of scientific theories. The theory of probability, he said, 'is a portion of mathematics' rather than 'a branch of the general science of evidence which happens to make much use of mathematics' (Venn 1962: vii). For a frequentist, there is no sense in attributing a numerical probability as a measure of our degree of belief in a theory. If we did, we would be saying that a certain proportion of theories of this type are true, but nothing other than an arbitrary decision would enable us to count a theory as being one of this 'type'. Venn acknowledged that, in describing a belief as probable, we are not always referring to a frequency, but he did insist that, in so far as our confidence in the belief is measured by the mathematical theory of probability, then we will have to understand the extent of that confidence as a frequency. If the belief in question concerns a scientific theory and we cannot therefore understand our degree of confidence in it as a frequency, then we are mistaken in thinking that we can use the resources of probability theory in trying to assign a measure to that degree of confidence. In supposing otherwise, we would 'be obtaining solutions about matters on which the human intellect has no right to any definite quantitative opinion' (Venn 1962: 186). In effect, Venn's view was that the mathematics of probability has no more to do with the kind of reasoning we associate with scientific method than it has to do with reasoning of any other kind. The degrees of certainty that we have, or ought to have, in the conclusions reached by scientific method are not probabilities; degrees of certainty are subjective in that they report on our mental states, whereas probabilities are objective in that they report on frequencies we observe to hold respecting objects and events in a real world.

Not surprisingly, Venn doubted the worth of most attempts to use inverse probabilistic reasoning to quantify degrees of certainty in particular scientific conclusions. He rejected Arbuthnot's conclusion that the consistent slight preponderance of male over female births should be attributed to divine intervention, on the grounds that the alternative conclusion – that, 'chance governs' – covered a wider variety of possible reasons for the facts than Arbuthnot had supposed. As Nicholas Bernoulli (nephew of Jakob and cousin of Daniel) and others had pointed out, the supposition that chance is the reason for the observed preponderance covers many possibilities, not just the one considered by Arbuthnot, namely that the chance of a male birth is exactly the same as the chance of a female birth. And in the case of Michell's reasoning, Venn made it clear that, although it was legitimate to draw the conclusion that stars are not distributed at random but 'have a tendency to go in pairs', no credence should be given to the attempt to calculate a value for the probability of this conclusion being correct. The scope of the alternative hypotheses, particularly the randomness hypothesis, is, he claimed, too vague and uncertain to allow of any calculation.

Venn's American contemporary, Charles Saunders Peirce, shared his empiricist view of probability. This is perhaps surprising, given his philosophical interests in scholasticism, in Kant and in post-Kantian idealism. He coupled those interests with considerable mathematical skills, and it was as a mathematician that he was led to explore some innovative ideas in logic, including inductive logic and probabilistic reasoning. Though his friends, colleagues and admirers provided him with lecturing opportunities, and in his early forties he taught logic at Johns Hopkins University, he shunned an academic career. Together with William James, John Dewey and Herbert Mead, he contributed to the formulation and development of that version of empiricism we know as pragmatism; indeed it was Peirce who coined the term 'pragmatism'. His ideas about logic and scientific method were, and have continued to be, particularly influential, even though much of what he wrote is in a fragmentary or incomplete form, and reflects changes of mind.

Like Venn, Peirce insisted that probabilities should be interpreted in a 'material' rather than a 'conceptual' manner. We should, that is, interpret probabilities in terms of frequencies or proportions, rather than in terms of degrees of belief. 'Probability', he said, 'to have any value at all, must express a fact'; and 'it is, therefore, a thing to be inferred upon evidence'. The fact stated by a probability judgement is a ratio, or fraction, 'whose numerator is the frequency of a specific kind of event, whilst its denominator is the frequency of a genus embracing that species' (Peirce 1931–58: 2.677, 2.747). There are, Peirce agreed, some important connections between probabilities as frequencies and probabilities as degrees of belief. If, for example, experience shows that the frequency of heads among throws of a coin is 1/2, then a reasonable degree of belief in a given throw yielding a head is 1/2. Such connections lie at the heart of Peirce's account of the probable reasoning used in science, for in general such reasoning is as concerned as any other kind of reasoning with inculcating belief.

In his *Studies in Logic* of 1883, Peirce distinguished three different kinds of probable reasoning. The first involved inferring a particular conclusion from a general statistical claim. For example, if only 2 per cent of people wounded in the liver recover, then there is only a 1/50 probability that some particular person wounded in the liver will recover. In concluding that the probability of recovery has this value, and thus that a corresponding degree of belief in recovery is justified, we mean, Peirce said, 'that if we were to reason in that way, we should be following a mode of inference which would only lead us wrong, in the long run, once in fifty times'. He called this kind of inference 'simple probable deduction'. It is, in effect, reasoning from knowledge of a population to a belief about a single member of that population. We introduce some complexity to probable deduction if we consider reasoning from knowledge of a population to a belief about a sample from it. For example, if we know that 'a little more than half of all human births are male', then 'statistical deduction' allows us to conclude that 'probably a little over half of all the births in New York during any one year are males' (Peirce 1931–58: 2.697, 2.700). We should notice that the probability of the conclusion, even though it is a frequency of some sort, is not quantified. In qualitative terms we can say that it will be smaller or greater depending on the size of the sample, for we assume or know that, in arguments of this type, the proportion of times that true premisses yield true conclusions is higher when the sample size is greater.

A second kind of probable reasoning involves an inversion of probable deduction. We know the proportion of A's that are B's in a sample, and we draw a conclusion about the proportion of A's that are B's in the whole population. For example, if we find that nine-tenths of the coffee beans in a handful taken from a sack of beans are perfect, then we can conclude that about nine-tenths of all the beans in the sack are perfect. A familiar application of this kind of probable reasoning occurs in induction by enumeration: if all of the A's in a sample are B's, i.e. all the observed A's are B's, we conclude that all of the A's in the whole population are B's, i.e. all A's are B's. Peirce used the terms 'induction' and 'quantitative induction' to cover not just this particular application but this kind of probable reasoning in general. Once again, the probability of the conclusion we draw being correct is dependent on the size of the sample, but we would also expect the conclusion drawn to change. So, in the coffee bean example, we may find that in a larger sample, say ten handfuls, the percentage of perfect beans is not 90 per cent but 87 per cent, and the conclusion about the percentage of perfect beans in the sack would not only be more secure, or more probably true, than the previous conclusion, but it would also be the conclusion that 87 per cent and not 90 per cent of the beans are perfect.

As in the case of probable deductions, Peirce did not suppose that we can measure in a direct manner the probability of a conclusion drawn in a quantitative inductive argument. This is because we have to understand this probability – a frequency – as signifying the proportion of arguments of this type with this size of sample that yielded true conclusions from true premisses. If, for example, we were to claim that our original conclusion about the coffee beans, namely that 90 per cent of all the beans in the sack are perfect, has a probability of 0.8 of being true, then we would be claiming on empirical grounds that the frequency of arguments yielding true conclusions from true premisses among all arguments of that type involving that size of sample is 0.8. Clearly, we would find it difficult in practice to properly justify such a claim. However, just as reasoning from a population to a sample – probable deduction – is direct probabilistic reasoning, the proportion in the population being, as it were, the 'cause' of the 'effect' we predict in the sample, so we can consider reasoning from a sample to a population – quantitative induction – as inverse probabilistic reasoning, the proportion we observe in the sample being the 'effect' whose 'cause' is the proportion in the population. This might suggest that, by using inverse probabilistic reasoning, we could evaluate the probability of the conclusion of a quantitative inductive argument indirectly. We could evaluate one conclusion specifying a 'cause' of the observed 'effect', as compared with other conclusions specifying other proposed 'causes'. It is possible, for example, that only 20 per cent of the coffee beans in the sack are perfect, even though 90 per cent of those sampled are perfect. We are, therefore, proposing to use inverse probabilistic reasoning to enable us to choose between the possible 'causes' of the observed 'effect' by assigning probabilities to the possible 'causes'. Our expectation is that the probability of the 'cause' being the fact that the proportion in the population is the same as the proportion observed in the sample will be greater than the probability of the 'cause' being some different fact about the proportion in the population. But although this is indeed what common sense leads us to expect, there is no way of using inverse reasoning to prove it unless we are able to assign prior probabilities to the possible 'causes'. And we cannot do this so long as we adhere to Peirce's view that probabilities are, fundamentally, frequencies. We must conclude, therefore, that there are formidable practical and theoretical objections to the measurement of the probabilities we assign to the conclusions of quantitative inductive arguments.

We here encounter a version of Hume's problem about inductive reasoning. For example, we examine a sample of tree frogs and we observe that all without exception are green. The sample, we may suppose, is large, varied and randomly selected. What we observe in the sample is the 'effect', and we wish to know its 'cause'. We wish to know, that is, what truth about the population of tree frogs we can judge to be responsible for our observations. It is natural to suppose that the 'cause' is nothing other than the fact that all tree frogs are green. We acknowledge that we could be wrong, and subsequent observations might prove that we are wrong. But nevertheless we think that this conclusion is the right one to draw, and certainly more probable than any other conclusion about the 'cause' of the fact that observed tree frogs are green. Do we, though, have any justification for thinking in this way? Suppose someone were to claim that a quite different conclusion about the tree frog population is the right one to draw and is more probable than any other conclusion, including the one that common sense suggests. For instance, someone could claim that the most probable 'cause' of what we have observed is the fact that, while every one of the tree frogs that we happen to have observed is green, none of those that we have not observed is green. Or it could be claimed that, while every one of the tree frogs that we happen to have observed is green, all but one of those that we have not observed is not green. There is, indeed, an indefinite number of such facts about the population of tree frogs, and, however implausible they might seem, any of them could be the 'cause' of what we have observed. We might allege, against the claim that one of these non-inductive 'causes' is the most probable, that probabilities must be understood as frequencies and that the frequency with which a true but non-inductive conclusion is produced by true premisses is very small. But the reply to this is that our experience is limited and in the long run the frequency with which we will derive a true conclusion from true premisses using a particular kind of non-inductive argument is greater than the frequency with which we will derive a true conclusion from true premisses using either an inductive argument or any other particular kind of non-inductive argument. Alternatively, we might try to show, using inverse probabilistic reasoning, that the probability of any of these non-inductive conclusions being correct is lower than the probability of the inductive conclusion. But, as we have seen, in order to do this we need to assign prior probabilities to each of the possible conclusions, and it seems that there is no principled way in which we can do this.

The third kind of probable reasoning recognised by Peirce relates more closely to scientific method. He called it 'hypothetic inference' or 'qualitative induction'. Its general form is as follows: a possible world in which a certain scientific hypothesis is true will have certain characteristics or qualities that follow from the truth of the hypothesis in this possible world. We observe that our actual world has a certain proportion of those characteristics or qualities. Consequently, it is probable that our world has a certain degree of likeness to that possible world. The argument, Peirce suggested, 'is simply an induction respecting qualities instead of respecting things' (Peirce 1931–58: 2.706). We take the qualities identified as characteristic of the possible world as a random sample of the qualities arising from the truth of the hypothesis in that world. We observe that a certain proportion of them is characteristic of the actual world, and we conclude that the actual world has a degree of likeness to this possible world. If unity represents the maximum degree of likeness, then it corresponds to the observation that all the qualities characterising the possible world also characterise the actual world, and therefore the hypothesis is true in the actual world. Zero degree of likeness corresponds to the observation that none of the possible-world qualities are actual-world qualities, and thus the hypothesis is false in the actual world. Degrees of likeness between one and zero represent the idea that the hypothesis is a more, or a less, satisfactory way of explaining the observed characteristics of the actual world. The hypothesis is, that is to say, closer to, or further away from, the truth about the actual world.

The conclusion we draw about the degree of likeness between our world and some possible world in which a hypothesis is true, or equivalently the conclusion we draw about the closeness to truth of that hypothesis, is never more than probable. Further observation may indicate that a quite different degree of likeness is more probable, and that a hypothesis which seemed a reasonable candidate for truth is much further from the truth than we had supposed. By analogy with induction we must acknowledge that we can draw an indefinite number of incompatible conclusions as to the degree of likeness of the actual world to the possible world in which the scientific hypothesis holds. So, for example, when the degree of likeness is one, we have the case in which we conclude that it is probable that our actual world is the same as the possible world, and that therefore the hypothesis in question is true. But it could be that, although all of the characteristics of this world so far examined have been characteristics of the supposed possible world, every unexamined characteristic fails to match anything in the possible world. This conclusion, as well as indefinitely many other and different conclusions, is consistent with the evidence available. Hume's scepticism, therefore, still applies. It challenges us to justify our common-sense belief that, because every examined characteristic of the actual world is also a characteristic of this supposed possible world, it is more probable that the degree of likeness between the two worlds is one than that it has any other value. Of course, the probability of the common-sense conclusion depends upon the extent to which observation is able to show that the actual world resembles the possible world. It could be quite insecure, i.e. have a low probability of truth, if there are only a small number of characteristics of our world that we have examined and found to be the same as qualities exhibited in the possible world where the hypothesis is true. It could be very secure, i.e. have a high probability, if there are a large number of such characteristics. But whether it be low or high, we believe that the probability in question is higher for the common-sense conclusion than for any other conclusion. Why, asks the sceptic, do we believe this?

There is, though, an important difference between induction and hypothetic inference. In both, the probability of the conclusion drawn depends on the relative size of the sample inspected. For induction, the sample size is easy to determine; we simply count the number of things inspected. But for hypothetic inference there is no way of determining sample size, because it is qualities, not things, that are being sampled, and qualities, Peirce acknowledged, are 'not subject to exact numeration'. We cannot count qualities. Nevertheless, he claimed, 'we may conceive them to be approximately measurable' (Peirce 1931–58: 2.704; cf. 2.706). Comparisons are possible even if they cannot be expressed in a quantitative form. And this will be sufficient. For, as we have seen in the case of induction, qualitative judgements of probability are all that we can in practice expect and express.

As an example of Peirce's analysis of hypothetic inference, consider Darwin's theory of evolution. We suppose that Darwin asked readers of *The Origin of Species* to imagine a possible world containing the sorts of organisms that we observe in our world. In the imaginary world, as in our world, organisms tend to reproduce their kind at a high rate and, consequently, there is competition for limited resources. In the imaginary world there is always some variation within a species and, because of this, some members of a species will be better able to survive and breed in their environments. Some of these variations will be inherited by offspring and, consequently, the prevalence of advantageous heritable variations in the population will slowly increase. On the other hand, in this imaginary world some variations will inhibit the ability of those possessing them to survive and breed, and in so far as these variations are heritable they will become less prevalent in the population. A species will, that is to say, evolve. This hypothesis of species evolution has certain implications, and we can work out what they are if we suppose that in other respects this imaginary world is the same as our world. We want to know how great a degree of likeness there is between this imaginary world and our real world. In particular, we want to know whether in our world, as in the imaginary world, the Darwinian hypothesis that species evolve is true. We cannot check this directly, because the rate at which species evolve is so gradual that it cannot be observed. We can only claim the hypothesis to be true in our world if we can establish that there is the highest degree of likeness between the two worlds. Reasoning has told us what the imaginary world is like; observation will tell us what our world is like. Reasoning will tell us, for example, that the finches on islands analogous to our Galapagos Islands will have beaks of a different shape to finches on the mainland, because even though they belong to the same species the environment on the islands has required the beak-shape of finches to change in a way not required by the mainland environment. During his voyage in the *Beagle* Darwin observed this effect – the beak-shape of Galapagos Island finches was indeed different from the beak-shape of mainland finches. So the results of reasoning about the imaginary world coincide with observations about the real world. Similarly, we can reason that in the imaginary world the fossil record will have certain characteristics, and observation in our world will show whether the fossil record does have those characteristics. Clearly, other evidence for the theory of evolution can be described in similar terms. Darwin's view was that, because of the close match between the results of observation and those of reasoning, he was right to claim the highest degree of likeness between his imaginary world and our world, i.e. he was right to claim that his species evolution hypothesis is true in our world. The large amount of evidence assembled by Darwin, and the extent of its agreement with the consequences of the evolution hypothesis, entitled him to declare that the conclusion he had reached was highly probable.

Both quantitative induction and hypothetic inference are contentious forms of probable reasoning when probability is understood in the way that Venn and Peirce advocated. We have to base any confidence we place in the conclusions of these kinds of reasoning on claims about the frequency with which arguments of particular kinds yield true conclusions from true premisses. Such claims have always been vulnerable to criticism, to doubt and to denial. Francis Bacon's dismissal of enumerative induction was based on his belief that simple quantitative induction does not yield true conclusions from true premises often enough for its conclusions to be trusted. Isaac Newton's refusal to employ hypothetic inference was based on his belief that the frequency with which such inferences give true conclusions from true premises is not high enough to justify any confidence in them. Moreover, quantitative inductive inferences from a sample to a population do not seem particularly relevant to interesting aspects of scientific method, and in the case of hypothetic inference we still have not addressed the question of choosing between different possible worlds, all of which have, so far as our evidence shows, the same degree of likeness to the real world. Faced with these misgivings we should notice, therefore, that Peirce drew attention to a feature of these kinds of reasoning which made them, he thought, valuable aids to the discovery of truth. This feature is that they are 'self-corrective', which is to say that their continued application will lead investigators closer to the truth. They have this feature because they are inferences used by investigators and, in Peirce's view, true beliefs are beliefs which investigators will in the long run accept. 'The opinion which is fated to be ultimately agreed upon by all who investigate is', he said, 'what we mean by the truth' (Peirce 1931–58: 5.407).

Quantitative induction is, therefore, self-corrective. When we begin using this method to determine the truth about a population, the sample size will be small and the conclusion we draw will be unreliable. But continued use of it means assembling more evidence, i.e. increasing the size of the sample, and as the sample increases so does the accuracy and reliability of the conclusion we draw about the population. By further use of quantitative induction we can make the difference between the conclusion reached and the truth about the population as small as we wish, for it is a feature of this kind of inference that, by using it consistently, we can be sure that in the long run most quantitative inductions will yield true conclusions from true premises. There remains, therefore, scope for radical doubt that, no matter how long we persist in using quantitative induction, the conclusion we reach could be erroneous, because the truth about the population is determined by facts about it which may remain undetected by enquiry, no matter how protracted that enquiry. On Peirce's view, investigators could ultimately agree that it is probable that all tree frogs are green, but on the frequency interpretation of probability, that is compatible with there being non-green tree frogs. Quantitative induction is self-corrective, but that is not to say that it is invulnerable to Humean scepticism.

Quantitative induction has built into it a method for proposing claims about a population; we simply propose that what observation shows to be true about a sample is also true about the population. If all observed tree frogs are green, we simply propose that all tree frogs are green; if only 90 per cent of those observed have that colour, then we propose that the same percentage of the whole population has that colour. Quantitative induction, that is to say, enables us to identify conclusions as well as to justify them. But hypothetic inference does not seem to be like this. By using it we can test and perhaps justify a hypothesis, but if testing reveals that the hypothesis is faulty, there is no logical machinery to suggest a replacement which might have fewer faults. This, though, is what is required if the method is to be self-corrective. Peirce tried to remedy the deficiency by representing hypothetic reasoning as an inference from a sample to a population, only in this case the sample and population are of qualities rather than of things. But the concept of degrees of likeness which he thereby introduced was of no use because it did not enable investigators to identify and test hypotheses which had ever-greater degrees of likeness. The knowledge that 90 per cent of tree frogs are green whereas the other 10 per cent are not might be of some use to naturalists, but it does not make sense to say that we might know, 'by sampling the possible predictions that may be based on it', that 90 per cent of the consequences of Darwin's hypothesis of evolution are true whereas the other 10 per cent are false (Peirce 1931–58: 7.216). Experiments and observations which enable us to know that any one of those consequences is false show that the hypothesis is false, without giving any indication of what hypothesis might be true.

If, then, hypothetic inference is to be self-corrective, we need to associate it with some procedure which will generate hypotheses likely to be true. It was with this in view that Peirce developed the concept of 'abduction'. Abduction is not simply guessing; guessing does not in general generate hypotheses likely to be true, and there is no guarantee that continued guessing will eventually generate the correct hypothesis. Abduction is reasoning and, Peirce thought, it does eventually yield hypotheses which hypothetic inference shows to be true. Given a phenomenon we want explained, we can, he said, rank the hypotheses which occur to us as capable of explaining it in accordance with their plausibility. Beginning with the most plausible, we test these hypotheses using hypothetic reasoning until we reach one which survives testing. We adopt it as true until further testing shows that it needs to be replaced by a hypothesis further down the list of plausible hypotheses. In answer to the question why the true hypothesis should appear at all on this list of plausible hypotheses, and so ensure that abduction will eventually generate it, Peirce replied that evolutionary processes have ensured that the human mind will make judgements of plausibility in such a way as to ensure the success of abduction. The evidence for this claim is to be found in the historical record of science – 'it has seldom been necessary to try more than two or three hypotheses made by clear genius before the right one was found' (Peirce 1931–58: 7.219). If we decide that the simplest and easiest-to-test hypotheses are the most plausible, that is because true hypotheses are likely to be the simplest and easiest to test. It might seem that judgements of plausibility are nothing other than judgements of prior probability, but Peirce rejected this connection on the grounds that prior probabilities are merely subjective assessments of degrees of belief, whereas plausibility judgements are objective, as indeed is the logic of abduction.

So the logic we use in scientific method is self-corrective in the sense that persistent recourse to it will bring us closer to the truth. The attention Peirce paid to establishing this claim was entirely appropriate, for in many ways it had been at the heart of debates about scientific method since the seventeenth century. Those, like Newton and Mill, who defended versions of what Peirce called quantitative induction, did so on the grounds that it was the most reliable method for ascertaining truth, and we could justifiably claim that it had this characteristic because it is self-correcting. Their critics, such as Herschel and Whewell, believed that quantitative induction was too restrictive to serve the needs of science. They, therefore, defended versions of what Peirce called hypothetic inference on the grounds that it, too, was a reliable method for ascertaining truth. Doubts about its reliability could be dispelled by showing that this form of reasoning, like quantitative induction, is self-corrective. One strategy for showing this was to regard it as self-corrective, but facts about the reliability or self-corrective character of such reasoning in the past, even if accepted, provide no secure basis for that conviction. We cannot cogently argue from what has been done, even from what has been successfully done, to a conclusion about what, rationally, should be done.

FURTHER READING

For the background to Venn's and Peirce's ideas about probability, see:

De Morgan, A. (1845) 'Theory of probabilities', in *Encyclopaedia Metropolitana*, vol. 2, London: B. Fellowes *et al.*

Ellis, R. L. (1863) *The Mathematical and Other Writings of Robert Leslie Ellis*, edited by W. Walton, Cambridge: Deighton, Bell.

Jevons, W. S. (1874) *The Principles of Science*, 2 vols, London: Macmillan.

Boole, G. (1952) *Studies in Logic and Probability*, La Salle, Ill.: Open Court.

For Venn on probable reasoning, see:

Venn, J. (1962) *The Logic of Chance*, fourth edition, New York: Chelsea. This is a reprint of the third edition of 1888.

Peirce's essays and papers on logic, induction and probability are best consulted in:

Peirce, C. S. (1931–58) *Collected Papers*, 8 vols, eds C. Hartshorne, P. Weiss and A. Burks, Cambridge, Mass.: Harvard University Press.

Peirce's ideas are discussed in:

Burks, A. W. (1946) 'Peirce's theory of abduction', *Philosophy of Science* 13: 301–6.

Rescher, N. (1978) *Peirce's Philosophy of Science: Critical Studies in His Theory of Induction and Scientific Method*, Notre Dame, Ill.: Notre Dame University Press.

Hacking, I. (1980) 'The theory of probable inference: Neyman, Peirce and Braithwaite', in D. H. Mellor (ed.), *Science, Belief and Behaviour*, Cambridge: Cambridge University Press.

Levi, I. (1980) 'Induction as self-correcting according to Peirce', in D. H. Mellor (ed.), *Science, Belief and Behaviour*, Cambridge: Cambridge University Press.

Hookway, C. (1985) *Peirce*, 'Arguments of the Philosophers', London: Routledge.

The development of statistical thinking in the nineteenth century is explored in:

Stigler, S. (1986) *The History of Statistics: The Measurement of Uncertainty before 1900*, Cambridge, Mass.: Harvard University Press.

Hacking, I. (1990) *The Taming of Chance*, Cambridge: Cambridge University Press.

9 John Maynard Keynes and Frank Ramsey
Probability logic

There was another respect in which Peirce linked together quantitative induction and hypothetic inference, for with regard to both he insisted on the importance of what he called 'predesignation'. Consider, for example, Michael Faraday's first law of electrolysis, which states that when an electric current passes through an electrolytic solution for a certain period of time, the mass of the material separated by the passage of the current is proportional to the strength of the current. We can, of course, collect experimental evidence relevant to this law. We examine, in effect, a sample of electrolytic solutions and find that, in each case, material is separated by the passage of an electric current in accordance with the law. In the light of this evidence we conclude that it is probable that the law is true. But, Peirce claimed, it is essential to the soundness of this probable argument that we begin our examination of electrolytic solutions knowing what characteristic we are concerned with, namely their capacity to deposit material in accordance with Faraday's law. We must, that is, specify or 'predesignate' the characteristic identified in the law beforehand. For suppose we do not do this, but instead simply examine and perform experiments with electrolytic solutions, looking for some undesignated characteristic which they all have in common. We might, if we are particularly lucky, notice that they all have the characteristic identified in Faraday's law. But there will be an indefinite number of other characteristics common to all the electrolytic solutions in the sample, no matter how large the sample. In most cases, their sharing the characteristic is no more than a fortuitous coincidence, and it would be a mistake to use quantitative induction to conclude that all electrolytic solutions have that characteristic. They might, for example, all have been experimentally examined on days other than Sundays. Or they might all have been experimentally examined in Faraday's laboratory in the Royal Institution. But an inductive conclusion based on these and other 'artificial' characteristics would be false. So, if we predesignate no characteristic of a sample, quantitative induction from the sample to a population is illegitimate.

Peirce similarly stressed the importance of predesignation in hypothetic inference. No matter how much evidence we might have regarding a particular scientific question, there is always an indefinite number of different and incompatible ways of answering it. When selecting from among these alternatives, what matters is the ability of a hypothesis to predict correctly, or at least to account for phenomena which had not previously been considered. So, if we take Faraday's law of electrolysis as a hypothesis rather than as the conclusion of a quantitative induction, then our confidence in it depends not on the fact that its truth would account for the evidence we have assembled but upon its ability to predict correctly. But if we are predicting that electrolytic solutions will have the characteristic identified in Faraday's law, then we are, in effect, predesignating that characteristic.

To insist on predesignation is, in effect, to rule 'that a hypothesis can only be received upon the ground of its having been *verified* by successful *prediction*' (Peirce 1931–58: 2.739). Peirce acknowledged that such a rule was not new. We have seen that John Herschel and William Whewell, among others, had given it their support. What Peirce did not mention was that there was opposition to this view, for Mill had refused to recognise that the successful predictions of a hypothesis gave us good grounds for believing it to be true. Peirce had no very high opinion of Mill, so he may have thought that his opposition could be ignored. If so, he was mistaken, because opposition to the rule was forcibly expressed by Keynes in his *Treatise on Probability* of 1921.

Keynes's fame rests chiefly on his association with the 'Bloomsbury Group' of writers and artists, and on his influence as an economist. He first came to public attention when, soon after the end of the 1914–18 war, he published a book – *Economic Consequences of the Peace* (1919) – which drew attention to the economic, political and social instability created by the reparations imposed on Germany. Later, in his *General Theory* (1936), he pioneered some revolutionary new ideas about economic theory and policy which have ever since been associated with his name. But before he turned to economics, much of his thinking and writing was concerned with probability, not as 'algebraical exercises', he said, but 'as a branch of Logic' (Keynes 1921: v). His view of probability contrasts sharply with that of John Venn, who, as we have seen, took the opposite view.

As a student at Cambridge, Keynes had developed an interest in philosophy and had felt the influence of men such as Bertrand Russell and, especially, G. E. Moore. In his famous *Principia Ethica* (1903), Moore had declared that in reasoning about good and bad conduct we have to consider the consequences of what we do, and because many of these consequences are to one degree or another uncertain, this means we have to consider probabilities. There is, as Keynes put it, a 'curious connection between "probable" and "ought"' (quoted in Skidelsky 1983: 151), and the dissertation he wrote for a Cambridge fellowship in 1908 was concerned with developing ideas about probability which would help to make this connection in a way consistent with the individualistic morality that he and other members of the 'Bloomsbury Group' promoted. His view was that probabilities are not relative frequencies based on observation, as Moore seems to have believed and as so many of his hard-headed empiricist colleagues at Cambridge supposed, but degrees of rational belief determined by reason. In deciding how we should act, we should be guided by our own beliefs about what is likely to follow from our actions, rather than by any statistical regularities about the consequences of supposedly similar actions. Clearly, Keynes was committed to an understanding of probability at variance with that of Venn and Peirce. For them, probabilities were relative frequencies, and it was therefore natural to speak of events, or rather kinds of events, as being probable, whereas for Keynes probabilities were degrees of belief, and it was necessary not only to attribute probabilities primarily to propositions, but also to recognise that propositions are always probable in relation to other propositions. In effect, Keynes endorsed the 'conceptual' or 'classical' idea of probability associated with Leibniz and Laplace.

The fellowship dissertation eventually turned into *A Treatise on Probability* (1921). That book opens, appropriately, with the declaration that its 'subject matter . . . was first broached in the brain of Leibniz' (Keynes 1921: v), so it comes as no surprise to find that the ideas about scientific method associated with Bayes and Laplace are subjected to an examination which, though severe, is sympathetic. Reasoning in science is probable reasoning, and for Keynes this meant that it results in the attribution of some degree of rational belief to a conclusion. A degree of rational belief has nothing to do with how frequently conclusions 'of this kind' follow when we use reasoning 'of this type'; rather, it is a function of the logical relations between the conclusion and the reasons we give for its truth. That is to say, logicians should recognise not only that propositions can entail, or contradict, other propositions, but also that propositions can 'partially' entail, or 'partially' contradict, other propositions. Probabilities arise because there can be such relations between propositions. Just as we say that the conclusion of some reasoning must be true when it is entailed by premises we accept, so we can say that a conclusion is probably true when it is 'partially' entailed by premises we accept. In other words, whereas entailed conclusions are necessary in relation to premises, partially entailed conclusions are probable in relation to premises. Probability, Keynes declared, comprises 'that part of logic which deals with arguments which are rational but not conclusive' (Keynes 1921: 217). It is a branch of logic, not mathematics.

So, for instance, if a certain cause is capable of producing a certain effect, and we observe the occurrence of that effect, then in certain circumstances it is rational for us to believe that the cause has occurred. For example, Henri Becquerel found that luminescent crystals of potassium uranyl sulphate produced 'penetrating rays' which, like Roentgen's x-rays, affected photographic plates. Experimental evidence enabled him to attribute the cause of these 'penetrating rays' – or radioactivity as we now call it – to the presence of uranium in the crystals. The crucial factor on which the rationality of such an attribution depends is the prior probability of the occurrence of the cause. If there are no good grounds for believing in the occurrence of the cause independently of the effect, then it is not rational for us to believe in its occurrence on the grounds that the effect has occurred. For example, we have no grounds for believing in the operation of non-human spiritual powers on the grounds that such a belief would enable us to account for some unusual or unexpected phenomenon, unless there is some reason, independent of this effect, for supposing that such a cause is present. And in science, too, Keynes acknowledged that if the only reason for believing a hypothetical axiom, or believing in the existence of a theoretical entity 'such as the ether or the electron', is that such beliefs have consequences that are true, then 'we can never attribute a finite probability to the truth of such axioms or to the existence of such scientific entities' (Keynes 1921: 300). This is not to say, he thought, that these axioms and entities have no place in science, for it may be 'convenient' to adopt them for the sake of their consequences. But adopting them for this reason is, Keynes implied, distinct from believing them to have some finite probability of being true. The confirmed experimental consequences of beliefs in hypothetical truths and entities do not, that is to say, even partially entail those beliefs. Epistemological scepticism led him, as it has led others, to scientific anti-realism.

For Keynes, in assigning a prior probability to a hypothesis we are stating the degree to which it is rational for us to believe the hypothesis, given that other statements, which do not include statements about evidence whose relevance we are estimating, are true. These other statements partially entail the hypothesis, and therefore make our belief in its truth rational to a degree represented by the figure we assign to its prior probability. We may know, because of subsequent evidence, that the hypothesis cannot be true, but nevertheless the hypothesis will have a prior probability. For example, if we have just been exploring a habitat in which some tree frogs are not green, we will know that it is not true that all tree frogs are green, but still the prior probability of the hypothesis could be quite high if we have examined a number of other habitats and, in each of them, all observed tree frogs are green. Sometimes the point is expressed by saying that the knowledge with respect to which we estimate a prior probability is 'background' knowledge. Such knowledge partially entails the hypothesis to a degree represented by the prior probability we assign to it. This can, though, be misleading if it gives the impression that the knowledge is of a rather general character with only an indirect bearing on the hypothesis in question. It must be recognised that the 'background' knowledge with respect to which we judge the prior probability of a hypothesis includes all of the evidence we have which bears on the truth of the hypothesis, with the sole exception of the evidence whose relevance is being considered.

This understanding of 'background' knowledge is relevant to Keynes's criticism of Peirce's allegation that correct predictions of a hypothesis carry more weight in supporting its truth than do known facts which the hypothesis explains or 'accommodates' (Keynes 1921: 304–5). What matters is our ability to compare the probability of the evidence, given the truth of the hypothesis, with its probability independent of the hypothesis. In making such comparisons we do not judge the probability of evidence to be unity simply because the evidence is already available to us; events can be surprising and, in that sense, improbable, even though they have occurred and we know that they have occurred, just as other events can be unsurprising even though they have not yet occurred. The 'background' knowledge with respect to which we judge the probability of the evidence, and which we take into account when we judge the probability of the evidence given the truth of the hypothesis, does not include the knowledge of the evidence. This is why evidence can be surprising unless the hypothesis is true. We can have, then, good reasons for believing a hypothesis which 'accommodates' known facts, provided that these facts are surprising and have a low probability given only 'background' knowledge. For in that case there is a significant difference between the probability of those facts independent of the hypothesis and their probability given the hypothesis. Conversely, we might not have good reasons for believing a hypothesis which 'predicts' unknown facts, if those facts are unsurprising and have a high probability given only 'background' knowledge. For then there is little difference between their probability independent of the hypothesis and their probability given the hypothesis.

The point is perhaps most easily seen with the help of a simple version of Bayes's theorem:

$$p(h, e\&b) = \frac{p(h, b)\, p(e, h\&b)}{p(e, b)}$$

where h represents the hypothesis, e the evidence relevant to its truth and b the 'background' knowledge available to us, i.e. everything we know apart from e. It is clear that for fixed $p(h, b)$ – the prior probability of h – $p(h, e\&b)$ will have its greatest value when $p(e, h\&b)$ is as large as possible and $p(e, b)$ is as small as possible. We secure these conditions by requiring that e should be a consequence of the truth of the hypothesis when combined with background information, so that $p(e, h\&b)$ is one, and by requiring that, in the light of the background information alone, e is unlikely or surprising, so that $p(e, b)$ is as small as possible. Evidently, e can be unlikely or surprising in this sense even if it has already occurred, and can be likely or unsurprising even if it has yet to occur.

Peirce had tried to persuade his readers that the ability of a hypothesis to 'accommodate' known facts was a poor recommendation for its truth, on the grounds that hypotheses known to be false had once been accepted for this reason, and also that we could support certain prima facie implausible hypotheses in such a way. For example, a law associated with two eighteenth-century astronomers, Bode and Titius, had identified a simple numerical relationship between a planet's ordinal position in the solar system and its distance from the Sun. The relationship $d = 0.4 + (0.3 \times 2^{n-2})$, where d is the average distance of a planet from the Sun expressed in astronomical units (i.e. the average Earth–Sun distance is used as the unit) and n is its ordinal position, expresses the putative law. It 'accommodated' the evidence available to Bode and Titius, but eventually had to be abandoned once data concerning Uranus and Neptune, first identified in the nineteenth century, were scrutinised. But, Keynes claimed, it had never derived much support from the original evidence because none was sufficiently surprising to make a large difference between its probability independent of the Bode–Titius hypothesis and its probability given the hypothesis. It would have made no difference to the degree to which the evidence was unsurprising if some of the data used by Bode and Titius had been successfully predicted, rather than simply accommodated. True, the law had been used to predict, successfully, the presence of asteroids between the orbits of Mars and Jupiter. This undoubtedly contributed to the confidence that some astronomers placed in the law at the end of the eighteenth century, but it did so not because the law successfully predicted rather than simply accommodated the presence of asteroids, but because this was a surprising consequence of the law (Keynes 1921: 304).

Another example was Playfair's suggestion that the specific gravities of the allotropic forms of chemical elements are equal to the different roots – square, cube, etc. – of the atomic weights of those elements. This hypothesis, though it may now appear rather fanciful, accommodates reasonably well a limited range of known facts about specific gravities, namely those concerning the three allotropic forms of carbon – diamond, graphite and charcoal. But Peirce claimed that the adoption of the hypothesis on these grounds 'can only serve to suggest a question, and ought not to create any belief', because 'the character in which the instances agree [had] not . . . been predesignated' (Peirce 1931–58: 2.738). There is, though, as Keynes pointed out, a rather obvious alternative reason why we are reluctant to accept Playfair's hypothesis on these grounds, namely that the evidence produced is so very meagre. The fact that three facts share some common characteristic is, once again, insufficiently surprising to make a large enough difference between the probability of the evidence independent of the hypothesis and its probability given the hypothesis for us to count the evidence as supporting the hypothesis to a significant extent. Had there been many more facts sharing Playfair's arithmetical characteristic, our inclination to believe the hypothesis would have been much greater, simply because that evidence is so much more surprising. Moreover, contrary to Peirce's claim, we would not be less inclined to accept the hypothesis in these circumstances if it accommodated rather than predicted this surprising evidence (Keynes 1921: 305).

Keynes's view about the nature of reasoning in empirical science was that such reasoning is fundamentally dependent on what he called 'the methods of Analogy and Pure Induction' (Keynes 1921: 217). To see what he meant by this, consider again Faraday's first law of electrolysis and the way that experiments support it. An investigator might begin with a particular electrolytic solution, such as copper sulphate, and design an experiment which shows that the quantity of copper separated from the solution by the passage of an electric current through it is directly proportional to the quantity of electrical charge used, i.e. the product of current strength and time. It seems clear that further experiments with other samples of copper sulphate, even though they provide further positive instances of Faraday's law, will do little if anything to enhance the probability of its truth. Having found that an initial sample of copper sulphate conforms to Faraday's law, it will come as no surprise to find that a subsequent sample also conforms. Subsequent samples will do little or nothing to enhance our degree of belief in the law. To proceed, then, with the method of pure induction – a method which requires only that we accumulate positive instances – will not necessarily lead to an increased degree of belief in the law. The method of analogy, however, requires that an investigator should assemble particular kinds of positive instance, namely those resulting from experiments with electrolytic substances which differ from each other in their chemical composition and in their physical circumstances. The nature and circumstances of electrolytic substances vary from each other in many ways, and experiments which yield positive instances of the law despite this variety increase what Keynes termed the 'negative analogy' of the instances of the law. By proceeding in accordance with the method of analogy, an investigator can, Keynes claimed, assign a high probability to the truth of the law. If the respect in which the instances of the law count as instances, in that they are all electrolytic, is made as comprehensive as possible, the respect in which they count as positive instances, in that the quantity of material separated is directly proportional to the quantity of electrical charge, is made as specific as possible, and the respect in which the instances are dissimilar is made as great as possible, then 'the stronger is the likelihood or probability of the generalisation we seek to establish' (Keynes 1921: 220).

The methods of pure induction and analogy are nothing other than the methods of enumerative and eliminative induction. Like Bacon and Mill, Keynes favoured the latter; in his view pure, or enumerative, induction is of little value except in so far as it leads to an increase in the negative analogy between positive instances, and thereby to an increase in the 'variety' of evidence. But he recognised that, although we might accept and adopt this as a practical mode of reasoning, we must defend these kinds of probable reasoning by examining their logic. Accordingly, in his analysis he asked and tried to answer two questions. The first was the question of what we would have to assume if we are to prefer eliminative to enumerative induction. The second question was how we could justify as true any assumptions so identified. To answer these questions he made use of a mathematical analysis of his concept of probability.

Keynes first showed that a further positive instance of a generalisation does not always increase the probability of its being true. In particular, if we can predict with certainty, on the basis of the already collected positive instances, that this further instance must also be positive, then its being so will not increase the probability of the generalisation. For example, if the evidence we have in favour of Faraday's first law of electrolysis makes us sure that the results of an experiment we are about to conduct will provide a further positive instance, then that instance, if positive, cannot increase the probability of the generalisation. Thus, if experiments with copper sulphate have made us sure that a further experiment with this electrolytic solution will provide a further positive instance of Faraday's law, then the experimental evidence of its being positive will not increase the probability that the law is true. This shows that we are right to claim that assembling positive instances of a generalisation is, in itself, of little or no use in probable reasoning. What we need are positive instances which we do not expect, on the basis of the evidence available, to be positive. This will happen if the instance is as different to previous instances as possible, because its negative analogy is as great as possible. In other words, Keynes's examination of the logic of probability showed that we are right to think that, in using inductive reasoning, we should rely on what he called 'the method of Analogy', or eliminative induction (Keynes 1921: 236–41).

This conclusion was challenged by Jean Nicod in his *Le Problème logique de l'induction* (Nicod 1969). Evidence providing positive instances of a generalisation can, Nicod thought, increase the degree of our belief in that generalisation without also providing negative instances of alternative generalisations. The issue turns on when instances of a generalisation count as different instances. For example, if in a laboratory class on a particular day, several people perform the same experiment and obtain the same results, should we say that one experiment, or that several simultaneous experiments, have taken place? Or, if the same experiment is performed on several successive days with the same result, should we say that one experiment, or that several successive experiments, have taken place? On behalf of the view that only one experiment has taken place, Keynes claimed that the several places or times where and when it took place do not differ in any 'significant' or 'relevant' way. Accordingly, given the result obtained in any one place, or on any one occasion, we are entitled to be certain that we would obtain the same result at other places and on other occasions. In support of this view, he urged that our conviction that 'nature' is 'uniform' is nothing other than a conviction that differences in place or in time are insignificant and irrelevant to the truth or falsity of generalisations. Of course, generalisations we accept may nevertheless fail to be true in places or at times uninvestigated by our experiments; but Keynes's view was that, if this happens, it is always because of differences other than those of place or time (Keynes 1921: 226). The alternative view pressed by Nicod claims that we should not misconstrue as identity the qualitative similarity of experiments performed in different places or at different times, however extensive that similarity. For the grounds on which we claim that experiments are qualitatively similar cannot include the results of those experiments. We must, that is to say, allow that qualitatively similar experiments will yield different results even though we believe, perhaps very firmly, that they will not. But if this is so, then the experiments are not identical and, as we have seen, it is only if they *are* identical that they will fail to increase the probability of a generalisation (Nicod 1969: 232–5).

The dispute between Keynes and Nicod about the identity conditions of instances of generalisations had important implications for the question whether the method of 'Analogy' can ensure that positive instances will eventually increase the probability of a generalisation so that it approaches certainty, or even so that the generalisation is more likely to be true than false. This was a question Keynes had to face because of his wish to use his probability theory, with its various axioms and theorems, to illuminate the inductive reasoning used by scientists to justify their conclusions. An inductive sceptic such as David Hume could acknowledge the existence of evidence in the form of positive instances of a generalisation, and there is no reason why he or she should not also accept that such evidence must display variety, or 'negative' analogy, if it is to be of any use. What the sceptic will doubt is whether any evidence, however extensive and however varied, entitles us to believe that a generalisation is true or probably true. Even if, as

Keynes thought, eliminative methods are superior to enumerative methods, that is not a sufficient reason for conceding that inductive reasoning is capable of yielding conclusions which a rational person should accept. Our experiments, and the positive instances they have yielded, may have increased the probability of Faraday's law being true, but that does not show that further experimental evidence, leading to further increases in probability, will eventually make it more rational to believe that the law is true than that it is false. For the increases in probability could diminish in such a way that the probability of the law never exceeds one-half.

Keynes showed that the inductivist's response to this depends on the claim that there is a sufficiently small probability of all the examined instances being positive if the generalisation is false. In the case of the electrolysis law it would not have been particularly surprising to investigators in the first third of the nineteenth century if extensive experiments with copper sulphate provided evidence in conformity with the law even though the law was itself false. That is to say, there is a high probability of those experiments providing that evidence even if the law is false. On the other hand, it would be very surprising if experiments with a wide variety of electrolytes provided evidence in conformity with the law despite its falsity. There is, in other words, a small probability of these experiments providing this evidence despite the law's falsity (Keynes 1921: 235–6). We should notice that, although the most effective way to secure a small probability for experimental evidence, given the falsity of the hypothesis under investigation, is often to assemble as much evidence as possible and to increase its variety as much as possible, we can sometimes achieve the same outcome with a single experiment yielding a result which we would not expect were it not for the truth of the hypothesis.

But even if this condition is satisfied, we will not have thwarted inductive scepticism unless we can also show that the prior probability of any hypothesis we wish to accept on the basis of inductive evidence has a non-zero value. This is not unexpected, for in general the legitimacy of inverse probable reasoning depends on non-zero prior probabilities. In this context, though, the condition is hard to satisfy, for the probability we require to be non-zero is the probability of a *universal* generalisation prior to the availability of *any* evidence, whether positive or not. We have to assume, that is, that any universal general-isation whatsoever has a finite, if small, probability of being true if we consider it independently of any evidence. Our inclination is to suppose that we could continue indefinitely a list of generalisations which are mutually exclusive but which thoroughly exhaust all possibilities, and that in the absence of evidence we would therefore not be able to justify a non-zero probability to any generalisation on the list. Again, Faraday's electrolysis law serves to illustrate the difficulty. The law states that for any electrolyte there is a *direct* relationship between the quantity of electrical charge used and the quantity of material separated; if the quantity of electrical charge is doubled, the quantity of material separated is doubled. But we could easily formulate other laws which specify some different relation between the two quantities. Perhaps one quantity is related to the cube, or the square root, or the logarithm, of the other quantity. There are, it seems, an indefinite number of distinct and incompatible laws which we could formulate about the behaviour of electrolytes when an electrical charge is applied. In the absence of any evidence we have no reason for preferring any one to any other, even though only one of the possible laws, at most, is true. Prior to evidence becoming available, we would not be able to assign a non-zero probability to any of these possible laws. But if this is so, then, according to Keynes, we will never be in a position to claim that any of the possible laws is more probably true than false, no matter what evidence we assemble (Keynes 1921: 258).

A remarkable feature of Keynes's account is that the conditions he identifies as necessary for the legitimacy of inductive reasoning are entirely general. They would need to be satisfied just as much if our concern were with the acceptability of some non-empirical claim that we wished to justify inductively, as if our concern were with the acceptability of empirical claims such as Faraday's law. For example, we would need assurance about these conditions if we wanted to establish the acceptability of the claim that every even number is the sum of two prime numbers (Goldbach's conjecture) by investigating particular even numbers, or if we wished to establish the acceptability of the claim that the sum of the number of vertices and the number of faces of any polyhedron is always equal to the number of edges plus two (Euler's hypothesis) by investigating particular polyhedra. We need to agree that these claims have some non-zero probability of being true before we have any evidence which supports them, and we have to agree that the facts we use to support the claims would be improbable if the claims were false.

But it is in the context of the natural world rather than mathematics that we normally use inductive probabilistic reasoning, so the question arises about what has to be true of the natural world if we are to satisfy Keynes's conditions. Consider first the condition requiring that the supporting evidence is improbable given the falsity of the supported hypothesis. Clearly, if this condition holds, not every positive instance of a hypothesis is a supporting instance. This is precisely what Bacon and Mill had urged, in favouring eliminative over enumerative induction. A positive instance is a supporting instance if it is sufficiently different from previous supporting instances to make it improbable that it would be positive if the hypothesis supported were false. If, for example, experiments with a particular electrolyte have provided us with positive instances of Faraday's law, then we cannot generate further support by further experiments with that same electrolyte. This is because, given the falsity of Faraday's law, we would not judge improbable any positive evidence yielded by those further experiments. We need experiments which investigate the behaviour of different electrolytes. We need, that is to say, to eliminate the possibility that it is some property of the substance first investigated other than its electrolytic character which is responsible for the fact that it provided a positive instance of Faraday's law. We will need still further experiments to eliminate hypotheses which, though compatible with the evidence so far provided, are incompatible with Faraday's law. Such experiments will help to yield evidence which it is improbable we should obtain if one or other of the competitors to this law were true.

Is it really true, though, that there is only a very small probability of obtaining the evidence we use to support Faraday's law if that law is false? Can we not envisage that further evidence will show that Faraday's law is false and that there is another law about electrolytes, incompatible with it, which is just as well if not better supported by our evidence? In short, should we accept Keynes's condition that supporting evidence should be improbable given the falsity of the supported hypothesis? To see how we might answer such questions, suppose that Faraday's law is, in fact, false even though we have no evidence which shows this; what is the probability that the next experimental test of the law will yield a falsifying instance, given that all evidence so far available is positive or confirming? If there are only a finite number of instances of the law, then we can envisage that we will eventually reach a point in accumulating positive instances at which it is reasonable to claim that a falsifying instance is improbable. But if there are an infinite number of instances, then we will not reach such a point. This is, indeed, the point of Hume's inductive scepticism: positive confirming instances, however many we accumulate, give us no better reason for disbelieving that a negative falsifying instance will occur than no instances at all. To satisfy Keynes's condition, therefore, we will have to defend the claim that, in some appropriate sense, there are only a finite number of instances of a scientific law. The role of what Keynes called his 'hypothesis of the limitation of independent variety' was to help provide that defence (Keynes 1921: 260–4).

To see what Keynes meant by this, consider a collection of items, such as books in a library, or chemicals in a laboratory, or animals in a zoo. The collections may be large and the items in them may differ from each other in numerous ways. But there will be connections between the differences. For example, in most libraries there is a connection between variation in the subject matters of books and variation in their shelf marks; books have different shelf marks because they are about different subjects. In such cases, one variety in respect of a characteristic is dependent upon another variety in respect of a different characteristic. Other differences are unconnected. Zoo animals are provided with different habitats; they also differ in size. But there is no connection between these two dimensions of variety; they are independent of each other. If we can assume that the number of independent ways in which any item in the collection can differ from any other item is limited, then, however large the collection, there is a sense in which the number of distinct items in it is limited. Items in a collection are distinct in this sense if they display a variety which makes them belong to different kinds. So if we consider the instances of a scientific law as items in a collection, then however large that collection, the items in it will, according to Keynes's hypothesis, display limited variety, and consequently there are a limited number of distinct instances. In the case of Faraday's law, the several positive instances of it resulting from experiments using copper sulphate in a school laboratory would not count as distinct instances. Another laboratory class which produced further positive instances using a different electrolyte would, though, provide a distinct instance.

But even if we accept the hypothesis of limited independent variety and agree that the number of genuinely distinct instances of a scientific law is therefore limited, we have still not conceded enough to satisfy Keynes's condition that supporting evidence should be improbable given the falsity of the supported law. For unless we know not only that there is a limit to the number of distinct instances but also what that limit is, we shall still never be in a position reasonably to claim that, given the positive confirming evidence accumulated, it is improbable that a falsifying negative instance will occur. We can express the point schematically by supposing that we have just one positive instance of a law which has ten distinct instances. On the basis of that evidence it would not be reasonable to believe that all of the remaining nine distinct instances are positive, and none is falsifying. But then it is clear that, no matter how many positive instances of a law we might accumulate, the limit to the number of distinct instances could be such that we cannot justifiably believe that no falsifying instance will occur. It is only if we know what the limit to the number of distinct instances is that we can judge how far we need to go in accumulating positive instances before we can justify the belief that no falsifying instances will occur (Nicod 1969: 239).

Keynes's claim, then, was that positive instances of a generalisation or law are not relevantly different and therefore supporting unless they put the generalisation or law at risk. And we do intuitively believe that some positive instances count for more than others. In defence of his claim, and of our intuitions, Keynes invoked his hypothesis of limited independent variety. According to this hypothesis there are only a limited number of truly distinct instances of a generalisation, even though it is possible that there are an indefinite number of instances. It is because of this that we seek distinct positive instances and the new information they provide, and tend to ignore positive instances which provide no new information. That is to say, a further instance is not a distinct probability-increasing instance unless, in the light of the evidence so far obtained, it is unlikely to be a positive instance of the generalisation unless the generalisation is true. This, as we have seen, was denied by Nicod. If the generalisation or law is false, then any instance, whether or not it was expected to support or increase the probability of the generalisation, could make it false. We may not expect a negative instance, but since negative instances are possible, Keynes is mistaken in supposing that we can ignore them. Accordingly, for Nicod, there is no special class of supporting instances among positive instances of a generalisation. Our intuition that some positive instances count for more than others has no rational foundation, and the hypothesis of limited independent variety has no role to play. In short, if inductive reasoning is probable reasoning in the sense indicated by Keynes, then we can have no justification for the preference for eliminative over enumerative induction.

Keynes also used his hypothesis of limited independent variety to ensure that the prior probability of a law would always have a non-zero value. Consider, for example, Lavoisier's claim that acids contain oxygen. This claim links together two properties, namely that of being an acid and that of containing oxygen. Keynes's hypothesis means that each of these properties, and indeed any other property, belongs to one of a limited number of 'generator' groups of properties. If we suppose that a number n represents the limit of the independent variety we find in nature, and therefore the number of 'generator' groups, then in the absence of any evidence $1/n$ represents both the probability that being an acid belongs to a particular 'generator' group and the probability that containing oxygen belongs to that same group. So in the absence of any evidence, the probability that both properties belong to the same group, and that consequently the two properties are linked as in Lavoisier's claim, is therefore $1/n^2$. Since n must be finite, even though perhaps large, this probability must have a non-zero value. Consequently, it is possible for positive instances of Lavoisier's hypothesis to increase its probability so that it approaches certainty. This conclusion follows, however many kinds of acids, or kinds of substances containing oxygen, there are. Provided that there is some limit to independent variety, there could be no limit to the kinds of acids or kinds of oxygen-containing substances.

In terms of eliminative induction, Keynes's hypothesis of limited independent variety was an attempt to ensure that, by eliminating some competitors, we will increase the probability of survivors. For if there were an indefinite number of competitors in the first place, then it would be logically impossible to eliminate all except one. Conversely, if it is logically possible to conclude that some generalisation is true, or probably true, on the grounds that other generalisations are false, then we must assume that independent variety is limited. But this opens the possibility that we might be quite unable to justify a conclusion as true or probably true, even though the independent variety principle holds. We may, that is to say, find that we cannot tell whether all except one of a limited number of competing hypotheses have been eliminated. For example, perhaps we can be sure that there are only a finite number of possible causes of an allergic reaction to food. Steps could be taken to eliminate, in a systematic fashion, some possible causes. But given that the cause of the allergy could be a complex of alternatives and/or combinations of different foodstuffs, it is quite possible that, despite our efforts, we have no justification for drawing any positive conclusion. This is because, although the limited independent variety hypothesis ensures a non-zero a priori probability of the conclusion we wish to draw, we cannot satisfy Keynes's other condition, namely that the positive evidence is improbable given the falsity of the law. As we have seen, this condition is the more demanding because it requires us to know how much independent variety there is, not simply that this variety has a limit (von Wright 1957: 76–8).

As we have seen, Keynes understood probability judgements as judgements about the degree to which certain statements – the 'evidence' – entail another statement – the 'hypothesis'. We may, or may not, know this degree. We will know it if the entailment is complete rather than partial, though in that case we will judge the hypothesis either certain or impossible, rather than probable or improbable, in relation to the evidence. In some cases, Keynes thought, we could know degrees of probability by judiciously employing a 'Principle of Indifference'. This principle is closely related to ideas about the comparative ease or facility with which nature can produce different outcomes or cases, used by Leibniz and Bernoulli in their probability calculations. Keynes's Principle of Indifference claims that, if there is no known reason why the evidence available to us should favour one rather than another of several alternative hypotheses, then we should judge the evidence to entail each of the alternatives and partially to the same extent, and we should therefore assign the same probability to each alternative hypothesis. Keynes was aware that the Principle of Indifference, so expressed, is subject to powerful objections. It can lead, in particular, to inconsistent and absurd assignments of probability. For example, our evidence may not allow us to favour any one of four alternatives a, b, c and d over any other, in which case the principle indicates that we should distribute the probability that one or other is true equally over each of the four alternatives. But the same evidence does not allow us to discriminate between the three alternative (a or b), c, and d, in which case we should distribute that same probability equally over each of these three alternatives. Clearly, though, this results in assigning different probabilities to the same hypothesis in relation to the same evidence. Given Keynes's views about the nature of probability judgements, this consequent is inconsistence and unacceptable.

Keynes examined these and other objections with some care, and came to the conclusion that, because of their force, quantitative probability judgements were often impossible. There is some scope for the Principle of Indifference, even though it is much less than is sometimes supposed. 'In those cases . . . in which a reduction to a set of exclusive and exhaustive *equiprobable* alternatives is practicable', he said, 'a numerical measure [of probability] can be obtained' (Keynes 1921: 65). Very often, because this reduction is impossible or impracticable, we cannot measure, or even compare, numerical probabilities. For example, if the grounds on which we claim truth for a pair of generalisations are very different, because one is based on numerous but similar positive instances while the other is based on fewer but varied positive instances, it may be impossible to compare, let alone measure, the probabilities in question. By pointing out that quantitative estimates of probabilities are not always available, Keynes was committing himself to the view that, although reasoning in science should conform to the principles embodied in Bayes's theorem, this is sometimes not enough to generate quantitative degrees of confidence in the truth of the conclusions we draw. He does not claim that this results from our assigning an infinitely small, or zero, prior probability to hypothetical axioms; it would be impossible to justify such probability assignments as rational degrees of belief. It results, rather, from our inability to compare prior and posterior probabilities.

But whatever the scope of quantitative probability judgements, there is a more fundamental question we must ask about any calculation resulting in a degree of probability: what is the aim of measuring probability? When a scientist undertakes an experimental investigation and concludes, perhaps by using the eliminative reasoning favoured by Keynes, that a hypothesis has a certain probability of being true, what does that probability signify? One answer to this question is that it signifies the degree of belief of the scientist in the hypothesis; if one hypothesis is more probable than an alternative, then a scientist making that judgement will have a greater degree of belief in the hypothesis than in the alternative. But, as we have seen, Keynes's view of probability was that it represents a logical relationship between statements. Probabilities in this sense do not necessarily have any connection with degrees of belief, because our degree of belief in one statement given another statement, to which it is logically related, may be based upon a misapprehension of that logical relation. Even in those cases where the entailment of one statement by another is not partial but is complete, our degree of belief in the entailed statement, given the truth of the entailing statement, may fall short of certainty simply because we have not recognised the entailment as complete. Probabilities, as degrees of belief, are psychological and subjective; probabilities, as degrees of entailment, are logical and objective. There is, no doubt, a stronger connection between a Keynesian probability and a rational degree of belief, or the degree of belief we ought to have in a statement made probable by the truth of another statement. But this is of little avail so long as rational degrees of belief are inaccessible to us, because their determination depends on a Principle of Indifference which has limited legitimate scope. Keynesian probabilities may, that is, be incapable of guiding practical belief.

This would be a disappointing conclusion to draw about an understanding of probability which has a long and distinguished history. Leibniz, the Bernoullis, Bayes and Price, Laplace, Herschel and Jevons had tried to identify and elucidate general principles governing sound probable reasoning, and for them probabilities represented rational degrees of belief. In scientific method we need probabilities because we need degrees of belief; these degrees of belief are rational in so far as we calculate them in accordance with rational principles. Critics such as John Venn and Charles Peirce had pointed to difficulties and uncertainties in the concept of rationality used or implied in this approach. In particular, the rationality of a degree of belief, as measured by a probability, depended upon principles about 'indifference' or 'insufficient reason' which were of questionable consistency, let alone rationality. Keynes defended tradition by limiting the scope of such a principle so that it would lead only to valid judgements of equiprobability. But the price of the defence was high; many of the quantitative and comparative judgements of probability that we need to make in elucidating scientific method are founded on an indefensible use of an indifference principle. There is, though, a quite different way of responding to difficulties with the classical account of probability. For if we can estimate degrees of belief directly, instead of by way of probabilities, then the way is open for a different approach to the rationality of those estimates. The prospects of such an approach are encouraged by the thought that beliefs, and degrees of belief, are mental or psychological characteristics.

This was the line of thought pursued by a young Cambridge contemporary of Keynes, Frank Ramsey, who in his short life made substantial contributions to philosophy, to mathematics and mathematical logic, and to economics. His 'Truth and probability' showed that we can recognise the subjectivity of the degrees of belief we have in propositions without sacrificing the prospect of constraining those degrees of belief so that they count as rational. The essay, unpublished in his lifetime, incorporated material from a review of *A Treatise on*

Probability that Ramsey had written for the *Cambridge Magazine* in 1922 (Ramsey 1989). Probability, he said, has both objective and subjective aspects. Sometimes when we speak of probabilities we are thinking of proportions: 'for example, if we say that the probability of recovery from smallpox is three-quarters, we mean, I think, simply that that is the proportion of smallpox cases which recover' (Ramsey 1978: 60). Such probabilities represent objective features of the world we encounter in experience. So far, at least, Venn and Peirce were correct. But sometimes probabilities are, or seem to be, degrees of belief. So, for example, if the only fact we know about a person is that he or she has recently swallowed arsenic, and we therefore say that it is highly likely the person will be dead in the next half hour, what we mean is that our degree of belief in this conclusion is high. If we then learn that the person has taken an emetic, our degree of belief in the conclusion will become less high. This is not because degrees of belief, being subjective, are liable to change, but because probabilities, which represent degrees of belief, are always relative to evidence. When evidence changes, probabilities and therefore degrees of belief also change. Keynes's view was that probabilities understood as representing degrees of belief are objective because they represent features of a real world which are, sometimes, measurable. But we encounter them in thought rather than in experience, because they are logical relations of partial entailment between propositions expressing conclusions in which we have degrees of belief and propositions expressing the evidence for those conclusions. Such features are, to say the least, contentious items of reality, and in Ramsey's view they are no more than the product of an over-fertile philosophical imagination. For him, probabilities as degrees of belief are subjective rather than objective; they represent psychological states. 'There really do not seem to be any such things', Ramsey declared, 'as the probability relations he describes' (Ramsey 1978: 63). We do not perceive them in any straightforward sense, and Keynes had produced no substantial argument for their existence.

Ramsey's critique opened up a new way of thinking about scientific method. We should understand the rationality of the probability judgements expressing partial beliefs arising from scientific investigation as a matter, not of their correspondence to something external to them, or of their derivability from a supposedly objective indifference principle, but of the relation of the beliefs to each other. Specifically, probability judgements are rational when the degrees of belief they express are 'consistent' with each other in the sense that they conform to the formal requirements of the probability calculus. For many, this 'subjective' or 'personalist' interpretation of probability has supplanted the classical interpretation of Laplace, Herschel, Jevons and Keynes as the chief alternative to the frequency, or statistical, interpretation. The accounts of scientific reasoning which are based on this subjective interpretation are known as Bayesian accounts, because they are able to supply, in a quite unproblematic way, the prior probabilities which are required when we use Bayes's theorem. The issues raised by these accounts are at the centre of many current debates about scientific method.

FURTHER READING

For general background, see:

Russell, B. (1948) *Human Knowledge: Its Scope and Limits*, London: George Allen and Unwin.

von Wright, G. H. (1951) *A Treatise on Induction and Probability*, London: Routledge and Kegan Paul.

von Wright, G. H. (1957) *The Logical Problem of Induction*, second edition, Oxford: Blackwell.

Cohen, L. J. (1989) *An Introduction to the Philosophy of Induction and Probability*, Oxford: Clarendon Press.

Gillies, D. (1991) 'Intersubjective probability and confirmation theory', *British Journal for the Philosophy of Science* 42: 513–33.

For Keynes on probable reasoning and scientific method, see:

Keynes, J. M. (1921) *A Treatise on Probability*, London: Macmillan.

For biographical information about Keynes, see:

Skidelsky, R. (1983) *John Maynard Keynes: Hopes Betrayed 1883–1920*, London: Macmillan.

Bateman, B. W. (1988) 'G. E. Moore and J. M. Keynes: A missing chapter in the history of the expected utility model', *American Economic Review* 78: 1098–1106.

Skidelsky, R. (1992) *John Maynard Keynes: The Economist as Saviour*, London: Macmillan.

For philosophical scrutiny, see:

Gillies, D. (1988) 'Keynes as a methodologist', *British Journal for the Philosophy of Science* 39: 117–29.

For Nicod, see:

Nicod, J. (1969) *Geometry and Induction*, London: Routledge and Kegan Paul.

For Ramsey's views, see:

Ramsey, F. P. (1978) 'Truth and probability', in *Foundations: Essays in Philosophy, Logic, Mathematics and Economics*, edited by D. H. Mellor, London: Routledge and Kegan Paul.

Ramsey, F. P. (1989) 'Mr Keynes on probability', *British Journal for the Philosophy of Science* 40: 219–22.

For philosophical discussion of Ramsey on probability, see:

Watt, D. E. (1989) 'Not very likely: a reply to Ramsey', *British Journal for the Philosophy of Science* 40: 223–27.

Runde, J. (1994) 'Keynes after Ramsey: In defence of A Treatise on Probability', *Studies in the History and Philosophy of Science* 25: 97–121.

10 Hans Reichenbach and Karl Popper
The (in)dispensability of induction

In his well known 'shilling shocker' of 1912 – *The Problems of Philosophy* – Bertrand Russell included a chapter on inductive arguments. He claimed that such arguments are relevant not only to our confidence in ordinary common-sense beliefs, like the belief that the Sun rises every day, that bread is nourishing, etc., but also that they are relevant to scientific beliefs. We use inductive reasoning, he said, to justify 'the general principles of science, such as the belief in the reign of law, and the belief that every event must have a cause' (Russell 1912: 38). For Russell, then, an adequate defence of induction was central to the defence of the rationality of reasoning in science. And he retained this basic approach in later books such as the 1948 volume, *Human Knowledge: Its Scope and Limits.*

In the induction chapter of *The Problems of Philosophy*, Russell makes it clear that the aim of inductive arguments is, given the truth of their premisses, to make their conclusion probably true. This aim is evidently distinct from that of deductive arguments, where we require that conclusions are necessarily true, given the truth of their premisses. If, therefore, we are sceptical of inductive reasoning, we cannot be so on the grounds that it fails to satisfy the aim of deductive reasoning. So long as such reasoning does yield probably true conclusions from true premisses, and therefore does meet its aim, inductive scepticism is unjustified. The crucial question is whether this condition for confidence in inductive reasoning is satisfied.

Russell's understanding of probability, at least in this context, was the same as that of Keynes. A statement is only probably true in relation to other statements, whether or not we explicitly identify those other statements. In inductive reasoning we do identify those other statements, because they are the premisses of the reasoning; they constitute what we would naturally call the evidence for the truth of the statement we describe as probable. Russell used the example of the claim that it is probable that all swans are white to illustrate this relational feature of probability statements. The claim is not refuted by the observation of a black swan, because the evidence in relation to which it is probable that all swans are white cannot include any observations of black swans, for if it did it would no longer be probable that all swans are white. Of course, the claim that all swans are white is refuted by the observation of a black swan, but this simply shows that whatever is the case about probability, truth itself is not relational (Russell 1912: 37).

Russell also shared Keynes's view that what we mean in declaring a conclusion probably true in relation to evidence is that it is rational to believe the conclusion when that evidence is all the relevant evidence we have. So the question whether inductive reasoning yields conclusions that are probably true is the question whether it is rational to believe those conclusions. Rationality is no doubt a matter of degree, so our belief in one conclusion can be more or less rational than our belief in another. But this conveniently reflects the fact that probability, too, is a matter of degree and that, therefore, the truth of one conclusion can be more or less probable than the truth of another. How, though, can we establish the rationality of a belief? What are the criteria of rationality we should use? We naturally think of rationality as a matter of logic; someone is rational in so far as they think logically. But this criterion is of little use, for logical thinking is either thinking in accordance with the principles of deduction or thinking in accordance with the principles of induction. If we choose the former we will restrict the scope of rationality and conclude that we cannot rationally believe inductive conclusions because they are not deductive conclusions. If we choose the latter we face the impossible task of identifying principles of induction when we have yet to establish that inductive reasoning is logical reasoning. We know what deductive rationality is and we also know that, in this context, it is inappropriate as a criterion; we do not yet know what inductive rationality is and therefore cannot appeal to it as a criterion.

Since David Hume in the eighteenth century, philosophers have accepted that it is possible to explain why we believe the conclusions of inductive arguments; evidence creates expectations which make it natural, and perhaps even inevitable, for us to believe the conclusions it leads to. But however tightly our psychological propensities, or 'habits', as Hume called them, constrain our beliefs, that does not in itself make them rational. So long as we wish to retain the concept of a belief being rational, we will want to allow for the possibility that people could find themselves psychologically obliged to believe things which they should not believe.

In *The Problems of Philosophy*, Russell's answer to the crucial question about why we are justified in believing the conclusions of inductive arguments involved an appeal to a 'principle of induction'. This principle states that, in the case of a general scientific law, if we have a 'sufficient number' of positive instances and no negative instances, then we can be 'nearly certain' that the law is true. And in the case of a specific prediction, the probability of a new positive instance is 'nearly a certainty', provided we have a 'sufficient number' of positive instances and no negative instances on which we base the prediction. In both cases the criterion of sufficiency in the number of positive instances is related to the criterion for a conclusion to be nearly certain.

This principle, if we can show that it is true, would justify our confidence in induction by enumeration. But can we show that it is true? As Russell noticed, if probability is understood in the way he advocated, we could never have an empirical reason for denying the truth of this principle. For to produce a counter example to the principle, we would have to show, not simply that a law judged to be nearly certain by the use of the principle is in fact false, but rather that a law is rendered uncertain or false by a 'sufficient number' of positive instances and no negative instances. And this is impossible. But by the same token we could never have empirical reasons for affirming the principle; it cannot, as Russell said, be '*proved* by an appeal to experience'. And this is just as well, because if there were such reasons they would have to be inductive reasons, and we have yet to establish that inductive reasons are good reasons. But if we do not and cannot have empirical grounds for either accepting or rejecting the principle of induction, why should we accept, or indeed reject, it? To this question Russell replied by presenting his readers with a dilemma: 'we must', he said, 'either accept the inductive principle on the ground of its intrinsic evidence, or forego all justification of our expectations about the future' (Russell 1912: 38). This, though, is hardly an answer: we know which of the two alternatives presented by the dilemma is the one we prefer; but we need to know which is the right one to choose, and why. Russell was in no doubt that the principle must be accepted, and in saying that the ground for this acceptance was its 'intrinsic evidence' he was claiming that our belief in the principle is a priori, or independent of experience. With the same point in mind, he called it a 'logical' principle, and thereby associated it with principles of deductive reasoning. But even so, we have a further dilemma to face. For our belief in the principle will be a priori if it is true, simply by virtue of the meanings of the words we use to express it, in particular the meanings of 'probable' and 'nearly certain'. But in that case, it is by no means clear that the conclusion is justified by the principle, such as the conclusion that a scientific law is 'nearly certain' has the meaning that we would customarily assign to it. Perhaps all that it means is that we have a 'sufficient number' of positive instances of the law and no negative instances, in which case we still have no good reason for thinking that the law will provide us with reliable predictions. Alternatively, our belief in the principle will be a priori if the principle is true by virtue of what reason, rather than experience, tells us about the natural world. But in that case we find ourselves committed to the view, incompatible with empiricist scruples, that some significant reasons for believing what we do about the natural world are independent of experience of that world.

Russell himself was prepared to sacrifice empiricism in order to defend his principle, and thereby the rationality of induction. 'Science', he declared in a later study of inductive reasoning, 'is impossible unless we have some knowledge which we could not have if empiricism, in a strict form, were true' (Russell 1948: 393). But many have thought, and continue to think, that the sacrifice of empiricism is an unnecessary price to pay.

An influential representative of these critics was Hans Reichenbach. He was born in Hamburg, where his father was a prosperous merchant. In 1910–11, he studied engineering briefly at the Technische Hochschule in Stuttgart, but it did not satisfy his theoretical interests and he turned to a study of mathematics, physics and philosophy. Before the outbreak of the First World War in 1914 he was fortunate to have among his teachers the mathematician David Hilbert, the physicists Max Planck, Arnold Sommerfeld and Max Born, and the philosopher Ernst Cassirer. In a dissertation which formulated a mathematical probability calculus, examined its philosophical significance, and explored its applicability to the physical world, he brought together the knowledge and skills he had acquired as a result of their teaching. After the war he furthered his knowledge of modern physics by attending Einstein's seminar on relativity theory at Berlin University. In 1920 he began a teaching career and, six years later, returned to that university as its Professor of the Philosophy of Physics. Though he was never a member of the Vienna Circle of logical positivists, he was in sympathy with its aims and had established contact with several of its members, including Rudolf Carnap. In 1930, with Carnap, he founded and edited the journal *Erkenntnis*. This became a successful means for promoting the ideas of the Vienna Circle and those of a similar group of philosophers and scientists in Berlin. His Berlin group, together with the Vienna Circle, organised several conferences at which philosophical and scientific approaches were able to interact with each other. In 1933, shortly after the Nazis' assumption of power, and as a consequence of the liberal politics he adopted and expressed, he was dismissed from his post. He subsequently taught in Turkey and in the USA. He died in 1953.

In the early part of his career Reichenbach was indeed receptive to the rationalism of Russell's approach, but by the time he turned his attention to writing his *Theory of Probability* in the 1930s, his advocacy of a thoroughgoing empiricist philosophy of science was unwavering. 'All forms of rational belief in synthetic statements', he said, 'whether they appear in the form of a synthetic *a priori*, or an animal faith, or a belief in the uniformity of the world, or a principle of insufficient reason . . . are remnants of a philosophy of rationalism, which holds that human reason has access to knowledge of the physical world by other means than sense observation' (Reichenbach 1949: viii). Such notions, he claimed, are superfluous, and at the heart of his opposition was his rejection of the Keynes–Russell understanding of probability in favour of a relative frequency concept which, like that advocated by Venn and by Peirce, was based on empirical facts rather than logical relations. For Keynes, as for Russell, 'the validity of the inductive method does *not* depend on the success of its predictions' (Keynes 1921: 221); but for Reichenbach the probability of an inductive conclusion implies its predictive success. Not surprisingly, his conclusions about scientific method contrast sharply with those of Keynes; 'the manifold forms of induction', he said, 'including the hypothetico-deductive method, are expressible in terms of deductive methods, with the sole addition of induction by enumeration' (Reichenbach 1951: 243). The task of finding a justification for enumerative induction is, as Russell had shown, a formidable one, but we will consider, first, why Reichenbach thought that its accomplishment was sufficient for the rationality of scientific method.

Reichenbach's general view about scientific method was that, although in practice it takes a sophisticated form, enumerative induction remains its core. 'All forms of inductive inference', he claimed, 'are reducible to one form, to the inference of induction by enumeration'. On the face of it, this seems sharply opposed to the views of Bacon, of Mill, and indeed of Keynes, all of whom had criticised the adequacy of enumerative induction. It seems, too, to be in conflict with the practice of science; rarely if ever do scientists interest themselves in establishing experimental or observational generalisations by collecting positive instances of them. Yet these impressions are misleading. As Reichenbach pointed out, Mill had acknowledged that his theory of scientific method, though it promoted eliminative induction, depended upon assumptions which could only be established by enumerative induction; in this sense his theory was also reducible to enumerative induction. Moreover, Reichenbach was quite clear that enumerative induction is not, by itself, sufficient to account for scientific method, and to that extent his disagreement with those who disparage it is verbal rather than real. Scientific method, in his view, involves more than the use of inductive inferences, even though those inferences are always enumerative. Thus, if we consider the eliminative methods of Bacon and Mill we find that, by incorporating 'a trivial use of *deduction*', they supplement, rather than supplant, enumerative induction. With Bacon's table of absence and Mill's canon of difference, for example, we can prove, deductively, that a possible universal generalisation is false; in such cases 'deduction is employed in a trivial form to rule out impermissible inductive conclusions'. But the addition of simple deductive logic still generates only a weak theory of scientific method, incapable of accounting for most of the logical aspects of scientific reasoning. It accounts only for what Reichenbach called 'primitive knowledge', by which he meant that it provides a method, namely enumerative induction, for 'finding probabilities' when we know none. Primitive knowledge, then, is of probabilities, but it is based upon knowledge which is not of probabilities, but of what did or did not happen in particular circumstances that we have observed. For 'advanced knowledge' we need other methods which, though they cannot themselves generate probabilities, allow us to construct 'concatenations of inductions' by deducing new probability statements from ones already accepted. These methods require the resources of the mathematical calculus of probability, which we apply in this context, as in others, only in so far as we understand probabilities as frequencies. 'In advanced knowledge', Reichenbach said, 'the whole technique of the calculus of probability is at our disposal and can be adduced to justify the methods employed, whereas primitive knowledge requires other means of justifying inductive inferences' (Reichenbach 1949: viii, 364, 429).

Prominent among the methods required for advanced knowledge is what Reichenbach called the method of 'explanatory inference'. It 'consists in the inference from certain observational data to a hypothesis, or theory, from which the data are derivable and which, conversely, is regarded as being made probable by the data' (Reichenbach 1949: 431). The 'method of hypotheses', and the 'hypothetico-deductive method' are other names for this inference. It involves the deduction, using 'the rule of Bayes', of the probabilities of hypotheses or theories, from 'antecedent' probabilities. These antecedent probabilities may be provided by other explanatory inferences on the basis of other antecedent probabilities, but ultimately the source of all probabilities is the only method capable of yielding them without reference to other probabilities, namely enumerative induction.

According to a relative frequency conception of probability, when we assign a probability to the occurrence of a specified type of event in a specified kind of circumstance, we are simply stating an empirical fact about the limit of the relative frequency with which events of that type occur in that kind of circumstance. So, for example, to say that the probability of heads when a coin is tossed is one half is to say that if we were to toss the coin an infinite number of times, a head would turn up on half of them. On the face of it, this understanding of probability seems quite different from what is needed for probable reasoning in science; when we judge a scientific law to be 'nearly certain' or probably true, it does not seem that we are stating a fact about the limit of a relative frequency. Nevertheless, in Reichenbach's view, this is what is happening in such cases; the probabilities of laws, of theories and of hypotheses can and must be understood as relative frequencies, for 'there is only *one* concept of probability, the same for phenomena and for scientific theories' (Reichenbach 1978: vol. 2, 385).

We can best see how this is so by considering a straightforward case of a universal scientific law which is made probably true by 'sufficiently numerous' positive instances and the absence of negative instances. A suitable example is the claim that copper is fusible (i.e. can be made liquid). The relative frequency of the property of fusibility in the samples of copper we have tested is one, for all such samples have provided positive instances of the claim. From this observed frequency we infer, or rather 'posit', that the long-run frequency of this property in copper generally is also one; we infer, or posit, that all copper is fusible. And the inductive rule that we use to make this inference is the rule of induction by simple enumeration: if the relative frequency of fusible copper in the copper samples we have tested for fusibility is one, then the relative frequency of fusible copper in the entire population of copper samples is also one. But because the conclusion that all copper is fusible is inductive and we have yet to establish whether such conclusions are acceptable, we cannot claim that it is true that all copper is fusible, or even that it is probable that all copper is fusible. That is why we posit rather than assert the conclusion; we 'deal with it', Reichenbach said, 'as a true proposition' (Reichenbach 1938: 313). At this stage it is a 'blind' posit, because we have no way of telling whether it is a good posit or not. We need to find some way of 'appraising' the 'weight' of the posit, and we can do this, Reichenbach thought, by turning our attention to other materials, such as iron, zinc, tin, etc. We know that in the case of most of them we have as a blind posit the inductive conclusion that they, too, are fusible. But there are, or there might be, exceptions; for some materials we have no direct evidence that they are fusible. Our blind posit of the fusibility of copper is, therefore, one among other similar blind posits, and since the overwhelming majority of them attribute fusibility to materials, the observed frequency of fusibility in a wide range of materials is close to one. Using the rule of enumerative induction we infer, or posit, that the long-run frequency of fusibility in materials is close to one. And finally, we transfer this limiting frequency, as a probability or rather as a 'weight', to the case of the fusibility of copper and conclude that it is highly probable that all copper is fusible. We have thus 'appraised the weight' of the posit that all copper is fusible. It needs to be treated with a degree of caution, because most, but not all, of the conclusions we have drawn from our experiments enable us to attribute fusibility to chemical elements; the relative frequency with which we have been able to draw such conclusions has been less than one, and we should therefore infer, inductively, that the limit of this relative frequency is less than one. Accordingly, we should judge each of the inductive conclusions we have drawn, including the conclusion that copper is fusible, to be probably true, in the sense that it belongs to a class of conclusions most, but not all, of whose members are true.

So we begin by positing, solely on the basis of observation and experiment, a probability which is understood as a long-run frequency. The posit takes the form of a universal or statistical generalisation; if the probability posit is one, the generalisation will be universal, and if it is less than one, the generalisation will be statistical. The rule of enumerative induction, or the 'straight rule' as it is sometimes called, enables us to acquire this 'primitive' knowledge. We then decide how seriously to take this posited probability. We decide what 'weight' it has, where 'weight' is simply a term for the second-level probability that our original first-level probability posit is true. In order to be consistent in understanding probability as a frequency, we will have to judge this 'weight' by assigning our original posit to an appropriate reference class of similar posits in order to determine the frequency within this class of posits with the characteristic, i.e. the probability of our original posit. The same rule of enumerative induction will then allow us to posit a 'weight' for the original posit. We will thereby know how much, if any, confidence to place in our original universal or statistical general- isation. This knowledge, too, would count as 'primitive' knowledge in Reichenbach's sense. 'Probability of hypotheses', Reichenbach claimed, 'is simply a probability of higher order' (Reichenbach 1978: vol. 2, 378).

One apparent difficulty with this way of understanding probable reasoning is that it seems to lead to an infinite regression. For the evaluation of an original 'posit' is itself a second-level posit which needs evaluation, and this third-level evaluation is a posit requiring evalu- ation, and so on indefinitely. In order to evaluate posits we need to compare them, as probabilities and thus as claims about limits of relative frequencies, with relevant facts, but the only facts that are ever available leave room for doubt as to whether the claims about relative frequencies are correct. In positing that they are correct we introduce a higher level probability and therefore a further claim about a limit of relative frequency. There seems no way of stopping the regression so that conclusions about probabilities can be stated as true (Russell 1948: 434–5; cf. Reichenbach 1978: vol. 2, 405–11).

There are significant difficulties, too, facing Reichenbach's views concerning the justification of advanced knowledge. His aim was to show how, using the mathematical calculus of probability, and par- ticularly 'the rule of Bayes', explanatory inferences could yield judge- ments about the probable truth of scientific hypotheses and theories. Bayes's theorem enables us to calculate the contribution that evidence makes to the probability, or weight, of a hypothesis when that evidence is explained by the hypothesis. The bases of the calculation are 'antecedent' probabilities, or weights, by which is meant probabilities which take into account only what we can take for granted before considering the relevance of this evidence to this hypothesis. All probabilities, whether antecedent or not, will have to be understood as relative frequencies if Reichenbach is to sustain his claim that the only inductive inference required in scientific method is enumerative induction. But it does not seem at all plausible to suppose that the antecedent probability of a hypothesis, which is one of the probabilities we need to know in order to apply Bayes's theorem, could be understood as a relative frequency. For consider what would be involved in an attempt to adhere to the frequency conception of probability in this case. We will have to identify an appropriate reference class of 'similar' hypotheses, and since it is the truth attribute of hypotheses that interests us, we will have to determine, using the rule of induction by enumeration, the relative frequency of that truth attribute in this reference class. Only when we have completed these tasks will we be able to transfer this frequency, as an antecedent probability or weight, to the member of that reference class that we are interested in, namely our hypothesis. But the tasks do not seem capable of completion unless we can identify the relevant reference class to which our hypothesis belongs. For instance, if we wish to judge the antecedent probability of Newton's inverse square law of gravitational attraction, should we identify its relevant reference class as also containing 'the law of the conservation of energy, . . . the law of entropy, etc.' (Reichenbach 1949: 440)? Admittedly, Newton's law is, like those laws, a law of physical science, but it is also like a great many other claims, most of which may not have anything to do with physics. To put the problem in its starkest terms, it is easy to find a reference class of other laws, all or most of which are thought to be true, and to conclude that, since the relative frequency of truth in this reference class is close to one, the appropriate probability to assign to Newton's law is also close to one. But it is equally easy to find a different reference class of other laws, all or most of which are thought to be false, and to conclude that, since the relative frequency of truth in this reference class is close to zero, the appropriate probability to assign to Newton's law is also close to zero. Reichenbach's insistence that probabilities of hypotheses are relative frequencies leaves us with no way of choosing between these alternatives.

It is true that the problem we face is comparable to that of assigning a probability, understood as a relative frequency, to a single event, such as happens when we say that 'it is improbable that Julius Caesar was in Britain'. For just as a single event either occurs or it does not, so also a hypothesis is either true or false. But probabilities, so understood, are defined only for types or classes of events, and since a single event belongs to any number of different reference classes, it would appear that it can have any number of possibly different probabilities. One response to this difficulty is to say that individual events do not have probabilities. The implication of this for our context is that individual hypotheses do not have probabilities, in which case Bayes's theorem cannot be applied and consequently probability ideas are of no use in justifying advanced knowledge. Alternatively, we can decide that, in assigning a probability to a particular event, we select as the relevant reference class the narrowest class for which we have reliable statistics. In this way, the 'pseudoconcept of a probability of a single case must be replaced by a substitute constructed in terms of class probabilities'. This indicates that the probability of a hypothesis is, similarly, a pseudoconcept which needs to be replaced by, or understood in terms of, a probability understood as a relative frequency in a suitable reference class – presumably the narrowest reference class for which reliable statistics are available. But, as Reichenbach acknowledged, we have yet to reach the stage of having sufficient statistics on theories and hypotheses to enable us to make such replacements, and until we can, the selection of a reference class will remain 'ambiguous'. 'The selection of a suitable reference class', he said, 'is always a problem of advanced knowledge'. Even if we grant that 'the probability of hypotheses offers no difficulties of principle to a statistical interpretation', the practical problems of assigning justifiable probabilities to hypotheses prevent us from making use of Bayes's theorem and thereby justifying any advanced knowledge. Reichenbach claimed that the practical problems were the consequence of 'insufficient data', and that therefore 'crude estimates' of probabilities of hypotheses would have to be used. But this is to underrate the nature of the problems, which arise not so much from a lack of relevant data as from a lack of clarity as to what data is relevant (Reichenbach 1949: 336, 375, 440, 442).

So far we have assumed that primitive knowledge, or knowledge based not on other probabilities but upon observed or experimental facts, is justified knowledge. We have assumed, that is, that the rule of enumerative induction – the straight rule – is reliable. Clearly, without this rule, advanced knowledge is impossible, because it provides us with our only means of establishing the probability values which need to be used when applying theorems of the probability calculus, notably Bayes's theorem. We must now, though, test this assumption to see whether it is capable of withstanding the weight placed upon it by Reichenbach.

The straight rule tells us that if a property B occurs with a certain relative frequency in a sequence of observed A's, then we can posit that same relative frequency of the property B in the whole population of A's. When more A's are observed, the relative frequency of the property B may change, in which case our posit will change to match it. For example, suppose that experiments with samples of a radioactive isotope of bismuth indicate that, over a period of five days, half of the material in each of the samples has been subject to radioactive decay. We posit, using the straight rule, the statistical law that the half-life of this radioactive isotope is five days. Our posit is 'blind' in the sense that we have no grounds as yet for attributing any weight to it. Suppose, though, that as a matter of fact there is no law, statistical or universal, which governs the radioactive decay of our isotope. Suppose, more generally, that despite the uniformities and regularities we constantly observe, there are in fact no laws which govern the behaviour of things, the character of natural phenomena, or the sequence of states of affairs. Even though it appears otherwise, the natural world is not subject to scientific laws; nor are any scientific hypotheses, proposed or not, true; nor are any scientific theories, invented or not, applicable. In such circumstances, any blind posit that we make using the straight rule is worthless, whether we realise it or not. But so too is any other posit that any other rule might enable us to make. If there is no such thing as the relative frequency of the property B among all A's, then all posits which attempt to identify it, on the basis of any rule, will be equally worthless. Evidently, then, the natural world must be governed by laws, hypotheses and theories if the straight rule is to stand any chance of yielding posits of any value. Why, though, are the posits yielded by the straight rule in such circumstances better than posits yielded by any alternative rule? An answer to this question is essential if we are to use the straight rule to justify primitive knowledge; it is essential if Reichenbach is to counter Hume's scepticism.

In assuming that the natural world is law-governed, we are assuming that in some cases there exists a relative frequency of the property B in the total population of A's. So long as that relative frequency exists, we can tolerate the prospect that even though all observed A's have displayed the property B, we are mistaken in our straight rule posit that all A's display B; our posit could be reasonable even though mistaken, and further observations could show that this is so. The straight rule is, in the circumstances we are now envisaging, self-correcting in the sense that persistent use of it will eventually yield a posit as close to the relative frequency as we wish. But the same is true of an indefinite number of other rules. Consider, for example, the rule so contructed that it yields posits which are incompatible with straight rule posits for all observed samples except when the sample approaches the size of the whole population, when it produces posits which converge with straight rule posits. For example, on the basis of sample testing the straight rule posits that all copper is fusible, whereas on the same sample basis an alternative 'crooked' rule posits that, say, only 90 per cent of all copper is fusible. As the sample increases in size, the 'crooked' rule differs less and less in its posit from the posit of the straight rule. Thus, once the sample has reached a certain size, it might yield the posit that 95 per cent of all copper is fusible. The rule can be formulated in such a way as to ensure that, although the rate at which the difference between its posits and those of the straight rule diminishes can be as slow as we please, it disappears entirely in the long run. In fact, given any finite sample of A's and any value for the relative frequency of the property B in that sample, there is a rule which posits any other value for the relative frequency of the property B in the whole population of A's. Such a rule can always be formulated so as to yield a posit which does not differ from the straight rule posit if it is applied to a sample sufficiently larger. However strange and arbitrary such a 'crooked' rule might appear, it has as much right to be considered as a legitimate rule for justifying posits as does the more familiar straight rule. If we prefer the posits of the straight rule to the posits of such a rule, we have yet to find a reason for our preference.

Reichenbach himself thought that simplicity considerations could justify the preference. But since we wish to use a preferred posit to anticipate correctly what will happen in the future, the simplicity of the preferred posit must be connected with its truth. However, unless we are to give up the empiricism which lies at the heart of Reichenbach's thinking, that connection between simplicity and truth will have to be established on empirical grounds, which means we will be relying on inductive reasoning. Clearly this takes us in a circle: we have to assume the reliability of inductive reasoning in order to justify our preference for the conclusions of inductive reasoning.

We have seen why Reichenbach thought that scientific method requires only one addition to the resources of deductive reasoning, including deductive reasoning concerning probabilities, namely induction by enumeration. We have also considered the difficulties confronting this view. To use the rule of enumerative induction we must assume, perhaps wrongly, that the natural world is governed by laws. Accordingly, in so far as we have no good reason for believing that the world is so governed, we have no good reason for using this rule. In addition, we have noticed that this rule is one among many rules yielding posits of relative frequencies or probabilities. Deductive reasoning cannot give us any assurance that we are right to choose the posits yielded by one rule rather than another. Using the rule of enumerative induction, we posit that the long-run relative frequency of a property in a population is the same as the observed relative frequency of that property in a sample, but our posit is 'blind . . . since it is used without a knowledge of how good it is' (Reichenbach 1949: 446). This would not matter quite so much if it were the only defensible posit we could make. But it is not. We could posit a long-run relative frequency which differs in any way we wish from the observed relative frequency, and there would be a defensible rule which would yield this posit. Consequently, our ignorance of how good the posits yielded by the inductive rule are prevents us from justifying the choice we make in their favour.

We have also seen that, even if these difficulties with enumerative induction could be overcome, there would still be obstacles to the use of its results in justifying advanced knowledge. For the relative frequencies or probabilities we obtain from the inductive rule need appraisal before we can use them in, for example, Bayes's theorem. Thus the rule of induction may posit that all copper is fusible, but we need to know how probable it is that this universal generalisation is true, and, because this probability, like any other, is a relative frequency, this means assigning the generalisation to an appropriate reference class for which we have the statistical information allowing us to determine this probability. We have, though, no clear criteria for deciding whether a reference class is appropriate; and in most cases we completely lack the relevant statistical data for classes of generalisations or laws. Reichenbach himself did not consider that these obstacles were insuperable. In his view, we should no more be discouraged about assigning probabilities to scientific laws than we are about assigning probabilities to particular events, though we know that particular events, like scientific laws, belong to any number of distinct classes.

Few shared his optimism, and in the year preceding the appearance of his principal study of probabilistic reasoning, there was also published an account of scientific method which depended upon ideas sharply opposed to Reichenbach's. Its author was a young Austrian schoolteacher named Karl Popper. He was born in Vienna in 1902. His father was a lawyer with an interest in academic matters, and his mother a pianist, so the family in which he grew up provided him with an environment in which scholarship and culture were valued. At the age of sixteen he became impatient with the shortcomings of formal education, left school, and enrolled as an unmatriculated student at the University of Vienna. The independent studies he then took up enabled him to encounter, and respond to, philosophical ideas. In due course he qualified as a schoolteacher. During the 1920s he studied educational psychology, acquiring a PhD in 1928. It was at this time that he began to give sustained attention to the philosophy of science and to develop the ideas for which he has since become renowned. He read the published work of Wittgenstein and Carnap, and his first contacts with members of the famous Vienna Circle of philosophers and scientists took place in the late 1920s. He was never himself a member of this circle, but nevertheless it was those contacts which stimulated him to write a book explaining his ideas. His *Logik der Forschung* is, Popper has claimed, no more than a brief summary of those ideas. It was published in 1934 and immediately attracted favourable attention, including praise from members of the circle. Shortly afterwards he was invited to lecture in England, and the favourable impression he created there helped him to secure an appointment to a lectureship at the Canterbury University College of the University of New Zealand. He, like others of his Viennese contemporaries, was therefore able to escape the baleful and growing power of National Socialism in Austria. This was just as well, for his Jewish origins and his liberal politics would have made him particularly vulnerable to Nazi activities at the time of the Anschluss and after. After the war, in 1946, he returned to England, first as a reader and later as a professor of logic and scientific method at the London School of Economics. *Logik der Forschung* was translated into English and published in 1959 as *The Logic of Scientific Discovery*. It contained much new material in the form of footnotes and appendices. Popper's intention was that its publication should be accompanied by a companion volume entitled *Postscript: After Twenty Years*. In the event, it was not until 1982 that this elaborate sequel, reviewing and developing his ideas about the philosophy and methods of science, was published. Fortunately, two important collections of his essays, *Conjectures and Refutations* (1963) and *Objective Knowledge* (1972), kept Popper's readers informed about those developments and their implications. In Britain at least, his ideas have been influential not only in philosophical circles but also, as his election in 1976 as a Fellow of the Royal Society testifies, among practising scientists. His influence also extended to political philosophy, though he did not count himself as a political philosopher and would have been surprised and perhaps not a little disappointed to have seen those several obituary notices appearing after his death in 1995 which focused on this aspect of his work, sometimes to the point of neglecting his theory of scientific knowledge.

Popper's claim about inductive reasoning is crucial to an understanding of his methodology. Such reasoning cannot and should not, he said, be part of any rational decision-making process in science, for inductive reasoning is fallacious reasoning. His uncompromising response to Hume's scepticism was not to find a way of defending induction but rather to abandon it altogether. Plainly, induction fails to satisfy the standards appropriate to deductive reasoning, but in Popper's view there are no other legitimate standards. He was, we might say, an atheist rather than an agnostic about the existence of good inductive arguments: 'there simply is no such logical entity as an inductive inference' (Schilpp 1974: 1015). We cannot deduce the truth of theories, hypotheses and laws that are used in science from the observations and experiments that we think, though wrongly, provide inductive support for them. And since inductive reasoning must be abandoned, we cannot deduce, either, their probable truth. All that we can do, so it seems, is deduce the falsity of theories, hypotheses or laws from our acceptance of reports of observations and experiments which are inconsistent with them. Thus accepted reports of experiments showing that the atomic weight of chlorine is 35.5 enable us to deduce that the hypothesis which claims the atomic weight of any element to be an integral multiple of the atomic weight of hydrogen, namely one, must be false. There are circumstances in which we can, therefore, deductively falsify a scientific belief, but there are no circumstances in which we can inductively verify it.

This difference, Popper claimed, arises because scientific beliefs are universal in character, and have to be so if they are to serve us in explanation and prediction. For the universality of a scientific belief implies that, no matter how many instances we have found positive, there will always be an indefinite number of unexamined instances which may or may not also be positive. We have no good reason for supposing that any of these unexamined instances will be positive, or will be negative, so we must refrain from drawing any conclusions. On the other hand, a single negative instance is sufficient to prove that the belief is false, for such an instance is logically incompatible with the universal truth of the belief. Provided, therefore, that the instance is accepted as negative we must conclude that the scientific belief is false. In short, we can sometimes deduce that a universal scientific belief is false but we can never induce that a universal scientific belief is true.

It is sometimes argued that this 'asymmetry' between verification and falsification is not nearly as pronounced as Popper declared it to be. Thus, there is no inconsistency in holding that a universal scientific belief is false despite any number of positive instances; and there is no inconsistency either in holding that a universal scientific belief is true despite the evidence of a negative instance. For the belief that an instance is negative is itself a scientific belief and may be falsified by experimental evidence which we accept and which is inconsistent with it. When, for example, we draw a right-angled triangle on the surface of a sphere using parts of three great circles for its sides, and discover that for this triangle Pythagoras' Theorem does not hold, we may decide that this apparently negative instance is not really negative because it is not a genuine instance at all. Triangles drawn on the surfaces of spheres are not the sort of triangles which fall within the scope of Pythagoras' Theorem. Falsification, that is to say, is no more capable of yielding conclusive rejections of scientific belief than verification is of yielding conclusive acceptances of scientific beliefs. The asymmetry between falsification and verification, therefore, has less logical signific-ance than Popper supposed.

We should, though, resist this reasoning. Falsifications may not be conclusive, for the acceptances on which rejections are based are always provisional acceptances. But, nevertheless, it remains the case that, in falsification, if we accept falsifying claims then, to remain consistent, we must reject falsified claims. On the other hand, although verifications are also not conclusive, our acceptance or rejection of verifying instances has no implications concerning the acceptance or rejection of verified claims. Falsifying claims sometimes give us a good reason for rejecting a scientific belief, namely when the claims are accepted. But verifying claims, even when accepted, give us no good and appropriate reason for accepting any scientific belief, because any such reason would have to be inductive to be appropriate and there are no good inductive reasons. Thus, Foucault and Fizeau constructed a deductive argument, based on the acceptance of experimental results, for the falsity of Newton's belief that light travels faster in water than in air. There is not, never was, and never could be any deductive argument, based on the acceptance of experimental results, for the truth of that belief. And the absence of any deductive argument means, in Popper's view, the absence of any good argument.

Despite Popper's rejection of induction, there is an affinity between his thinking and some aspects of eliminative induction. For whether or not we think that the elimination of some hypotheses makes other hypotheses more likely to be true than they would otherwise be, it certainly makes the eliminated hypotheses false in just the way that Popper supposes. Hypotheses are eliminated, perhaps provisionally, on the grounds that their truth is incompatible with accepted experimental results. So far, at least, there is common ground between Bacon's tables of absence and presence, Mill's methods of agreement and difference, and Popper's deductivist account of scientific method. There is, though, an important difference between Popper's account and eliminative induction, for in the latter the elimination of some hypotheses is used to argue for the truth, or rather probable truth, of other hypotheses. But so long as there are an indefinite number of hypotheses compatible with the available evidence, such an argument is non-deductive and inconclusive. In Popper's view, no such argument is of any value; the elimination or falsification of some hypotheses, no matter how many, does not legitimately imply that any other hypothesis is true or even probably true. Bacon, Mill, and those of their successors who promoted the superior virtues of eliminative induction are therefore mistaken in their conviction that, by seeking variety in evidence, or by undertaking controlled experiments, we can establish the truth or enhance the probability of any scientific belief.

Still, the limited affinity between Popper's ideas and the views of those who advocate eliminative induction helps to explain why the weight of his attack against inductivist conceptions of scientific method is directed against those, like Reichenbach, supporting the view that induction by enumeration is fundamental to any such conception. He agreed with Reichenbach that, with the aid of a 'principle of induction', if only it could be established, 'we could put inductive inferences into a logically acceptable form'. And he also agreed with Reichenbach that in such inferences we 'pass from *singular statements* (sometimes also called "particular" statements), such as accounts of the results of observations or experiments, to *universal statements*, such as hypotheses or theories'. A suitable principle of induction, therefore, would be a principle of enumerative induction. But to establish this principle, we would need to treat it either as empirically valid, in which case it would have to be established inductively and so would assume its own validity, or alternatively as a priori valid, in which case we would be faced with the task of providing an a priori justification for an empirical statement (Popper 1959: 27–9). For both Reichenbach and Popper, the first alternative was logically unacceptable and the second incompatible with empiricist convictions. Reichenbach's response was to acknowledge that we could not establish the truth of the principle, but nevertheless to argue that, if we can assume that the natural world is governed by stable laws, then this principle is superior to any other. Popper agreed that we cannot establish the truth of the principle, but his conclusion was that, because of this, we should abandon it altogether and construct an account of scientific method which does not depend in any way on inductive reasoning. We have seen that there are unanswered difficulties facing Reichenbach's approach, and in their light we might well think we should adopt Popper's alternative approach.

For Popper, then, an inductive account of scientific method would have the shape given it by Reichenbach, with a principle of enumerative induction at its core. His fundamental reason for rejecting an inductivist scientific method was his conviction that this principle could not be justified. But Popper was also sure that, even if the principle of enumerative induction were used, it would not be capable of generating, as Reichenbach required, conclusions about the probability of hypotheses. For that would require us to understand such a probability as a relative frequency: we 'call a hypothesis "probable" if it is an *element of a sequence of hypotheses* with a definite truth-frequency' (Popper 1959: 259). In Popper's view there could be no such understanding, for, in the first place, we would have to overcome the difficulty of knowing which of any number of sequences of hypotheses we should choose, and, in the second place, we would have to address the problem of establishing a definite truth-frequency for the chosen sequence. He placed particular stress on the latter, claiming that, since no hypothesis is known to be true, we must either tolerate the conclusion that the truth-frequency in any sequence of hypotheses is zero, and therefore that all hypotheses are false, or, if we assign a truth-frequency of less than one to a sequence of hypotheses, attribute a probability determined by that truth-frequency to each hypothesis in the sequence, including those we know are false. Both alternatives seem unacceptable. In effect, Popper's objection was that the relative frequency conception of probability is ill suited to the understanding of the probability of hypotheses.

Popper did, then, have reasons for rejecting an inductivist account of scientific method. Will, though, the resources of deductive logic be sufficient to create an alternative account? Popper believed that they are. A key question is whether deductive reasoning alone can account for scientists' preferring one rather than another of the uneliminated or unfalsified hypotheses capable of accounting for some range of phenomena. We have seen that, in eliminative induction, we justify such a preference by restricting the number of hypotheses that have to be considered. Popper did not accept this as legitimate. Instead, he appealed to his concept of 'corroboration' in order to discriminate between uneliminated or unfalsified hypotheses. Some unfalsified hypotheses, he claimed, are *better corroborated* than others, by which he meant, not that we have better reasons for thinking them true or probably true, but simply that they have survived severer tests. So to say of one hypothesis that it is more highly corroborated than another hypothesis is to report a fact about what has happened – namely that the former has survived more severe tests than the latter; it is not to propose a conjecture about what will happen in the future. Why, though, should Popper have been interested in the past record of a hypothesis, with regard to corroboration or any other matter, since his opposition to induction prevents him from claiming that the past record of a hypothesis is a reliable guide to its future performance? A hypothesis may have survived the severest tests we can devise, and thus be highly corroborated, but that can be no good reason in Popper's view for the belief that it will survive further tests.

In answer to this question, Popper claimed that the fact that a hypothesis has survived a severe test and is thus corroborated is important, because if the hypothesis is false it is more likely to fail a severe test than a non-severe one. This may be true, but it does not help with the central issue of why we should prefer those unfalsified hypotheses which are highly corroborated. Consider a case where we have to choose between several hypotheses which could account for a range of phenomena. None of the hypotheses have been eliminated, but one, we suppose, is more highly corroborated than any of the others because, unlike them, it has been subjected to severe tests and has survived. Why should we prefer this corroborated hypothesis? One answer to this question is that we prefer the corroborated hypothesis because it is unlikely that it would have survived those severe tests unless it were true, or at least close to the truth. Surviving severe tests, and hence corroboration, is important because a severe test of a hypothesis is a test we expect it to fail unless it is true or approximately true (Popper 1963: 112). So, severe tests are important, not just because when they are failed we are able to eliminate falsified hypotheses, but also because when they are passed we are able to prefer some unfalsified hypotheses over others. And this preference, Popper claimed, involves no inductive reasoning.

However, induction in a broad sense does seem to be involved in justifying, in this way, the preference for well-corroborated hypotheses. For consider again the case where we have several hypotheses which can account for a range of phenomena, one of which is more highly corroborated than the others. Of this corroborated hypothesis it is said that it is unlikely that it would have survived the severe tests to which it was subjected unless it were, at least, approximately true. But there will be other hypotheses, hitherto unidentified and incompatible with each other and with this corroborated hypothesis, which would also have survived those same severe tests. Unless we think that for some reason they should not be considered, we can say of each of them that it is unlikely that they would have survived the tests unless they were, at least, approximately true. But if they are mutually incompatible we know that all except at most one must actually be false, despite having survived the tests. The problem is not that we think less well of a highly corroborated hypothesis because there are other hypotheses which are just as highly corroborated; it is rather that we must, it seems, think equally well of those competing hypotheses. But if we think equally well of a number, perhaps an indefinite number, of competing hypotheses, we seem to have no grounds on which to choose one rather than another. An inductivist such as Reichenbach can use Bayes's theorem to agree that, given survival of a test by a hypothesis, the hypothesis is unlikely to be false (and is therefore to be preferred) provided, among other things, that survival of this test is unlikely unless the hypothesis is true. But, even if those other things are equal, there may well be other hypotheses, perhaps unlimited in number, which would also have survived that test, and of each of which we can say that its survival is even more unlikely unless it is true. However, Popper's rejection of induction prevented him from supplying the prior probabilities needed to apply Bayes's theorem so that he could obtain a conclusion as to which of the surviving hypotheses he should prefer. Indeed, Popper claimed that, since no probabilistic theory of induction is acceptable, whether or not of the variety proposed by Reichenbach, the probability of any universal law, whatever evidence we take into account, is always zero. For him, therefore, Bayes's theorem is inapplicable.

It would appear, then, that Popper has not provided a deductive reason for preferring a hypothesis on the grounds that it is highly corroborated. This is not just because, in saying of a hypothesis that it is highly corroborated, we are reporting on its past success in passing severe tests, which cannot be a good ground for Popper to declare that it will in the future pass other severe tests. It is also because there will always be other hypotheses which are equally highly corroborated in Popper's sense (see Salmon: 1981: 115–25; Watkins 1984: 340–41).

There is, though, another reason Popper gave for preferring a corroborated hypothesis. This reason depends on the idea that we can rank corroborated hypotheses with respect, not to their prior inductive probability, but rather with respect to their 'verisimilitude'. Roughly speaking, to say of one hypothesis that it has more 'verisimilitude' – or is closer to the truth – than another hypothesis, is to say its truth content is the greater while its falsity content is not (or that its falsity content is the lesser while its truth content is not). By the truth content of a hypothesis we are to understand the set of deductive consequences of the hypothesis which are true, and by the falsity content we are to understand the set of its false deductive consequences. Together, the set of true consequences and the set of false consequences make the content of the hypothesis. Popper showed that if, among the hypotheses which are equally well corroborated, we select one which is bolder or stronger than the others, in the sense that its content is greater than theirs, then, provided its falsity content is not greater, it would have greater truth content and would therefore have greater verisimilitude. This hypothesis should therefore be the one we prefer. We can say of it, as we can say of its competitors, that it is unlikely it would have survived the severe tests to which it has been subjected unless it were true. But we can also say that it, unlike its competitors, is closer to the truth, even if it, like them, should turn out to be false in the light of further tests. And because this is so, we have a justification – a deductive justification – for preferring it.

I have used, as Popper did, the language of 'preferring' one hypothesis to another. We need to clarify the implications of this terminology, for it can easily seem that his concept of corroboration is implicitly inductive. We prefer corroborated hypotheses with the greatest verisimilitude because our aim in science is to approximate as closely as we can to the truth, even though we know that our approximations are false. In preferring an approximation, therefore, we are not committed to the belief that it is true; nor are we preferring it in the sense that we accept it as true; nor are we preferring it in the sense that we are willing to rely on its truth; nor are we preferring it in the sense that we expect that the choices we base upon it will be successful choices. For, Popper claimed, we can only have inductive reasons – and therefore bad reasons – for believing any hypothesis, for accepting it, for relying upon it, or for expecting its practical success. The only sense in which we are entitled to prefer a hypothesis is in the sense that, although it is probably false, it is less false than other hypotheses, even if we have yet to show that those other hypotheses are false. We have, Popper insisted, good deductive reasons for this preference. The science which results from the exercise of preferences for which we have deductive reasons is unjustified, is untrue, and is not to be believed, but this is the inevitable nature of science without induction (Popper 1972: 21–2; cf. Miller 1978: 129).

Much depends upon whether we can make the concept of verisimilitude sufficiently robust to bear the weight which Popper needed to place on it. This is no easy task. Popper's original account of the concept, as he acknowledged, was not satisfactory. For we have seen that, according to that account, one hypothesis – A – counts as having greater verisimilitude than another – B – only if the falsity content of A is less than or equal to the falsity content of B. But if A is in fact false, it is hard to see how this necessary condition can be satisfied, for B itself will have to be counted in the falsity content of B whereas it will not be in the falsity content of A. And, even more damagingly, whether A is in fact true or in fact false, we will find ourselves drawing the general conclusion that its falsity content is less than the falsity content of B on the basis of limited evidence, and the only way that this general conclusion can be drawn from that evidence is by using induction by enumeration. 'If we fail to refute [A]', Popper said, 'or if the refutations we find are at the same time also refutations of [B], then we have reason to suspect, or to conjecture, that [A] has no greater falsity content than [B], and, therefore, that it has the greater degree of verisimilitude'. This 'reason to suspect, or to conjecture', it would appear, is an inductive reason, and to this extent judgements of greater verisimilitude are inductive judgements (Popper 1972: 53; cf. Grunbaum 1976a: 122). To set aside such judgements, as Popper intended, is to lack the means for comparing verisimilitudes.

Reichenbach contributed a review of Popper's *Logik der Forschung* to *Erkenntnis*, the 'house journal' of the Vienna Circle. His view was unambiguous: 'the theses presented in Popper's book . . . appear to me to be completely untenable'; and 'I am . . . unable to understand why Popper believes his investigation to constitute even the smallest step forward in resolving the problem of induction' (Reichenbach 1978: vol. 2, 372, 385). He acknowledged, to be sure, that no-one had yet succeeded in justifying the inductive reasoning which he considered to be indispensable in science. Such reasoning must be, in fact, either rational or irrational; we have not yet found out which it is, but since the rationality of scientific method depends upon the rationality of enumerative induction, we should continue our search for the truth about its rationality. Reichenbach's claim that the straight rule of enumerative induction gives the best conclusion, if any conclusion is true, was an important part of his contribution to that search. Popper, by contrast, was impressed by how meagre such contributions were. We are, he thought, so far away from being able to show that inductive reasoning is rational rather than irrational that we should take the apparent impossibility of justifying induction as indicating that it is not justified. So, if we wish to reason rationally, then the safe decision to take is that induction is irrational. And, he thought, this decision can be reconciled with a recognition of the rationality of scientific method, because we can show that, despite appearances, it does not make any use of inductive reasoning.

Both Reichenbach and Popper, then, were committed to the exposure of appearances as deceptive. For Reichenbach the task was to show that the apparent irrationality of induction was illusory; for Popper the task was to show that the apparent indispensability of induction was illusory. In both cases the illusions, if that is what they are, have stubbornly resisted their attempts to expel them. If induction really is rational, then we have seen some of the good reasons for thinking that Reichenbach did not show that it is. And if induction really is dispensable, then we have seen some of the good reasons for thinking that Popper did not show that it is. But nevertheless, with the aid of the insights provided by these two philosophers, we have been able to see more clearly some of the important issues that divide enumerative from eliminative approaches to scientific method. Reichenbach inherited, elaborated and transformed a tradition of thinking about scientific method rooted in Newton's rules of reasoning, questioned by David Hume, and continued by John Venn and Charles Peirce. Correspondingly, Popper inherited, elaborated and transformed a tradition of thinking which began with Francis Bacon and was developed by Mill and Keynes (see Urbach 1987). But there are, as we have seen, other traditions, and many of the insights into scientific method yielded by studies in the latter part of the twentieth century have been related to those traditions.

FURTHER READING

For Reichenbach, see:
Reichenbach, H. (1938) *Experience and Prediction: An Analysis of the Foundations and the Structure of Knowledge*, Chicago, Ill.: University of Chicago Press.
Reichenbach, H. (1949) *The Theory of Probability: An Inquiry into the Logical and Mathematical Foundations of the Calculus of Probability*, translated by E. H. Hutten and M. Reichenbach, Berkeley and Los Angeles: University of California Press. First published in 1935.
Reichenbach, H. (1951) *The Rise of Scientific Philosophy*, Berkeley and Los Angeles: University of California Press.
Reichenbach, H. (1978) *Selected Writings, 1909–1953*, edited by M. Reichenbach and R. S. Cohen, 2 vols, Dordrecht: Reidel.

For discussion of his views, see the essays in:
Salmon, W. (ed.) (1979) *Hans Reichenbach: Logical Empiricist*, Dordrecht: Reidel.

For an influential defence of a Reichenbach approach to scientific reasoning, see:
Salmon, W. (1966) *The Foundations of Scientific Inference*, Pittsburgh, Pa.: Pittsburgh University Press.

For Popper's views, see:
Popper, K. (1959) *The Logic of Scientific Discovery*, London: Hutchinson. First published in 1935.
Popper, K. (1963) *Conjectures and Refutations: the Growth of Scientific Knowledge*, London: Routledge and Kegan Paul.

Popper, K. (1972) *Objective Knowledge: An Evolutionary Approach*, Oxford: Clarendon Press.

Popper, K. (1982a) *Realism and the Aim of Science*, Postscript to the *Logic of Scientific Discovery*, vol. 1, edited by W. W. Bartley III, London: Hutchinson.

Popper, K. (1982b) *The Open Universe*, Postscript to the *Logic of Scientific Discovery*, vol. 2, edited by W. W. Bartley III, London: Hutchinson.

Popper, K. (1982c) *Quantum Theory and the Schism in Physics*, Postscript to the *Logic of Scientific Discovery*, vol. 3, edited by W. W. Bartley III, London: Hutchinson.

Popper, K. and Miller, D. (1983) 'A proof of the impossibility of inductive probability', *Nature* 302: 687–8.

Popper, K. and Miller, D. (1984) 'The impossibility of inductive probability', *Nature* 310: 434.

Essays discussing Popper's ideas are collected in:

Schilpp, P. A. (ed.) (1974) *The Philosophy of Karl Popper*, Library of Living Philosophers, La Salle, Ill.: Open Court.

Levinson, P. (ed.) (1982) *In Pursuit of Truth: Essays in Honour of Karl Popper's 80th Birthday*, Hassocks: Harvester.

For further defence and criticism, see:

Settle, T. (1970) 'Is corroboration a nondemonstrative form of inference?', *Ratio* 12: 151–3.

Jeffrey, R. C. (1975a) 'Probability and falsification: critique of the Popper programme', *Synthese* 30: 95–117.

Miller, D. W. (1975b) 'Making sense of method: comments on Richard Jeffrey', *Synthese* 30: 139–47.

Miller, D. W. (1975c) 'The accuracy of predictions', *Synthese* 30: 159–91.

Miller, D. W. (1975) 'The accuracy of predictions: a reply', *Synthese* 30: 207–19.

Grunbaum, A. (1976a) 'Is the method of bold conjectures and attempted refutations justifiably the method science?', *British Journal for the Philosophy of Science* 27: 105–136.

Grunbaum, A. (1976b) 'Is falsifiability the touchstone of scientific rationality? Karl Popper versus inductivism', in R. S. Cohen and M. W. Wartofsky (eds), *Essays in Memory of Imre Lakatos*, Dordrecht: Reidel.

Miller, D. W. (1978) 'Can science do without induction?', in L. Jonathan Cohen and M. Hesse (eds), *Applications of Inductive Logic*, Proceedings of a Conference at The Queen's College, Oxford, 21–24 August 1978, Oxford: Clarendon Press.

Salmon, W. (1981) 'Rational prediction', *British Journal for the Philosophy of Science* 32: 115–25.

Watkins, J. (1984) *Science and Scepticism*, London: Hutchinson.

Eells, E. (1988) 'On the alleged impossibility of inductive probability', *British Journal for the Philosophy of Science* 39: 111–16.

Gemes, K. (1989) 'A refutation of Popperian inductive scepticism', *British Journal for the Philosophy of Science* 40: 183–4.

Howson, C. (1991) 'The last word on induction', *Erkenntnis* 34: 73–82.

11 Rudolf Carnap
Scientific method as Bayesian reasoning

With the notable exception of Karl Popper, philosophers of science have accepted that the reasoning scientists use in order to establish their conclusions is, or is in part, inductive reasoning. There have been, and there continue to be, different views about what induction is, but there is considerable agreement that induction has some degree of cogency, even though it is incapable of the conclusiveness of deduction. Inductive conclusions drawn from given evidence are accepted, that is to say, with a certain degree of confidence. But if scientific reasoning is entitled to its customary reputation, then we need to justify these degrees of confidence as rational, and for this we must have a good way of understanding degrees of confidence. The traditional view, which, as we have seen, we can trace back to Leibniz in the seventeenth century, is that they are nothing other than probabilities. So the rationality of inductive conclusions depends on the rationality of probabilities. This dependence, though, will not enable us to clarify our understanding so long as we are confronted with alternative accounts of probability. The arguments of Keynes and Reichenbach plainly showed that different particular interpretations of probability yielded different specific accounts of what counts as sound inductive reasoning. They reflect the contrast, which began to emerge in the nineteenth century, between rationalist a priori and empiricist a posteriori accounts of scientific method.

Both Keynes and Reichenbach took it for granted that there are useful analogies between inductive and deductive reasoning, but their different interpretations of probability generated different views about how we could use these analogies. In the case of deduction, when we are given true premises we feel certain of the truth of the conclusion we validly derive from them. We need, though, to explain why we are entitled to this feeling of psychological certainty. What makes it rational for us to be completely confident that the conclusion is true? The traditional view, traceable to Aristotle, is that the confidence arises from, and is analysable in terms of, the necessity of the conclusion given the truth of the premises. Such necessities are objective in the sense that they characterise the relation between premises and conclusion, whether or not we recognise that they do. It is these objective necessities which justify our psychological attitudes to deductive conclusions, when those attitudes are justifiable. Analogously, our psychological confidence in the conclusion of an inductive argument stands in need of justification, and we turn for that justification to the probability of the conclusion given the truth of the premises. Probabilities justify our psychological attitudes to inductive conclusions when those attitudes are justifiable. If, as Reichenbach thought, probabilities are relative frequencies, then it is empirical facts about the world which justify our confidence in inductive reasoning. For him, as for others with similar views about the interpretation of probability, there are important disanalogies between induction and deduction in that, whereas the reliability of induction depends upon truths, whether knowable or not, about the way the world is, the reliability of deduction depends upon truths of logic alone. For Keynes, on the other hand, probabilities are like necessities in that they also express objective truths about the logical relations between statements. Just as a deductive necessity derives from a logical fact about the relation between premises and a conclusion deduced from them, so also an inductive probability derives from a logical fact about the relation between premises and a conclusion induced from them. This, indeed, is the reason why it is appropriate to use the term 'logical' to describe both deductive necessity and inductive probability.

How, though, were logical truths about necessary and probabilistic relations between statements to be ascertained? Keynes did not answer this question. He may not have thought it important. Nevertheless, it became possible to answer it following the impressive progress made in formal deductive logic at the end of the nineteenth century by Gottlob Frege. In a history that we can trace back to Aristotle, the Stoic philosophers and the medieval logicians, parts of formal logic had, indeed, been explored in some depth. But prior to Frege's *Begriffsschrift* of 1879 there was no unified structure which helped to make sense of what had been achieved and which was capable of completing puzzling gaps in understanding how deductive reasoning worked. However, because the forbidding and cumbersome appearance of the notation Frege used to express his conceptual innovations did not encourage wide readership, some thirty years elapsed before Bertrand Russell and Alfred Whitehead, in their *Principia Mathematica*, adopted Giuseppe Peano's symbolism and thereby succeeded in bringing those innovations to the attention of philosophers and logicians.

The basic idea for understanding logical relations between statements is that of a model or interpretation. Thus, in the case of a deduction with one or more premises and a validly derived conclusion, to say that the truth of the premises makes it necessary that the conclusion is true is to say that every model or interpretation in which the premisses are true is also a model or interpretation in which the conclusion is true. For example, taking a familiar syllogistic deduction, the premisses 'All Greeks are men' and 'All men are mortal' satisfy, or are true in, a number of models or pictures about how the world is or, as in this case, might be. If each and every one of these models is also a model satisfied by the conclusion 'All Greeks are mortal', then the truth of the premisses makes it necessary that the conclusion is also true. By contrast, if the premisses were 'All men are Greeks' and 'All men are mortal', then their truth would not make it necessary that the conclusion 'All Greeks are mortal' is also true. For there is a model satisfied by the premisses but not by the conclusion, namely a model of Greek people in which the men are mortal and the women immortal.

In the case of induction, to say that the truth of the premisses makes it probable that the conclusion is true is to say that a certain proportion of all those models or interpretations in which the premisses are true are also models or interpretations in which the conclusion is true. The greater this proportion is, the greater will be the probability. For example, taking a familiar if naive enumerative induction, the premisses 'All examined and tested metals conduct electricity' and 'No examined and tested metal fails to conduct electricity' satisfy, or are true of, each member of a set of distinct models or pictures of how the world is or might be. The conclusion 'All metals, including those unexamined, conduct electricity' will satisfy, or be true in, some but not all of these models. The ratio of the number of those models in which both premisses and conclusion are satisfied to the number of those models in which the premisses are satisfied, is the probability of the conclusion given the premisses.

There are a number of questions raised by this development of the analogy between induction and deduction. If we have satisfactory answers to these questions and can create procedures for determining inductive probabilities as effective as those developed for establishing deductive necessities, then we will have an inductive logic on which we can base our understanding of scientific method. It was Rudolf Carnap who did most to identify the relevant questions and who undertook an extensive investigation of the prospects for inductive logic. He was persuaded that the formalisation of logic, which had led to a much improved understanding of how deductive reasoning works, could also contribute to a better grasp of inductive reasoning and to a resolution of the outstanding problems associated with it. Induction and de-duction are, as it were, applications or particular cases of a generalised logic. Those unconvinced by Carnap's project or by the strength of the analogy on which it is based have commonly expressed their opposition by rejecting the idea of inductive logic.

Carnap was born in 1891 – the same year as Reichenbach, who

became his friend and colleague. At the age of eighteen he left north-west Germany, where he had been brought up, for Jena University, in order to study mathematics, physics and philosophy. Frege was teaching logic in Jena at this time, though his ideas remained neglected and ignored by mathematicians and philosophers. Carnap's acquaintance with logic was derived from attending Frege's lectures on his 'conceptual notation' [*Begriffsschrift*], though it was not until somewhat later that he appreciated the power and philosophical significance of the innovative ideas developed in these lectures. In 1913 he began experimental research for a doctoral degree in physics, though this was soon interrupted by the outbreak of war. Throughout his military service, at the Western Front and later in Berlin, he maintained his interest in physics and philosophy, and after the war began his philosophical work with a dissertation on the foundations of geometry. At this time, as well as later, Frege and Russell were the principal influences on his thinking, with the former providing the clear concepts needed for a new and more powerful logic, and the latter showing how we can use this logic to solve outstanding philosophical problems. During the 1920s he met Hans Reichenbach and, through him, Moritz Schlick who, in 1926, secured a post for him teaching philosophy at Vienna University. With Schlick and Otto Neurath, Carnap became a leading member of the famous Vienna Circle, and many of his most characteristic views are closely connected with the logical positivism developed in the circle. Though he remained in close contact with members of the Vienna Circle, he left Vienna in 1931 for a professorship in natural philosophy at Prague University. But he found the political environment in Czechoslovakia and in Austria increasingly unacceptable, and emigrated to the USA in 1936, accepting a position at University of Chicago. Later he taught philosophy at Princeton University and at University of California in Los Angeles. He began working on probability and inductive logic shortly after his arrival in the USA. His *Logical Foundations of Probability* was published in 1950, and was planned as the first in a two-volume account of the results of an extensive programme of research. It was followed shortly afterwards by *The Continuum of Inductive Methods*, which showed that this programme was too narrowly conceived, and subsequent studies have indicated that the scope of the research envisaged by Carnap needs to be broader still. The programme remained incomplete at his death in 1970, though colleagues and associates have continued to contribute to it.

Carnap believed that, just as logical implication is the key concept for deductive logic, so degree of confirmation is the key concept for inductive logic. Logical implications between statements, as for example between the premisses of a deductively valid argument and its conclusion, can, as we have seen, be expressed as relations of logical necessity between the statements and understood in terms of the idea that any model satisfied by the implying statements, or premises, is also satisfied by the implied statement, or conclusion. Similarly, we express degrees of confirmation between statements – for example between evidence and hypothesis in an inductive argument – as relations of logical probability between statements, this being understood as signifying that of all the models satisfied by the confirming statement – or evidence – a certain proportion are also satisfied by the confirmed statement – or hypothesis. Clearly, since logical necessities do not admit of degrees, neither do logical implications, whereas because there are degrees of logical probability it is entirely appropriate that there should be degrees of confirmation.

It is not the aim of inductive logic to ascertain or discover the hypotheses which are confirmed by the evidence available to us, any more than it is the aim of deductive logic to ascertain conclusions implied by premisses. Rather, just as deductive logic is concerned with whether a conclusion, however discovered, is logically implied by given premisses, so inductive logic is concerned with whether a hypothesis, however it may be discovered, is confirmed by given evidence, and if it is, the degree of that confirmation. For example, 'a report concerning observations of certain phenomena on the surface of the sun is given', and a physicist has found 'a hypothesis concerning the physical state of the sun . . . which, in combination with accepted physical laws, furnishes a satisfactory explanation for the observed facts'. He wishes to know 'whether [the hypothesis] is indeed highly confirmed by [the report]'. He wishes, more specifically, to know the degree to which the report confirms the hypothesis. In inductive logic we need to develop techniques which will enable us to identify that degree of confirmation (Carnap 1962a: 194–6).

To make this identification possible, Carnap defined both logical implication and degree of confirmation with the help of what he called the 'range' of a statement. By this he meant a certain set of other statements, called 'state-descriptions', these being the most complete descriptions, capable of being expressed in the language used, of models or possible states of affairs. The criterion for inclusion in the set of 'state-descriptions' which is the 'range' for a certain statement is that a 'state-description' contain that statement. If, for example, we wish to specify the range of the statement 'All examined and tested metals conduct electricity', then we must survey all the state-descriptions expressible in the language we are using and select from that survey the set of all those state-descriptions which contain or imply this statement. It may, of course, be necessary to restrict the expressive powers of a language in order to ensure that the state-descriptions it can contain are surveyable.

In the case of logical implication, where the implied conclusion is necessarily true in relation to the implying premisses, the set of state-descriptions that is the range of the conclusion includes all members of the set of state-descriptions that constitute the range of the premisses. And in the case of confirmation, where the confirmed hypothesis is probably true in relation to the confirming evidence, the set of state-descriptions that is the range of the hypothesis includes a proportion of the set of state-descriptions that is the range of the evidence. This proportion, which simply depends on the relative size of two sets, does not in itself determine the degree of confirmation, or the probability, of the hypothesis given the evidence. For we cannot simply assume that state-descriptions are of equal weight or significance, and that therefore only their number matters. We need also to determine a method of measuring ranges that takes into account any variable weight or significance we should attribute to state-descriptions. Figure 2 shows these relations by representing ranges, measured by some appropriate method, as areas (see Carnap 1962a: 297).

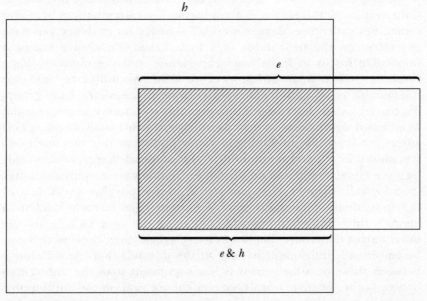

Figure 2 The shaded part of the diagram represents that part of the range of *e* which is included in the range of *h*.

How, though, should we choose a suitable method for measuring ranges? Bearing in mind that degrees of confirmation represent logical relations between hypotheses and evidence statements, our measurement of ranges must also depend only on logical considerations, and not on any empirical facts. Our evaluations of degrees of confirmation, or logical probabilities, are, if correct, analytically true. The choices we make concern the requirements that should be satisfied by an acceptable method for measuring ranges and assessing degrees of confirmation, and our measurements and assessments are, if correct, analytic relative to those choices. We would, for example, choose the requirement that the degree of confirmation of a hypothesis should not remain the same whatever evidence we produce. We can, we believe, learn from experience. We might also choose the requirement that the degree of confirmation of a universal law should not always be zero no matter how much supporting evidence we produce. The non-zero values for the degrees of confirmation of universal laws resulting from this choice are, provided we have calculated them correctly, analytically correct.

In choosing a method for measuring ranges we are, in effect, choosing an inductive logic. For example, we might choose to measure the range of a statement by giving equal weight and significance to each of the state-descriptions in the set constituting its range. If we think of each state-description as a description of a possible world, then we are proposing that we count each logically distinct world equally. But, as Carnap showed, this results in an inductive logic – symbolised by $c^{\dagger}$ and sometimes called the 'dagger method' – where no evidence can have any effect on the probability of a hypothesis. Our choice makes it impossible for us to learn from experience, and the inductive logic resulting from it is, accordingly, of no value. An inductive logic that does enable us to learn from experience results, however, from grouping together state descriptions with the same structure, and giving equal weight and significance to groups which are structurally distinct. This corresponds to the method sometimes known as the 'star method', symbolised by c^*, and it amounts to the proposal that possible worlds be given equal weight and significance when they are empirically rather than logically distinct. For example, if, in one possible world, half of the individuals it contains have a certain characteristic, and in a logically different possible world containing the same individuals, the other half of them have that same characteristic, then these worlds may be empirically indistinguishable. On the grounds that the difference between these possible worlds is less significant than the differences between other possible worlds, we may choose to apply the indifference principle in a different way. In effect, different ways of measuring ranges result from different ways of resolving the inherent ambiguity of the indifference principle. The choice between them, and thus between different ways of determining degrees of confirmation, or probabilities, will be a matter of convention. As Carnap and his co-workers have shown, there are an indefinite number of different ways of measuring ranges and thus degrees of confirmation. Though some will seem more reasonable or simpler than others, the use of one rather than another depends on choices of requirements that, far from being trivial or obvious, are substantial and contentious.

Given the analogies between deductive and inductive logics, it is not surprising that Carnap's characterisation of degree of confirmation, like Frege's and Russell's definition of logical consequence, should be abstract and formal. In both contexts, central concepts were introduced with reference to artificial languages representing, more or less adequately, only some of the features of the natural languages we use when we reason. In the case of deductive logic, this means that the reasoning being analysed often bears only a tenuous relation to real arguments that people actually use. And yet there are sufficient links between the formality of deductive logic and the informality of practical deductions to enable the former to illuminate the latter. Carnap's expectation was that a similar pattern would emerge in the case of the inductive logic he wished to develop. Certainly there would be a gap between the artificiality of the inductive logics developed for languages with only very limited expressive powers, and natural inductive reasoning. Nevertheless, by judicious selection of an inductive logic and by developing its use in a language with greater expressive resources, the gap could be reduced to the extent necessary for the logic to play an illuminating role with respect to natural inductive reasoning, such as the reasoning used in scientific contexts.

One problem that Carnap faced in his attempts to bridge the gap between abstract logical theory and its practical application to scientific reasoning was that the inductive logics he created and discussed led to the conclusion that the degree of confirmation, and the logical probability, of any universal scientific law is zero, no matter how much supporting evidence we may have. In particular, the 'star method' favoured by Carnap as satisfying to the greatest degree requirements for rationality assigns zero probability to all scientific laws. This consequence, he acknowledged, is inconsistent with our inclination to attribute probabilities and degrees of confirmation, sometimes high probabilities and degrees of confirmation, to scientific laws. Let us be clear, first, why this is a consequence of his approach.

Consider Figure 2 (see p. 217). The degree of confirmation of hypothesis h on evidence e is given by the ratio of that part of rectangle e falling inside the rectangle h to the whole of the rectangle denoted e. As we have seen, the sizes of the rectangles e and h are fixed by the method we use to measure the ranges of e and h, and this depends in part at least upon our counting state-descriptions. If the language we are using to provide state-descriptions contains only limited resources for identifying the individuals featuring in them, then when h is a universal scientific law and e the evidence for it, we may expect the ratio of areas to have a non-zero value. Depending on how extensive the language limitations are, the area of e may be large, and if we have assembled a large amount of positive data the part of it falling inside h may be large in proportion. But the language we use for expressing scientific truths is not limited in its resources for identifying individuals, so the number of state-descriptions helping to measure the range of *e*, and thus the size of the area of the rectangle *e*, is infinitely large. Within the infinitely large rectangle *e* there will be some – but not infinitely many – state-descriptions which also satisfy *h*, but nevertheless the ratio of the part of *e* which thus falls within *h* to the whole of *e* is zero. Since it is this ratio which is the degree of confirmation, or logical probability, of the universal law *h* in relation to the evidence *e*, we must conclude that the degree of confirmation of any universal law on any evidence is zero.

Because this conclusion is so much at variance with our convictions about confirmation and probability, it might seem that Carnap's attempt to create an inductive logic is a failure. Such a reaction, though, would be premature. For this is a case, he thought, where our intuitions do not oblige us to abandon principles that otherwise seem reasonable. We can, Carnap thought, reconcile our intuitions with our principles and their consequences. In particular, we should distinguish between the reliability of a universal scientific law and its degree of confirmation or probability. For when an engineer, say, claims that a universal physical law is very reliable, 'he does not mean to say that he is willing to bet that among the billions of billions, or an infinite number, of instances to which the law applies there is not one counterinstance'. The implication is that this is precisely what we would mean to say if we were to claim that the degree of confirmation of the law is high. Instead of using betting quotients, or degrees to which universal laws are confirmed, we should judge the reliability of a law 'by the degree of confirmation ... of one or several instances' (Carnap 1962a: 572). A law is reliable if it is a law which, we have reason to believe, will not let us down the next time we depend on it, or on the next few times that we depend on it; it is not a law which, we have reason to believe, will never let us down. In terms of Figure 2, the ratio of the part of rectangle *e* falling within rectangle *h* will approach one as more evidence is assembled and the size of *e* increases, because *h* will concern a finite rather than an infinite number of individuals and the area of *h* will therefore always be finite. If this is right, then, since we can assign to a prediction derived from a law a logical probability greater than zero, it will not matter that the logical probability of the law itself is zero. In effect, Carnap's proposal was that, instead of judging the reliability of a law by measuring its range, we should judge it by measuring the range of one or a few predictions derived from the law.

However, both the argument for the conclusion that universal laws have zero degree of confirmation, and Carnap's response to the argument, are questionable.

In the first place, a crucial step in the argument is taken when we claim that the range of e must be infinitely large. To make this step secure we would have to show that the claim remains true no matter which of the different ways of measuring the range of a statement we adopt. But in principle there seems to be no reason why the range of any statement should be infinite. If, as Carnap claimed, we have some control over how ranges are measured, then we should, if we can, choose a measure which gives a non-zero value to the degree of confirmation of a scientific law. Further development of Carnap's ideas has shown that this can indeed be done. The details of this development are technical, but in general they show that, by making conventional choices about the scope of an indifference principle and about how it should be applied, we can measure ranges in such a way that the logical probability of a universal law can have a non-zero value.

Second, if, as Carnap suggested, we identify the degree of reliability of a universal scientific law with the degree of confirmation of a limited set of its instances, then we will have to concede that laws known to be false can nevertheless have high degrees of reliability. This is not especially surprising, given the vagueness of our concept of reliability; we often rely on laws, such as the laws of classical mechanics, knowing that these laws have been shown to be false. It does, however, mean that we have no rational basis for our belief that, while some reliable laws are false, others are true. For example, the law that the mass of an object is independent of its velocity is falsified by objects travelling at velocities comparable with that of light, but we believe that in most contexts we can rely on the truth of its implications. We might express this by saying that the law, though falsified, is reliable. On the other hand, Newton's inverse square law of gravity has been successfully tested, and we believe that, irrespective of the context we are using, we can rely on all its implications. We might express this by saying that the law is highly confirmed and reliable. So even if we accept Carnap's suggestion about how we should understand reliability, what we say in these cases will have no justification unless universal laws can have non-zero degrees of confirmation.

The problem of zero probability for universal laws is but one aspect of a more general problem about Carnap's programme. For in his attempt to build on the achievements of Frege, Russell and others in deductive logic, it was inevitable that he would turn towards formal and abstract treatments of inductive logic. The development of axiomatic bases for mathematical probability was a further contributing factor in the prospect of a generalised formal logic. But the price to be paid for the development of this programme was that its account of the inductive reasoning we think necessary to an understanding of scientific method became ever more remote from the reasoning characteristic of real science. The resolution of questions about the most general features of induction has preoccupied Carnap and his colleagues, and the need to create and discuss artificial languages within which these questions can be addressed has resulted in a yet wider gulf between what we require for a theory of inductive logic and what we require for a theory of scientific method. If inductive logic requires that the probability of universal scientific laws be zero, then, we might think, so much the worse for the relevance of inductive logic to scientific method. Carnap recognised this problem in making his distinction between inductive logic, which is a theoretical study of logical relations between statements, and the methodology of induction, which is a practical enquiry into how that theory may be applied. Some contributors to a theory of scientific method, such as the seventeenth- and eighteenth-century founders of probabilistic reasoning, had been concerned with inductive logic, whereas others, such as Bacon and Mill, had focused their attention on the methodology of induction (Carnap 1962a: 202–5). Carnap's own work, of course, was principally concerned with the theory rather than the application of inductive logic, so he certainly saw himself as contributing to the ideas introduced by Leibniz, Jakob Bernoulli, Bayes and Laplace. We can find, indeed, a version of Laplace's rule of succession proved as a 'theorem' in Carnap's system of inductive logic (Carnap 1962: 568).

Although the choice of an inductive logic is conventional, it would not be right to claim that it is an arbitrary matter. Carnap laid down certain requirements, or axioms, which any 'admissible' inductive logic would have to satisfy in order to count as rational. But the number of inductive logics satisfying these axioms, he acknowledged, 'is still infinite' (Carnap and Jeffrey 1971: 27). Our choice of an 'admissible' inductive logic cannot, however, be objectively right or wrong, in the sense that it represents, or fails to represent, the logical facts. There are no such logical facts, or at least none that are accessible to us. So whether one statement confirms, or makes probable, another statement, and if so to what degree, is not determined independently of our choice of an inductive logic. As Carnap said in his 'Autobiography' (Carnap 1963), 'it seems that an observer is free to choose . . . an inductive logic'. No doubt we would prefer an inductive logic which is consistent with our intuitive understanding of which statements confirm which other statements. But this may well be a matter of selecting among inductive logics, none of which is entirely consistent with those intuitions, an inductive logic that in our judgement is the best fit with them. But, as Carnap also acknowledged, intuitions may vary from one person to another; in drawing inductive conclusions 'we find that the person X . . . is more cautious than Y' (Carnap 1963: 75). Some element of subjectivity, therefore, seems to be implied by Carnap's treatment. So, when we use Bayes's theorem to calculate the probability of a hypothesis given certain evidence, our conclusions will be subjective to a certain extent. Two people, using the same evidence, could legitimately attribute different probabilities to a hypothesis on the basis of that evidence. This is because Bayesian calculations require us to make judgements about the probability of the hypothesis independently of the evidence, and about the probability of the evidence independently of the hypothesis, and these judgements are not objectively validated by requirements for rationality or prudence, though they are constrained by them.

If, as seems to be the case, Carnapian constraints on probability judgements do not suffice to legitimate a unique probability, the question arises whether we can legitimate those judgements in some other way. Are there ways of constraining subjective probability judgements so that, despite their subjectivity, they can count as rational? Modern Bayesian personalism is built around the conviction that the answer to this question is yes. Personalists agree with Carnap that rational degrees of confirmation are probabilities, but instead of these probabilities being unique abstract logical relations between statements, they represent the extent or degree to which a person believes a statement claimed to be probable. Probabilities are personal degrees of belief. Thus, my belief in the truth of a statement, say a scientific conclusion, can be more or less strong, and if we can find a way of measuring the strength of this personal belief then, under certain conditions, what we measure can count as the probability of the belief. Clearly, personal degrees of belief are subjective; so too, then, are probabilities. Contrary to Carnap's view, there is not a single fraction, which we may or may not know, representing the probability of a given hypothesis with respect to a set of statements constituting the evidence for it; the probability of that hypothesis given that evidence, because it corresponds to a personal degree of belief, will vary from one person to another.

An advantage of seeing probabilities as personal degrees of belief varying from one person to another, rather than as abstract relations between statements with a unique, if undetermined, value, is that they become accessible and measurable. For, as Ramsey put it, 'the old-established way of measuring a person's belief is to propose a bet' (Ramsey 1978: 74). We can, that is, assess the degree of belief that a person has in a statement, and thus its probability for that person, by ascertaining the odds on the truth of the statement he or she accepts as fair. If a person judges bets at odds of $s:t$ on the truth of a statement as fair, then for that person the corresponding fair betting quotient is $t/(s + t)$, and this ratio will measure the degree to which he or she believes the statement. Fair odds are those which the person judges to confer neither an advantage nor a disadvantage when offered a bet on the truth of the statement (Howson and Urbach 1993: 75). A person judges a bet fair, that is to say, when he or she is indifferent to the choice of being bettor or bookie. There is, of course, no presumption that what counts as fair odds will remain stable from one person to another; fair odds as well as fair betting quotients are only subjectively fair.

But if fair betting quotients, personal degrees of belief and probabilities have only subjective validity, how can probabilities have anything to do with what it is rational for us to believe? Keynes and Carnap had identified probabilities with rational degrees of belief, so for them we could come to know the degree to which it is rational for us to believe the truth of a hypothesis in relation to evidence, and thus the probability of that hypothesis in relation to that evidence, by ascertaining the unique logical relation between the hypothesis and the evidence. This, though, is much easier to say than to do, and many would share Ramsey's comment on Keynes's claim that we can, sometimes at least, perceive these relations: 'there really do not seem to be any such things as the . . . relations he describes', he said, and 'I do not perceive them, and . . . I shrewdly suspect that others do not perceive them either' (Ramsey 1978: 63). But whatever the difficulties with this way of establishing rational degrees of belief, it cannot be any more satisfactory to establish them on the basis of personal degrees of belief measured by means of fair betting quotients. There may be little or no connection between the extent to which I believe a hypothesis in relation to evidence and the extent to which I am entitled to believe that hypothesis in relation to that evidence.

The personalist's response to this criticism is to claim that it depends upon a mistaken view about what it is for a degree of belief to be rational. What matters for the rationality of the degree of belief I have in the truth of a hypothesis is not the degree of belief itself, which may be quite different for different people, but the relation of this degree of belief to other degrees of belief in other hypotheses. Consider the following simple illustration. Two people may have very different degrees of belief in a certain hypothesis; one degree of belief may be close to one, the other close to zero. Both these degrees of belief, though quite different, may be rational. What cannot be rational is for the person who attributed a near-zero degree of belief in the hypothesis to also attribute a near-zero degree of belief in its negation, or for the person who attributed a near-one degree of belief in the hypothesis to also attribute a near-one degree of belief in its negation. The reason for this is that these degrees of belief are determined by fair odds, and if either of these two people were to place bets in accordance with the odds corresponding to their supposed degrees of belief, they would be sure to lose or win. The person who attributes a near-zero degree of belief to both h and $-h$ will, if he or she should place bets in accordance with those degrees of belief, suffer a loss irrespective of whether h or $-h$ is true. In the case of the person who attributes a near-maximum degree of belief to both h and $-h$, he or she is bound to gain by placing bets in accordance with those degrees of belief, provided only that a gullible bookie can be found to accept them. There are, then, constraints on any set of degrees of belief which can count as rational, arising from the claim that these degrees of belief are determined by fair betting quotients. It can be shown, indeed, that degrees of belief, when rational, are probabilities and are subject to the basic principles governing probabilities. Personal degrees of belief not satisfying this condition are counted as inconsistent or incoherent because, if anyone were to place bets in accordance with these degrees of belief, not knowing whether they were bettor or bookie, they would be certain to sustain a loss. They would be victims of what gamblers call a 'Dutch book'.

The principles of probability depend on just three axioms, which stipulate that all probabilities are greater than or equal to zero, that the probability of a tautology is one, and that if two statements are mutually exclusive then the probability that one or the other is true is equal to the sum of their probabilities. In addition, we need to define the 'conditional' probability of a statement, or the probability of that statement given the truth of another, as the probability of the truth of both statements divided by the probability of that other statement. The simplest version of Bayes's theorem is a straightforward consequence of this definition, and we can easily derive other versions of the theorem by using the probability axioms and the principles which follow from them. The so-called Dutch book argument shows that a set of degrees of belief, and the fair betting quotients which would measure them, is invulnerable to a Dutch book if and only if the set conforms to the probability axioms and the principles which follow from them. For example, one of these principles states that if the probability of a hypothesis is p then the probability of its negation must be $1 - p$, so we can see immediately that, in assigning the same high, or low, degree of belief to a hypothesis and to its negation, we allow a Dutch book to be made. Such assignments of degrees of belief would not, therefore, be rational. But there is nothing irrational in assigning a high degree of belief to any hypothesis provided that we also assign degrees of belief in other statements in such a way as to ensure consistency, or coherence. Assignments of degrees of belief will continue to be personal in the sense that they may not coincide with another person's degrees of belief, but this is no bar to their rationality.

It might seem that, if we are to measure degrees of belief by fair betting quotients, we cannot assign anything other than zero degree of belief to any universal generalisation which, like a proposed scientific law, has or might have an infinite number of instances. For bets on the truth of such generalisations, though they can be lost, cannot be won. One negative instance is sufficient to lose the bet, but however many positive instances we have, we cannot guarantee that no negative instance will occur, though that is what we would have to guarantee if we wish to win the bet. So if degrees of belief are correlated with actual betting behaviour, then the conclusion that putative laws have zero degree of belief and thus zero probability seems unavoidable. But we are not obliged to accept behaviouristic analyses of psychological characteristics on which this reasoning depends. People can, we know, still be intelligent, amusing, kind, angry, etc. even though they do not, for one reason or another, behave in the ways we associate with these characteristics. Perhaps the circumstances in which these people would behave intelligently, amusingly, kindly or angrily have not occurred. Similarly, a person can have a non-zero degree of belief in a universal generalisation even though that person does not and would not bet in accordance with that degree of belief. The circumstances in which it would make practical sense for betting behaviour to reflect a degree of belief in a universal generalisation never occur, for they can never reveal that the universal generalisation is true. There remains, of course, a question about the basis on which we attribute an unobserved psychological attribute like having a certain degree of belief in a hypothesis when, for whatever reason, we cannot use observed behaviour. We would have to use, it seems, conjectures about what betting behaviour we would observe in a possible world, remote as it may be from the actual world, where we can correlate this behaviour with degrees of belief.

There is, then, a constraint on the degree to which it is rational to believe in the truth of a statement given that we have assigned degrees of belief to other statements; personal degrees of belief are only rational in so far as they conform to the axioms and principles of probability. But this constraint is weak; coherence in assigning degrees of belief to items in a set of statements is compatible with a great deal of eccentricity in those assignments. We could retain a high degree of belief in any discredited hypothesis provided our degrees of belief in other hypotheses were adjusted so as to make the set coherent. This is not, in itself, especially surprising, for it is a version of Duhem's claim that eccentric or discarded hypotheses can be retained in the face of any evidence provided we are prepared to make the necessary adjustments in our other beliefs. We need, Duhem had said, 'good sense' to guide us in our decisions about what we should retain and what we should abandon in the light of our experimental evidence. Similarly, a Bayesian personalist needs to be guided by 'good sense' as well as by coherence in distributing degrees of belief. It is to 'good sense' that we would appeal when we ask whether, among the infinity of evaluations of degrees of belief that can be made coherent, 'one particular evaluation [is] ... *objectively correct* ... or ... is better than another' (Finetti 1964: 111). But Duhem gave his readers no account of what they were to understand by 'good sense'; to say that it justified a decision was no more than a rhetorical flourish. And, so long as we lack that account, we must acknowledge that 'good sense' can vary, perhaps widely, from one person to another. It is true that many probabilists had, in effect, sought to constrain what could count as judgements displaying 'good sense'. Bernoulli's principle of insufficient reason, Keynes's principle of indifference and Carnap's conditions of adequacy for measures of ranges can all be seen as attempts to limit probabilities or degrees of belief. Each such attempt, however, faces difficulties which have yet to be overcome. So if we are seeking an 'objectively correct' evaluation of a degree of belief, or more modestly an evaluation which a rational person should prefer to alternative evaluations, then an appeal to 'good sense' is no more than an empty gesture, and we might as well recognise that no such evaluations can be justified.

In considering a set of statements at a particular time, the Bayesian personalist recognises no legitimate constraint upon the degrees of belief we attach to each statement, except that the degrees of belief must be coherent in the sense that they function in the same way as probabilities and are subject to the axioms and principles of probability. However, these degrees of belief will change over time, if only because new statements will join the set and the degrees of belief we attribute to them will affect our degrees of belief in the existing statements. These changes are subject to an important additional constraint, for they must take place in accordance with Bayes's theorem. Thus, if we add a statement describing new evidence, e, to our set, then our degree of belief in the hypothesis, h, to which this evidence related should change in accordance with the 'rule of conditionalisation', so that the new degree of belief in h, $p_n(h)$, is equal to the old conditional degree of belief, $p_o(h,e)$. This latter is equal, by Bayes's theorem, to the old degree of belief in h, $p_o(h)$, multiplied by the old conditional degree of belief, $p_o(e,h)$, divided by the old degree of belief in e, $p_o(e)$. If e contradicts h then $p_o(e,h)$ is zero, and so too, therefore, are $p_o(h,e)$ and, by conditionalisation, $p_n(h)$. If e is a consequence of h, then $p_o(e,h)$ is one, and $p_o(h,e)$ and $p_n(h)$ are proportional to $p_o(h)$ – the prior probability of h – and inversely proportional to $p_o(e)$ – the degree to which the occurrence of e is surprising.

Consider, for example, Paul Dirac's theory of the electron, which predicted the existence of positrons. This prediction counted as unexpected because neither the background information available to physicists in the 1920s, nor any alternative electron theory, had it as a consequence. So although the probability of the prediction given Dirac's theory is high, indeed it is one, the probability of the prediction being true given only the background information and any available alternatives to Dirac's theory is very low. Bayes's theorem tells us that, in such circumstances, the probability of Dirac's theory given the truth of its prediction is greater, perhaps much greater, than the prior probability of the theory, or its probability independently of the prediction. So once the predicted existence of positrons was confirmed in 1932, physicists needed to change their degree of belief in Dirac's theory in accordance with the rule of conditionalisation; to remain coherent in their attribution, overt or tacit, of degrees of belief, they needed to increase their degree of belief in Dirac's theory. This coincides exactly with what our intuitions about scientific reasoning tell us. Confirmation of the existence of positrons made it reasonable for physicists to accept Dirac's theory because, without that theory, their existence would have been unsuspected (see Franklin 1986: 113–23).

A further schematic example of 'conditionalisation' is provided by Mendeleev's hypothesis, developed in the 1870s, that chemical elements can be classified in accordance with a periodic law which results in a tabular arrangement known as the periodic table. The blank spaces in the proposed table implied that there were undiscovered elements with predictable characteristics. For example, Mendeleev predicted on the basis of his hypothetical periodic table the existence and characteristics of a new element he called eka-silicon. This element, which we now know as germanium, was subsequently discovered, and there was a remarkable degree of agreement between its measured properties and Mendeleev's predictions. If we use h as an abbreviation for Mendeleev's hypothetical periodic table, and e as an abbreviation for his prediction, then $p_o(e,h)$ is one, since the prediction was deduced from the hypothesis. The probability of, or degree of belief in, h prior to our knowing the truth or falsity of this prediction is $p_o(h)$; let us take the view of sceptical contemporaries of Mendeleev and suppose it to be no more than 0.05. The probability of, or degree of belief in, the truth of e is $p_o(e)$; suppose e to be unexpected and to have, therefore, a probability 0.25. Then Bayes's theorem allows us to claim that $p_o(h,e)$ > $p_o(h)$, for we calculate $p_o(h,e)$ as $(0.05 \times 1)/0.25$, or 0.2, which is four times greater than 0.05, the value we had assigned to $p_o(h)$. Mendeleev's sceptical contemporaries, then, remain unpersuaded of the truth of the hypothesis, for its probability remains low. But in accordance with the rule of conditionalisation the sceptics' new degree of belief in the hypothetical periodic table is significantly greater than their old degree of belief. Were there to be further evidence, equally unexpected, a further application of Bayes's theorem yields a new degree of belief of 0.8, and the sceptics would be persuaded. Other sceptics, starting with still lower prior probabilities, would need further evidence, perhaps a great deal of further evidence, before accepting Mendeleev's hypothesis. Since there is no lower limit to the prior probability of h, though it cannot be zero, we may be unable to produce sufficient evidence to persuade some of them.

But so long as this is the case, a critic might say, we are a long way from understanding how reasoning works in science. For reasoning is used to persuade colleagues that, in the light of evidence, they should accept a hypothesis or a theory which had previously seemed too speculative or too undeveloped. Mendeleev wanted to convince chemists, including sceptical chemists, that his periodic table hypothesis should be accepted, not just that the evidence available made it more probable or more believable than it would otherwise have been. If, as personalist Bayesians claim, there are no justifiable restrictions of the choice of prior probabilities for hypotheses, provided those probabilities are coherent, then no-one need be persuaded by the success of Mendeleev's prediction, or by any evidence, however strong, to accept his hypothesis. The new probability of the hypothesis may be greater than its old probability but it may still be quite insufficient to justify acceptance of the hypothesis. Scientific method is about arguing for the acceptance, or rejection, of scientific claims; personalist Bayesians offer only an account of 'personal inference' which does not necessarily lead to either acceptance or rejection (see Glymour 1980: 75).

There are at least two ways of responding to this charge that personalist Bayesianism is too subjective to be of use in understanding scientific reasoning. In the first place we can claim that, as we change our degrees of belief in accordance with the rule of conditionalisation, the significance of the prior probabilities with which we began decreases. Two scientists might begin with widely divergent views about the credibility of a hypothesis, and this difference will be reflected in the widely different degrees of belief they assign to the hypothesis. But over a period of time, and in the light of the evidence, their degrees of belief will converge. The effect of different prior probabilities will, therefore, be 'swamped' or 'washed out' by experience. There is, of course, a question about how long that period of time will be, and consequently a doubt about the value of the truth that differences in prior probabilities will eventually become irrelevant. Second, we can insist that there is no more reason to place restrictions on the prior probabilities which form the basis of inductive probabilistic reasoning than there is to place restrictions on the premises we may use in deductive reasoning. Deductively valid arguments remain deductively valid whatever premises we use; similarly, inductively valid arguments remain valid whatever prior probabilities we adopt. Rationality does not require restrictions on the premises we use in deduction; it should not require restrictions on the prior probabilities we use when we reason inductively and change our degree of belief in a hypothesis in the light of evidence with the aid of Bayes's theorem. We need, though, to take care that disanalogies between induction and deduction do not undermine this defence. In inductive reasoning, though not in deduction, we need not only premises but degrees of belief in them, for the reasoning is essentially concerned with changes in degrees of belief brought about by applying, consciously or unconsciously, Bayes's theorem. In other words, although premises in deduction do not have to be believed, we do have to believe the premises in induction, and prior probabilities represent the strength of our belief. Beliefs, and the strength of our commitment to them, as well as our inferences, can be more or less rational.

As we have seen, one of the important criteria for rationality is that the rule of conditionalisation should govern the way a person's beliefs change over time, in the light of relevant evidence. This suggests that it is only new evidence which can be effective in changing degrees of belief. Old evidence is part of the background information taken into account in determining the prior probability of a hypothesis. More especially, information which was used to justify the introduction of a hypothesis cannot have a role in enhancing our degree of belief in it. If, for example, Dirac's electron theory had been put forward in order to explain the existence of positrons, then their existence would have done nothing to increase the probable truth of the theory. Similarly, the existence of silicon, unlike the existence of germanium, does not increase the probable truth of Mendeleev's periodic table hypothesis, for that hypothesis was constructed in the knowledge of silicon's existence. Again, if in a medical context a hypothesis about how a disease is transmitted is put forward to explain known facts about its speed of transmission, then those facts do not make the truth of that hypothesis any greater than it would otherwise be. We can express this by saying that its probability given the evidence of those facts is no greater than its prior probability and, by referring to Bayes's theorem, we can easily see that the reason for this is that the probability of the evidence, because it is known evidence, is one. Whenever $p(e)$ is one, $p(h,e)$ cannot be greater than $p(h)$.

There is, though, something puzzling about this line of reasoning. For scientists often use old and familiar evidence to increase the probability of new hypotheses and theories. The known existence of interference fringes in optical experiments was used to enhance the probability of wave theories of light in the nineteenth century. Newton used Kepler's laws in arguing for his inverse square law of gravitation, even though those laws were known and accepted. Einstein used the known anomalous advance of Mercury's perihelion to claim that his general theory of relativity deserved a higher degree of belief than would otherwise be the case. All scientists would regard these uses of evidence as entirely legitimate. It is, therefore, an 'absurdity' to imply, as Bayesianism seems to imply, that 'old evidence cannot confirm new theory' (Glymour 1980: 86).

The issue is an old one. As we have seen, it divided inductive logicians in the nineteenth and in the early twentieth century. Herschel, Whewell and Peirce were sure that, in seeking support for a theory, we should only use facts predicted by it, and not those 'accommodated' by it. Mill and Keynes took the contrary view that our confidence in a theory can be increased just as well by accommodated truths as by predicted truths.

Arguments for and against these positions have remained finely balanced. On the one hand, new and unexpected evidence becomes old and familiar, so why should we distinguish between prediction and accommodation? Our degrees of belief in predicted outcomes become little different from our degrees of belief in accommodated inputs, once we learn that the predictions are correct. Yet it seems absurd to claim that a predicted outcome, once known to be correct, cannot increase our degree of belief in the theory which has it as an outcome. Indeed, the rule of conditionalisation depends on our being able to increase that degree of belief in just these circumstances. On the other hand, if the appropriate degree of belief in predicted outcomes and accommodated inputs is, or becomes, one because we know the outcomes and inputs to be true, then Bayesianism offers little or no help in the understanding of scientific reasoning.

A distinction which could be important in resolving this issue is that between evidence deliberately accommodated, in the sense that the relevant theory is designed to fit or explain that evidence, and evidence accidentally accommodated, in that although this evidence was available it was ignored in constructing the theory. This suggests that, although accommodated evidence cannot be new, the 'evidence' or knowledge that the theory accommodates it can be new. And this helps to bridge the gap between prediction and accommodation, and so reduce the extent of disagreement. Those who claim that facts accommodated by a theory cannot inductively support it are right because some of those facts, namely those deliberately accommodated, cannot increase the probability of the theory. But there will normally be some facts which a theory accommodates accidentally, and these facts can increase its probability, so those who claim that accommodated facts are of use in supporting a theory are also right. For example, there are good grounds for thinking that Einstein's relativity theory was not designed to explain the failure of the famous Michelson–Morley experiment to detect any optical effect of an aether, even though that failure was known and accepted by Einstein. His degree of belief in the Michelson–Morley result was, or should have been, one. However, the 'evidence' or knowledge that his relativity theory could explain this result was new, at least for a short time. And, to the extent that he did not expect this 'evidence', his degree of belief in it would be less than one. By taking this into account we can, it is suggested, understand how the existing and accommodated evidence provided by the Michelson–Morley experiment could support Einstein's theory. By contrast, Einstein did intend to accommodate the known anomaly in the advance of Mercury's perihelion. So the facts concerning that anomaly could not be used to support his theory.

But this distinction will be of little value if it leads to conclusions which cannot be reconciled with the relevant historical information and with the firmly held views of scientists about which evidence inductively supports which theory. In the case of Einstein's relativity theory, the complex historical evidence does little or nothing to encourage the suggestion that this proposal does lead to a suitable resolution of the issue. Mercury's anomalous perihelion advance, though intentionally accommodated by the general theory of relativity, did and still does contribute to an increased degree of belief in the theory. It would appear, indeed, that the contribution it makes is, for many scientists, greater than the contribution made by successful predictions of the theory, such as the prediction confirmed by Eddington's 1919 British eclipse expedition that light should be deflected as it passes close to the Sun (see Brush 1989: 1124–9; cf. Earman 1992: 119). In general, the fact that a theory has been constructed in order to explain known data does not, in itself, seem to prevent us from appealing to that data in order to increase the probability of the theory.

Another way of approaching the issue turns on the idea that what matters is not whether evidence has been predicted or accommodated but rather how unexpected or surprising it is. We can still be surprised by what has happened, even though we know it has happened. Conversely, we can be unsurprised by a prediction, even though it is a correct prediction. To this extent, what has happened can be unexpected, and what has yet to happen can be expected. For example, ten consecutive heads when I tossed a fair coin yesterday remains surprising and unexpected although the evidence that it has occurred is incontrovertible, whereas six heads and four tails when I toss the same coin tomorrow is unsurprising and reasonably expected. How, though, can we use this distinction between the surprising and the unsurprising in a Bayesian account of reasoning? One way to do it is to revive the claim insisted on by Keynes and Carnap that the probabilities which we need to understand inductive reasoning, whether in Bayesian terms or not, are relational. When we judge the probability of a hypothesis, or the probability of evidence relevant to it, we judge relative to some information. The so-called 'prior' probability of a hypothesis is not its probability relative to no information, for there cannot be any such probability. There will always be some 'background' information, more or less extensive, relative to which we judge the prior probability of the hypothesis, so that $p(h)$ should always be understood as elliptical for $p(h,b)$ where b signifies that background knowledge. Similarly, in the case of the probability of the evidence we intend to use to change our degree of belief in the hypothesis, this probability, too, is always relative to background information, including information about alternative ways of accounting for the evidence, if there are any. So $p(e)$ should always be understood as elliptical for $p(e,b)$. Of course, if we include the evidence in the background information on the grounds that it has been used to construct the hypothesis in question, then $p(e,b) = 1$ and it will be impossible for the evidence to affect the degree of belief in the hypothesis. But our aim is to suggest a way of interpreting $p(e,b)$ that will reflect the degree to which e is surprising or unexpected. We must therefore judge the probability of the evidence relative to background information that does not contain that evidence. In effect, we are proposing that $p(e,b)$ should measure the degree to which you would have expected the evidence had it not been available to you, or the degree to which you would have believed e true given the background information b had not included e. If we can evaluate this counter-factual degree of belief, then normally $p(e,b)$ will be less than one, and sometimes it will be much less than one, even though we know that e is true. And in these circumstances accommodated evidence, even deliberately accommodated evidence, can increase our degree of belief in the accommodating hypothesis. On the other hand, even when the background information cannot include e because e is predicted rather than accommodated, $p(e,b)$ may still be close to one if the truth of e is expected and unsurprising, in which case the truth of e will do little if anything to increase our degree of belief in the hypothesis.

It is, however, by no means clear that the practice of scientists in sometimes using old evidence to support new theories can be reconciled with a Bayesian account of reasoning. Much depends on whether the concept of evidence being surprising or unexpected can be elucidated in terms of counter-factual degrees of belief. Actual degrees of belief can be associated with real dispositions that a person has, if not with his or her real behaviour when obliged to bet on the truth of beliefs. But degrees of belief that a person would have had in circumstances other than those that obtain, or possible degrees of belief, have no such associations. Nevertheless, perhaps possible degrees of belief, like the possible worlds in which they exist, are no less obscure or puzzling than actual degrees of belief and the actual world in which they exist. And even if there is some difficulty in accepting this, we face an even greater difficulty if we reject it. For by accepting it we are able to claim that the reasoning used in science is, in essence, Bayesian; by rejecting it we imply that some alternative account of scientific reasoning is needed, and currently there is no such account which has so many of Bayesianism's advantages and so few of its disadvantages.

FURTHER READINGS

For Carnap, see:

Carnap, R. (1962a) *Logical Foundations of Probability*, second edition, Chicago: University of Chicago Press. The first edition was published in 1950.

Carnap, R. and Jeffrey, R. C. (eds) (1971) *Studies in Inductive Logic and Probability*, vol. 1, Berkeley: University of California Press.

Carnap, R. (1974) *An Introduction to the Philosophy of Science*, previously published as *Philosophical Foundations of Physics,* edited by M. Gardner, New York: Basic Books; Part I.

For an account of Carnap's life, see:
Carnap, R. (1963) 'Autobiography', in P. A. Schilpp (ed.), *The Philosophy of Rudolf Carnap,* Library of Living Philosophers, La Salle, Ill.: Open Court.

For discussions of Carnap's ideas, see:
Schilpp, P. A. (ed.) (1963) *The Philosophy of Rudolf Carnap,* Library of Living Philosophers, La Salle, Ill.: Open Court.
Hintikka, J. (1965) 'Towards a theory of inductive generalisation', in Y. Bar Hillel (ed.), *Proceedings of the 1964 Congress for Logic, Methodology and Philosophy of Science,* Amsterdam: North-Holland.
Hintikka, J. (1966) 'A two-dimensional continuum of inductive methods', in J. Hintikka and P. Suppes (eds), *Aspects of Inductive Logic,* Amsterdam: North-Holland.
Salmon, W. C. (1967) *The Foundations of Scientific Inference,* Pittsburgh, Pa.: Pittsburgh University Press; ch. 5.
Kuipers, T. A. F. (1978) *A Survey of Inductive Systems,* Dordrecht: Reidel.
Popper, K. (1982a) *Realism and the Aim of Science,* Postscript to the Logic of Scientific Discovery, vol. 1, edited by W. W. Bartley III, London: Hutchinson; Part 2, ch. 2.
Cohen, L. J. (1989) *An Introduction to the Philosophy of Induction and Probability,* Oxford: Clarendon Press; esp. ch. 17.

Others who developed inductive probability along lines similar to those in Carnap include:
Jeffreys, H. (1957) *Scientific Inference,* second edition, Cambridge: Cambridge University Press.
Jeffreys, H. (1967) *Theory of Probability,* Oxford: Oxford University Press.

For modern Bayesianism, see:
Finetti, B. de (1964) 'Foresight: its logical laws, its subjective sources', in H. E. Kyburg and H. E. Smokler (eds), *Studies in Subjective Probability,* New York: John Wiley and Sons, Inc. Originally published in French in *Annales de l'Institut Henri Poincaré* 7 (1937).
Shimony, A. (1970) 'Scientific inference', in R. Colodny (ed.), *The Nature and Function of Scientific Theories,* Pittsburgh, Pa.: Pittsburgh University Press. Reprinted in A. Shimony, *Search For A Naturalistic World View, vol.1: Scientific Method and Epistemology,* Cambridge: Cambridge University Press, 1993.
Hesse, M. (1974) *The Structure of Scientific Inference,* Berkeley: University of California Press.
Rosenkrantz, R. D. (1977) *Inference, Method and Decision: Towards a Bayesian Philosophy of Science,* Dordrecht: Reidel.
Ramsey, F. P. (1978) *Foundations: Essays in Philosophy, Logic, Mathematics and Economics,* edited D. H. Mellor, London: Routledge and Kegan Paul; ch. 3.
Hesse, M. (1980) 'What is the best way to assess evidential support for scientific theories?', in M. Hesse and L. J. Cohen (eds), *Applications of Inductive Logic,* Oxford: Clarendon Press.
Earman, J. (1992) *Bayes or Bust? A Critical Examination of Bayesian Confirmation Theory,* Cambridge, Mass.: MIT Press.
Howson, C. and Urbach, P. (1993) *Scientific Reasoning: The Bayesian Approach,* second edition, La Salle, Ill.: Open Court.

The applicability of Bayesianism to real scientific reasoning is explored in:
Franklin, A. (1986) *The Neglect of Experiment*, Cambridge: Cambridge University
   Press.

An influential criticism of modern Bayesianism is to be found in:
Glymour, C. (1980) *Theory and Evidence*, Princeton, NJ: Princeton University
   Press, ch. 3.

12 Conclusion
Experimental interventions and social constructions

Besides the continuing debate about how far Bayesianism is capable of representing the kind of reasoning scientists use in justifying their conclusions, there are other issues which are currently prominent for philosophers of science. There are questions about the experimental character of scientific method. How do, or should, scientific experiments contribute to the growth of scientific knowledge? Can experimental enquiry proceed independently of theoretical commitment? There are questions about the social character of scientific method. Are the conclusions which are established by using scientific methods determined less by reason than by the social, political and economic environment within which the methods are endorsed? In what way, if at all, are scientific facts constructed for scientists rather than discovered by them? There are questions about the nature and basis of claims about scientific method. Do these claims purport to be true generalised descriptions of how scientists proceed and of how they reason when establishing their conclusions, or are they rather attempts to prescribe standards to which good scientific reasoning should aspire? And there are questions about the need for, and existence of, any 'rules' about good reasoning in science. In the light of historical evidence about how science has proceeded, why not concede that any reasoning, how ever absurd in some circumstances, may be entirely appropriate and legitimate in other circumstances? Why not allow that scientists are 'epistemological opportunists' or 'methodological anarchists'? Why not allow that they should be? In this concluding chapter we will consider some connections between these issues, some questions they have raised, and some answers that have been proposed.

It is tempting, and indeed natural, to see experiments as essential features of scientific enquiry. Physics, chemistry, biology, geology and at least some parts of psychology are 'laboratory' sciences, and therefore experimental, whereas mathematics, whether pure or applied, is not a laboratory science, and not experimental. We are told that physics became a science when Galileo made it experimental; that although alchemists and chemists had laboratories long before Lavoisier's time, his quantitative experiments made a science of chemistry; that biology grew apart from natural history and into a science when it became experimental. No such transformations affected mathematical enquiry; from the time of Euclid and Plato its status as a rational exploration of an ideal world, accessible to thought but not to the senses, had remained secure. It is, perhaps, only the honorific connotations of the words 'science' and 'scientific' that dissuade us from claiming that only laboratory sciences are, in the fullest sense, sciences. The real world of laboratories and experiments is the proper province of natural science; the ideal world of abstract thought is the proper province of mathematics. Distinctive skills are required in the laboratory sciences, and though no doubt they are of various kinds, they are of a different order to the skills required in the mathematical sciences. Good experimenters in the laboratory sciences and good problem-solvers in mathematics have acquired practical abilities, but they are different abilities. Scientific methods are, essentially, experimental methods and a mathematician will have little or no use for them. Consequently, mathematical knowledge differs significantly from scientific knowledge. This is not to say that either type of knowledge is more valuable than the other; scientific knowledge, though worth having, may be less valuable than mathematical knowledge, or vice versa.

The weakness of this reasoning is easy to see. In the first place the laboratory sciences are not the only sources of scientific knowledge. Many of our ideas about scientific methods and about what is characteristic of scientific knowledge developed in the context of an important non-experimental science – astronomy – that, until relatively recently, required sharp and accurate observation rather than the skilful dexterity needed to make effective use of laboratory equipment. There are, it is true, many important links between astronomy and physics, which is an experimental science, but nevertheless astronomers can only observe, not manipulate, the objects they study. Astronomers cannot intervene in the world to change it in the way that an experimenter can. They must base claims about what would happen if the world were to change on inference rather than upon observation. Of course, observational astronomy has always been an elaborate and sophisticated enterprise using techniques and sense-extending instrumentation which demand skills like those needed in an experimenter. This shows that observation is not always as straightforward and passive as we sometimes suppose. Telescopic observation, for instance, requires the abilities of an experimenter, even if experiment is not the same as observation. The same is true of other instruments, such as those used in microscopy.

In the second place the concepts of experiment and laboratory are much broader than the reasoning recognises. Mathematicians experiment; so do most people much of the time. Thus, in developing a proof for a theorem, mathematicians might experiment with various approaches because they believe that experiment, if only in the form of trial and error, is a good way of achieving their object. Similarly, gardeners will experiment with alternative horticultural aids in order to obtain a better display of sweet peas, or with different layouts in their gardens so as to make the best of their labours. Neither the mind nor the potting shed is a scientific laboratory, but even so there is nothing especially metaphorical about our saying that experiments are taking place in these laboratories. We can, it is true, observe the outcomes of these experiments, but it is the ingenuity, the reliability and the patient application of the techniques and methods used to obtain these outcomes which are of importance and which are the mark of a good experimenter.

A scientific experiment is a species of experiment, and of that species there are very many varieties. Seeing it in this light draws attention, in a natural way, to some features of any experiment which we might otherwise overlook. For example, the experiments of mathematicians and of gardeners are not so much tests of hypotheses or theories as explorations and investigations of unfamiliar territory. The primary thought is not 'is such-and-such true?' but rather 'what would happen if . . .?' Mathematicians wonder what would happen if the theorem for which a proof is sought is false, and discover that if it were they could deduce a contradiction. The investigating experiment has led to the discovery of a *reductio ad absurdum* proof of the theorem. For example, mathematicians seeking to prove that $\sqrt{2}$ is a number which cannot be represented as a fraction experiment with the claim that it can. They suppose, that is, $\sqrt{2} = n/m$, where n and m are whole numbers and their ratio n/m cannot be expressed as a simpler ratio. From this supposition it follows that $2 = n^2/m^2$, or $n^2 = 2m^2$. This means that n^2 must be an even number, which in turn implies that n itself is also even. Since n is even it can be divided by 2, so $n/2$ is a whole number – say p. So n^2, which we already know equals $2m^2$ also equals $4p^2$. Therefore $2m^2 = 4p^2$, or $m^2 = 2p^2$. But this means that m^2 must be an even number, which in turn means that m is also even. However, it cannot be the case that both n and m are even numbers, because if they were the ratio n/m would not be expressed in its simplest terms, which is contrary to our supposition. We started by assuming that $\sqrt{2}$ is expressible as a fraction, n/m, where n and m are not both divisible by 2; our reasoning from this assumption leads to the conclusion that n and m are divisible by 2; the conclusion we must draw is that $\sqrt{2}$ is not expressible as a fraction.

Similarly, gardeners seeking to improve the aspect of a shady and gloomy part of their gardens wonder what would happen if they moved plants from here to there, if they grew trees near here, if they rearranged patio containers, etc. Sometimes what they do will have no effect, or no interesting effect; sometimes what they do will make things worse. But that is what exploration in general is like. When we visit an unfamiliar city for the first time we are sometimes disappointed and sometimes pleasantly surprised in our experimental explorations. We can say that we are 'testing' implicit 'hypotheses' about how interesting it would be to venture down this or that street, but it seems doubtful whether we could, or would wish to, find a suitable way of expressing such a 'hypothesis' so that it would make good sense to speak of a 'test' for it. If we think of experimental exploration as nothing more than hypothesis testing, we are liable to mistake the role and significance of experiments; if we think of hypothesis testing as requiring the initiative and skills associated with experimental exploration, we acquire an enhanced appreciation of what testing involves.

Scientific experiments have this exploratory character. Is there, psychologists asked in the 1960s, a chemical which will help to improve the memorising abilities of animals? Some explored this question by extracting chemicals from animals who had learned how to perform a task, and subsequently supplying them to other animals who had not, in order to discover whether those supplied were able to learn that task more easily or more quickly. Learning, whether of worms, mice, rats, goldfish or people, is of course a matter of degree, and if those supplying chemicals and those supplied by them learn, at most, only a very little, then the results of the exploration might be very limited and questionable. The data purporting to show that learning had taken place were disputed, with some claiming that the phenomenon does exist and that failure to detect it reflects on the experimenters' lack of skill and experience, while others maintained that there is no such phenomenon and the data supposed to be evidence for it are artefacts of the experiment and its environment. Experiments have not yielded a clear answer to a test; rather they have explored the limitations of certain techniques and procedures (Collins and Pinch 1993: ch. 1).

For a second example, consider a famous experiment conducted in the 1880s. How fast, asked Albert Michelson, does the Earth travel through the invisible aether which acts as a medium for the trans-mission of optical, gravitational and electrical effects from one place in the universe to another? If the speed is small and its effects marginal, it will be difficult to detect with the optical interferometer device he and his colleague Edward Morley built, which made the speed depend on the almost undetectable difference in the time taken for light beams projected at right angles to each other to return to their source having traversed the same distance. Unable to detect the difference he thought should exist, Michelson did not conclude that the Earth travels at zero speed through the aether; he concluded, rather, that despite the care and precautions taken the device was too susceptible to extraneous factors, such as temperature and vibration, and was not suitable for measuring that speed. His exploration failed, he thought, to yield the interesting data he had hoped for. He could have sought an explanation for his 'null' outcome other than the inadequacy of his interferometer. If he had had sufficient confidence in the non-existence of the effect he tried to measure, he might have looked for a theoretical explanation. As it was, within a few years Albert Einstein had developed a theory from which it followed that the looked-for effect does not exist. Not that his theory ended the exploration. For perhaps, despite Einstein's theory, Michelson's effect does exist and it really was the inadequacies of his device which prevented him from detecting it. There have been enough surprises in the history of physics to make us cautious in ruling out the possibility of such a result (Collins and Pinch 1993: ch. 2).

Such examples also draw attention to another important feature of scientific experiments, namely their function of identifying, stabilising and characterising phenomena. Experiments always produce an outcome or data. Often something happens as a consequence of an experiment, and what happens is the outcome of the experiment; even when nothing happens, that is an outcome. But different experiments sometimes produce different data. This is almost invariably the case with experiments of different types and, if they relate to a particular question, it may be difficult if not impossible to reconcile the different data. For example, experimental determinations of temperature using different kinds of thermometer are unlikely to deliver the same data. Experiments of the same type – replica experiments – also sometimes produce different data, for reasons of which experimenters are unaware and over which they have no control. Replicated experiments can and perhaps should replicate data, but laboratory experience indicates that we cannot assume they will. For example, experimental determinations of temperature, by different people or at different times, using the same kind of thermometer – perhaps even the same thermometer – will sometimes deliver different data. So the data yielded by experiments will exhibit differences, perhaps inconsistencies, which will make it difficult to judge their significance. The data may or may not have sufficient coherence and consistency to show either that a specific phenomenon does or does not exist. Thus the data yielded by experiments involving the extraction and transfer of chemicals thought to be connected with memory in animals was so diffuse, variable and contradictory that no clear conclusion could be drawn as to the existence or non-existence of the chemical transfer of memory. There were plenty of experimental data but, some claimed, no new phenomenon revealed by them. Similarly, the data yielded by the Michelson–Morley experiment were insufficiently consistent to reveal reliable information about a phenomenon assumed to exist, namely the speed of the Earth through the aether. Later, when the question was whether the aether exists at all, those data were similarly inconclusive. Certainly, some of the data showed, not that the predicted optical effect did not occur, but rather that it was very much smaller than expected (see Hacking 1983: 220–32; Bogan and Woodward 1988).

So the phenomena revealed in scientific experiments are often elusive and difficult to identify, to stabilise and to characterise. In optics, for example, interference patterns resulting from diffraction phenomena are now easy to produce, and everyone who has studied physics at school knows how to create them. But it was not always so. Thomas Young, who earned considerable credit for his experimental investigation of diffraction, found it difficult to obtain the results that enabled him to produce reliable descriptions of the phenomena. It was, indeed, the introduction of Fresnel's wave theory, rather than experimental work, that provided a good account of diffraction phenomena. Similarly, the phenomenon of constant acceleration under gravity is harder to establish by experiment than we often suppose. Galileo may have dropped different weights simultaneously from the top of a tower, but it is unlikely that the data he obtained about the coincidence, or lack of it, in their arriving at the foot of the tower would have encouraged confidence in the phenomenon. He would have found that blocks of wood and of stone released simultaneously from the same height do not reach the ground simultaneously. However, this data must be set alongside that from Galileo's famous thought experiment before a conclusion is drawn as to the existence and nature of the constant acceleration phenomenon.

It is a commonplace that experimenters need skills. As Thomas Kuhn, among others, has pointed out, 'the operations and measurements that a scientist undertakes in the laboratory are not "the given" of experience but rather "the collected with difficulty"' (Kuhn 1970a: 103). But we do not so readily acknowledge the wide scope of these skills. Imagination and ingenuity are clearly important; so are interpretative and manipulative capacities. But so also are rhetorical abilities. Words, as well as apparatus, are powerful components of the experimenter's repertoire, and the skill of wielding them effectively has often been important. Galileo is a conspicuous example, but so too are others such as William Harvey, Joseph Black, Henry Cavendish, Jakob Berzelius and Michael Faraday. Rhetoric, even the rhetoric of experiment, can work against the development of good science, but, contrary to the impression sometimes given, it often co-operates with reason. Many scientists are naturally sceptical, and replacing their scepticism by conviction is difficult even when conviction is the more reasonable alternative. For such scientists, rhetoric is a legitimate means for trying to effect the change. Sceptical scientists do not have to have good reasons for being convinced by experiments; it is enough if there are good reasons why they should be convinced by experiments.

We are also apt to overlook the implications of the fact that there are different degrees to which experimenters possess appropriate skills. If an experimenter using certain equipment reports that there is good evidence for a novel phenomenon, whereas another experimenter using the same equipment reports that no evidence for the phenomenon has been found, we would need to make a judgement about the relative expertise of the experimenters in order to express a view. Often this will not be easy; sometimes it will be impossible. Experimental expertise is related to experience and to reputation, both of which can, of course, vary widely. We saw one example in Newton's experimental work with prisms, which his contemporaries found difficult to replicate. Another example would be the painstaking work of Berzelius in determining the atomic weights of elements. Even noticing and observation require expertise (see Hacking 1983: 180). The ability to recognise something out of the ordinary, something other than the expected, is important whether experimenting in a biochemical laboratory or observing the night sky. Such expertise is not confined to those familiar with the theoretical assumptions which might encourage an observer or experimenter to notice the unexpected or the interesting; we find it in anyone whose training and experience has enabled them to develop the required skills.

The attention philosophers have paid to the nature of the reasoning involved in science has led, then, to a distorted image of experiments. Phenomena produced in experiments are used to test scientific theories; depending on whether what does happen in the experiment conforms with what, according to the theory, should happen, the theory will be confirmed or falsified, and the logic of scientific method will tell us what confidence to place in any confirmation or falsification. But in practice the production of experimental phenomena can be a protracted process, following a 'logic' of its own and involving 'negotiation' between experimenters. New techniques will be introduced; ways of eliminating or reducing significant sources of error will be found; the relevance of other experiments will be explored; the expertise of those experimenting will be judged. In these and other ways, experiments have lives of their own independent of any theory. Moreover, experiments are not always tests of theories or hypotheses. Evaluating an innovative technique, exploring a novel topic, measuring or remeasuring a physical constant, identifying the characteristics of a new synthetic chemical, or simply observing the effects on animal behaviour of controllable variables, are all legitimate modes of experiment. Sometimes, indeed, experiments are designed simply so that we can get nature to behave in unfamiliar ways and thereby illuminate its more familiar ways. We have, in short, reasons for 'intervening' in the world, or 'interrogating' nature, other than that of finding out whether our guesses are correct or not.

Although there are isolated experimenters, just as there are solitary theorists, experimentation has always been an activity undertaken with, or on behalf of, others. It is a socially established and co-operative human activity, like building a house, selling insurance, managing a business, playing football, etc. The scientific laboratory is a place where people meet to report, to witness, to agree and disagree, to negotiate, and to interact, as well as a place where hypotheses are tested, problems solved, questions raised, difficulties eased, frustrations compounded, time wasted, etc. Similarly, demonstration-lectures, such as those associated with the Royal Institution, and made famous by Humphry Davy and Michael Faraday, are social occasions replete with cultural associations. Though not perhaps explicitly acknowledged, the social role of the laboratory and lecture as scenes for the operation of the experimental method have been prominent since the seventeenth century. The Royal Society of London is an obvious manifestation of this. In the early days of the society the performance of experiments before members was an important way of assuring the reliability of the phenomena they revealed. The truth or otherwise of some general theory might be accessible only to God, but the reliability of a report of an experiment, perhaps relevant to the theory, was a matter of social credibility. The skills of an experimenter such as Robert Hooke could be, and were, bought; but those who witnessed his experiments were required to have social standing in the community if they wished others to believe their reports (see Shapin 1994). It is as though the social fabric determines what will be believed and accepted.

In one sense, of course, there have to be constraints on what any person believes and accepts. We can, after all, believe only what we have had an opportunity to consider, and there are physical and personal, as well as social, limitations on what at a particular place and time we can consider. Nevertheless, it does not follow that the truth of what a person believes and accepts is determined by physical, personal or social circumstances. Just because our beliefs are carefully built up and constructed in the light of the evidence we have been able to assemble, it does not follow that the facts or the reality which those beliefs concern are also made, or built, or constructed by us. Unless we beg questions and say that the world is constantly changing in order to fit the latest views of scientists, we must allow that even universally adopted scientific beliefs are sometimes mistaken. We must allow, that is, a distinction between truth and belief, between fact and conviction, between reality and acceptance. The distinction is sometimes hard to maintain, for although one person can and often does distinguish between what other people believe and what is true, she cannot distinguish what she believes from what is true even though she may think that some of her beliefs are false. From the inside, or from what we might call a 'first person perspective', the distinction between belief and truth is a distinction which does not make a difference. It is only from the outside, or from a 'third person perspective', that the distinction does make a difference.

Questions about the role of social factors in the development of scientific enquiry were raised in an interesting manner by Thomas Kuhn's famous book, *The Structure of Scientific Revolutions* (Kuhn 1970a). In the first place, he claimed that theoretical and experimental work in natural science takes place within frameworks or paradigms which are identified, in part at least, in a sociological manner. For a paradigm, he said, consists in 'the entire constellation of beliefs, values, techniques, and so on shared by the members of a given community' (Kuhn 1970a: 144), so in identifying a paradigm we *ipso facto* identify a social network of scientists. The structures of such networks are studied by sociologists and historians, who develop criteria for membership based upon education, expertise, professional recognition, etc. Typically there will be standard means of communication within a network, helping to sustain it and carrying its work forward. Journals consulted, conferences attended, societies joined and authorities cited will often be useful indicators of a community. The interactions represented by these activities are, in a broad sense, social, and we should expect therefore that the shared paradigm will contain elements reflecting the interests that social groups have. What is said in the journals, at conferences and society meetings, and by authorities, will contribute to the articulation of a paradigm. But so, too, will what is not said but implied. Unstated attitudes and outlooks, as well as stated beliefs and values, will play a significant part in motivating the work scientists do and in securing its positive reception.

Second, the choice of a paradigm cannot be determined by facts about the world. In part this is because the facts accessible to scientists are insufficient to justify a choice. Different incompatible paradigms can be made to fit the facts, and our decision to adopt one rather than another is under-determined by them. Historical investigation purports to show that cultural, political and ideological convictions are brought to bear on the decisions scientists make; to this extent the scientific beliefs incorporated in a paradigm are socially constructed. The same conclusion follows from the recognition that it is beliefs about the facts rather than the facts themselves which influence the scientist's decision-making, and because of the inclusive scope of paradigms these beliefs are inevitably part of that paradigm. We cannot brings facts from 'outside' the paradigm to bear on our judgement of its adequacy, for in trying to do this we have to formulate beliefs about the facts and this is bound to bring them within its scope. It is not that paradigms are under-determined by facts; it is rather that there are no paradigm-independent facts we can use to justify the adoption of one rather than another. The choices scientists make are conventional rather than rational, and relate, allegedly, to the prevailing cultural, political and ideological values of the society supporting their investigations.

A paradigm then has broad cognitive and evaluative scope, as well as having social significance as the defining characteristic of a community of scientists. From within such a community it will, it seems, be impossible to distinguish in any practical way between what is believed, valued and accepted, and what is true. Only if a scientist finds a way to step outside the community and think from within a different paradigm will he or she be able to appreciate the distinction. But the beliefs and values of a community, as determined in the paradigm shared by its members, are created, constructed and negotiated by the community. We should not and do not expect the beliefs characteristic of one paradigm to be found in a preceding or succeeding paradigm. There is nothing puzzling or alarming in the fact that beliefs change, if not from day to day, then from time to time and from place to place. But there is something puzzling in the claim that the reality which is the subject matter of these beliefs also changes from one time to another, and from one place to another. Yet this is what might seem to follow from the claim that belief is relative and that belief and truth are indistinguishable. We will, as Kuhn pointed out, be tempted to say, for example, that 'after Copernicus, astronomers lived in a different world', and that 'after discovering oxygen, Lavoisier worked in a different world'. We will need to 'learn to make sense of' the claim that, though the world does not change with a change of paradigm, 'the scientist afterward works in a different world' (Kuhn 1970a: 96–9; cf. Hacking 1993: 275–310).

It is no wonder, then, that the crucial transformations that have taken place in natural science are seen as having social and psychological explanations. When scientists adopt a paradigm they do so because of the social, political and ideological preconceptions prevailing in the community to which they belong. This in itself does not mean that paradigms, or the scientific conclusions which result from their adoption, are 'social constructs' in the sense that they are formed out of the ideologies and values of the societies within which they are accepted. For there could be rational justifications as well as social explanations for the changes in question; the conclusions reached by scientists working within a paradigm could provide a reliable guide to the way the natural world really is. But if paradigms are such that there cannot be good reasons for, but only social and ideological causes of, their adoption, then natural science will be no more than one among many other ways we have of conversing with one another. In particular, if the way the world is exercises no control over what scientists believe and what they accept, then natural science itself no longer counts as a body of more or less reliable theories about a real world, and the experimental method is no more than a practice characteristic of a type of 'discourse' or 'narrative' having no independent force or validity. Outside of the different discourses to which they belong, reliable theories are no more credit-worthy or less arbitrary than irrational superstitions. 'Science', according to this view, 'is not a body of knowledge; it is, rather, a parable, an allegory, that inscribes a set of social norms and encodes, however subtly, a mythic structure justifying the dominance of one class, one race, one gender over another' (Gross and Levitt 1994: 46).

Kuhn himself does not endorse this cognitive relativism. There is an accessible mind-independent world, and the paradigms scientists work with will contain theories which vary in the their 'accuracy, scope, simplicity, fruitfulness and the like'. Judgements of these qualities are problematic in the sense that not everyone will always agree on which theories have the greatest accuracy, scope, simplicity or fruitfulness, and also in the sense that not everyone will always agree about the relative importance of these qualities. But in adopting a paradigm on the basis of an estimate of these qualities, scientists are looking for accuracy in representing the facts, scope in accommodating the facts, simplicity in accounting for the facts, and fruitfulness in predicting the facts. In short, we can, and perhaps should, think of these values as truth-making. The greater the accuracy, scope, simplicity and fruitfulness of the theories incorporated into a paradigm the greater the confidence we have in their truth-likeness and in its adequacy. Because scientists will differ on the extent to which they accept these qualities as truth-making, they will place different values on them and they will reach different conclusions in the same situations. This does not, though, mean that the conclusions they do reach are arbitrary, that they are conventional or that they are 'socially constructed' (Kuhn 1970b: 261; cf. Kuhn 1977: 320–339).

Nevertheless, sociological explanations of what scientists do have led to the neglect and even dismissal of rational justifications; revealing descriptions have tended to replace pontificating prescriptions. Scientific method has been surrendered to sociologists and anthropologists, and to judge by what is currently being written in the philosophy of science, the idea of a method characteristic of scientific enquiry is not popular. Many would set aside the imperialism of Newtonian method, of the method of hypotheses, of Bayesianism, etc., in favour of a more eclectic approach in which the task of understanding what various scientists variously do supersedes attempts to pontificate about what all scientists should always do. 'Scientists', says one writer, 'should not be constrained by the rules of the methodologist'. Fruitful violations of rules cannot, he says, 'be anticipated and legislated for in advance'. New practices will alter methodologies 'and for this reason the notion of a universal, a-historical account of method that can serve as a standard, not only for the present but also for future knowledge, is an absurdity'.

Such remarks echo Paul Feyerabend's influential claim to be 'against method' (Chalmers 1982: 135, 183; cf. Feyerabend 1975).

Superficially, at least, the case against method proceeds something like this: some facts about the way science is actually practised are presented as inconsistent with a principle of scientific method. Almost invariably, principle is obliged to give way in favour of practice. So, for example, Galileo's preference for telescopic evidence about the surface of our Moon, or about the satellites of Jupiter, conflicted with the views of his contemporaries that our unaided senses provided superior testimony, and we are invited to reject the latter views as inadequate by accepting Galileo's preferred practice as successful.

The crude falsificationism inherent in this reasoning is obvious: where our thinking – as embodied in general principle – is inconsistent with reality – as exemplified in particular practice – then we must adjust our thinking to fit reality. But we know from science itself that, with the aid of ingenuity and perhaps audacity, we can reconcile any practice with any principle. Take, for illustration, a falsificationist principle itself, namely: every genuine test of a theory is an attempt to falsify it. Those who question this principle, on the grounds that it does not fit what scientists actually do, soon find that any practice is consistent with this principle. They learn, in fact, that falsificationist principles fit the history of science 'like a glove'. For if we wish to attack it by identifying some test of a theory which is not an attempt to falsify it, we cannot do so without deciding that the test in question counts as genuine. Given the provisional nature of such decisions it is clear that falsificationists could protect their principle by deciding differently about the test.

If there is no right way to reason in science, then the justification or rationality of a scientific conclusion is determined not by reference to universal standards but by reference to local conventions, needs, habits, etc. What is justified or rational is what we think is justified and rational. As is so often the case with relativistic views, doubts about their coherence are well founded. For example, the relativist will argue that we should abandon the rule which requires scientists to reject any theory which is incompatible with the facts as revealed in careful observations and well conducted experiments. They should relinquish this rule because it is incompatible with what actually happened in some crucial episodes in science. Newton, for example, did not abandon his inverse square law of gravitation even though he was unable, for a long time, to reconcile the truth of this law with the observed behaviour of the Moon. Had the proposed rule been followed, the law would have been rejected as false. But this argument is clearly using a mis-match between a rule and what really happens in order to justify the rejection of a rule, even though the rule used and the rule rejected are the same rule. How can relativists reconcile their rejection of a rule with their need of it to justify that rejection?

More generally, there is a substantial and insufficiently noticed difficulty for relativism about scientific method in that, by adopting it, we eliminate any possibility of its being properly supported by evidence. For it seems clear that the criticism of scientific method in the light of scientific practice cannot be effective unless that practice is successful. How, though, can we recognise this success? In particular, can we distinguish between real and merely apparent success? Pre-Galilean practice of natural philosophy must have seemed successful to many of Galileo's predecessors, yet no-one would wish to suggest that his principles of method might have to be adjusted or abandoned in the light of that success. And the reason for this is clear: our own standards and principles are, we believe, closer to those of Galileo than to those of his predecessors, and it is quite natural, therefore, that we judge the success of Galileo's practice to be, on the whole, real, and the success of his predecessors' practice to be, for the most part, only apparent. But this entails the supposition that our standards are, in turn, closer to some objective truth about these matters. For unless we do suppose some mind-independent standard of correctness here, the distinction between what seems right, effective and successful, and what is right, effective and successful will collapse. It is hard, therefore, to see how relativism about scientific method can be supported properly by an appeal to the history of science without covertly assuming an objective conception of scientific method. It is true, of course, that this objection shows only that a familiar way of trying to establish relativism about scientific method is faulty, and not that that doctrine is itself false, incoherent or inconsistent. Nevertheless, an important reason for the doctrine's popularity is its supposed conformity with historical evidence, so if, as claimed, this reason is spurious, then the attractions of the doctrine are liable to fade.

A further argument against method which may be implicit in appeals to scientific practice is one that mirrors a familiar argument for realism in science, namely that the predictive and explanatory success of a scientific theory is a strong reason for the belief that the theory is a true, or approximately true, report of the real causes of the events predicted and explained. The success of a theory would otherwise be, it is claimed, miraculous. The suggestion so far as scientific method is concerned is that the efforts of philosophers of science to formulate theories of method which would be of any assistance to scientists, or which would help explain scientific practice, have been conspicuously unsuccessful. We are told, sometimes at wearisome length, that no account of scientific method so far proposed has even come close to enabling us to understand anything other than the coarsest outlines of the authenticating practices used in science. And, so the argument continues, the best explanation for this fact is, quite simply, that there is no such thing as objective, mind-independent, a-historical truth in any such accounts.

The continued failure of philosophers of science to achieve even approximate truth would, so to speak, be miraculous if truth in method were achievable. In other words, just as the instrumental efficacy of scientific theories would be difficult to explain unless they can be understood as providing access to observation-transcending facts, so the continued instrumental futility of accounts of scientific method is best explained as a natural consequence of the absence of any practice-transcending facts for such accounts to state.

The worth of this argument seems as questionable as the corresponding argument about scientific theories (see Laudan 1984). Most conspicuously, the kind of argument in use here is not one which anyone who accepts its conclusion can take seriously. For its conclusion is that there is no such thing as objective truth about scientific method, yet the argument invoked manifestly requires that this conclusion is, itself, an objective truth. It may well be a consequence of the non-existence of scientific method that theories of it are instrumentally inadequate, but the observed truth of this consequence is not a legitimate ground upon which anti-realists can advance their anti-realism.

The sheer fact of disagreement about scientific method is another feature which seems to have impressed the sceptics and fostered their relativism. In general, it is claimed, views about scientific method can vary dramatically, not only between different scientists working at different times or in different subject areas, but also between scientists working at the same time and in the same subject area. For example, though we, like Galileo, may deem perverse the notorious refusal of some of his colleagues to make use of telescopic observations, members of the intellectual community in Italy at the time may have viewed that refusal as entirely apposite. After all, Galileo had great difficulty in persuading others that the data provided by his new device were good evidence for real celestial phenomena rather than evidence for illusory products of the lenses used (Geymonat 1965: 44–5). But, so the sceptical argument continues, such 'disputes' cannot be settled in the absence of an objective standard of rationality. By declaring for one side or the other of a dispute, we simply expose our allegiance to one rather than another conception of rationality. All we can say, it seems, is that conflicting judgements are simply products of distinct systems of beliefs, coherent within their own terms, about scientific method. We will search in vain for any 'fact of the matter' which could resolve the disagreement; a Popperian judgement is not truer than a Bayesian judgement, for there is nothing for it to be truer to. There are no facts about the right or best way to justify scientific conclusions. So although there can be change in our views about what is right or best, there can be no progress, for there is no such thing as a true theory about method in science.

The issue here is a familiar one from other contexts: it is not easy to tell whether a conflict of beliefs about some topic obliges us to relinquish any idea that the beliefs are answerable to an objective subject matter, or whether, instead, we are faced simply with a difference in concepts. Dispute about the validity of, say, a precept involving the use of moral concepts, or the truth of a law using scientific concepts, cannot be assumed to imply disagreement about the truth value of the precept or the law; it is at least as likely that it implies, rather, a difference about the scope of the concept involved. For example, claims about the role of experience, observation and experiment in science may be contentious, not because a claim about their role is disputed, but because of disagreement about the scope of experience, of observation and of experiment.

However, to challenge a view about scientific method, or a view about the standards of reasoning appropriate to science, or a view about the right or best way to justify conclusions in science, is not thereby to undermine the more fundamental claim that there is a right or best way to justify conclusions, that there are standards of reasoning, that there is scientific method. In this context as in others, we can disagree about what is true without implying that there is no truth. In their theories of method, people can and do make mistakes. The view that scientific conclusions should always and everywhere be supported on the basis of unaided observations is mistaken, even though there may have been justification for it in particular circumstances. Scientific views are often challenged, yet we do not for that reason abandon realism in science, so why should a challenge to views about scientific method oblige us to discard realism about science? Error in what we say about science, like error in what we say in science, can sometimes be corrected by rational means; in neither case is it always and everywhere a matter of the inexplicable replacement of one more or less arbitrary view by another. If the mistakes of scientists, because they can be explained and corrected, do not oblige us to abandon realism in science, why should the explicable and correctable mistakes of philosophers of science in their account of scientific method threaten realism about science? Provided we can show that the changes which have taken place in scientific method have come about in an explicable and non-arbitrary manner, relativism will not be a good explanation of disagreement about scientific method.

One further source of relativism about scientific method deserves some mention. It is often assumed that rules for good reasoning in science are relative, in the sense that their admissibility or appropriateness depends upon the aims of the scientists subject to them. Since these aims are, or can be, a matter of choice, so also are the rules that embody them. There can, therefore, be no question about the objective validity of these rules. Thus, since Aristotle took the view that scientific enquiry should aim at knowledge of the 'reasoned' fact, we expect demonstrative reasoning and formal logical techniques to feature prominently in an Aristotelian theory of method. We expect, too, the concepts of reason, authority, enlightenment and understanding to be of central importance in such a theory. But, as is now plain to see, there is no obligation to accept this account of what science should achieve. Euclid's *Elements* and the geometrical science of positional astronomy, despite their intellectual and practical virtues, are in many ways misleading models of what is possible in science. The new and some-times surprising models that were created in the seventeenth century led eventually to a different conception of science, and to a suitably transformed methodology. Such concepts as hypothesis, conjecture, evidence, probable belief and ampliative reasoning, which had pre-viously been neglected, shunned or unknown, began to assume the important role that they now have. Our requirements are not those of Aristotle, and it is a mistake, therefore, to suppose that we can compare our standards in any useful way with his.

But in this case, too, we should exercise more caution. We may acknowledge that there have been in the past different conceptions of scientific enquiry and its aims. But this is not to say, as required by the relativist, that there are different concepts of scientific enquiry and its aims. Though the relativist will deny, he does not refute the realist thought that certain aims for scientific enquiry have turned out to be too limiting and distorting. Moreover, there need to be arguments for the key assumption that accounts of scientific method reflect aims, in that they can have force and application only for those who decide to pursue those aims. Aims themselves require justification, and it is misleading to represent them merely as conditions contributing to the motivational basis for principles of method. Whatever may be the motivation for a scientist's adoption of a rule or a standard, it will be appropriate, because of his adoption of it, to ascribe to him the corresponding aims. Accordingly, the explanation for his pursuit of these aims will be the same as the explanation for his adoption of the rule or standard.

It is true, of course, that history reveals diversity in method as well as diversity in science itself, but we should not be so impressed by the diversity that we ignore the connections. It is, after all, we and not Aristotle who label some parts of this work 'scientific'. The belief that scientific truth is created rather than discovered has proved difficult to sustain; we should not suppose that the idea of a true scientific method being a variable fiction of our philosophical imagination, rather than an account of how, objectively, things stand, will be easier to defend.

We can misuse history; but can we use it? Is a history of scientific method, like a history of science, a luxury? Is such a history from a philosopher's point of view, like most history of science from a scientist's point of view, little more than a record of superstition, error and inaccuracy? Such questions are part of a more general one about the relation of a theory of scientific method to matters of fact about the rules and standards that scientists have used. No one doubts that there is such a relation, yet its nature is puzzling. Illustrative accounts of the reasoning used to justify conclusions are used to 'support' or 'suggest' claims about scientific method, and yet we are told that such claims cannot be based on 'descriptive accounts of the research behaviour of scientists' (Hempel 1965: 44). We are urged to notice the confusion engendered by failure 'to pay attention to some very obvious facts' about the actual science, and, at the same time, we are encouraged to favour those philosophers of science who 'were bold enough to stick to their theses even in those cases where they were inconsistent with actual science' (Feyerabend 1968: 13, 24). Such prevarications are as harmful as they are unnecessary. They openly invite the accusation that, if philosophers are as muddled about the relation of theory to fact, so far as scientific method is concerned, there is little hope that they will say anything clear and true about the relation of theory to fact, so far as science is concerned.

The debate seems to arise in the following way. If we represent the rules of science as based upon, or reducible to, a priori propositions of logic and epistemology, it can be difficult to see how they relate to the practice of science. For in analysing these rules in terms of eternal verities or semantic decisions which are independent of experience, we are apt to overlook, misconceive or at least minimise their practical substance and their relation to what actually happens in science. The theory and practice of scientific method thus become separated and, sooner or later, the relevance of theory is challenged. We cannot evade this challenge by dismissing the practice of science as having nothing to do with theory because belonging to the province of historians, sociologists, psychologists, etc. Rather, a theory of scientific method must be constructed in such a way as to capture those features of practical procedure which we take to be characteristic of science.

One easy way to meet this requirement would be to identify scientific method with generalisations about the practice of science. The task would then be to describe, in suitably general terms, the procedures which are or have been used with success in science. Such an uncompromising empiricism would be concerned, presumably, with whatever might happen to be common to superior scientific achievements, but would have no power to prescribe characteristics of future achievements.

These 'Euclidean' and 'anti-theoretical' approaches, as they have been called (Lakatos 1976: 35), generate accounts of scientific method implying that we can appraise standards independently of their consequences. Thus a 'Euclidean' approach yields standards which we judge irrespective of their consequences for the historical record of achievement in science. If it forces us to evaluate Newton's *Principia*, say, in a way that conflicts with conventional wisdom, then so much the worse for conventional wisdom and, indeed, for Newton's *Principia*. This 'Euclidean' approach is, of course, encouraged by the half-truth that scientific method is a conceptual matter and thus a fit subject for armchair philosophical reflection. An 'anti-theoretical' approach, on the other hand, takes its cue from the half-truth that scientific method is a practical matter and thus a fit subject for glib, rule-of-thumb generalities. This approach requires that we consult the traditions of science in formulating our account of scientific method, and such rationality as it possesses when so formulated is secured by its faithfulness to these traditions. But we cannot secure genuine rationality in this way without some restriction on which traditions we should consult. In effect, an 'anti-theoretical' approach yields standards which are judged irrespective of their consequences for rationality in science.

These contrasting views about the right method to use in justifying theories of scientific method have become familiar in recent years. It is remarkable, though, how similar in structure they are to opposed views about the right method to use in science. Consider, for example, Mill's description of what he called the 'chemical' and the 'geometrical' methods in science. The 'chemical' or 'experimental' method, he said, is characteristic of those who, 'for the direction of their opinions and conduct . . . profess to demand, in all cases without exception, specific experience'. It is favoured by those who eschew 'metaphysical dogma', preferring 'to ground their conclusions on facts'. 'Chemical' methodologists will think of themselves as 'true Baconians', and of their opponents as 'mere syllogisers and schoolmen'. They will collect their facts 'without the assistance of any theory', and use one or other of Mill's methods of experimental enquiry to draw their conclusions. Mill observed that the empiricism embodied in this 'chemical' method is not capable of doing justice to what he called the deductive aspects of the mature sciences. Devotees of this method, he thought, 'should be sent back to learn the elements of some one of the more easy physical sciences' (Mill 1961: 574; Book VI, Chapter 7, Section 1). He would not be surprised to learn that those who ignore this advice become mesmerised by puzzles about simple empirical generalisations, and are unable to proceed beyond them. The 'geometrical' or 'abstract' method, by contrast, is said to be 'peculiar to thinking and studious minds', and 'could never have suggested itself but to persons of some familiarity with the nature of scientific research'. Proponents of this method are inclined to emphasise the enlightenment offered by the abstract general principles upon which their theories are based, and to take an indulgent view of any lack of fit between their theory and the facts. These theories, because they deal in abstractions which are not precisely instantiated in the real world, are threatened by anomalies capable of compromising their applicability, and it is only by overlooking or minimising the effect of these anomalies – by making allowances – that the theories survive. 'But', Mill said, 'it is not allowances that are wanted'. What is needed, rather, is a theory of 'sufficient breadth in its foundations' that such compensations would be unnecessary. It is, he continued, 'unphilosophical to construct a science out of a few of the agencies by which the phenomena are determined, and leave the rest to the routine of practice or the sagacity of conjecture'. Mill would have found our talk of 'paradigms', 'frameworks' and 'conceptual schemes', with their emphasis upon the explanatory value of a small number of abstract general principles, symptomatic of an allegiance to the 'geometrical' method. We should, he thought, deplore rather than applaud a method which encourages us to 'bestow a disproportionate attention upon those [facts] which our theory takes into account, while we misestimate the rest, and probably underrate their importance' (Mill 1961: 578–9; Book VI, Chapter 8, Section 1).

These two debates, one about how to do scientific method and the other about how to do science, interact with each other. Defenders of Mill's 'chemical' method can afford to be ill informed and simpleminded about science because they have a sophisticated philosophy and logic to fall back on. They will use a 'Euclidean' method in methodology to defend the 'chemical' method in science. Admittedly, real science will rarely if ever live up to their expectations, but this, they will claim, is no disadvantage. After all, real triangles, real circles, etc., fail to live up to the expectations of Euclidean geometry, and yet we do not, for this reason, consider those expectations useless. Conversely, defenders of Mill's 'geometrical' method will quickly dismiss a condemnation of it as unphilosophical, because it is nevertheless the method which evidence shows to be the method used by scientists. They pay such serious and close attention to real science that they can afford to neglect or ignore a demonstration of its rationality. In short, they will use an 'anti-theoretical' method in methodology to defend the 'geometrical' method in science.

One explanation for the employment of contrasting methods in science and in methodology goes as follows. Philosophy, of which methodology is a part, is concerned with what should be, rather than with what is; with what should count as knowledge, as rational, as explanatory, as evidence, as justification, as a cause, etc., rather than with what does count as these things. Questionnaires, surveys, interviews and so on might elicit interesting information about, say, whether scientists regard so-called statistical explanations as explanatory, but such information could throw no light whatsoever upon whether statistical explanations are really explanatory. Statistical explanations might not be explanatory despite universal opinion to the contrary. In short, the subject matter of methodology is distinct from the subject matter of science. We should expect, therefore, that the methods appropriate to one will be different from the methods appropriate to the other.

This argument should not satisfy us. In the first place, it does not follow from the alleged fact that science and methodology differ in their subject matter that they must differ in their methods. Astronomy and zoology differ in their subject matter, yet no-one supposes that, simply for this reason, they must differ in their methods. For the argument to be valid, we must show and not just assume that methodology and science differ in the right kind of way. Second, the premiss of this argument, though supported by an array of familiar distinctions, has been attacked by a formidable and equally familiar battery of arguments. If the aim of methodology were a priori analyses, and the aim of science true empirical conjectures, then no doubt that would be the right kind of difference to justify a difference in method. But the distinction between a priori and empirical has proved difficult to defend. To describe our conclusions about scientific method as a priori certainties, which impose limits and constraints upon what is epistemologically legitimate, seems no more than a ploy designed to protect those conclusions from the effect, possibly falsifying, of evidence. Again, it will not do to attribute to scientific method normative or legislative power and to science merely descriptive power. Just as methodologists might say 'every genuine test of a theory is an attempt to falsify it', and intend the word 'genuine' to have a normative significance, so scientists might intend that word to have a similar significance when they say 'every genuine acid contains oxygen'. Scientists may, as in this example, be mistaken about the laws which give their claims normative significance; methodologists, too, will sometimes be mistaken. But normative vocabulary is as much part of the language of science as it is part of the language we use to talk about science. And finally, even if this argument were valid and its premiss correct, it would still fail to establish part of what it needs to establish. If methodologists are concerned with what is really rational, or justified, as opposed to what is said to be rational or justified, why should they pay attention to facts about what is said and done by scientists? They can legitimately ignore facts about the practice of science when they conflict with the deliverances of an account of scientific method which seeks to strip away the misleading appearances to reveal the reality which they conceal. It would seem, then, if we are to support the employment of double standards in science and methodology in this way, that we must use non-empirical methods to establish conclusions about scientific method. It is, it would seem, sheer muddle to suppose that empirical methods could have any role in methodology.

A more plausible argument for double standards is one that construes the difference between science and methodology in terms of their aims, rather than their subject matter. Between 'geometrical' and 'chemical' methodologists, there will be sharp disagreement about what the aim of science and the aim of methodology are, but they can at least agree that they are different and that this difference implies that the methods of science and methodology must be distinct. But is there such a thing as the aim of science, or the aim of methodology; and even if there is, could we specify it in such a way that we could identify a clear method for achieving that aim? Different scientists have different, if related, aims. Indeed, talk of 'the aim of science' would seem to be anthropomorphic shorthand for talk about a presupposed common element in the aims of individual scientists. Little, if any, argument or evidence is provided to justify this presupposition. It may perhaps be true that 'there is something characteristic of scientific activity' (Popper 1972: 191), but methodologists have not undertaken the kind of scrutiny of science that might help to identify this characteristic. Much the same is true of the supposed aim of methodology. The stated aims of methodologists are sufficiently diverse to justify doubts about the existence of a single purpose. Mill's aim was to construct a theory which would 'embody and systematise the best ideas . . . conformed to by accurate thinkers in their scientific inquiries' (Mill 1961: iii). Carnap identified the aim of inductive logic as the formulation of rationality requirements for credibility functions which would aid us in determining rational decisions (Carnap 1962b: 317). Popper said that his aim was to articulate a set of necessary and consistent rules for playing the game of science (Popper 1959: 53). If, despite these differences, we feel that there is some common characteristic of methodological activity, then it is surprising that no-one has attempted to vindicate this feeling by identifying it.

Some will claim that to emphasise the diversity of aims among scientists and methodologists is to play into the hands of those who would have us be 'geometrical' in our science and 'anti-theoretical' in our methodology. For, it will be said, a theory of method in science must amount to an identification of the aim of science, and to deny that science has an aim is to concede, rather too easily, that there is no such thing as the scientific method. To take a parallel from within science, it is as though we were so impressed by the diverse behaviour and properties of individual gases that we dismissed the very idea of a general theory about gases. On the other hand, if we reject the emphasis on diversity and accept the premiss that science has an aim and that this aim differs from that of methodology, then our argument will, once again, prove only part of what it was intended to prove. A theory of scientific method which is, at the same time, an identification of the aim of science must count as an attempt to cut through the superficial diversity of aims among scientists to a reality which unifies them. Clearly, we could not accomplish such a task by an anti-theoretical method; method in methodology would have to be 'Euclidean', method in science 'non-Euclidean'. As a justification of double standards, then, this argument fails. If sound, it shows only that a 'Euclidean' method in methodology may be combined with a 'chemical' method in science, not that a 'geometrical' method in science may be combined with an 'anti-theoretical' method in methodology.

Of course, no methodologist is in practice exclusively 'Euclidean' or rigorously 'anti-theoretical'. Nevertheless, it is difficult to see how either a legitimate 'Euclidean' method or a legitimate 'anti-theoretical' method can brook compromise. Much as we might wish it were otherwise, there is no *via media* between the two. Consider, for example, the following apparently reasonable suggestion. We are told that 'a logic of science differs from a descriptive study of methodology' in that 'it supplements mere description with normative considerations' (Hesse 1974: 6). A 'logic of science' cannot be arbitrary; we must test it against historical examples. Sometimes it will be appropriate to modify the logic in the light of examples; sometimes it will be appropriate to criticise cases in the light of the logic. 'The relation of logic and cases', it is said, 'will be one of mutual comparison and correction' (Hesse 1974: 6–7). But the difficulty with this is that it leaves us with no indication as to when and in what circumstances it is appropriate to treat theory (or logic) as authoritative, and when it is appropriate to treat practice (or cases) as authoritative. Scientists, faced with a task or a problem, will form a view as to what they should do in order to accomplish the task or solve the problem. Typically, this view will be shared by other scientists and, to that extent, will count as a 'received view'. But it may nevertheless be a view which conflicts with the implications of a methodological theory or logic of science. It is all very well to be told that such conflicts call for a mutual comparison and correction of logic and cases, but unless we can draw a distinction between those questions we answer by appealing to logic and those questions we answer by appealing to received opinion, the advice is useless. Short of dispensing with methodological theory altogether, the only way of resolving a conflict between theory and received opinion is by treating theory as authoritative and not allowing received opinion to modify it in any way.

'Reflective equilibrium' between logic and cases is, therefore, inherently unstable. A normative logic of science whose function is to settle methodological questions cannot consistently allow that received opinion can force any change in that logic. It is possible, of course, that we cannot formulate a logic of science, except in the vaguest of terms, with reference to received opinion. Consequently, some interaction between logic and cases may be inevitable. But the fact, if it is one, that we are obliged to temper the rigidity of a 'Euclidean' method in methodology with gestures in the direction of what we take to be real science does not mean that a relaxed 'Euclidean' method is acceptable. The way we do methodology is, perhaps, both inevitable and unacceptable.

We can perhaps explain the employment of different methods in science and methodology even if we cannot justify it. For the position we have identified is one effect of a much more general syndrome, namely the irreconcilable tension between empiricism and naturalism.

By empiricism is understood the view that human beings occupy a special and privileged place in our picture of the world, because it is only in terms of human experience that we can construct and understand that picture. The world is a mirror of the mind and, accordingly, the language we use to describe it is meaningful only to the extent it connects appropriately with human experiences. For an empiricist, there is no prospect of inventing mind-independent structures and processes to explain experience, for we could not meaningfully describe them. Explanatory entities exist only in so far as we can relate them satisfactorily to experience, and in general what there is or might be in the world is a subjective, or least inter-subjective, matter. Twentieth-century empiricists have not been slow to exploit developments within the physical sciences which, they think, reinforce their philosophy.

By naturalism is understood the view that human beings, together with their capacities and abilities, belong to an objective natural order, and that we should explain their relation to the world in terms appropriate to that order. The human capacity to know, for example, is a natural phenomenon as is the behaviour of the planets, and, just as we have a science which studies the latter, so we might have a science which studies the former. There is nothing special or central about human experience which entitles us to treat it as authoritative. For naturalism, therefore, there is no warrant which requires that we automatically refer all questions to the tribunal of experience. What lies beyond or behind experience may be no less real than what does not. Initial impressions or appearances can provide no more than a record of the passing show in which we discern useful generalities. Naturalism urges us to erect theories which will enable us to understand such a record, to complete the gaps in it, and sometimes to correct it.

The theories of method in science which are most consonant with empiricism as it has been outlined here are those whose history is traced in the preceding chapters of this book. But the way these theories are justified and defended expresses something quite different, for they bear a relation to relevant evidence which would be regarded as intolerable in the case of scientific theories. What matters for these theories of scientific method is not the superficial record of what scientists have done and do, but the real, objective, rational standards which they attempt to identify, and which lie behind or beyond that record. This reality, as expressed and described in theories of scientific method, is what enables us to understand, to complete and sometimes to correct the record. There are characteristically empiricist claims about the right method to use to justify claims within science, but those claims themselves are justified using an altogether different method in which empiricism gives way to naturalism. We do not judge empiricist theories of scientific method – logics of science – by empirical evidence; rather, we base their warrant upon decisions concerning the nature of the rational reality which, we think, must lie behind and must explain the remarkable achievements of science.

The traditional accounts of scientific method, then, offer a logic of science which is biased more or less heavily in favour of an empiricist epistemology and ontology. This bias, though, is offset by an implicit naturalism in the way the logic is presented, justified and defended. Faced with the sharp differences between empiricism and naturalism, many would have us try to develop some sort of compromise between the two, and perhaps a traditional logic of science is an attempt to effect such a compromise. The implicit naturalism associated with such a logic is, at least, an indication that it is impossible to maintain a thorough-going and comprehensive empiricism.

Some recent views about scientific method, including the view that attempts to identify it are futile, unnecessary and damaging, approach the same central issue from the opposite direction. The conviction that observations and experiments are shot through with theoretical allegi-ances, and the belief that paradigms, conceptual schemes, etc. have an all-pervasive power, can be understood as signifying a rejection of empiricism as the central component of an account of scientific method. So, too, can the claim that, although scientific theories disclose reality, it is a reality socially and ideologically constructed so as to serve as a subject matter for the discourses and narratives in which some people elect to participate. But those who subscribe to these newer views find that the empiricism they eject through the front door returns surreptitiously by the back door. For they base their claims, including their dismissal of traditional accounts of scientific method, on facts about what scientists actually do. They 'observe' the 'behaviour' of scientists in their laboratories and explain it using favoured theories in psychology, sociology and anthropology. They would reform, indeed abandon altogether, scientific method, but would disclaim any concern with reforming science itself. They exhibit a reverence for the evidence provided by the history of science and by their own field-work observa-tions which they would consider merely superstition if displayed by a scientist towards his evidence. For them, accounts of what scientists have done and do can only be properly expressed in the language of description. To suppose that there is anything beyond or behind the description is, they would urge, to deal in gratuitous mysteries. They claim that method in science is richer in its details and less dogmatic in its outline than we are apt to credit. We will, they believe, learn more that is useful to us by paying attention to the rich detail in the record of achievement in science than we ever should by exploring the fictitious superstructure of abstract idealist analysis that has, for too long, passed for scientific method.

The explanation for this sharp contrast between a naturalistic attitude to what is done within science and an empiricist attitude to what we say about science could be, as before, that we like to think the attractions of naturalism compatible with those of empiricism. It shows, at least, that naturalism, like empiricism, is too stark and inflexible a philosophy. A consistent, thoroughgoing and comprehensive naturalism is the only naturalism we are entitled to adopt, but it may nevertheless be impossible to maintain.

FURTHER READING

Some background for the questions explored in this chapter can be found in:

Kuhn, T. S. (1970a) *The Structure of Scientific Revolutions*, second edition, Chicago: University of Chicago Press.

Lakatos, I. and Musgrave, A. (eds) (1970) *Criticism and the Growth of Knowledge*, Cambridge: Cambridge University Press.

Feyerabend, P. (1975) *Against Method: Outlines of an Anarchist Theory of Knowledge*, London: New Left Books.

Lakatos, I. (1976) 'History of science and its rational reconstruction', in C. Howson (ed.), *Method and Appraisal in the Physical Sciences*, Cambridge: Cambridge University Press.

Newton-Smith, W. (1981) *The Rationality of Science*, London: Routledge.

Chalmers, A. (1982) *What Is This Thing Called Science?*, Milton Keynes: Open University Press.

Some philosophical issues about scientific experiments are discussed in:

Hacking, I. (1983) *Representing and Intervening*, Cambridge: Cambridge University Press.

Franklin, A. (1986) *The Neglect of Experiment*, Cambridge: Cambridge University Press.

Galison, P. (1987) *How Experiments End*, Chicago: University of Chicago Press.

Bogan, J. and Woodward, J. (1988) 'Saving the phenomena', *Philosophical Review* 97: 303–52.

Ackermann, R. (1989) 'The new experimentalism', [essay review of A. Franklin, *The Neglect of Experiment*], *British Journal for the Philosophy of Science* 40: 185–90.

Gooding, D., Pinch, T. and Schaffer, S. (eds) (1989) *The Uses of Experiment*, Cambridge: Cambridge University Press.

Collins, H. and Pinch, T. (1993) *The Golem: What Everyone Should Know About Science*, Cambridge, Cambridge University Press.

Franklin, A. (1993) 'Experimental questions', *Perspectives on Science* 1: 127–46.

For consideration of the social dimension of scientific method, see:

Goldman, A. (1987) 'Foundations of social epistemics', *Synthese* 73: 109–44.

Worrall, J. (1988) 'The value of a fixed methodology', *British Journal for the Philosophy of Science* 39: 263–75.

Longino, H. (1990) *Science as Social Knowledge: Values and Objectivity in Scientific Inquiry*, Princeton, NJ: Princeton University Press.

Gillies, D. (1991) 'Intersubjective probability and confirmation theory', *British Journal for the Philosophy of Science* 42: 513–533.

Kitcher, P. (1992) 'The naturalists return', *Philosophical Review* 101: 53–114.

Kitcher, P. (1993) *The Advancement of Science*, Oxford: Oxford University Press; ch. 8.

Gross, P. R. and Levitt, N. (1994) *Higher Superstition: The Academic Left and Its Quarrels with Science*, Baltimore and London: The Johns Hopkins University Press.

Shapin, S. (1994) *A Social History of Truth: Civility and Science in Seventeenth-Century England*, Chicago: University of Chicago Press.

Bibliography

Achinstein, P. (1990) 'Hypotheses, probability, and waves', *British Journal for the Philosophy of Science* 41: 73–102; reprinted in Achinstein, P. (1991) *Particles and Waves: Historical Essays in the Philosophy of Science*, Oxford: Oxford University Press.

Ackermann, R. (1989) 'The new experimentalism', [essay review of A. Franklin, *The Neglect of Experiment*], *British Journal for the Philosophy of Science* 40: 185–90.

Alexander, H. G. (ed.) (1956) *The Leibniz–Clarke Correspondence*, Manchester: Manchester University Press.

Alonso, M. and Finn, E. T. (1992) *Physics*, Wokingham: Addison Wesley.

Bacon, F. (1915) *The Advancement of Learning*, edited with an introduction by G. W. Kitchin, London: Dent.

—— (1985) *The New Organon and Related Writings*, edited with an introduction by F. H. Anderson, New York: Macmillan.

Bateman, B. W. (1988) 'G. E. Moore and J. M. Keynes: A missing chapter in the history of the expected utility model', *American Economic Review* 78: 1098–106.

Bayes, T. (1763) 'An essay towards solving a problem in the doctrine of chances', *Philosophical Transactions of the Royal Society of London* 53: 370–418. Reprinted in *Biometrika* 45 (1958): 296–315, and in E. S. Pearson and M. G. Kendall (eds), (1970) *Studies in the History of Statistics and Probability*, London: Charles Griffin.

Bentham, M. A. (1937) 'Some seventeenth-century views concerning the nature of heat and cold', *Annals of Science* 2: 431–50.

Bernoulli, J. (1975) *Die Werke von Jakob Bernoulli*, vol. 3, Basel: Basel Naturforschende Gesellschaft.

Bogan, J. and Woodward, J. (1988) 'Saving the phenomena', *Philosophical Review* 97: 303–52.

Boole, G. (1952) *Studies in Logic and Probability*, La Salle, Ill.: Open Court.

Bradley, L. (1971) *Smallpox Inoculation: An Eighteenth Century Mathematical Controversy*, Nottingham: Adult Education Department, University of Nottingham.

Brady, J. E., Humiston, G. E. and Heikkinen, H. (1982) *General Chemistry: Principles and Structure*, 3rd edition, New York: John Wiley and Sons.

Bricker, P. and Hughes, R. I. G. (eds) (1990) *Philosophical Perspectives on Newtonian Science*, Cambridge, Mass.: MIT Press.

Brush, S. G. (1989) 'Prediction and theory evaluation: the case of light bending', *Science* 246: 1124–9.

Burks, A. W. (1946) 'Peirce's theory of abduction', *Philosophy of Science* 13: 301–6.

Burtt, E. A. (1932) *The Metaphysical Foundations of Modern Physical Science: A Historical and Critical Essay*, second edition, London: Routledge and Kegan Paul.

Butts, R. E. (ed.) (1989) *William Whewell: Theory of Scientific Method*, Indianapolis: Hackett.

Carnap, R. (1962a) *Logical Foundations of Probability*, second edition, Chicago: University of Chicago Press.

—— (1962b) 'The aim of inductive logic', in E. Nagel, P. Suppes and A. Tarski (eds), *Logic, Methodology and Philosophy of Science*, Stanford, Calif.: Stanford University Press.

—— (1963) 'Autobiography', in P. A. Schilpp (ed.), *The Philosophy of Rudolf Carnap*, Library of Living Philosophers, La Salle, Ill.: Open Court.

—— (1974) *An Introduction to the Philosophy of Science*, previously published as *Philosophical Foundations of Physics*, edited by M. Gardner, New York: Basic Books.

Carnap, R. and Jeffrey, R. C. (eds) (1971) *Studies in Inductive Logic and Probability*, vol. 1, Berkeley: University of California Press.

Chalmers, A. (1982) *What Is This Thing Called Science?*, Milton Keynes: Open University Press.

Clarke, D. M. (1982) *Descartes' Philosophy of Science*, Pennsylvania: Pennsylvania State University Press.

Cohen, I. B. (1971) *Introduction to Newton's 'Principia'*, Cambridge: Cambridge University Press.

Cohen, L. J. (1989) *An Introduction to the Philosophy of Induction and Probability*, Oxford: Clarendon Press.

Collins, H. and Pinch, T. (1993) *The Golem: What Everyone Should Know About Science*, Cambridge: Cambridge University Press.

Condorcet, Marquis de (1955) *Sketch for a Historical Picture of the Progress of the Human Mind*, ed. S. Hampshire, trans. by J. Barraclough, London: Weidenfeld and Nicolson.

Daston, L. (1979) 'D'Alembert's critique of probability theory', *Historia Mathematica* 6: 259–79.

—— (1988) *Classical Probability in the Enlightenment*, Princeton, NJ: Princeton University Press.

Davie, G. E. (1961) *The Democratic Intellect: Scotland and Her Universities in the Nineteenth Century*, Edinburgh: Edinburgh University Press.

De Morgan, A. (1845) 'Theory of probabilities', in *Encyclopaedia Metropolitana*, vol. 2, London: B. Fellowes *et al.*

Descartes, R. (1984–5) *The Philosophical Writings*, trans. J. Cottingham, R. Stoothoff and D. Murdoch, 2 vols, Cambridge: Cambridge University Press.

Donkin, W. F. (1851) 'On certain questions relating to the theory of probabilities', *The London, Edinburgh and Dublin Philosophical Magazine and Journal of Science*, 4th series 1: 353–68.

Drake, S. (1967) 'Galileo: A biographical sketch', in E. McMullin (ed.), *Galileo: Man of Science*, New York: Basic Books.

—— (1975) 'The role of music in Galileo's experiments', *Scientific American* 232: 98–104.

—— (1978) *Galileo at Work: His Scientific Biography*, Chicago: University of Chicago Press.

—— (1990) *Galileo: Pioneer Scientist*, Toronto: Toronto University Press.

Duhem, P. (1954) *The Aim and Structure of Physical Theory*, trans. by P. P. Wiener, Princeton, NJ: Princeton University Press.

—— (1969) *To Save the Phenomena*, trans. by S. L. Jaki, Chicago: University of Chicago Press.

Earman, J. (1992) *Bayes or Bust: A Critical Examination of Bayesian Confirmation Theory*, Cambridge, Mass.: MIT Press.

Eells, E. (1988) 'On the alleged impossibility of inductive probability', *British Journal for the Philosophy of Science*, 39: 111–16.

Elkana, Y. (ed.) (1984) *William Whewell: Selected Writings on the History of Science*, Chicago: University of Chicago Press.

Ellis, R. L. (1863) *The Mathematical and Other Writings of Robert Leslie Ellis*, edited by W. Walton, Cambridge: Deighton, Bell.

—— (1905) 'Preface', in Robertson, J. M. (ed.), *The Philosophical Works of Francis Bacon . . .* , London: George Routledge and Sons Ltd.

Emch-Deriaz, A. S. (1982) 'L'inoculation justifée – or was it?', *Eighteenth Century Life* 7,2: 65–72.

Fauvel, J., Flood, R., Shortland, M. and Wilson, R. (eds) (1988) *Let Newton Be!: A New Perspective on his Life and Works*, Oxford: Oxford University Press.

Feyerabend, P. K. (1968) 'How to be a good empiricist – a plea for tolerance in matters methodological', in P. Nidditch (ed.), *The Philosophy of Science*, Oxford: Oxford University Press.

—— (1975) *Against Method: Outlines of an Anarchist Theory of Knowledge*, London: New Left Books.

Feynman, R. (1965) *The Character of Physical Law*, Cambridge, Mass.: MIT Press.

Finetti, B. de (1964) 'Foresight: its logical laws, its subjective sources', in H. E. Kybug and H. E. Smokler (eds), *Studies in Subjective Probability*, New York: John Wiley and Sons.

Fisch, M. (1991) *William Whewell: Philosopher of Science*, Oxford: Oxford University Press.

Fisch, M. and Schaffer, S. (eds) (1991) *William Whewell: A Composite Portrait*, Oxford: Clarendon Press.

Forbes, J. (1849) 'On the alleged Evidence for a Physical Connexion between Stars forming Binary or Multiple Groups, arising from their Proximity alone', *Philosophical Magazine*, 3rd series, 35: 132–3.

—— (1850) 'On the alleged Evidence for a Physical Connexion between Stars forming Binary or Multiple Groups, deduced from the Doctrine of Chances', *Philosophical Magazine*, 3rd series, 37: 401–27.

Franklin, A. (1986) *The Neglect of Experiment*, Cambridge: Cambridge University Press.

—— (1993) 'Experimental questions', *Perspectives on Science* 1: 127–46

Fuller, S. (1987) 'On regulating what is known: A way to social epistemology', *Synthese* 73: 145–83.

Galilei, Galileo (1989) *Two New Sciences, including Centres of Gravity and Force of Percussion*, trans. with new introduction and notes by S. Drake, second edition, Toronto: Wall and Thompson.

Galison, P. (1987) *How Experiments End*, Chicago: University of Chicago Press.

Gaukroger, R. (1989) *Cartesian Logic: An Essay on Descartes' Conception of Inference*, Oxford: Oxford University Press.

Gemes, K. (1989) 'A refutation of Popperian inductive scepticism', *British Journal for the Philosophy of Science*, 40: 183–4.

Geymonat, L. (1965) *Galileo Galilei: A Biography and Inquiry into his Philosophy of Science*, New York: McGraw-Hill.

Giedymin, J. (1982) *Science and Convention: Essays on Henri Poincaré's Philosophy of Science and the Conventionalist Tradition*, Oxford: Pergamon Press.

—— (1991) 'Geometrical and physical conventionalism of Henri Poincaré in Epistemological Formulation', *Studies in the History and Philosophy of Science* 22: 1–22.

Giere, R. (1984) *Understanding Scientific Reasoning*, second edition, New York: Holt, Rinehart and Winston.

Gillies, D. (1987) 'Was Bayes a Bayesian', *Historia Mathematica* 14: 325–46.

—— (1988) 'Keynes as a methodologist', *British Journal for the Philosophy of Science* 39: 117–29.

—— (1991) 'Intersubjective probability and confirmation theory', *British Journal for the Philosophy of Science* 42: 513–33.

—— (1993) *Philosophy of Science in the Twentieth Century: Four Central Themes*, Oxford: Blackwell.

Gillispie, C. C. (1960) *The Edge of Objectivity: an Essay in the History of Scientific Ideas*, Princeton, NJ: Princeton University Press.

Glymour, C. (1980) *Theory and Evidence*, Princeton, NJ: Princeton University Press.

Goldman, A. (1987) 'Foundations of social epistemics', *Synthese* 73: 109–44.

Golinski, J. V. (1990) 'Chemistry in the Scientific Revolution: Problems of language and communication', in D. C. Lindberg and R. S. Westman (eds), *Reappraisals of the Scientific Revolution*, Cambridge: Cambridge University Press.

Gooding, D., Pinch, T. and Schaffer, S. (eds) (1989) *The Uses of Experiment*, Cambridge: Cambridge University Press.

Gower, B. (1987) 'Planets and probability: Daniel Bernoulli on the inclinations of the planetary orbits', *Studies in the History and Philosophy of Science* 18: 441–54.

—— (1991) 'Hume on probability', *British Journal for the Philosophy of Science* 42: 1–19.

Gross, P. R. and Levitt, N. (1994) *Higher Superstition: The Academic Left and Its Quarrels with Science*, Baltimore and London: The Johns Hopkins University Press.

Grunbaum, A. (1976a) 'Is the method of bold conjectures and attempted refutations justifiably the method science?', *British Journal for the Philosophy of Science* 27: 105–36.

—— (1976b) 'Is falsifiability the touchstone of scientific rationality? Karl Popper versus inductivism', in R. S. Cohen and M. W. Wartofsky (eds), *Essays in Memory of Imre Lakatos*, Dordrecht: Reidel.

Hacking, I. (1975) *The Emergence of Probability*, Cambridge: Cambridge University Press.

—— (1978) 'Hume's species of probability', *Philosophical Studies* 33: 21–37.

—— (1980) 'The theory of probable inference: Neyman, Peirce and Braithwaite', in D. H. Mellor (ed.), *Science, Belief and Behaviour*, Cambridge: Cambridge University Press.

—— (1983) *Representing and Intervening*, Cambridge: Cambridge University Press.

—— (1990) *The Taming of Chance*, Cambridge: Cambridge University Press.

—— (1993) 'Working in a new world: the taxonomic solution', in P. Horwich (ed.), *World Changes: Thomas Kuhn and the Nature of Science*, Cambridge, Mass.: MIT Press.

Hall, A. R. (1983) *The Revolution in Science 1500–1750*, second edition, London: Longman.

—— (1992) *Isaac Newton: Adventurer in Thought*, Oxford: Blackwell.

Harré, R. (1983) *Great Scientific Experiments*, Oxford: Oxford University Press.

Hempel, C. G. (1965) *Aspects of Scientific Explanation*, New York: Free Press.

Herschel, J. F. W. (1830) *A Preliminary Discourse on the Study of Natural Philosophy*, London: Longmans, Rees, Orme, Brown, and Green.

—— (1848) *Outlines of Astronomy*, London: Longmans, Green.

—— (1850) 'Review of Quetelet's Lettres á S. A. R. Le Duc règnant de Saxe-Cobourg et Cotha sur la Théorie des Probabilités appliquée aux Sciences Morales et Politiques' (Brussels, Hayez, 1846), *Edinburgh Review* 92: 1–57.

Hesse, M. (1964) 'Francis Bacon's philosophy of science', in D. J. O'Connor (ed.), *A Critical History of Western Philosophy*, New York: Free Press.

—— (1974) *The Structure of Scientific Inference*, Berkeley: University of California Press.

—— (1980) 'What is the best way to assess evidential support for scientific theories?', in M. Hesse and L. J. Cohen (eds), *Applications of Inductive Logic*, Oxford: Clarendon Press.

Hintikka, J. (1965) 'Towards a theory of inductive generalisation', in Y. Bar Hillel (ed.), *Proceedings of the 1964 Congress for Logic, Methodology and Philosophy of Science*, Amsterdam: North-Holland.

—— (1966) 'A two-dimensional continuum of inductive methods', in J. Hintikka and P. Suppes (eds), *Aspects of Inductive Logic*, Amsterdam: North-Holland.

Hobbes, T. (1839) *The English Works*, London: John Bohn.

Hookway, C. (1985) *Peirce, Arguments of the Philosophers*, London: Routledge.

Horton, M. (1973) 'In defence of Francis Bacon: A criticism of the critics of the inductive method', *Studies in the History and Philosophy of Science* 4: 241–78.

Howson, C. (ed.) (1976) *Method and Appraisal in the Physical Sciences*, Cambridge: Cambridge University Press.

—— (1991) 'The last word on induction', *Erkenntnis* 34: 73–82.

Howson, C. and Urbach, P. (1993) *Scientific Reasoning: The Bayesian Approach*, second edition, La Salle, Ill.: Open Court.

Hume, D. (1955) *An Inquiry Concerning Human Understanding*, edited with an introduction by C. W. Hendel, Indianapolis: Bobbs-Merrill.

Huygens, C. (1962) *Treatise on Light. In which are explained the causes of that which occurs in reflexion, and in refraction. And particularly in the strange refraction of Iceland crystal*, trans. by S. P. Thompson, New York: Dover.

Jaki, S. L. (1987) *Uneasy Genius: The Life and Work of Pierre Duhem*, Dordrecht: Nijhoff.

Jeffrey, R. C. (1975) 'Probability and falsification: Critique of the Popper programme', *Synthese* 30: 95–117.

Jeffreys, H. (1957) *Scientific Inference*, second edition, Cambridge: Cambridge University Press.

—— (1967) *Theory of Probability*, Oxford: Oxford University Press.

Jevons, W. S. (1874) *The Principles of Science*, 2 vols, London: Macmillan.

Kant, I. (1933) *Critique of Pure Reason*, trans. by N. K. Smith, London: Macmillan.

—— (1953) *Prolegomena To Any Future Metaphysics That Will Be Able To Present Itself As A Science*, trans. by P. G. Lucas, Manchester: Manchester University Press.

—— (1970) *Metaphysical Foundations of Natural Science*, trans. by J. Ellington, Indianapolis: Bobbs-Merrill.

Keynes, J. M. (1921) *A Treatise on Probability*, London: Macmillan.

Kitcher, P. (1992) 'The naturalists return', *Philosophical Review* 101: 53–114.

—— (1993) *The Advancement of Science*, Oxford: Oxford University Press; ch. 8.

Krane, K. S. (1983) *Modern Physics*, New York: Wiley.

Kuhn, T. S. (1970a) *The Structure of Scientific Revolutions*, second edition, Chicago: University of Chicago Press.

—— (1970b) 'Reflections on my critics', in I. Lakatos and A. Musgrave (eds), *Criticism and the Growth of Knowledge*, Cambridge: Cambridge University Press.

—— (1977) *The Essential Tension*, Chicago: Chicago University Press.

Kuipers, T. A. F. (1978) *A Survey of Inductive Systems*, Dordrecht: Reidel.

Lakatos, I. (1974) 'Popper on demarcation and induction', in P. A. Schilpp (ed.), *The Philosophy of Karl Popper*, La Salle, Ill: Open Court.

—— (1976) 'History of science and its rational reconstruction', in C. Howson (ed.), *Method and Appraisal in the Physical Sciences*, Cambridge: Cambridge University Press.

Lakatos, I. and Musgrave, A (eds) (1970) *Criticism and the Growth of Knowledge*, Cambridge: Cambridge University Press.

Laplace, P. S. de (1951) *A Philosophical Essay on Probabilities*, trans. by F. W. Truscott and F. L. Emory, New York: Dover.

Laudan, L. (1971) 'William Whewell on the consilience of inductions', *Monist* 55: 368–91; reprinted in Laudan, L. (1981) *Science and Hypothesis*, Dordrecht: Reidel.

—— (1981) 'The medium and its message', in G. Cantor and M. Hodge (eds), *Conception of the Ether*, Cambridge: Cambridge University Press; reprinted as 'The epistemology of light: Some methodological issues in the subtle fluids debate', in Laudan, L. (1981) *Science and Hypothesis*, Dordrecht: Reidel.

—— (1984) 'A confutation of convergent realism', in J. Leplin (ed.), *Scientific Realism*, Berkeley: University of California Press.

Leibniz, G. W. (1969) *Philosophical Papers and Letters*, edited by I. E. Loemker, Dordrecht: Reidel.

Levi, I. (1980) 'Induction as self-correcting according to Peirce', in D. H. Mellor (ed.), *Science, Belief and Behaviour*, Cambridge: Cambridge University Press.

Levinson. P. (ed.) (1982) *In Pursuit of Truth: Essays in Honour of Karl Popper's 80th Birthday*, Hassocks: Harvester.

Lindberg, D. C. and Westman, R. S. (eds) (1990) *Reappraisals of the Scientific Revolution*, Cambridge: Cambridge University Press.

Locke, J. (1975) *An Essay Concerning Human Understanding*, edited by P. H. Nidditch, Oxford: Clarendon Press.

Longino, H. (1990) *Science as Social Knowledge: Values and Objectivity in Scientific Inquiry*, Princeton, NJ: Princeton University Press.

Mach, E. (1960) *The Science of Mechanics*, trans. T. J. McCormack, new introduction by K. Menger, sixth edition, La Salle, Ill.: Open Court.

McMullin, E. (1967) 'Introduction: Galileo, man of science', in E. McMullin (ed.), *Galileo: Man of Science*, New York: Basic Books.

—— (1978) 'The conception of science in Galileo's work', in R. E. Butts and J. C. Pitt (eds), *New Perspectives on Galileo*, Dordrecht: Reidel.

Maehle, A. H. (1995) 'Conflicting attitudes towards inoculation in Enlightenment Germany', in R. Porter (ed.), *Medicine in the Enlightenment*, Amsterdam: Editions Rodopi.

Mandelbaum, M. (1964) *Philosophy, Science, and Sense Perception: Historical and Critical Studies*, Baltimore, Md.: The Johns Hopkins University Press.

Michell, J. (1767) 'An inquiry into the probable Parallax and Magnitude of the Fixed Stars from the quantity of Light which they afford to us, and the particular Circumstances of their Situation', *Philosophical Transactions of the Royal Society of London* 57: 234–64.

Mill, J. S. (1961) *A System of Logic, Ratiocinative and Inductive: Being a Connected View of the Principles of Evidence and the Methods of Scientific Investigation*, London: Longmans, Green.

—— (1963) *Collected Works. Volume XIII. The Early Letters . . . 1812–1848*, edited by F. E. Mineka, Toronto: University of Toronto Press and Routledge and Kegan Paul.

—— (1973–4) *Collected Works. Volumes VII–VIII. A System of Logic*, edited by J. M. Robson, Toronto: University of Toronto Press and Routledge and Kegan Paul.

Miller, D. W. (1975a) 'Making sense of method: comments on Richard Jeffrey', *Synthese* 30: 139–47.

—— (1975b) 'The accuracy of predictions', *Synthese* 30: 159–91.

—— (1975c) 'The accuracy of predictions: a reply', *Synthese* 30: 207–19.

—— (1978) 'Can science do without induction?', in L. J. Cohen and M. Hesse (eds), *Applications of Inductive Logic*, Proceedings of a Conference at The Queen's College, Oxford, 21–24 August 1978, Oxford: Clarendon Press.

Milton, J. R. (1987) 'Induction before Hume', *British Journal for the Philosophy of Science* 38: 49–74.

Naylor, R. H. (1989) 'Galileo's experimental discourse', in D. Gooding, T. Pinch and S. Schaffer (eds), *The Uses of Experiment: Studies in the Natural Sciences*, Cambridge: Cambridge University Press.

Newton, I. (1934) *Mathematical Principles of Natural Philosophy*, trans. A. Motte, rev. F. Cajori, Berkeley and Los Angeles: University of California Press.

—— (1979) *Opticks, or A Treatise of the Reflections, Refractions, Inflections and Colours of Light*, based on the fourth edition of 1730, New York: Dover.

Newton-Smith, W. (1981) *The Rationality of Science*, London: Routledge.

Nicod, J. (1969) *Geometry and Induction*, London: Routledge and Kegan Paul.

Peirce, C. S. (1931–58) *Collected Papers*, edited by C. Hartshorne, P. Weiss and A. Burks, 8 vols, Cambridge, Mass.: Harvard University Press.

Pérez-Ramos, A. (1988) *Francis Bacon's Idea of Science and the Maker's Knowledge Tradition*, Oxford: Oxford University Press.

Pickering, A. (ed.) (1992) *Science as Practice and Culture*, Chicago: University of Chicago Press.

Poincaré, H. (1914) *Science and Method*, trans. by F. Maitland, London: Thomas Nelson.

—— (1946) *The Foundations of Science: Science and Hypothesis; The Value of Science; Science and Method*, trans. G. B. Halsted, Lancaster, Pa.: The Science Press.

—— (1952) *Science and Hypothesis*, New York: Dover.

—— (1958) *The Value of Science*, trans. by W. J. G., New York: Dover.

Popper, K. (1959) *The Logic of Scientific Discovery*, London: Hutchinson.

—— (1963) *Conjectures and Refutations: the Growth of Scientific Knowledge*, London: Routledge and Kegan Paul.

—— (1972) *Objective Knowledge: An Evolutionary Approach*, Oxford: Clarendon Press.

—— (1982a) *Realism and the Aim of Science*, Postscript to the *Logic of Scientific Discovery*, vol. 1, edited by W. W. Bartley III, London: Hutchinson.

—— (1982b) *The Open Universe*, Postscript to the *Logic of Scientific Discovery*, vol. 2, edited by W. W. Bartley III, London: Hutchinson.

—— (1982c) *Quantum Theory and the Schism in Physics*, Postscript to the *Logic of Scientific Discovery*, vol. 3, edited by W. W. Bartley III, London: Hutchinson.

Popper, K. and Miller, D. (1983) 'A proof of the impossibility of inductive probability', *Nature* 302: 687–8.

—— (1984) 'The impossibility of inductive probability', *Nature* 310: 434.

Price, R (1764) 'A demonstration of the second rule in the essay towards the solution of a problem in the doctrine of chances', *Philosophical Transactions of the Royal Society of London* 54: 296–325.

Ramsey, F. P. (1978) 'Truth and probability', in D. H. Mellor (ed.), *Foundations: Essays in Philosophy, Logic, Mathematics and Economics*, London: Routledge and Kegan Paul.

—— (1989) 'Mr Keynes on probability', *British Journal for the Philosophy of Science* 40: 219–22.

Rees, G. (1986) 'Mathematics and Francis Bacon's natural philosophy', *Revue Internationale de Philosophie* 40: 399–426.

Reichenbach, H. (1938) *Experience and Prediction: An Analysis of the Foundations and the Structure of Knowledge*, Chicago, Ill.: University of Chicago Press.

—— (1949) *The Theory of Probability: An Inquiry into the Logical and Mathematical Foundations of the Calculus of Probability*, trans. by E. H. Hutten and M. Reichenbach, Berkeley and Los Angeles: University of California Press.

—— (1951) *The Rise of Scientific Philosophy*, Berkeley and Los Angeles: University of Chicago Press.

—— (1978) *Selected Writings, 1909–1953*, edited by M. Reichenbach and R. S. Cohen, 2 vols, Dordrecht: Reidel.

Rescher, N. (1978) *Peirce's Philosophy of Science: Critical Studies in His Theory of Induction and Scientific Method*, Notre Dame, Ill.: Notre Dame University Press.

Robertson, J. M. (ed.) (1905) *The Philosophical Works of Francis Bacon. . .*, London: George Routledge and Sons.

Rosenkrantz, R. D. (1977) *Inference, Method and Decision: Towards a Bayesian Philosophy of Science*, Dordrecht: Reidel.

Runde, J. (1994) 'Keynes after Ramsey: In defence of A Treatise on Probability', *Studies in the History and Philosophy of Science* 25: 97–121.

Ruse, M. (1975) 'Darwin's debt to philosophy: an examination of the influence of the philosophical ideas of John F. Herschel and William Whewell on the development of Charles Darwin's theory of evolution', *Studies in the History and Philosophy of Science* 6: 159–81.

Russell, B. (1912) *The Problems of Philosophy*, Oxford: Oxford University Press.

—— (1948) *Human Knowledge: Its Scope and Limits*, London: George Allen and Unwin.

Salmon, W. (1966) *The Foundations of Scientific Inference*, Pittsburgh, Pa.: Pittsburgh University Press.

—— (ed.) (1979) *Hans Reichenbach: Logical Empiricist*, Dordrecht: Reidel.

—— (1981) 'Rational prediction', *British Journal for the Philosophy of Science* 32: 115–25.

Schaffer, S. (1989) 'Glass works: Newton's prisms and the uses of experiment', in D. Gooding, T. Pinch and S. Schaffer (eds), *The Uses of Experiment: Studies in the Natural Sciences*, Cambridge: Cambridge University Press.

Schilpp, P. A. (ed.) (1963) *The Philosophy of Rudolf Carnap*, Library of Living Philosophers, La Salle, Ill.: Open Court.

—— (ed.) (1974) *The Philosophy of Karl Popper*, Library of Living Philosophers, La Salle, Ill: Open Court.

Schmitt, C. B. (1975) 'Science in the Italian Universities in the Sixteenth and Early Seventeenth Centuries', in M. P. Crosland (ed.), *The Emergence of Science in Western Europe*, London: Macmillan.

Settle, T. (1970) 'Is corroboration a nondemonstrative form of inference?', *Ratio* 12: 151–3.

Shafer, G. (1978) 'Non-additive probabilities in the work of Bernoulli and Lambert', *Archive for the History of the Exact Sciences* 19: 309–70.

Shapin, S. (1994) *A Social History of Truth: Civility and Science in Seventeenth-Century England*, Chicago: University of Chicago Press.

Shapin, S. and Schaffer, S. (1985) *Leviathan and the Air-Pump: Hobbes, Boyle, and the Experimental Life*, Princeton, NJ: Princeton University Press.

Shapiro, A. E. (1993) *Fits, Passions, and Paroxysms: Physics, Method, and Chemistry and Newton's Theories of Coloured Bodies and Fits of Easy Reflection*, Cambridge: Cambridge University Press.

Sharratt, M. (1994) *Galileo: Decisive Innovator*, Oxford: Blackwell.

Sheynin, O. (1972) 'D. Bernoulli's work on probability', *Rete. Strukturgeschichte der Naturwissenschaften* 1: 273–99.

Shimony, A. (1970) 'Scientific inference', in R. Colodny (ed.), *The Nature and Function of Scientific Theories*, Pittsburgh, Pa.: Pittsburgh University Press.

—— (1993) *Search For A Naturalistic World View, vol. 1: Scientific Method and Epistemology*, Cambridge: Cambridge University Press.

Shoesmith, E. (1987) 'The Continental controversy over Arbuthnot's argument for divine providence', *Historia Mathematica* 14: 133–46.

Skidelsky, R. (1983) *John Maynard Keynes: Hopes Betrayed 1883–1920*, London: Macmillan.
—— (1992) *John Maynard Keynes: The Economist as Saviour*, London: Macmillan.
Sklar, L. (1976) *Space, Time, and Spacetime*, Berkeley: University of California Press.
Skorupski, J. (1989) *John Stuart Mill*, London: Routledge.
Spedding, J., Ellis, R. L. and Heath, D. D. (eds) (1857–74) *The Works of Francis Bacon*, 14 vols, London: Longman and Co.
Stigler, S. M. (1982) 'Thomas Bayes's Bayesian inference', *Journal of the Royal Statistical Society* (A) 145: 250–8.
—— (1986) *The History of Statistics: The Measurement of Uncertainty before 1900*, Cambridge, Mass.: Harvard University Press.
Strong, J. V. (1978) 'John Stuart Mill, John Herschel, and the "Probability of Causes"', in *PSA 1978* 1, East Lansing, Mich.: Philosophy of Science Association.
Stump, D. (1989) 'Henri Poincaré's philosophy of science', *Studies in the History and Philosophy of Science* 20: 335–63.
Swijtink, Z. G. (1986) 'D'Alembert and the maturity of chances', *Studies in the History and Philosophy of Science* 17: 327–49.
Thayer, H. S. (ed.) (1953) *Newton's Philosophy of Nature: Selections from his Writings*, New York: Macmillan.
Toraldo di Francia, G. (1981) *The Investigation of the Physical World*, Cambridge: Cambridge University Press.
Urbach, P. (1987) *Francis Bacon's Philosophy of Science: An Account and a Reappraisal*, La Salle, Ill.: Open Court.
Venn, J. (1962) *The Logic of Chance*, fourth edition, New York: Chelsea. [This is a reprint of the third edition of 1888.]
von Wright, G. H. (1951) *A Treatise on Induction and Probability*, London: Routledge and Kegan Paul.
Vuillemin, J. (1986) 'On Duhem's and Quine's theses', in L. E. Hahn and P. A. Schilpp (eds), *The Philosophy of W. V. Quine*, Library of Living Philosophers, La Salle, Ill.: Open Court.
Wallace, W. A. (1984) *Galileo and his Sources: The Heritage of the Collegio Romano in Galileo's Science*, Princeton, NJ: Princeton University Press.
Watkins, J. (1984) *Science and Scepticism*, London: Hutchinson.
Watt, D. E. (1989) 'Not very likely: a reply to Ramsey', *British Journal for the Philosophy of Science* 40: 223–7.
Weisz, P. B. (1961) *Elements of Biology*, New York and London: McGraw-Hill.
Westfall, R. (1980) *Never at Rest: A Biography of Isaac Newton*, Cambridge: Cambridge University Press.
—— (1988) 'Galileo and the Jesuits', in R. S. Woolhouse (ed.), *Metaphysics and Philosophy of Science in the Seventeenth and Eighteenth Centuries: Essays in Honour of Gerd Buchdahl*, Dordrecht/Boston/London: Kluwer.
Wisan, W. L. (1978) 'Galileo's scientific method,' in R. E. Butts and J. C. Pitt (eds), *New Perspectives on Galileo*, Dordrecht: Reidel.
Woolhouse, R. S. (1988) *The Empiricists*, A History of Western Philosophy 5, Oxford: Oxford University Press.
Worrall, J. (1988) 'The value of a fixed methodology', *British Journal for the Philosophy of Science* 39: 263–75.
—— (1989) 'Fresnel, Poisson and the white spot: the role of successful prediction in the acceptance of scientific theories', in D. Gooding, T. Pinch and S. Schaffer (eds), *The Uses of Experiment: Studies in the Natural Sciences*, Cambridge: Cambridge University Press.
—— (1957) *The Logical Problem of Induction*, second edition, Oxford: Blackwell.

Yeo, R. (1985) 'An idol of the marketplace: Baconianism in nineteenth-century Britain', *History of Science* 23: 251–98.

—— (1986) 'Scientific method and the rhetoric of science in Britain, 1830–1917', in J. Schuster and R. Yeo (eds), *The Politics and Rhetoric of Scientific Method: Historical Studies*, Dordrecht: Reidel.

—— (1991) 'William Whewell's philosophy of knowledge and its reception', in M. Fisch and S. Schaffer (eds), *William Whewell: A Composite Portrait*, Oxford: Clarendon Press.

Zabell, S. (1989) 'The rule of succession', *Erkenntnis* 31: 283–321.

Index